~ Captain Blakeley and the *Wasp*

Captain Blakeley *and* the *Wasp*

THE CRUISE OF 1814

STEPHEN W. H. DUFFY

NAVAL INSTITUTE PRESS

Annapolis, Maryland

Naval Institute Press
291 Wood Road
Annapolis, MD 21402

Library of Congress Cataloging-in-Publication Data
Duffy, Stephen W. H., 1960–
    Captain Blakeley and the Wasp : the cruise of 1814 / Stephen W. H.
Duffy.
        p.   cm.
    ISBN 1-55750-176-9 (alk. paper)
    1. Blakeley, Johnston, d. 1815. 2. United States—History—War of 1812—
Naval operations, American. 3. Wasp (Sloop). 4. United States. Navy—
Officers Biography. 5. Ship captains—United States—Biography. I. Title.
    E353.1.B57D84   1999
973.5'25—dc21   99-26571

Printed in the United States of America on acid-free paper ⊗
08 07 06 05 04 03 02 01   9 8 7 6 5 4 3 2
First printing

To Naomi, for patience, support, and love

Contents

Acknowledgments

The author owes special, alphabetical thanks to the following generous individuals: Brina J. Agranat of Mobile, Alabama, who shared her research on naval disappearances, specifically with regard to the tales of shipwrecks upon the African coast; Eleanor Baily of the Historical Society of Old Newbury; naval historian Roman Barzana of Tampa, Florida, a noted authority in Cuban maritime history, for his help in deciphering several interesting aspects of the capture of the American *Frolic;* Evelyn Bechtel of the New Hampshire Historical Society, Concord, who helped secure data on the Hall, Toscan, and Langdon families of Portsmouth; Duane Borchers, for digging through the RG217 receipts at the National Archives; historian and shipwright Harold Bosche of Islip, New York; Charles E. Brodine Jr., of the Naval Historical Center, for finding and sharing far too many small historical tidbits to mention here, and especially for reviewing my first draft manuscript; Sean Callahan of Dublin, Ireland, for research on the Jones-Blakeley lineage; James W. Cheevers, senior curator of the U.S. Naval Academy Museum in Annapolis, Maryland, for sharing his institution's Blakeley and Geisinger manuscripts; Michael J. Crawford of the Naval Historical Center for searching through the ZB file; Dr. Kevin J. Crisman of the Department of Nautical Archeology, Texas A&M University in College Station, Texas, for sharing his expertise on two of the *Wasp*'s stablemates, the *Eagle* and the *Jefferson;* Robert H. Davis Jr., of the New York Public Library, for helping to obtain copies of the *Frolic* journal; James Tertius de Kay of Stonington, Connecticut; Dr. William S. Dudley Jr., senior historian of the Naval Historical Center, Washington, D.C.; my dear friend and mentor, the late Dr. William M. P. Dunne of the University of New York, for opening his "Naval Scribe" data files and for his prodding and encouragement in turning my initial *Wasp* manuscript into a full-fledged Blakeley biography—I will always be grateful; Ira Dye of Virginia Beach, Virginia, whose book on the cruise of the *Argus* and whose advice were of great inspiration; Carolyn Eastman of Portsmouth, New Hampshire, Athenaeum; Richard L. Eddy of Tallahassee, Florida; Peter Fitzgerald, Water Transport Collections assistant for the London Science Museum; Donna K. Flowers, of the North Carolina Department of Cultural Resources, Raleigh, who provided access to contemporary North Carolina newspapers; Dr. Naomi Fontaine, loyal cofounder of the Institute for Advanced Blakeley Studies; historian John C. Frederiksen of Warwick, Rhode Island; Katherine H. Griffin, Massachusetts Historical Society, Boston, for her assistance in obtaining access to the Frederick Baury Papers; William L. Harrell of the CEL Regional Library, Savannah; Nancy C. Hayward of the Essex Society of Genealogists in Lynnfield, Massachusetts, for her help on the Bartlett clan; Dr. Donald Higginbotham, professor of history at the University of North Carolina, Chapel Hill, for helping to obtain a photograph of Blakeley's portrait; fellow *Wasp* researcher Bert Hubinger of the U.S. Naval Academy; James H. Hutson of the Library of Congress for helping to secure a copy of the David Geisinger journal; Capt. Kenneth A. Johnson, USN, for his invaluable information on the *Wasp*'s armament; Dr. George Kleine of the University of South Florida; Dorothy LaFrance, head librarian of the Newburyport Public Library; Dr. Linda M. Maloney of The Liturgical Press, Collegeville, Minnesota; Cdr. Tyrone G. Martin, USN, Ret., of Tryon, North Carolina, who not only helped in many aspects of Blakeley's early history, especially where it related to the *Constitution,* but also invited me to participate with him in the 1993 Naval History Symposium at the Naval Academy in Annapolis (and who proofed my less than perfect first draft), to whom I will always be extremely grateful; Capt. Joseph R. McCleary, USN, Nautical Research Guild director of Williamsburg, Virginia, for access to his *Epervier* data files; Christopher McKee, librarian of Grinnell College, Grinnell, Iowa, for generously opening up his extensive biographical data files on the *Wasp*'s officers; Archie Motley of the Chicago Historical Society, for providing the missing pages of the *Frolic* journal; Robert Napier of the Nautical

Research Guild, Newburyport, Massachusetts, for his help in understanding the history, culture, and geography of the Merrimack River; Robert E. Richardson of the Cartographic and Architectural Branch, National Archives, for providing drafts of the *Wasp* and many of her contemporaries; Graham K. Salt of Research Services, Ltd., of Fareham, England, who painstakingly dug through the uncataloged stacks at the Public Records Office in Kew; Robert W. Schoeberlein, manuscripts librarian with the Maryland Historical Society in Baltimore, for providing a copy of the *Atalanta* portion of the Geisinger journal; Graham Slater and David Lyons of the National Maritime Museum, Greenwich; Norman Swales of Doncaster, England, for sharing his knowledge of British shipbuilding; John E. Vajda of the Naval Historical Center, Washington, D.C.; Richard A. Von Doenhoff of the Military Reference Branch, National Archives; Jane E. Ward of the Essex Institute, Salem; Taylor K. Warren of the Mariners' Museum, Newport News, Virginia; and finally Richard E. Winslow III of the Portsmouth Public Library, for sharing his knowledge of early nineteenth-century Portsmouth history.

Chronology

Oct. 1781	Johnston Blakeley born in Ireland
Fall 1783	Blakeley family immigrates to the United States
1796–99	Blakeley attends University of North Carolina at Chapel Hill
5 Feb. 1800	Receives midshipman appointment
July 1800	Assigned to the frigate *President*
June 1801–Apr. 1802	Mediterranean cruise onboard the *President*
Sept. 1802	Blakeley assigned to the *John Adams*
8 May 1803	*John Adams* battles forces off Tripoli; blockade of Tripoli begins
16 Apr. 1804	Blakeley transferred to *Congress*
9 Nov. 1804	Transferred to *Constitution*
24 Sept. 1805	Assigned to the *Hornet*
July 1806–7	On furlough from the navy; serves in the merchant service
10 Feb. 1807	Promoted to rank of lieutenant
Sept. 1807–Apr. 1808	At Norfolk, Va., station with gunboat flotilla
Apr. 1808	Assigned to brig *Argus*
June 1808	*Argus* captures prize, the brig *Charles*
1809–10	Blakeley serves onboard corvette *John Adams; John Adams* becomes his first unofficial independent command

1811–13	Serves onboard *Enterprize,* first permanent command
18 June 1812	War Hawks declare war on Great Britain; War of 1812–15 begins
1 June 1813	British *Shannon* captures *Chesapeake*
24 July 1813	Blakeley receives rank of master commandant; assumes command of new sloop of war *Wasp*
11 Sept. 1813	New corvette (sloop of war) *Frolic* launched in Charlestown, Mass.
18 Sept. 1813	*Wasp* is launched
27 Dec. 1813	Blakeley marries Jane Anne Hoope in Boston
28 Feb. 1814	*Wasp* sails from Newburyport, Mass., to Portsmouth, N.H.
Apr. 1814	New sloop of war *Peacock* captures British *Epervier*
18 Apr. 1814	*Frolic* surrenders to the British
2 May 1814	*Wasp* begins cruise
3 June 1814	*Wasp* captures first prize, barque *Neptune*
14 June 1814	*Wasp* captures brig *William*
17 June 1814	*Wasp* captures brig *Pallas*
22 June 1814	*Wasp* captures carrier *Henrietta*
27 June 1814	*Wasp* captures letter of marque *Orange Boven*
28 June 1814	*Wasp* battles and defeats sloop of war *Reindeer*
5 July 1814	*Wasp* captures brig *Regulator*
6 July 1814	*Wasp* captures schooner *Jenny*
July–Aug. 1814	*Wasp* at L'Orient, France, repairing damage received during battle with *Reindeer*
27 Aug. 1814	*Wasp* leaves L'Orient at noon
31 Aug. 1814	*Wasp* captures brig *Lattice*
1 Sept. 1814	*Wasp* captures brig *Bonacord*
2 Sept. 1814	*Wasp* captures brig *Mary; Wasp* battles sloop of war *Avon*
13 Sept. 1814	*Wasp* captures brig *Three Brothers*
14 Sept. 1814	*Wasp* captures brig *Bacchus*
21 Sept. 1814	*Wasp* captures brig *Atalanta*
23 Sept. 1814	*Atalanta,* with prize crew aboard, departs company from *Wasp*
4 Nov. 1814	*Atalanta* arrives in Savannah Harbor
10 Nov. 1814	Blakeley's daughter, Udney Maria Blakeley, is born
24 Nov. 1814	Blakeley promoted to rank of captain

~ Captain Blakeley and the *Wasp*

PART ONE

The Captain

I. Choose Now for Mr. B

October 1781–June 1800

On a sweltering July day in the year 1800, a quiet young man passed through the gates of the New York Navy Yard, where his future home lay rocking against the almost imperceptible swells. He was embarking upon a new life, one that he himself had chosen. This change in the young man's life calling, from lawyer to warrior, had come about rather suddenly, unexpectedly—and certainly much later than it ought to have done. Home was now the U.S. frigate *President,* commanded by Commo. Thomas Truxtun, Esquire, and no longer the comparatively free and undisciplined university at Chapel Hill, North Carolina. The *President,* a new vessel, was this day being fitted out at Corlaer's Hook for a long cruise, its very first.

The North Carolinian stood in stark contrast to the flood of humanity washing before him among the boxes, bales, and barrels. Both officers and enlisted men alike wore workaday sailor's slops on that beautiful clear morning. To this immaculately gilt-laced young gentleman, the masses seething all about him embodied a wholly unexpected and entirely unromantic side of the new nation's naval service. But there was no time for ceremony.

America was in the second year of its undeclared naval war with France. The young man had long ago bid farewell to family and friends and collected those few practical belongings he believed might be of use to him—

or might provide him at least a minimal degree of comfort. Confined within his high-collared jacket, he remained rigid, both with excitement and trepidation. Somewhere before him upon the vast spar deck paced his new captain. Defeating the most formidable pair of armed adversaries during this present quasi-conflict (the French frigates *L'Insurgente* and *La Vengeance*), Truxtun had become the first of only two American post–Revolutionary War captains to conquer more than one nominally equal antagonist during a single war. The commander who would tie this achievement, a decade and a half later, a man who would, in fact, upstage Truxtun by accomplishing these feats while out upon a single cruise—and at both a younger age and a lower rank—had just now come aboard. His name was Johnston Blakeley.

Ireland, more specifically Seaford in County Down, a small hamlet located in the outskirts of Belfast, was the birthplace of America's most accomplished martial mariner. Little is known about this branch of the reasonably prolific Blakeley family, other than that the boy's father, John Blakeley, was a successful wine merchant and grocer when his son Johnston was born on 11 October 1781.[1] John was a "landed" man of note, possessing a small amount of real property. The Blakeley family's ancient lineage is rooted in County Down, as too is that of the Johnstons, whose motto, *Nunquam Non Paratus* ("Never Unprepared"), fits the attributes of Johnston Blakeley to a tee. "His first name, that of a great family of southern Scotland and northern England," wrote an early biographer of identical descent, "suggests that he belonged to the Scotch-Irish race, which has been conspicuous . . . for intelligence, pluck and all manly virtues."[2] More than likely, however, in this case the name Johnston simply meant "the son of John." The central image of the coat of arms of the Blakeley family (which oftentimes spelled its name "Blakely") is a bold and rampant lion set loose upon a blue shield and contained within a bright red, dovetailed border. Lest anyone confuse this crest with that of an English cousin, the Blakeley lion is liberally sprinkled with small green shamrocks.

Johnston's mother, Marie, brought at least one other son into the world during their short stay in Seaford, prior to their flight to the New World in the fall of 1783. The American War of Independence had just ended, and North America would provide boundless opportunities for the Blakeley family. After selling off his properties, John, Marie, and their sons immigrated to the city of Philadelphia, the new nation's burgeoning capital, "with a view of engaging in business." Finding things there not to his liking, John removed after only a few months to Charleston, South Carolina. He met with little more in the way of encouragement there, and moved once again to his final destination, Wilmington, North Carolina. Vast numbers of immigrants from both Scotland and Ireland were drawn to the Carolinas, and that fact no doubt influenced John's decision to take up residence there. "Soon after his establishment at this place," wrote an early biographer, "Mr. Blakeley was deprived, one by one, of his wife and all of his children, except his son Johnston."[3]

John Blakeley never remarried, but labored relentlessly to provide a living for himself and young Johnston. By the dawn of the 1790s, in partnership with a Mr. Vance, the elder Blakeley had become one of Wilmington's most successful grocers. The enterprise soon expanded into waterfront real estate, primarily warehouses, with both men investing heavily in commercial and residential properties. John took out many advertisements in the local papers, announcing, for example, "excellent London Porter in bottles, by the cask or dozen," along with other items such as ripened produce and "freshly ground meats."[4]

Johnston received the first rudiments of his education at Fayetteville.[5] The death of his other family members induced the elder Blakeley to send his remaining son north to preparatory school, far from the "insalubrious" southern coastal climate so particularly unfavorable to the young. In 1790 young Johnston arrived at "a highly celebrated academy," most certainly Erasmus Hall,[6] in Flatbush, New York, "at that time much resorted to by young men from the south." John Hoope, a respectable merchant from the island of St. Croix and apparently also a long-time acquaintance of the senior Blakeley, agreed to watch over Johnston. After "assiduously" pursuing his studies for five years, Johnston returned home to Wilmington "without any particular pursuit or occupation." Since John was obviously not happy with his son's lack of direction, he asked the influential Wilmington attorney Edward Jones for help. John particularly desired his son to study law in the state's new university at Chapel Hill.

The friendship between the Jones and Blakeley families dated back to their relatively penniless days in Ireland. After John's death in February 1797, Edward Jones would agree to care for Johnston until he reached manhood. Edward's wife, Mary Mallet Todd-Jones, was the closest thing to a mother that Johnston ever knew.

Born in 1762 in Lisburn, near Belfast, Edward Jones was a descendant, by his mother's side, of the eminent Bishop Jeremy Taylor, a man once called the "Shakespeare of theological literature" and the "most eloquent and imaginative of all the divines of the English Church." Edward's father, Dr. Conway Jones, owned a great estate called Homera outside Belfast, but, as Edward lived in a country in which the rights of primogeniture entitled the eldest son to all properties, nearly everything passed on to his older brother, William. Edward's only chance of inheriting his father's vast holdings was for William Jones, later a renowned Irish patriot, to die a childless bachelor. This happened in 1818 when, at the age of sixty-three, his carriage overturned during a trip to Parliament (of which he was an "esteemed member"). But it was too late for Edward; deeply in debt, William had already been forced to sell off nearly all his lands.

The younger (and therefore lesser) son had not been sent to college, nor had he been provided with any sort of literary education; he had instead been apprenticed to a linen merchant. Unable to converse freely about the classical authors and "lacking a strong taste for polite letters," Edward was cruelly segregated from the "cultivated" society that his elder brother so freely enjoyed. In the fall of 1783, after completing his apprenticeship "to merchandise," the twenty-one-year-old Edward departed for Philadelphia alongside his most particular friend, John Blakeley. Neither would ever see his native land again.

Edward was not an immediate success in the New World. In Ireland he had enjoyed the somewhat "free expenses of a family of easy circumstances," according to his contemporary biographer. He was subsequently unprepared for the "vital habits of economy and steady industry" so essential for success in the competitive marketplace.[7] In spite of this, he ran in some heady circles. Edward soon formed a valuable and intimate friendship with the influential Peter Stephen Du Ponceau, a "profound jurist, learned philosopher, and liberal patriotic citizen." Soon after emigrating from France in 1777, the seventeen-year-old Du Ponceau had received his captain's commission in the Continental army and soon became the aide-de-camp to then Major General Steuben at Valley Forge. Now an enthusiastic member of the Pennsylvania Supreme Court, Du Ponceau was one of the leading experts in civil, foreign, and international law, due in no small part to his mastery of a great many languages.[8]

Edward Jones moved to Wilmington in 1786 and was cordially received by John Blakeley.[9] He was no more successful there as a merchant than he had been in the nation's capital.[10] Edward himself wrote that the "recent upheavals in Europe," most certainly the French Revolution, were to blame for his business failures. Things became so bleak at one point that Edward gave serious thought to retiring to India and starting anew. Influenced by Du Ponceau, however, he remained in the United States. Pursuing a law career, in 1789 he began legal studies under the direction of Archibald

McClaine, one of the leading jurists of the South. Edward was elected to the North Carolina legislature in 1788, while still a law student. He was proving to be nearly as successful in his newly adopted frontier home as Du Ponceau had been in the more civilized Pennsylvania. Edward was elected solicitor general of North Carolina in 1791, and he would hold that prestigious post for several decades. In 1793, Counselor Jones wed Mary Mallet Todd-Jones, who immediately placed young Johnston under her protective wing.

The low coastal climate carried away the first three Jones children in their infancies, including baby Peter Du Ponceau Jones. "If I die," the unsuspecting Edward had written to his late first-born's godfather and namesake, "I leave him to you." Du Ponceau responded that he would concede it to be "a pride and pleasure to consider [him] as my own." Edward could not foresee that he himself would play just such a paternal role for another. The fever that had so ravaged Wilmington during the fall of 1796 was most certainly contributory, if not entirely responsible, for the elder Blakeley's death that following February. John was not yet forty years old. His obituary appeared in the form of an advertisement on the front page of the leading Wilmington weekly: "For sale, a pew at the church," proclaimed the *Gazette*. "Apply to John Blakeley."[11]

Although nobody had yet made the connection between the yellow fever and its mosquito carriers that thrive in stagnant coastal waters, North Carolina's early legislature at least had the good sense to choose an elevated inland county as the site of the new university. Chapel Hill was far from the "bad air" thought to produce, or at least encourage, the illness. To Edward Jones, the loss of John Blakeley, coupled with the memory of his own recent triple tragedy, was too much to bear. If he were to ensure the survival of any future children, his wife, and indeed himself, he would have to leave this lethal, low-lying region. Leaving the city that had cost him so dearly, Jones purchased a large estate in Chatham County, about eight miles west of the town of Pittsboro.

Accounts vary concerning the exact location and description of Edward's new country seat, which he quaintly named Rock Rest. It may have been real estate offered in *Hall's Gazette* the previous April.[12] The advertisement was placed by Henry Lutterich, and it had run unsuccessfully since February. Lutterich begged all those who might be interested to contact his attorney, Edward Jones, Esquire, of Wilmington. It is quite possible that Jones bought this particular parcel for his own use. The riverfront property reportedly consisted of 450 "finely timbered" acres that included a valuable crossing called Clark's Ferry, a large although unfinished grist mill, and a brickyard. The estate boasted "a good house, out house, stable . . . [located] . . . on the main road from Fayetteville to Hillsborough" in the heart of "plentiful wheat country." The only concrete detail known about Jones's Rock Rest is that it was located "on the Banks of the Haw River."[13] Counselor Jones's Chatham County retreat would become not only a safe haven for his family but also a frequent destination for Johnston, during his remaining college years as well as throughout his naval career. While away at school, Johnston always declared himself to be "from Chatham," not Wilmington.

"As it was the intention of his father to bring him up to the law," wrote Moses Thomas, Blakeley's first biographer, "and with a view towards qualifying him towards that profession, he was placed in 1796 at the University of North Carolina." Blakeley remained there until 1799 "with occasional intermissions."[14] Another biographer agrees with the date of admission: "When sufficiently advanced to enter college, he was removed to that of Chapel Hill, in North Carolina, in 1796."[15] But this latter biographer states another field of interest, "mathematics and its application to navigation, surveying and the like." Still another biographer states that "young Blakeley entered the university in 1797."[16] Regardless, university records show that Johnston was a member of the class of 1801. Political and religious upheavals would soon envelop the campus, however, and only half a dozen members of Blakeley's class would graduate.

Johnston most likely bounded confidently off to Chapel Hill, firm in the conviction that he would, as his father had so ardently wished, master the legal profession. Dr. James Johnson, a Blakeley biographer, states that Johnston instead sought a mathematical education so that he might excel in his naval career, but no such program was offered at this landlocked college. Math and geometry would not become available to Johnston in any depth until his second year, although the strict disciplines of philosophy and logic would have prepared him well for any calling. To have been admitted at Chapel Hill, Johnston would have had to have passed several written and oral examinations on Greek and Latin grammar and would have been required to know the major works of Virgil, Sallust, and Ovid. In his first year at Chapel Hill, Johnston would have deepened his knowledge of these subjects. Not until his sophomore year would the more practical disciplines— mathematics, bookkeeping, and geography—come his way. The third year, which was for Blakeley his final year, was to mandate the more complex mathematical studies, including both a rigorous continuation of geometry and an introduction to trigonometry and calculus.

Today's picturesque town of Chapel Hill was then a spartan outpost in the wilderness. Fresh stumps still covered the grounds of the presiding professor's unpainted clapboard house when Johnston first strode onto campus. The University of North Carolina, the oldest such institution in the country, had been literally hewn out of the woods. As the year progressed and money vanished, many of Johnston's schoolmates walked to their classrooms barefoot; the town contained neither shoemakers nor cobblers. What's more, the dormitory was soon besieged by bedbugs, or "sabines," despite the students' best efforts to control them. One classmate, John Pettegrew, wrote to his mother during Blakeley's freshman year remarking that none of the boys would need the customary and dreaded bleeding by a physician, since the sabines were so voracious in their thirst. "There is one comfort," he added. "There are no mosquitoes."[17]

Chapel Hill was not, however, entirely immune from disease. Of the eighty-six students enrolled in 1797, nearly half came down with the dreaded mumps during the course of that year. The lone brick dormitory, the largest structure on campus, was severely overcrowded; it contained the entire student body with all their personal belongings crammed into fourteen small rooms. This was good conditioning, however, for one about to join the navy. When the weather permitted, the boys retreated into the cool, dark privacy of the woods. Many erected cabins and even primitive Indian lodgings for solitude. But fearing that such unsupervised forest dwellings might "interfere with discipline," the faculty ordered the dozens of teepees and wigwams torn down.

"In the Philanthropic Society, of which he was a member," wrote Blakeley's most enthusiastic biographer, Dr. Johnson, "he was elected to every office, from the Presidency on down, and was placed on all the important committees."[18] The Philanthropic Society records contain numerous references to young Johnston from 1797 through 1799. He is not listed as a society president, but he was elected (or possibly reelected) treasurer on 26 March 1799.[19] From these same records, Johnston is known to have "read on Jacobisms" during one meeting. On another less serious occasion he was fined fifteen cents for repeatedly bursting into laughter during a colleague's speech. He was "punctual in debating," and in one debate he argued against the question "Is luxury always the cause of the downfall of nations?" The society voted in his favor. Another issue of debate was: "Are ladies or wine the most deleterious to students?" Women seemed to them the greater evil. A somewhat less lighthearted question was presented in February of 1797: "Is there just cause of war by the United States against France?" No, not yet.

But by the following March, when ships of both nations had begun firing upon each other, the question earned a nearly unanimous agreement. "Should the United States further negotiate with Algiers?" Certainly not, they reasoned, for there had been enough talk and now it was time to act. Last, and of greater relevance to the life of Johnston Blakeley, "Should our navy be increased?" Blakeley contributed his emphatic yes to the overwhelmingly positive verdict.

The student body assembled at Chapel Hill in those years was, to say the least, rough. One disgusted professor recalled that students continually displayed the "vile and detestable" practice of swearing in a manner "which sailors divert themselves with." The failing that most worried the faculty was that "their favorite book was Paine's *Age of Reason.*" Thomas Paine's fierce attack upon established religious doctrine was anathema to all those who believed in the sacred traditional Christian values. These same values, in fact, had been specifically mandated to be taught in the new university. Blakeley and his companions, daily struggling through the tortures of *Wittenhall's Greek Grammar* and *Young's Latin Dictionary,* no doubt agreed with Paine's assertion that schools should cease expounding the "barren study" of dead languages. All the useful works, Paine argued, had already been translated into the modern tongue. It was the philosophies of the Greeks and Romans that were important, not their languages. If students were preoccupied with Latin and the like, wrote Paine, they would have less time and energy for questioning true philosophies and the honesty of the established system of Western faith. Paine promoted the values of experimental science and natural philosophy and openly questioned the core beliefs of traditional Christianity. Quite naturally, most of his contemporaries viewed Paine as an anarchist, and they despised him and his "atheistic" views. However, any views condemned by the established generation will always be willingly embraced by rebellious and curious youth. "Blakeley particularly spoke of having read Paine's *Age of Reason* in [the university] library," recalled Edward Jones's daughter, Frances, "and said that it had, for many years, been very injurious to him in his duties here, and his hopes hereafter."[20] Unfortunately the impoverished campus library failed to live up to expectations during those early days. "Blakeley spoke with regret that the college library was not in its collection more select and exclusive," recalled his "adopted" stepsister.[21]

The school's professor of mathematics was Joseph Caldwell. The son of a prominent New Jersey physician, Caldwell had graduated from Princeton University with the highest possible honors at the age of nineteen. Four short years later this proficient Scotch-Irish mathematician had become the department head at Chapel Hill. In its early years, the university had endured many difficulties in procuring qualified professors. The majority of educated northerners looked with contempt upon the "semibarbarian" South, scoffing at the meager salaries offered there to professors. Caldwell, mature beyond his years, was a bargain, and a qualified and extremely popular bargain at that. But he was deeply disturbed at what he found at Chapel Hill. He could deal with the more barren aspects of his new position in the wilderness, but thought his fellow faculty members were a "motley group" consisting of, among other things, "infidels and Roman Catholics." Few of his colleagues even possessed college degrees. Nonetheless, he worked on cheerfully with what he had, lamenting to himself that "the Age of Reason has finally come."

Caldwell had strong opinions against what was being promoted in the name of education. "The state appears to be swarming with lawyers," wrote the deeply religious Caldwell soon after his arrival. "It is almost the only profession for which parents educate their children." To his despair, he noted that religion was so little in vogue in North Carolina that shockingly few students wished any connection with it, despite the intense wishes of the university's founding trustees. The only channel by which students or faculty could gain social respectability, he observed, was by publicly disavowing the Sacred Scriptures. Thomas Paine had clearly gained a foothold here.

The 1799 term was explosive. No president had yet been chosen for the university, but only a "presiding professor," whose duty it was to supervise "all the teaching" and to enforce discipline. For some unexplained reason, Presiding Professor James Gillespie developed traits that one contemporary described as "personally obnoxious." The students soon broke into an all-out rebellion against him, the faculty, and the laws of the university. The collegians "waylaid" Gillespie, literally beating him into submission, before going on to stone another professor, Mr. Webb, into early retirement. After a week of almost total anarchy, the rebellious scholars demanded that Professor Caldwell take over the presidency. The effect of this well-publicized disorder was to sharply decrease the number of new students applying for admission. The year 1800 had only three graduates and nearly the entire faculty tendered their resignations. There was, in fact, the very real danger of the university failing for a want of both students and teachers.

The meager surviving records from this early period make it nearly impossible to identify the true causes of the infamous 1799 riots, but there are clues and speculation. Caldwell charged the influential professor Samuel Holmes, a renegade "apostate" and formerly a Baptist minister, with being a devout "anarchist" and a follower of "that filthy atheist" Thomas Paine.[22] He had, among other things, Caldwell alleged, been teaching the boys that there was no such thing as personal virtue. They must bend their wills to the circumstances of the times, Holmes preached, to best advance their vested ambitions and personal interests. But Holmes was a Republican and Caldwell a Federalist. The Republican followers of Thomas Jefferson were accused of seeking to introduce French-style mob rule, while the Federalists, in turn, were accused by their opponents of being monarchists. "Republican students thought it highly patriotic to insult and worry the professors who, they thought, were enemies of the rule of the people, seeking to introduce an aristocracy, if not a king." At one point during these riots, Caldwell and Blakeley clashed. The youngest daughter of Edward Jones recalled the incident:

> In the year 1810, during his last visit to our family, he [Blakeley] called upon Dr. Caldwell, President of Chapel Hill College, to make, as he said, an apology to the Doctor for having once spoken disrespectfully to him, while student under him, at the college. As the circumstances may give an insight into the characters of both parties, I will endeavor to state them, as Dr. Caldwell himself once did. He (Dr. C.) was himself at that time young and inexperienced in the discipline of a college and in mildly curbing the wayward dispositions of youth. Many of the young collegians were as wild as college blades generally are, and probably as their fathers had been before them. Some disturbances arose there, and as the Doctor was going round to discover the cause and the parties engaged in it, he opened Blakeley's door, and found him seated in a window. The Doctor questioned him as to the riot and authors of it. Blakeley answered truly that he had nothing to do with it, and could not say who the parties were. The Doctor replied with irritation and questioned his veracity; Blakeley resented the injury promptly and decidedly, the Doctor being still more irritated, threatened to throw him out the window. Blakeley then replied in a mild, but determined tone: "I beg sir that you will not try it, as it will oblige me to put you out."[23]

Why then did Johnston Blakeley leave the university in 1799 at the end of his junior year? The most common explanation was that his income "was entirely cut off by a destructive fire, consuming all the [ware]houses . . . [and] he suddenly lost by fire his whole means of support, about two years after his entering college."[24] This same source, however, states that John Blakeley died during Johnston's second year, which is not true. If Johnston was at the university in February of 1797 when his father died, he had not been there more than a couple of months, if even that. But Blakeley himself wrote during the peace of 1806 that a destructive fire had "recently" destroyed just such properties in Wilmington, inducing him to beg the secretary of the navy for a temporary leave of absence from the service to make a lucrative, year-long merchant cruise for the purpose of paying off his debts. The implication here is that Johnston maintained all or part of an outside income up until this later date. There may well have been two fires in Wilmington, seven years apart, and indeed both might have wrought financial havoc on poor Johnston. Given the lack of any specific evidence of a 1799 blaze, this popular explanation is unlikely.

"By some misfortune, of which we have never been able to obtain any distinct account," wrote the *Analectic*'s editor in 1816, "he was deprived of the support derived from his father."[25] Perhaps there were legal troubles with his father's surviving partner. It is not too insignificant that John's partner, Mr. Vance, took no interest at all in the welfare of the orphaned Johnston, a boy known to him for some time. Both the firm and the surviving partner did, after all, cease to advertise in the Wilmington papers immediately following John's death. The Reverend W. Hooper, Jones's biographer, insists the reason was wholly financial:

> It is right that I should here correct an error that has got abroad, and which I find in two published accounts . . . namely that Mr. Blakeley, was sent to the University of North Carolina, by Mr. Jones. Of this statement, a daughter of Mr. Jones makes the following correction: "There is an error as to the fact as to my father's advancing money for the expenses of J. Blakeley's education. He wished to do it, and pressed it on Mr. B., but he would not accept it, on the ground that my father had a young family, and ought not to add to his responsibilities. In this, I cannot be mistaken, as I learned it from my mother, and this was the reason too, of his entering the Navy."[26]

In the margins, the Reverend Hooper amended his statement: "I have learned, since the above was in press, that Mr. Blakeley was sent to the University by Mr. Jones, but would not consent to stay there at his expense, when he got old enough to assist himself." No doubt this was a contributory factor, but additional causes might have arisen elsewhere. Three unnamed students were expelled as a result of the 1799 riots, and untold numbers of others were suspended or took leave of absence. Also, threatening to throw the university president out of one's room—either by door or by window—was (and might still be) considered no small offense. If Johnston was expelled for any reason, none of his early biographers mentioned it.

Moses Thomas, writing in 1916, insisted that Johnston had long possessed a strong predilection for naval life, "which however, he had, with a self denial worthy of imitation, concealed from his father." If true, this desire was no doubt fueled by the presence of William Augustus Richards, the senior tutor in the Preparatory Department. Richards had last been employed by a traveling theatrical company before joining the staff at Chapel Hill at its inception. "His acquaintance with the stage," wrote the university's first historian, "in some degree vitiated his morals and gave an air of affectation to his manners."[27] Richards was a native of London and possessed a fair but incomplete education. For some unstated reason, he left his English university, as well as his native land, and enlisted as a common sailor, serving first on board a merchantman and then in His Majesty's Navy. When he died suddenly in 1798, his many devoted followers in the Philanthropic Society mourned wholeheartedly. That such a worldly man had left his own studies in order to go to sea could have left a strong impression on young Johnston. It is possible that Richards's firsthand and possibly personal views of English impressment, or the misbehavior of the Barbary States, strengthened Blakeley's resolve to join the navy. When Thomas Paine was an adolescent, he had also gone off to fight at sea, albeit only in a privateer. Also Peter Stephen Du Ponceau, certainly an influence on Blakeley by reputation if not by actual acquaintance, had abandoned his own religious and classical education to pursue a military career after the death of his father in 1775.

Unable to dissuade Johnston from pursuing a martial vocation, Counselor Jones reluctantly enlisted the help of two powerful allies to aid him in winning the ear of the first secretary of the navy, Benjamin Stoddert. Jones would go to the mat for his best friend's son, in spite of his own personal objections. Although prominent in North Carolina politics, Jones was virtually an unknown commodity in the nation's capital, and politics, as much as any other factor, separated the successful applicants from the unsuccessful. Stoddert was almost solely responsible for issuing the midshipmen's warrants, and he did so based upon the recommendations and influence of those around him. Federalist congressman William H. Hill, "an enlightened lawyer" from New Hanover and formerly a member of the North Carolina legislature, was Jones's most influential connection.

Johnston, perhaps a bit too overconfident in his prospective appointment as a midshipman, went further than most applicants and specifically requested that the secretary assign him to Commo. John Barry. Blakeley's attraction to Barry, one of the most successful captains of the Revolution, was most certainly based in their shared Irish ancestry. Edward Jones applied different criteria, however, and in his eyes Barry did not fit the bill, despite his heritage. Whoever took this rebellious youth under his wing would have to be skilled in the gentlemanly arts as well as the navigational and martial sciences. Someone had to wring any further riotous thoughts from young Johnston's mind while he was still malleable. Both representatives had objected to Barry for just this reason. A response from Congressman Hill survives within the text of Edward Jones's biography, albeit in a somewhat censored form:

> Mr. Hill, in a letter bearing the date Feb. 1800, informs us that "the Secretary has promised him that Johnston Blakeley shall be appointed midshipman, and that his appointment would be made out and forwarded in the course of a week or two. . . . I suggested to him," he continues, "that a wish existed that the young gentleman should be placed in a particular vessel, say, 'the United States,' Com. Barry, and I hoped if there were no important obstacle, the wish might be granted. I was assured it would be so if possible, the Secretary feeling himself perfectly disposed to accommodate. I know not the commanders of the several ships of war; but I have been told that B. is a mere tar, and that B., who commands the ship —, is a well bred gentleman."[28]

At the time this tantalizing letter was printed in 1856 in Jones's biography, many of those who knew these particular naval officers were still alive, so discretion was the order of the day. The "mere tar" unfairly refers, of course, to Barry. The "well bred gentleman" could have been either Samuel Barron, then fitting out the frigate *Chesapeake,* or William Bainbridge of the schooner *Retaliation.* Federalist congressman and general John Steel, later the first comptroller of the North Carolina treasury (and, along with both Jones and Hill, a founder of the university), was Counselor Jones's second Philadelphia liaison. His response survives in the same source and is similarly pruned:

> Mr. Blakeley, shall go on board any ship that he prefers, and with the advice in your power to give him, I have no doubt he will receive a Lieutenancy as soon as he himself would desire it. Talents, education,

attention to duty, willingness to be instructed and to perform, (without being required to do so) the laborious parts of seamanship, manly and elevated deportment, &c., are, I find, the surest means of deserving, and consequently of acquiring promotion. The Secretary of the Navy thinks highly of Capt. *B.*, who is to command the Frigate —. The *C.*, you know, is a mere tar. *T.* is clever as an officer and as a man, and has brought forward some young men very handsomely. *M.* is highly spoken of; I do not know him. Decatur is a good seaman and brave, but not as polished as others. *T.* is vain and too haughty to think of the youth under his care. Choose now for Mr. *B.*[29]

This latter congressman also unfairly used the degrading label "tar" to describe the *C.*, or the aforementioned commodore. The first *T.*, described as "clever," almost certainly suggests Thomas Truxtun, an officer who did indeed take a most handsome interest in the young gentlemen placed under his charge. The fact that Blakeley was finally sent off to that particular commander tends to confirm this first *T.*'s identity. The second *T.*, apparently both vain and haughty, might have been Silas Talbot of the frigate *Constitution* (although he was highly praised in many circles), or quite possibly Captain Thomas Tingey of the *Ganges,* a former officer of the Royal Navy. Finally, the highly spoken of *M.* might identify either Alexander Murray, commanding the frigate *Insurgente,* or Richard V. Morris of the frigate *New York.* At this early date, of course, "Decatur" refers to Stephen Sr., the celebrated Revolutionary War privateersman then commanding the frigate *Philadelphia,* and not his soon to become even more famous son.

The acceptance of Johnston Blakeley into the navy was not a certainty. At one point during the War of 1812, there were ten applicants for every opening. The situation was not nearly as bad during the Quasi-War, but there was still competition aplenty. Furthermore, Secretary Stoddert, based upon his own sound experience, had made the age of eighteen the unofficial upper limit for admission to the officer corps, unless an applicant already possessed considerable sea experience. Older minds were often more difficult to reform after that important benchmark age. There were exceptions, but many of the more successful officers had begun their careers relatively early. And so Johnston, destined to become nineteen in late autumn, was fast approaching the secretary's limit. In the plus column, however, he possessed a considerable education. Although not a graduate of Chapel Hill, he towered intellectually above most of the others. Many midshipmen possessed only a common "English" education, roughly equivalent to that of the modern elementary school; most of the others had obtained the higher "Latin," or preparatory, schooling, similar today to a high school education. Johnston's unique combination of educational merit and political influence did the trick, and he was granted his cherished appointment on 5 February 1800. Benjamin Stoddert forwarded the warrant to Congressman Hill, who in turn sent it to Edward Jones. Before Johnston could officially become Mr. Midshipman Blakeley, however, he would first have to perform two formal yet vital tasks. He must swear his oath of allegiance to the United States before a local magistrate, and then return the printed oath, conveniently supplied by the secretary, to Philadelphia along with a formal letter of acceptance. It was in Blakeley's best interest to perform this second duty as quickly as possible, since his pay would not begin until the secretary received his acknowledgment. Blakeley's confirmation was dated 5 March and was postmarked Wilmington. Early in May, Secretary Stoddert ordered Blakeley to proceed immediately to New York and report to Mr. *T.*, Commo. Thomas Truxtun.

Just before Johnston departed Rock Rest, a substantial roadblock suddenly appeared in his path. According to Edward's youngest daughter, Frances, Johnston fell "desperately" in love with an attractive young woman, referred to only as "Miss *B.*" She too had been an orphan, graciously taken in by the ever-philanthropic Jones family. Needless to say, their mutual guardian did not encourage the liaison. Edward took Johnston aside and was both fatherly and firm. Out of the earshot of Mrs. Jones, Edward explained that when he had been Johnston's age, he too had been unlucky in love. He had been engaged to Stephen Du Ponceau's own sister, but the deadly yellow fever had cruelly stolen her from him. Not long afterward, he had fallen for the charms of another alphabetical lover, a "Miss *R.*" This enigmatic woman was not only exceptionally beautiful, as was Johnston's own Miss *B.*, but she was also the very belle of Philadelphia society. Her parents wanted nothing to do with the Irish pauper, however, and they made their irrevocable sentiments clear. Edward had been like Johnston, poor and unknown to fame. He and Miss *R.* secretly courted and were for a while the favorite topic of gossip in that city of brotherly love. Several popular songs were reportedly written about their illicit passion. But the young lady's father remained adamant, and so Edward went south to begin a new life, hoping to create the financial success that would eventually win the respect of his love's family. The two kept up a secret correspondence for many years, using the pen names of Armide and Elvira lest their notes should fall into the wrong hands. Neither married or seriously courted for many years, but finally Miss *R.*, subject to the unrelenting encouragement of her parents, succumbed to the charms of another suitor of wealth and "good character."

Now, looking back with the wisdom that only hindsight can provide, Edward Jones admitted regret over the time and effort lost in pursuing the unobtainable. Had things not turned out as they had, Edward added in an aside, he would not have met Mrs. Jones. And so, he concluded, everything worked out well in the end. Johnston reluctantly acquiesced.[30] Not long after his departure, the mysterious and beautiful Miss *B.* married a "wealthy and respectable" gentleman and retired with him to Savannah, Georgia. This was to be Johnston Blakeley's last such dalliance for some time. He was now an officer in the United States Navy.

2. PRESIDENTIAL STUDIES

July 1800–August 1802

When the French government sent their envoy to the United States in 1793, they had every reason to expect enthusiastic assistance against the counterrevolutionary confederation of Britain, Spain, Austria, and Prussia. They had put both their lives and their money on the line during the American Revolution and now, they reasoned, it was payback time. But the United States did not yet possess a navy, and what little army it did have was not sufficient to deal with the troubles along its own borders. To side with France must necessarily mean taking up arms against its foes. The valuable northwestern fur-trading posts, which were supposed to have been ceded following the Revolution, still remained in British hands. The Spanish for their part were openly inciting the southern Indians to rebel against the settlers in Georgia and along the Mississippi. America had little choice but to remain neutral. The nation's polite refusal distressed and angered the Paris government.

The Jay Treaty between the United States and Great Britain was the final straw. What had actually been intended to settle nagging territorial issues was instead interpreted by the French as a military and economic alliance between the two English-speaking nations. Paris issued decrees in retaliation, granting permission to French captains to seize American vessels. President John Adams longed for a peaceful settlement to the crisis and so dispatched Elbridge Gerry, John Marshall, and Charles Cotesworth Pinckney to Paris with the authority to conclude a face-saving deal. The French response to this delegation shocked even the loudest critics of appeasement. Representatives of the Paris Ministry demanded a bribe before negotiations could begin. The XYZ Affair, as it came to be known, created a war cry throughout the land and led not to the creation but to the completion of the U.S. Navy.

Construction of six frigates had already been authorized by Congress for use against the piratical state of Algiers, but when the latter signed a treaty of peace with the United States construction had ceased on three of the frigates. This latest security threat stimulated renewed building and inspired the purchase of a score of additional vessels. Hence the modern navy was born. The first three frigates, *Constitution, United States,* and *Constellation,* were already in such an advanced state of construction that they were able to put to sea in only a short time. The last three ships, still under construction into the second year of the war, were the *Congress* at Portsmouth, New Hampshire; the *Chesapeake* at Norfolk, Virginia; and the *President* at New York City. It was to this last ship that Midshipman Johnston Blakeley reported in the summer of 1800.

Blakeley could not have received his initial sea training at the hands of a more willing and capable officer. Commo. Thomas Truxtun had been Blakeley's second or perhaps even his third choice. Nevertheless, Truxtun was the only captain of the original six who went out of his way to encourage and enhance his young gentlemen's complete education. Midshipmen must not, he felt, simply become proficient in the necessary skills of their calling, but infinitely more. He took a dim view of many of his own peers, characterizing them as uninformed men who disliked reading and who lacked what he termed "studious application" to their own continuing education. To date, Truxtun had already published a textbook on the complex theory of navigation, which also included a proposed organizational plan for the country's new navy, "from the admiral on down to the most inferior officer." The bulk of this latter work was, most wisely, devoted to the instruction of the inexperienced midshipmen.[1]

Blakeley was one of twenty midshipmen assigned to the *President;* the sister frigates normally carried only a dozen or so. This voyage was going to be as much Truxtun's "school of the sea" as it was a fighting cruise. Blakeley, always described as somewhat compact, no doubt adapted better than most to the meager clearance beneath the beams, only slightly less commodious than the Chapel Hill dormitories. With his mind full of Greek, Latin, and

Paine—but totally devoid of any practical knowledge of the sea—Blakeley would have had little to do but overcome seasickness and befriend his new hammock-mates. Few of the other gentlemen were first-time voyagers, and Blakeley, the college boy, was probably snubbed and then taunted, teased, and, above all, tested. His reactions would determine the level of respect, or lack thereof, he would enjoy for the totality of the voyage. Before long, the adaptive, amiable Blakeley had learned the ropes and had slowly begun to fit into this strange sea-society.

The clock was slowly ticking down on the naval war with France, and Truxtun feared the inevitable news of an armistice. He had strong personal motives for quickly putting to sea, for he had left some unfinished business anchored off the Dutch-held island of Curaçao. "Truxtun is leaving and will do the impossible," observed one presidential confidant, "in order to have a second fight with the *Vengeance*. . . . What vain and unreasonable creatures most men are!"

Truxtun had won a credible victory against *L'Insurgente* in 1799 while commanding the *Constellation*, the post–Constitutional navy's first such victory, but his triumph was somewhat hollow. Although not the equal of the *President*, the *Constellation* was a very large 24-pounder frigate, rated at 38 guns but actually mounting 50, while the Frenchman was a mere 12-pounder ship, honestly rating and mounting 40. The press had been kind to Truxtun, reporting with a wink and a nod that a 38-gun American had captured a French 40-gunner. The *Constellation*'s second battle, with the French frigate *La Vengeance*, would be more fair.

Originally mounting thirty long 24-pounders on the main deck during its first commission in addition to nearly two dozen lighter pieces on its upper deck, this experimental French frigate was the most powerful single-decked ship of its day. By the time of the Quasi-War, *La Vengeance*'s commander had swapped his long 24s for an equal number of lighter long 18s to reduce weight and increase his ship's speed. Coincidentally, Truxtun had made the exact same swap with the *Constellation* immediately following his meeting with *L'Insurgente*. These 52-gunners were of the same length, breadth, and armament. A closer match could not have been possible. The French frigate *La Vengeance* was battered by Truxtun during a five-hour, moonlit match, and reportedly struck its colors three times, but to no avail. If Truxtun had realized that the prize had been thrice his for the taking, he could have sailed triumphantly home with one of the most phenomenal vessels then afloat. *La Vengeance* managed to escape to the temporary sanctity of Curaçao and Truxtun was unable to pursue his shattered foe because his ship lost its mainmast.

La Vengeance sat at Curaçao for six months, unable to acquire the spars and cordage needed to implement the extensive repairs. Truxtun had hoped to be standing off the Dutch island in the *President* by the time the Frenchman was readied for sea but he was not able to sail quick enough. A British frigate snatched up the still shattered Frenchman in the Mona Passage. *Vengeance* is mine, sayeth the lord, Sir David Milne, commander of the British frigate *Seine*. Truxtun's trophy was gone.

President Adams wanted his enormous namesake put to sea with all possible dispatch because there had recently been an increase in the number of French raids against American merchantmen near the Guadeloupe Station. Much of the last-minute, near-frantic provisioning fell upon the shoulders of Truxtun's five lieutenants. Three of them—Isaac Chauncey, the frigate's first lieutenant; John Dent, its second; and Philemon Wederstrandt, its fifth—would each take Midshipman Blakeley with them upon assuming their first commands. Such was the positive impression of the North Carolinian's abilities.

Truxtun's marine officer, Lieutenant Lewis, created a very different impression, however, because he was often absent. Truxtun felt that Lewis was far more concerned with his new wife ashore than with his official duties. On one occasion he even threatened the marine with arrest if he did not return on board posthaste and remain there.[2] Truxtun always openly pronounced himself "sensible to the unimportance of the Marine Corps." Able seamen, he reasoned, well trained in the use of small arms and boarding tactics, were far more efficient on board a sailing ship of war because they were of more use when the frigate was not engaged in battle. Truxtun could not foresee that during the summer of 1814, one of his underlings, then a master commandant, would be forced to put to sea in a ship devoid of all marines except four privates and a corporal. In an ensuing British trial, Johnston Blakeley would unintentionally prove his old captain's theory correct.

The *President* got under way from its anchorage in the East River on 5 August 1800, and stood out to sea after briefly watering at Sandy Hook. Six storm-tossed days later, Blakeley witnessed his first capture. The British ship *Ruth*, taken the previous morning by a 6-gun French privateer, somehow mistook the huge *President* for a friendly letter of marque and foolishly closed with it. The frigate and its new charge arrived safely at their station off the island of Nevis on the twenty-second. Dispatching his prize to St. Kitts the following day, Truxtun set off in pursuit of two strange sails. His quarries, however, proved to be the frigates *Philadelphia* and *John Adams*. Capts. Stephen Decatur Sr. and George Cross soon hove their respective ships to and came aboard to meet with their squadron commander. The *John Adams*, although the smallest of the trio, no doubt intrigued Blakeley. Built by the patriotic citizens of Charleston, South Carolina, it was the most "southern" frigate in the fleet of the new nation. It was floating proof that the southern states were as capable of producing complex war machines as their northern brethren. This pretty little frigate would also one day become Blakeley's first independent command—albeit in an unofficial and temporary capacity.

On 5 October Truxtun cruised between the Saints and Dominica with the schooner *Enterprize*, Lt. John Shaw commanding, in company. This tiny schooner was destined to become Blakeley's first permanent command eleven years later. When the duo caught up with the *John Adams* on the evening of 7 October Truxtun decided to put the ships' sailing qualities to the test. Setting its courses, topsails, topgallants, and flying jibs, the *President* quickly outpaced its companions. The master observed with some satisfaction, "We far outsail the John Adams." By early the next morning, Truxtun's struggling opponent was nearly two miles astern.[3] The schooner had by then already parted company, but it would try the same experiment five days later.

It was a general rule of thumb that vessels of the *President*'s bulk tended to perform better in heavy weather than those of the *Enterprize*'s waifish stature, the latter class excelling in lighter airs. But there were conditions under which the vessels could compete more equally. On just such a day, with the wind brisk, but not too brisk, just abaft the beam and "with all sail set fore and aft," the frigate's master recorded with subdued triumph, "Find we out sail the Enterprize."[4] The *President* returned to its Basseterre anchorage on 22 October and once again settled into the dull routine of provisioning.

Midshipman Blakeley was witness to a curious naval interaction on 25 October. The British 32-gun frigate *Southampton*, the old reliable of the West Indies station, arrived in port early that morning. Launched in 1756, the *Southampton* was both the oldest frigate in His Majesty's Service and the first single-decked "true frigate" ever built for the Royal Navy. A mere 671 tons, its ancient hull could have been demolished by a single, well-placed presidential broadside. Duly impressed by the American's relative invulnerability, Seaman Thomas Parker leapt from the *Southampton*'s forecastle into the green sea and swam the short, shark-infested distance to the *President*'s side. Standing dripping before the surprised commodore, Parker explained that he was an American who had been forcibly pressed into service to the Crown. The furious English captain could do little more than stare across at them in embarrassed silence.

There was still much for Blakeley to learn. On 5 November, for example, Truxtun specifically ordered Robert Thompson, the frigate's schoolmaster, to instruct the young gentlemen in the art of chart-making. After drawing their accurate representations of the local environs, the midshipmen were then to plot the frigate's cruises to date. Thompson was also to make sure that they thoroughly understood the principles of Mercator's astronomical projections. Within the week, however, Blakeley's teacher departed in the newly arrived *Chesapeake* because, as Truxtun explained, "The unhappy situation between Thompson and the other officers of the gun room seems incurable."[5] The day ended with a happy note, however. "Tried our sailing with the Chesapeake," wrote the increasingly giddy sailing master, "and find we beat her."

Sickness dominated these notoriously unhealthful waters, and Truxtun was not immune. His health, never good on this voyage, became steadily worse. By mid-December he was begging permission to come home, anxious once again to breathe the "pure northern air." His successful cruises on the *Constellation* had spoiled him, and he quickly grew tired of chasing neutral merchant schooners. Moreover the unwelcome news of the *Vengeance*'s capture vexed him.

His squadron was soon bolstered by the arrival of the new 36-gun *New York*, and when they at length chanced an impromptu race, the predictable *President* trounced it soundly.[6] In late November, a British packet informed the commodore that American diplomats had finally completed their treaty of amity in Paris. Once the Senate ratified this peace agreement, the war would be over.

The *President* made several short cruises about its assigned hunting grounds at year's end, but none proved successful. One December cruise took Truxtun past Martinique on the tenth; he then passed between that island and St. Lucia, standing about fifty leagues to windward in search of a reported French corvette. Truxtun next stretched northward about Dominica, Mariagallante, Petit Terre, Desirata, southward of Antigua and Montserrat, before returning to St. Barts and St. Martin. Joining forces with his temporary ally, the aging though still swift *Southampton*, they chased many a mysterious windward sail. Neither was successful in their pursuits and curiously the *President*'s master did not make any remarks about the ships' relative performances. At St. Barts on 26 December, Truxtun learned from a passing Swede that the French corvette was at Pointe-à-Pitre, ready to cruise. He dashed immediately off to the Saints in hope of getting windward of his quarry, but he was too late.[7]

Truxtun's cruise technically ended on 15 January, when the frigate *United States*, flying the broad pennant of Commo. John Barry, dropped anchor in St. Kitts. On the eighteenth Barry got under way, leaving the *President* and the *Chesapeake* with orders to return home. An unwelcome report arrived later that afternoon announcing the election of Thomas Jefferson as president. The Republican Jefferson was thought to oppose the existence of a navy, and there was the real possibility that the ship's company might all find themselves unemployed upon their return. After an uneventful passage of twenty-two days, the *President* arrived safely home in Hampton Roads, Virginia, its jittery officers preparing for the worst.[8]

Once on land they discovered that the lame-duck Congress, wisely electing to deal with naval matters before the Republicans came into power, had passed the Peace Establishment Act (PEA) hoping to minimize the looming reductions in naval expenditures. The outgoing Federalists made the preemptive cuts themselves, hoping that these drastic but not devastating cutbacks would satisfy the incoming Jefferson and his budget-slashing, isolationist followers. The PEA reduced the size of the navy from thirty-odd vessels to only thirteen frigates, the balance being sold out of the service. Of the remainder, all but six would be mothballed—laid up "in ordinary"—awaiting future use, which would be against the Barbary pirates. Fortunately, the half-dozen frigates destined to remain in commission at any given time were to be kept actively cruising, to train midshipmen. But the officer corps was also to be gutted. The current list of captains was slashed from twenty-eight to nine, and the lieutenants and midshipmen suffered in even greater proportion. Only those officers possessing the greatest combination of influence and individual merit would be spared. Johnston Blakeley was one of the lucky few.

The navy's records show that Blakeley reported on board the *President* in June of 1800 and that he remained there until March of 1802[9] and reference Blakeley's West Indian cruise.[10] The acting secretary of the navy, Samuel Smith, sent Commodore Truxtun his approved list of those officers to be kept on board the *President*.[11] He not only named each of the frigate's midshipmen who would be retained but also detailed the names of the other young gentlemen to be consolidated from other vessels. Midshipman Blakeley, retained because of his proven abilities, is listed among those meritorious souls to be kept "on board."

President Jefferson proved to be not quite as opposed to the navy as had been feared. Although he wholeheartedly disapproved of the use of the service against his Revolutionary allies, the French, he knew that the Barbary States respected only those nations with the power to defend themselves. Jefferson's America needed its navy. Three weeks after his inauguration, the president ordered a naval force to the Mediterranean to deal with the combined forces of Tripoli and Algiers. Corsairs had for centuries sailed from the four distant dependencies of the Turkish sultan: Tripoli, Tunis, Algiers, and the nearly independent Morocco. While the latter three states were momentarily quiet, Tripoli's saber rattling was kicking up quite a din. In the past, it had been America's established practice to pay annual tribute to purchase peace. The treaty with Morocco in 1786 was the first such agreement, followed soon after by arrangements with Algiers in 1795, Tripoli the following year, and Tunis the year after that. But the pasha of Tripoli, Yusuf Karamanli, had been throwing a tantrum ever since he learned that the dey of Algiers, Bobba Mustapha, had received more valuable presents. The pasha was now threatening to go to war, and Washington believed that unless a powerful squadron made an open display of forceful resolve—and did so quickly—his cruisers would once again put to sea. Truxtun was given a formidable squadron consisting of the frigates *President*, *Philadelphia*, and *Essex*, along with the useful, shallow-draft *Enterprize*, with which to carry out this mission.

Only Congress could declare war and it would not meet for several months. Secretary Smith had given strict orders in the interim for the squadron to act only defensively. Perhaps, Smith hoped, an adequate show of force might be enough to keep the pasha at bay. But Truxtun would have none of it. If he was to be prohibited from "acting decisively" against Tripoli and its allies, he declined the honor. A staunchly Federalist captain, he believed he could browbeat the incoming Republicans. If he had hoped to gain greater freedom by refusing the squadron's command, he was sadly mistaken. Truxtun's adoption of an I'll-resign-and-then-they'll-be-sorry policy backfired. On 28 April 1801 Secretary Smith transferred the command of the squadron to Commo. Richard Dale.

Dale was John Paul Jones's most loyal and highest-ranking subordinate during the Revolution. Dale had served as Jones's first lieutenant on board the *Bon Homme Richard* during his epic "I have not yet begun to fight" contest against the powerful English *Serapis* off Flamborough Head. Dale's telling of the tale of his cruise in the *Richard* would have impressed young Blakeley. Dale would have to call upon every ounce of political talent to implement his orders properly. The stakes were high. But the department saw fit to weigh him down with strict and detailed instructions for nearly every conceivable eventuality involving the four potentially hostile and possibly allied nations. He was to initiate nothing that would bring the United States into collision with any Barbary power. The acting secretary had threatened that, if he did so, he would be reprimanded "scrupulously and without indulgence." At the same time, he was not to stand for any insults to the flag.

The squadron departed the Chesapeake Capes on 2 June 1801, arriving in Gibraltar one uneventful month later. Dale's unofficial reception there included "the High Admiral of Tripoli," Murad Reis, the commander of a squadron that was in port watering. Reis soon came aboard, feigning delight at seeing so distinguished a commodore. No, declared Reis, there was no reason for apprehension on Dale's part, for their two nations were still at peace, and to prove it he produced a letter of friendship from Tripoli's American consul, James Leander Cathcart. Actually, Tripoli had indeed declared war against the United States on 14 May; Cathcart's otherwise legitimate letter had been written just days prior. Reis had been within hours of sailing into the western ocean in hopes of snatching up unsuspecting Yankee merchantmen when the American squadron unexpectedly appeared. Dale saw through Reis's guise, but lacking any definitive proof, which was required by his instructions, he could do nothing, especially in a neutral port. Leaving the powerful *Philadelphia* offshore to deal with Reis in case he tried to slip out, Dale sailed the balance of his squadron southeast to Algiers in compliance with the next phase of his orders.

News obtained at their destination revealed Tripoli's true belligerent status. This came as no surprise. As neither Algiers nor Tunis at present desired any trouble with the powerful *President* (the *Essex* had been dispatched eastward on convoy duty), Dale hurried off to Tripoli with the *Enterprize*. When they arrived on 24 July, Dale instantly dispatched a letter to the pasha, expressing both his surprise and regret upon learning that their two nations were at war. The pasha would therefore understand that his job was now to blockade Tripoli unless, of course, some sort of peaceful settlement could be reached. Nicholas Nissen, Tripoli's Danish consul, came aboard the following day to meet with Dale, and together they drew up plans to bombard the city. But Dale wanted at least one additional frigate alongside him. Since those few remnants of the pasha's fleet not bottled up in Gibraltar were being rapidly hauled up onto shore, Dale realized that his blockade might well be a long one.

On 27 September the *President* returned to Gibraltar Bay on a dual mission. First, a Greek transport attempting to run Dale's blockade had been intercepted and was carrying a large number of Tripolitan subjects on board. Since the pasha had refused any exchange of prisoners, the forty-odd guests had been forced to stay in the frigate long enough for "some form of influenza" to debilitate more than 150 hands. Second, although the Tripolitan admiral had laid up his ships and dispersed their crews, Dale found a difficulty of a more troubling sort brewing at the Rock. Gunboats and privateers operating out of Algeciras had begun a strict blockade of the British at Gibraltar. They apparently also thought that American merchantmen were fair game. Not only had this created another unwanted political headache for the commodore, but the bold Spaniards had taken the squadron's long-anticipated store ship as well. In an angry letter to the Spanish governor, Dale insisted upon immediate repatriation of all confiscated American ships and property and then demanded to know whether they considered themselves at war with the United States. It seems that not only did the governor of San Roque own three of the offending privateers, but he was also the impartial chief justice of the Spanish Admiralty Court.

Dale was disappointed with the contents of his store ship when it was recovered on 26 October. The ship contained no cheese, butter, molasses, candles, or the all-important rum. But there was some good news. First, his squadron had been augmented by the arrival of the frigate *Boston;* second, the King of Sweden was sending out four frigates with orders to act in concert with him against their common enemy. Furthermore, an encouraging rumor abounded that England and France had just signed a treaty of peace, although no official announcements had yet been made. The *President* departed Gibraltar Bay on 9 November and set out alone for its rendezvous with the Swedes off Tripoli. On the way, Commodore Dale made the nearly fatal decision to look into Port Mahon, Minorca, where the American consul at Algiers, Richard O'Brien, had warned him that a large and particularly powerful corsair was secretly being fitted out for the pasha. From his quarantine anchorage, Dale sent off a note to the governor of Minorca reminding him that even if the xebec-frigate were to sail with a Minorcan crew while flying English colors, he felt duty bound to engage it if it was the property of the pasha. The governor replied that the vessel had in fact been sold at auction to Tunis, not Tripoli. This seemed to pacify the commodore, but he made it publicly known that any "Imperial, Greek and Ragusan vessels" caught trading with Tripoli were to be considered legitimate prizes.

The harbor of Port Mahon, located on the southeastern edge of the island of Minorca, has long been considered the safest natural haven for shipping in the Mediterranean. Its uniformly deep anchorages made it ideal for the Royal Navy's needs, enabling even ships of the line close access to the quay and the victualing wharf. These accommodations were especially appreciated by Dale because the *President* drew as much water as an English 74. This particular naval base was one of the best protected, not only from the elements—stretching more than a league inland—but also from any potential seaborne attack, and the selective admission of visitors was ensured by the powerful batteries of Fort St. Philip. In fact, the mere ninety-fathom-wide, rock-ringed entrance alone might deter a direct naval invasion. This gave rise to one serious drawback. Unless the wind blew from the north, it was difficult, even hazardous, to attempt to take a ship out. But 30 November was just such a favorable day. Confident that his warnings had put an end to any threat, Dale put boldly back out to sea, his mind filled with the countless details and the endless potential glories of the upcoming multinational assault on Tripoli. His lone frigate was making from five to six knots with the wind on its larboard quarter when it struck the submerged stone bank. The unexpected shock threw most of the 409 men on board flat on the deck. As the frigate rolled heavily with the increasing swell, its frame ground against the barnacled rocks. To a man, the impression on board was that once the ship slid off the shelf into the channel, it would quickly fill and founder. And if it did not extricate itself at once, it must certainly beat to pieces. There would be no time to heave out the boats or rig the pumps. The frigid December seas would certainly consume most on board long before help might arrive from Fort St. Philip. All seemed instantly and irretrievably lost. Dale initially blamed the Mahon pilot for running the ship up on the rocks,[12] but soon afterward he admitted that it was "a man belonging to the ship."[13]

The ship was thus upon the rocks with the lower part of the stem and forwardmost section of the keel, a complex oddly shaped structure called the forefoot, at first maintaining an Atlas-like hold. Then the thick, composition metal bolts suddenly wrenched free in a tangle of split wood and twisted copper skin. The frigate dropped down off its perch and slid slowly astern into the channel, with the crushed, forwardmost section of the keel grinding away as it descended. To Dale's amazement, the frigate remained not only afloat but reasonably watertight as well. In the design of any other ship, the lowest strakes of adjacent planking would have torn violently away with the forefoot, opening the ship to such an enormous torrent of seawater that it would have gone down by the head in minutes. But the frigate's brilliant designer, Joshua Humphreys, had foreseen the possibility of such a calamity. In any other vessel, the leading butts of the forward planking would have been mortised snugly into a bevel called the rabbet, cut at the juncture of the forefoot and the stout backing timber called the apron. But the *President* and its two sisters instead terminated their planking into the apron. Thus the projecting forefoot had acted as a shock-absorbing, breakaway bumper.

The fitful gusts now increased in their violence as the dreaded mistral came on. Dale reasoned that even if he could successfully retreat into the temporary safety of Mahon, that naval base did not afford a drydock. The carpenter reported that the damage was far too low to come at otherwise, so the commodore charted a course to the closest yard so equipped. The French port of Toulon, although a mere 225 miles distant, was due north of both Minorca and the *President*. For eight anxious days the frigate labored northward against contrary winds, finally reaching the harbor on 7 December. The crew was exhausted, emotionally drained, and physically ill. Although the *President*'s repairs took over a month to accomplish, they were completed in "an excellent manner," and the vessel soon prepared to set sail for home. The *President* did not arrive at Hampton Roads until late April, however, since Dale elected to dawdle awhile in Toulon and Gibraltar.

Blakeley took a furlough to Wilmington immediately after this voyage. At this time, however, he began to suffer a professional change of heart. He had served two active years, under two reputedly enterprising commanders, in two different wars, aboard the finest single-decked fighting ship afloat. Blakeley, however, had never seen a great gun fired in earnest or in anger. His second cruise had been a major disappointment. Timidity by the acting secretary had hamstrung his new commander at a time when bold, decisive action might well have done some good. The great old Commodores Truxtun and Dale of lore, each returning from what would prove to be their final cruises,[14] had enjoyed fighting reputations, but Blakeley had not seen any firsthand evidence of it.

Midshipman Blakeley therefore wrote the secretary, begging for a temporary furlough to enter the merchant service. Robert Smith, who replaced acting secretary Samuel Smith in July 1801, responded positively and gave him permission for a nine-month leave of absence.[15] Johnston did not need the money merchant service would ensure because his father's Wilmington properties provided an income. He liked the life at sea and perhaps he thought that this might be a good time to explore what the merchant service had to offer. However, he did not act in earnest. Smith must have been surprised to find the midshipman still lingering at home a full five weeks after receiving permission to leave. His subsequent recall orders required the Carolina reefer to return at once to active service for another crack at the Tripolitans.[16] He was to be part of a new squadron commanded once again by Commodore Truxtun, but this time there were to be more aggressive guidelines. John Rodgers, the commodore's hard-driving protégé, was to be Blakeley's new captain, and the sweet, southern, shallow-draft *John Adams* was to be his new home.

3. Rodgers's Boy

September 1802–July 1805

verything seemed to go wrong with Midshipman Blakeley's cruise on the *John Adams*. Thomas Truxtun was not in command of the squadron, as Blakeley had hoped. The commodore had eagerly reported to his flag-frigate, the *Chesapeake*, early on, only to find it partially stripped, half decayed, and, because of numerous expired enlistments, sparsely populated, especially in the wardroom. Showing a characteristic lack of tact, the Federalist commodore demanded that the Republican secretary of the navy, Robert Smith, supply him with a subservient flag captain. Otherwise, he threatened, he would not only relinquish the command of the squadron but quit the service as well. The appointment of a flag captain was not possible, because the PEA had stripped the navy of all available junior captains, and the lesser rank of master commandant had been scrapped in its entirety. Glad to be rid of such a constant albeit extremely able pest, the secretary jumped at the chance and called his bluff. Shocked, Truxtun had no choice but to depart, regretting his error for the rest of his days.

The next available senior captain on the list, Richard Valentine Morris, assumed command of the squadron and quickly put to sea. The mission, however, was handicapped from the start. Although the combined force represented the largest American naval presence seen thus far in the

Mediterranean, the individual ships were at first scattered all along the Eastern Seaboard, in various stages of disrepair. Subsequently, their respective departures stretched over a period of several months.[1] Significantly the secretary had failed to supply Morris with any of the big 24-pounder ships, those best calculated to deal with harbor fortifications. As a result the entire squadron did not possess a single long gun heavier than an 18-pounder. Even worse, no sooner had the fleet assembled after much delay in Gibraltar in preparation for the upcoming campaign than Washington ordered the recall of Morris's largest frigates, the *Constellation* and the *Chesapeake*. Morris had to shift his flag to the identically rated but considerably weaker *New York*, his only remaining 18-pounder ship. His two smaller frigates, the confusingly named *Adams* and the *John Adams*, carried only 12-pounders on their main decks. The faithful old *Enterprize* carried only 6-pounders, and inasmuch as it had been used continuously since its purchase in 1799 without a major overhaul, the navy's lone schooner was quickly becoming unserviceable.

The expedition had not, however, been intended as a big one. The *Constellation, Chesapeake,* and *Adams* had been deemed sufficient to corral the pasha. But then a new threat from a grumbling and potentially dangerous Morocco added a complicating twist to their mission. The secretary had therefore sent the *New York* and Blakeley's *John Adams* out as an added measure of security. When the Republican Congress finally convened, one of their first tasks was to "unleash the navy" from its earlier constitutional constraints by passing an "Act for the Protection of the Commerce and Seamen of the United States against the Tripolitan Cruisers."[2]

Jefferson had mistakenly assumed that Dale had sufficiently lulled the pasha into a state of near submission the previous summer. A mere show of the American armada, Jefferson had hoped, might be enough to buy a peace for the United States on advantageous terms. The president therefore sent diplomat James Leander Cathcart, the former American consul to Tripoli, out with Morris in the *Chesapeake* with instructions from the secretary of state to open negotiations after some decisive strike, or, it was hoped, to take advantage of "the awe inspired by a display of force displayed before his eyes and capitol."

The *John Adams* crossed the Atlantic in five weeks and proceeded on to Valetta, on the island of Malta, arriving on 1 January 1803. Here Capt. John Rodgers learned that Dale's old nemesis, Admiral Reis, had at last made his way back to Tripoli, although he had been forced to leave behind both of his heavy cruisers. Reis was thought to be preparing to put to sea once again with whatever vessels he might scrape together, a force still thought to be considerable. On the last day of the month, Morris's three-frigate squadron set off confidently for Tripoli, awash with hopes of glory. "Ye Tripolitans beware," growled one of the *Chesapeake*'s midshipmen. "The Chesapeake, New York and John Adams are coming towards ye in battle array!" But, as was all too often the case, nature was not going to cooperate. A continuous gale blew out of the northwestern seas and that, combining with a strong easterly current, forced the squadron some thirty-five miles to the eastern lee of Tripoli. As the increasingly "boisterous" weather convinced Morris that his ships would soon be in imminent peril, he abruptly called off the mission and ordered his squadron away to Tunis in search of stores and perhaps to make a resolute show of force in that equally restless quarter.

From that seemingly low point of the cruise, fortunes slid downhill even further. On 23 February 1803, the *John Adams* dropped anchor in the Bay of Tunis, about "3 miles south of old Carthage." Rodgers found not only the balance of his squadron there but the schooner *Enterprize* as well. Three days later, Commodore Morris, Captain Rodgers, "and other officers and diplomats," with Blakeley quite possibly among them, went ashore to visit the bey. While out cruising independently, the *Enterprize* had the good fortune to capture the Tripolitan polacre *Paulina* but had made the grave mistake of bringing it along from Malta. The bey, believing that the polacre contained Tunisian property, demanded its immediate return, even threatening to go to war over the issue. A disagreement over some unpaid American tribute soon complicated the matter, and before the day was over the diplomatic mission found themselves trapped ashore. The bey had Morris arrested and threatened to make hostages of them unless the tribute was paid immediately. Since the Tunisian navy was more powerful than the American squadron, Morris and Cathcart were forced to comply, in spite of the national and personal humiliation.

Returning on board his frigate, Captain Rodgers found still more unpleasantries awaiting him. Under the impression that the situation might turn out to be a prolonged stalemate, Lt. George Cox had arbitrarily reduced all food rations on board, including those of the wardroom. The unhappy junior officers who had remained behind with Cox presented their returning captain with a polite, yet firm and somewhat amusing, note requesting a "sufficiency for supper this evening." They had, they explained, been deprived of this indulgence, even though the ship had not been officially placed on any restricted allowance. The undersigned officers did make a point of stating that it was to their certain knowledge that their fair-minded captain could not have known of this draconian measure. In the unusual circumstance that he might approve of the decision by Cox (who was never explicitly named), they would "at all times submit with cheerfulness" to any culinary restriction that he, Rodgers, would desire. Blakeley's name was not included in the long list of signatories, either because he sided with Cox or (more likely) because he had gone ashore with Rodgers.[3] The squadron soon arrived off Algiers, but as they found the reception there equally cold, no one went ashore. Instead, the squadron returned to Gibraltar on 23 March.

Many of the sailors had come to the end of their enlistments at this time, and Morris was forced to send them back home in the *Chesapeake*. The commodore then shifted his flag to the *New York*, but immediately sent it and the *John Adams* off to Málaga without him.[4] He instead remained in the nearly empty *Enterprize*, hoping to recruit a sufficiently large English-speaking crew before the imminent Franco-English conflict consumed their ranks. Blakeley's frigate arrived in the Spanish port on 12 April and began its return trip to Malta once the commodore caught up with them three days later.[5] During the lengthy fortnight-long passage back to the island, Rodgers desired to try his frigate's wings against those of its two consorts. The log concluded that day with "the New York beating us as usual and we [beat] the schooner Enterprize." This seemingly average performance was a bit disappointing, as the *John Adams* was no slug, although neither were its companions. The ship had earned a great name for itself during the Quasi-War for catching many unusually swift French privateers. In addition, it had raced against several British men-of-war, Caribbean cruising companions of a common purpose, and had "outdone them all in sailing."[6] The *New York* limped into Malta on 1 May after a fire adjacent to its magazine had consumed much of the inner works. Morris was therefore forced to spend much of his time from then on in the dockyards, while his acting flag captain scrounged for expensive replacement stores ashore. The flagship would be out of action for several weeks. So too would the *Enterprize*, for its bottom sheathing was torn and foul and the ship now required recoppering, a process of many days if not weeks. Thus it was under these circumstances that Morris had sent the lone *John Adams* off to Tripoli, and it was ordered to show what force it could and to inflict all the damage that was in its power.

The *John Adams* first sighted the port city of Tripoli bearing southwest just after sunrise on the brilliantly clear morning of 8 May 1803. The highlands of Tagiura, bright ocher against the rising sun, had already pushed themselves up over the mist nearly two hours before. Through his telescope, Captain Rodgers watched the frenzied activities in the harbor with grave interest: the coasters pulling in closer toward shore; the cavalry racing along the dunes; and the legions of turbaned men clambering about the great siege batteries of the Citadel, known to mariners as the dreaded French Batteries. The Americans had been seen and identified. In the inner harbor, Rodgers observed nine small yet lethal craft rowing slowly into the outer roads. Suddenly the teeth of the harbor's yawning mouth flashed out sharp and clear in the form of gunboats' triangular sails. The sun sparkled off their heavy brass guns as the Barbary pirates pulled toward a rock-strewn stretch of sea just to the east of town. Rodgers had by now stripped his frigate down to fighting canvas and had long ago cleared his decks for action. As the lateen-rigged corsairs advanced to greet the *John Adams*, it sailed slowly on, wholly undeterred and prepared to return any greeting instantly.

Midshipman Johnston Blakeley stood on the quarterdeck, just abaft the wheel. Beside him, also awaiting the upcoming action, were his immediate charges, a team of four able seamen, ready to attend to the mizzen topsail and cross-jack braces. Victory or defeat depended in no small part on the ability of his quartet of mizzen topmen to adjust their assigned mast's complex collection of sheets and braces when called upon, through the smoke and noise, to tack or wear. From his position, Blakeley could hear an order the instant that Rodgers or 1st Lt. George Cox gave it, without waiting for a messenger. He could carefully study every nuance of command under fire, and, above all, view the entire panorama of the battle. Many of the navy's most active and accomplished future leaders eagerly attended their posts on this same frigate as well. Midshipmen John B. Nicholson and Charles Ridgely, in command of the mainsail and main topsail braces, respectively, supervised their own people on the quarterdeck just forward of Blakeley's party, while gentlemen John Orde Creighton and William Allen stood behind their commander as aides-de-camp. High above, Midshipman John T. Shubrick conducted his small-arms men in the maintop, while down below, messmate James Renshaw made last-minute preparations as second in command of the forwardmost division of main deck guns.[7] The frigate's second and third lieutenants, Samuel Evans and Philemon C. Wederstrandt, both late of Dale's *President*, ran to and fro among the 223 eager souls in their finest azure and amber dress.

The petite *John Adams* was truly the copper-bottomed cradle of the U.S. Navy. At just under six hundred tons, it was small as far as frigates went. But the ship was beautiful in its proportions, swift in its sailing, and stout in its build. Most important, its present commander did not seem the type of man to shy away from a fight, whatever the odds, and his ship was quite alone on this otherwise pleasant morning.

At 12:30 P.M., when the *John Adams* was within "half-gunshot" of the anchored flotilla, the Citadel and the numerous smaller batteries opened up. But the Tripolitan gunners threw their shot too high. Rodgers instantly responded with his larboard main deck 12-pounders. As if by signal, the gunboats got under way once again and commenced their own rapid but ineffectual fire. Rodgers, in turn, discharged his starboard guns straight into their startled ranks and gave them reason to reconsider their attack. Believing it now unwise to venture beyond the shoals, the gunboats tacked and stood inshore, back toward the sanctuary of the town. But Rodgers would have none of it, and he followed them right in, evoking the wrath of the French Batteries once more. The *John Adams*'s accurate gunnery sent balls straight into the midst of the unnerved Tripolitans, causing endless confusion and inspiring a number to desert their posts, while many a shot flew well over the Citadel and into the town. "All was confusion in the city, running to and fro," wrote an observer, "[and] the next day when the J. Adams stood in for the city again, it cost the Bey several hundreds of dollars to hire men to man the guns, his own soldiers refusing." At least one ball struck the living quarters of the royal palace, alarming the pasha's harem and inducing his favorite wife to faint dead away.

By sunset Rodgers perceived that he had caused enough mischief for one day; he tacked ship and stood offshore. Just such a determined show of force by Dale in the mighty *President* during the summer of 1801, utilizing his longer range, battlement-smashing firepower, would probably have brought about the desired peace within a matter of hours. But Dale had been too cautious, and the navy had to return another day. After nearly three years of continuous service, Blakeley at long last had seen guns fired in fury.

On the following day the gunboats renewed their attack. Wishing to stay well outside the range of the *John Adams*'s 12-pounders, they hovered inshore, firing in concert with the batteries on the western bank. "None of their shot reached us by a mile," wrote the master, "[and they] made a useless expenditure of powder." The next day, the gunboats again approached under oars to within maximum range. They made two feeble discharges but then pulled quickly back into the harbor. An hour later, the Tripolitans came out again, fired once, and again retreated. On 13 May 1803, however, events turned more profitable. At five that afternoon a strange ship appeared alone in the southeast, standing on a wind to the westward, apparently trying to run into the city. Rodgers made all sail in chase while the stranger tacked to the northeast to escape. When it at length swung its broadside into view, the ship revealed its true identity. It was the cruiser so long blockaded at Gibraltar, the *Meshouda*. At one time it had been the *Betsey* of Boston, but Adm. Murad Reis had taken the cruiser in 1795 during its maiden Atlantic crossing. They had adorned it garishly: a bright yellow hull with a broad white stripe, twenty-six blood-red gun muzzles, and, across its lime-green transom, a painted woman's head resting on a bed of white flowers. It appeared "the very jackal of the seas." As the ship's stern had been cut down very low to accommodate its two standing stern-chase guns, it possessed a slinking or "down at the hind end" appearance.[8]

The *Meshouda* was deeply laden with contraband and was thus quite slow, which is no doubt why Rodgers had so little trouble catching it. Its small crew showed no inclination to fight, to the disappointment of the midshipmen. The ship had been sold to Morocco, its captain explained, and he had been given leave by Commodore Morris, at that time still recruiting in Gibraltar, to enter any Mediterranean port save Tripoli. "The John Adams caught it in the act," gloated one of the flagship's midshipmen. The Moorish commander openly admitted everything, noting in an aside that Admiral Reis was eagerly awaiting their return. After continuing the blockade for several more days, the *John Adams* returned triumphantly to Valetta with the pasha's heaviest cruiser in tow.

Captain Rodgers found the commodore ready to sail, and he put back out to sea the following day. The flagship first made out Tripoli at 9:00 A.M. on 22 May, and as soon as the squadron came within extreme range the shore batteries commenced a futile cannonade. "We hove to," recalled Midshipman Henry Wadsworth, "not noticing them." Morris next observed a strange sail inshore, a small unarmed felucca of about thirty tons, that had run itself up onto the sands. But as it did not seem worth the risk, they left it after a brief, distant inspection. This decision was, of course, poison to the impatient junior officers, who had been dying for a close brush with the enemy. Had the felucca been a mere oyster boat, Wadsworth reflected, "it would have been an amusement for us to skirmish a little." While he acknowledged being fond of the commodore, he nevertheless felt compelled to remark: "I esteem him very much, yet I thus privately note in my journal [that] I wish Captain [Rodgers] had command on today." Fearing that his writings might fall into the wrong hands, Wadsworth crossed out that final comment and jotted the word "mutiny" down beside it, before crossing that out as well.[9]

Morris did indeed conceive a bold plan of attack, but until his third frigate joined him, he did little but sail back and forth, exchanging the occasional random shot. When Capt. Hugh G. Campbell finally brought the *Adams* in on 27 May, Morris went right in after the harbor defenses with his entire force. About 5:00 P.M., a squadron of seven gunboats and a small ship (a corsair under escort attempting to get into port) was seen close in with the land, standing to the eastward toward Tripoli, then about five miles distant. Morris had hoped to cut off their escape and so "rob the Bey of all his gunboats and one of his small cruisers." But the wind died away with the setting sun. Morris formed his ships in line of battle during the waning moments of the afternoon with what little breeze remained. The experienced *John Adams,* by now well familiar with local topography and possessing the squadron's sole pilot besides, led the way in. It was followed by the flagship *New York,* quite imposing with its unbroken tier of spar deck guns in the center, while the *Adams* sailed astern giving the small yet dignified line a sense of symmetry. The *Enterprize* darted about to windward relaying signals and prepared to stand in where needed. The line approached the enemy flotilla with their starboard tacks aboard and with the shore under their lee. "A gentle breeze wafted us along," recounted one of the flagship's officers.

When Blakeley's frigate was within point-blank range of the surf, but still within the safety of fifteen fathoms of water, it laid its broadside to the beach and opened up with "both decks," utilizing the few short-range carronades.[10] Its three companions quickly imitated its actions, and the fight began in earnest. By now it was almost dark, and the American gunners could no longer see the enemy; only the flashes of their guns flared. The heavy shot from the gunboats characteristically flew well over their heads "and whistled all around," but not a single ball reportedly hit the quartet. "It was the most elegant sight," wrote Wadsworth. "The frequent flash and heavy report of the gunboats; the still more frequent broadsides of our squadron formed the most sublime scene you could imagine." But the *Adams,* half a cable's length away on the *John Adams's* weather beam, fired the greater part of its first broadside through the latter's rigging, cutting away its fore-topgallant bowlines. "By Captain Rodgers desire," the *Adams* quickly backed its main topsail and dropped astern. The flagship at the same time took a position about four cable lengths away on the *John Adams's* weather bow, but, finding three broadsides later that the only way it could hit the retreating gunboats was to throw its shot well over the point frigate, it too ceased firing for the night.

The Americans had engaged the Tripolitan navy that night under a great disadvantage. The enemy kept themselves close in with the high shore and were concealed within a "dark shade," whereas the frigates were distinct against the orange western horizon. Had the Tripolitans not been among the least skilled cannoneers in the entire Mediterranean, Morris's ships would have suffered horribly. "The moon [shone] against our sails and the light from our gun deck afforded them a sure mark," noted Wadsworth.[11] The *New York,* the *Adams,* and the *Enterprize* at length stood away to the westward at about 8:00 P.M., leaving Blakeley's little frigate alone on the scene of the action all night. In the morning, Rodgers spied his unpopular commodore and the remainder of the squadron eleven miles away to the northwest.

Believing that his little pyrotechnics show had nevertheless impressed the pasha with America's strength and resolve, Commodore Morris ordered the *Enterprize* to stand in toward the harbor under a flag of truce. The pasha provided Danish consul Nissen with a boat with which to venture out and test the waters, all the while, of course, feigning a complete lack of interest. He extended an offer to provide Morris with all the water and fresh provisions he might desire, implying that the blockade was completely ineffective, since the city had food to spare. This was no mere boast. "Tripoli this year is well provided with provisions by a rich harvest," wrote Nissen privately to James Cathcart. "There are plenty of European goods by the arrival of several ships." In a footnote to this letter, Nissen added, "What a glorious blockade!"[12] Several days later, the commodore sent Captain Rodgers into Tripoli. Accompanied by the pasha's minister of war, Sidi Mohammed Dghies, Rodgers met formally with the great ruler of Tripoli. The French consul, Bonaventure Beaussier, with the muscle of Napoleon's great navy behind him, had guaranteed Morris's complete safety should he choose to land. Satisfied, Rodgers returned to the flagship while Morris, Cathcart, and his suite went ashore to negotiate. Both sides hoisted white flags, agreeing that all hostilities were to cease during the parlay. Under these conditions, no Tripolitan cruiser could put to sea, but any homeward-bound corsair was to be allowed in unmolested. "The advantages are all on the side of the enemy," wrote Wadsworth. "Therefore let the truce be short."

And short it was. Dghies demanded, in the name of the pasha, two hundred thousand dollars in "ready cash" up front, and then an additional, annual tribute of twenty thousand more. He also insisted upon compensation for the war's expenses and an unspecified quantity of military and naval stores. The commodore's counteroffer consisted of five thousand dollars to be paid now as a gift of good faith, with an additional ten thousand dollars to be paid after five years, provided of course that the Tripolitans behaved themselves. After a very brief meeting with the pasha, the royal secretary returned to the scene of negotiations "in a rage" and asked whether the commodore had come ashore simply to mock them. The pasha then terminated all discussion. To everyone's dismay, he also ordered the flags of truce to be hauled down immediately, effectively trapping Morris and company on shore. But the French consul valiantly stepped forward and reminded the pasha of his guarantee ensuring the commodore's safety. France was a country mindful of its honor, he reminded his forgetful hosts, and it possessed a great navy capable of leveling the city. This threat had the desired effect, and the flags were rehoisted at daylight. The French consul, Bonaventure Beaussier, was under no obligation to get involved in the affairs of their late adversaries, especially since word had just come into the city of the renewed hostilities between England and France. For the second time in Blakeley's career, France had come to America's aid. There were to be no more negotiations.

To the surprise of many on both sides of the siege, Morris divided his squadron into two units. The *Adams* twins were to remain on active blockade, while the *New York* and the *Enterprize* proceeded back to Malta. It had been Morris's intention to cruise along the northern coast of the Mediterranean and to offer convoy to any American merchantman that might desire it. But when Morris reached Malta, he heard a disturbing rumor: The Tunisian navy was combining with the even larger Algerian navy, both nations intent upon capturing the American squadron piecemeal. Duly impressed with the validity of the source, the commodore felt obliged to keep "the whole of his squadron together." He recalled his two remaining blockaders, intending to move northward en masse, entirely out of harm's way. But in those few brief days that separated Morris's inglorious departure and Rodgers's subsequent recall, Johnston Blakeley would participate in one of the most exciting events of his career.

At 7:00 A.M. on 22 May the schooner *Enterprize,* having just arrived from Malta bearing Morris's recall orders, was observed from the deck of Blakeley's frigate some distance inshore flying a series of indistinguishable signal flags and firing several guns. Just the evening before, Captain Rodgers had noticed some activity among the gunboats in the harbor. He had rightly concluded that the enemy was preparing to escort some valuable but as yet unseen vessel. However, he could not ascertain whether the pasha had a warship bound out or whether all the commotion was in preparation to receive some important arrival, perhaps a returning cruiser trailing a long line of captures. Either scenario would certainly require an elaborate distraction if they were to run safely past the blockaders, regardless of the direction. Rodgers made the proper disposition of his forces to meet with either contingency. Any ill-timed recall would have to wait. He had, therefore, sent the *Adams* away to the westward and the *Enterprize* off to the east, while he remained abreast of the town. His vigilance was rewarded at 2:00 A.M., when the gunboats began creeping away to the east. Someone special was coming in. The *John Adams* clapped on all possible sail and rejoined Lt. Isaac Hull's vigilant schooner within the hour. There, for all to see, irrevocably trapped close to shore, lay the pasha's largest remaining corsair bound in after a completely unsuccessful cruise.

This heavily armed ship was thought by some to have been a recent gift of tribute from the French government, an old 18-gun corvette, or quite possibly another vessel known to have been purchased by the pasha in Smyrna in 1801. Now polacre-rigged, it mounted twenty-two guns, ten in each broadside plus two standing stern chasers. Its black sides were divided by a broad yellow streak that ran its entire length. While the ship bore only a modest white bird as a figurehead, an enormous, brightly painted phoenix covered the entirety of its transom, appearing, as one observer noted, as if it was rising up out of its cabin windows.[13] The enemy, by this time, was securely anchored with springs on its cables, safe within the confines of a deep, narrow bay about seven miles from the town. When the *John Adams* had itself anchored at about 8:30 A.M., Rodgers observed the nine now familiar gunboats close inshore, crawling quickly up to the polacre's assistance. Hull began to warp his schooner up to within six fathoms of water, and the corsair at last opened fire. The *John Adams* followed Hull in to within "point blank shot," backed main topsail, and then commenced a devastating fire that lasted for forty-five minutes. Many of the frigate's shot were observed to pass straight into the corsair's crowded decks, killing and wounding a great many. "Yet to the disgrace of Tripoli," wrote Rodgers, "we have received no injury." Rodgers ran in a little closer and then recommenced his punishing cannonade. After only a few more minutes, the polacre's crew deserted their guns "in a most confused and precipitate manner." While some pulled frantically ashore in the boats, others leapt overboard.

The *John Adams* was in the act of hoisting out its boats to take possession when one of the corsair's cutters was seen returning to the shattered polacre. The American frigate once again opened fire but abruptly ceased again when the Tripolitan flag fluttered down, the polacre firing both broadsides as it did so, the universal signal of surrender. In the next instant the phoenix took flight. The stern of the ship erupted in a tremendous explosion, its hull aft the main chains "dashing to attoms [*sic*]," flinging its main and mizzenmasts some 150 feet into the air with all their attendant yards, shrouds, and rigging attached. "There appeared a huge column of smoke," wrote Rodgers several days later, describing one of the "grandest spectacles" he had ever beheld, "with a pyramid of fire darting vertically through its center." Rodgers could ascribe no reason for its dramatic loss, nor did he try. The French consul, Bonaventure Beaussier, believed that the polacre's crew had fired the vessel deliberately on direct orders of the pasha to avoid capture.

The squadron departed Malta after eight busy days, stopping in Messina forty-eight hours later in an attempt to obtain the loan of several gunboats for the next assault. Commodore Morris found himself referred to the chief minister of the Kingdom of the Two Sicilies in Naples. On the way, the squadron sailed to within sight of the ancient volcano, Stromboli, and the *John Adams*'s logbook noted the fires of its repeated eruptions on the evening of 21 July. A mysterious lateen sail had been seen to windward earlier in the day, and as it had given every appearance of being an armed Barbary galliot, Captain Rodgers ordered his boats away in chase. A Tripolitan corsair was still thought to be active in these seas. Attention was suddenly distracted away from their quarry, however, when the men witnessed "Stromboli erupting violently." Still, they rowed defiantly on through the night and eventually took possession of the galliot. It proved to be a mere Naples-bound Tunisian, however, and they let it go. Midshipman Blakeley, whether from the boats or from the considered calm of the frigate, witnessed the scene. Here he was, in the center of the classical world, in the very land that he had so long studied, the black sea alive with ships in earnest chase, illuminated all the while by the hellish flash and glow of an erupting volcano.

The squadron reached Naples on 27 July, and Minister Sir John Acton graciously promised the use of gunboats for their next campaign. On 10 August the dome of St. Peter's Basilica in Rome, nearly thirty-five miles away to the northeast, was clearly visible from the upper yards of the *John Adams*. The roundabout cruise brought the squadron to Leghorn, Barcelona, and finally Alicante. Blakeley's frigate found Lt. Richard Somers there with his new schooner *Nautilus*, part of the relief squadron belonging to Commo. Edward Preble. The dispatches brought aboard by Somers contained some surprising new developments. Morris had been relieved of his command by an angry secretary, and Rodgers was appointed to succeed him. Secretary

Smith was most unhappy with the events of the past year, and he ordered Morris home to explain his actions. Commodore Rodgers shifted his berth over to the flagship *New York,* while the displaced Hugh Campbell transferred his command from the *Adams* to the *John Adams.*

When Morris returned to Washington, he was forced to endure an unpleasant inquiry into the merits of his conduct over the past year. The secretary was openly disdainful of his prolonged stays in port "without necessity or any adequate object." When Morris had at last managed to bring his diminished force to Tripoli, the commodore had proceeded to make a sad tactical show of it. Then, after the negotiations ashore had fallen through, he had abandoned the blockade "without necessity or any adequate object and never afterwards appeared on the coasts of Tripoli." As a result of the court's findings of indolence, Jefferson tossed Morris out of the service.

Commo. Richard Morris was neither lazy nor incompetent. He was just not the right man for the job. The secretary had perhaps unwisely loaded him down with too many peripheral instructions, overwhelming his inexperienced commodore with infinite possibilities regarding war with Morocco, Tunis, and Algiers. Morris's problem was that he had been unable to disassociate theoretical threats from real ones, and he was thus unable to concentrate his forces effectively and focus his efforts. One can only wonder what might have happened if Morris had aggressively sailed all five of his original frigates in line of battle across the harbor of Tripoli the year before. Had they exhibited the same type of effective gunnery and aggressive zeal that Rodgers's lone ship had displayed on its first day on the blockade, the pasha may have sued for peace. Although Blakeley had been part of a squadron that had proven unsuccessful overall, his particular association with Rodgers gave him much pride. Blakeley's squadron sailed for home on 19 October, after briefly combining the ships of both squadrons to deal with a potential Moroccan threat.

The secretary rewarded Rodgers with command of the beautiful 36-gun frigate *Congress,* part of a powerful squadron then fitting out under the command of Commo. Samuel Barron that was intended to relieve Preble. Rodgers brought three of his favorite midshipmen over with him, Robert Henley, William Allen, and Johnston Blakeley, a trio of men who would later cut their own capers during the coming war with Great Britain as the commanders of the *Eagle, Argus,* and *Wasp,* respectively.

The blockade of Tripoli continued and the many deeds of Preble and his famous flagship, the *Constitution,* are legendary. His squadron's repeated bombardments of Tripoli did more to bring about a peace than all the other missions combined.[14]

On board the *Congress*, Rodgers made Blakeley the frigate's acting third lieutenant, much to the dismay of William Allen, who had competed with him for the job. The *Congress* departed Hampton Roads on 5 July 1804, in company with the *President, Constellation,* and *Essex,* and arrived at Gibraltar on 12 August. Nothing of any significance occurred during the *Congress's* cruise, since the fighting was over by the time Commodore Barron brought his squadron across.

When Preble departed for home, Rodgers transferred over to the *Constitution,* taking many of his best officers with him, including Blakeley and Allen, both of whom would continue to act as lieutenants. Although the *Constitution* would remain Blakeley's home for the next eighteen months very little was accomplished during that period. Barron sent Rodgers's frigate off to Lisbon for repairs, and there it remained for most of the winter of 1804–5. With the memory of his Tunisian humiliation still fresh in his mind, Rodgers sailed his entire armada directly into Tunis Bay in line of battle and demanded to know whether there was to be peace or war. The bey backed down immediately and never stood up again. With this nagging problem successfully dealt with, the squadron sailed to Syracuse for the peaceful winter months. Commodore Rodgers took leave of his command in May 1805 and sailed home with Blakeley and his other loyal followers in the *Essex,* arriving back in Washington in July. This commission would mark the end of Blakeley's service in anything larger than a sloop of war, but it would also end his days as a mere midshipman.

4. THE SPIRIT OF YANKEE ENTERPRISE

August 1805–December 1808

During the early part of September 1805, Johnston Blakeley reported on board the newly commissioned brig *Hornet,* then fitting out in Baltimore under Mstr. Comdt. Isaac Chauncey. Although Blakeley was to act as the brig's second lieutenant, his official promotion had yet to be confirmed by the Senate. America was then still at peace, but the effects of the European war were becoming felt up and down the coast. British frigates and French privateers were playing a cat-and-mouse game all along the southern shores, and both sides were seemingly united in their quest to disrupt American commerce. The Royal Navy was halting neutral vessels at the approaches to nearly every major American port and impressing sailors as the need arose. As part of the squadron commanded by Commo. Alexander Murray in the frigate *Adams,* Chauncey was ordered to help restore America's freedom of movement. Their cruising ground would extend from Florida's St. Marys River up to St. George's Bank and then east "to the distance of the Gulf Stream." Murray was ordered not only to prevent unlawful seizures of American citizens and property but also to retake them, by force if necessary.[1]

On 19 December, "after a pleasant passage" of four days, the *Hornet* arrived at Charleston. The *Adams* was not there. Murray had sprinted away the day before, towing a shallow-draft gunboat in his wake. He had hoped to catch the privateer *Creole,* thought to be refitting in the St. Marys after a bloody fight with His Majesty's brig *Peterel* several weeks before. The coast was now temporarily free of the French. "There is but little chance of my gathering laurels on the coast of the Carolinas," lamented Chauncey. But the merchants of the city did not share his opinion. Four days after his arrival, the South Carolina Insurance Company sent him a letter. A number of American vessels then lying in port, ready for sea and containing "valuable cargoes, bonafide property of the citizens of the United States" were in need of convoying out of harm's way. Might the *Hornet,* asked the president of their board of directors, be willing to perform this essential service? Chauncey was delighted.[2]

Nature, not the warring Europeans, would prove to be the real enemy. On the second day at sea, a tremendous gale scattered the convoy off North Carolina, effectively ending the mission. When the tempest subsided, Chauncey discovered that the *Hornet* had sprung its mainmast and had received "considerable damage otherwise." The essential spar was so badly injured, in fact, that it had to be replaced, not simply repaired. This was both a time-consuming and, in the port of Charleston, an expensive proposition. With little to do afloat, Lieutenant Blakeley went ashore and looked up many old friends and perhaps found sufficient time on his hands for unrecorded adventures as well. He did, in fact, manage to run up a considerable tab during this brief period (Charleston was an expensive city in every respect), but as he regularly received income from his late father's real estate, he was not concerned. His insouciance would not last. He learned that a great fire had swept Wilmington earlier in the year, destroying all of his properties, which had apparently been uninsured. Now he had to rely on what the navy alone paid, and even after his promotion to lieutenant his salary was modest. He soon found himself in serious debt.

The brig's services now became required for foreign duty, and the repaired *Hornet* sailed to New York in early February 1806. Chauncey, in the interim, had been promoted to a full-fledged captain and was transferred out of the *Hornet* because a brig-sloop was the domain of a master commandant. John Herbert Dent was slated to be its new commanding officer, but he wanted nothing to do with the current wardroom occupants. With his own subordinates hovering in the wings ashore, Dent sent Blakeley and his messmates packing.[3] Blakeley was caught completely off guard. At a minimum the *Hornet* had been a rent-free roof over his head. But old friends, living "on Long Island, opposite the city of New York," agreed to put him up.[4] He wrote Smith:

> Sir, It is with reluctance I am compell'd to call your attention to my personal concerns at this time, but I trust my situation will plead as an apology. Enclosed is a statement of my account with the Brig Hornet by which it appears I am in debt to the department. This has been occasion'd by the frequency and length of time the Hornet was in port, and the unavoidable expenses attendant on this situation, particularly in the harbor of Charleston. Presuming upon remaining a much longer time in the brig, I had made no provision for the event which has taken place. Under these circumstances, I have to request you will be good enough to grant me an advance of $150 to enable me to return home, indeed to discharge those expenses here which my removal from the Hornet has necessarily occasion'd. The recent calamity by fire in the town of Wilmington in which most of my friends have suffered has left me no alternative and I hope will be a sufficient excuse for the trouble this application may bring. . . . As I am incurring expense every day here, permit me to request of you an answer as soon as your time will allow.[5]

Smith graciously instructed the New York navy agent to advance Blakeley whatever funds he might require. Such requests for cash were not always granted, so this must be considered as evidence of the special esteem in which the department held him.[6] Blakeley returned to Washington by the end of April and was ordered to report immediately on board the *Chesapeake*. For some unstated reason, however, Blakeley chose instead to wait for the frigate's new captain, Charles Stewart, to report first. This drew a terse letter from the secretary, reinstructing him to repair on board at once.[7] On 26 May the *Chesapeake*'s active status was canceled because of congressional restrictions on manpower, and Blakeley was left, once again, stranded high and dry.[8]

Usually, when a junior officer temporarily found himself without any seagoing assignment and was likewise strapped for cash, the secretary would recommend he make a brief voyage in the merchant service to fine-tune his navigational and seamanship skills.[9] Blakeley made just such a request. Secretary Robert Smith understood the value of this type of impromptu employment. Young Blakeley would learn the harsher side of sea life aboard a private vessel, and he would acquire the practical knowledge of the common sailor firsthand. By this point in his career Acting Lieutenant Blakeley would have achieved great competence as a navigator and as an officer of the watch. His position on board the merchantman would be that of a mate, the merchant service's equivalent rank. As the average midshipman knew only the relatively plush life of the naval wardroom, thought Smith, Blakeley must necessarily return home a more resourceful and self-reliant officer than most, and as such, he would be of infinitely greater value.[10] Nearly all of the victorious commanders in the War of 1812 belonged to this mercantile minority, a point not lost on a later secretary of the navy, William Jones, who compiled a careful list. Blakeley wrote Smith from Baltimore on 8 July: "Conformable to the furlough of the Navy Department of the 27th May, I have the honor to inform you, I am about to leave the United States in the Ship Bashaw of Baltimore, bound to the River de la Plate and home again."[11]

Fourteen months later, an older yet wiser Johnston Blakeley returned confidently home to Baltimore.[12] The great length of his absence suggests that his cruise had extended somewhat beyond his stated South American itinerary. Although he left no record of his experiences, he probably thought little of the merchant service. His former presidential messmate James Biddle made just such a trip the following year, and he found it "far from so pleasant as I could have wished," further noting a desire to "rub off those merchant service ideas" with an immediate naval cruise.[13] Although merchant life was difficult, even on the quarterdeck, it was at least lucrative, and for that Midshipman Blakeley was certainly grateful. Five months after his departure, the Senate finally confirmed the latest batch of lieutenancies. A printed list of "the relative rank of the officers that have at this time been promoted" awaited Blakeley along with his new commission in the Washington Navy Yard.[14]

Among the lieutenants, Blakeley was ranked twenty-fifth in seniority. The names of his soon-to-be-famous contemporaries, many of whom had sailed with him in the *President*, leapt out at him from the page. Joseph Bainbridge and Lewis Warrington were ahead of him at places seven and twenty-three, respectively. But he had beaten James Biddle by one position and William Allen by six, and he was firmly planted in the upper half of the sixty-odd men mentioned. Lieutenant Blakeley's next, brief assignment was the command of a small flotilla of gunboats stationed at Norfolk, Virginia. His primary duty during this monotonous time was to survey these light-draft craft for seaworthiness. Blakeley, like most naval officers of his day, thought little of the defensive gunboats, regardless of their condition. When orders arrived redirecting him to the brig *Argus*, his spirits soared. The *Argus* was, without question, the finest sailing sloop of war in the navy. Blakeley applauded his good fortune.

In November 1807 the British cabinet issued an Order in Council against all neutral vessels trading with France or any port on the European continent under Napoleon's domain. This order required that any American merchantman who wished to pursue such trade must first obtain an English license, available only in an English port, or else risk permanent seizure. Napoleon immediately responded with his own equally unjust "Milan Decree," which pronounced that any neutral vessel that obeyed this English order, or for that matter put into an English port for any reason at all, would be confiscated. Since President Jefferson had made no effective preparations for war, he returned to his "hallowed Republican doctrine" of commercial retaliation, calling for an immediate embargo against all overseas shipping. This policy, the longtime pet doctrine of Secretary of State James Madison, was designed to deprive both sides of desperately needed American products. Jefferson believed that raw American goods such as grain, cotton, and lumber were so vital to the wealthy and influential English merchant class that they would pressure their government to accede to American demands. France, who also required America's abundance, would have no choice but to reluctantly follow England's lead. The United States could do without the manufactured goods of either Britain or France because most imported items were expensive luxuries. In theory the United States, with a little perseverance combined with a firm patriotic unity, could work its peaceful will on Great Britain without ever having to fire a shot. Three days before Christmas of 1807, a naive Congress passed the Embargo Act.[15] With the exception of the coastal trade, nearly all maritime activity was summarily halted. Hundreds of ship masters and owners, however, still insisted upon making a living, law or no law. Blakeley's brig was thus assigned, alongside only two other vessels, the *Wasp* and the *Chesapeake,* the role of coastal policeman.

The *Argus's* commanding officer, Philemon Charles Wederstrandt, had also begun his naval career in the *President's* steerage. Being senior to Blakeley, he was promoted to lieutenant when Richard Dale took over command of the big frigate in 1800. He had also been one of John Rodgers's lieutenants on board the *John Adams* during the blockade of Tripoli. A Marylander, Wederstrandt had returned from a merchant voyage and found his coveted promotion to master commandant awaiting him.[16] He considered the new *Argus* a "charming vessel," and he could not have been happier.[17] Manpower shortages affecting the quarterdeck as well as the forecastle would set the tone of the upcoming cruise; Blakeley alone would wear the true lieutenant's epaulet this time out. The roles of second and third lieutenant, as well as that of sailing master, would all be performed by mere midshipmen.

"Presuming that the Argus will be ready for sea when you read this letter," read Commander Wederstrandt, "you will immediately weigh anchor and proceed to St. Marys, Georgia, for the purpose of enforcing the laws relative to the embargo." He was to take command of the gunboat squadron already on the river and, cruising together, they were to seize any American or foreign vessel found to be in violation of the embargo laws. Just across St. Marys lay Spanish Florida, the most accessible border crossing for illegal traders in the South. Secretary Smith strictly cautioned him to violate neither the jurisdiction nor any law of Spain. Wederstrandt would be briefed by the local revenue service officers and they would carefully define for him the precise southern boundaries of the United States. There must not, above all else, be any collision with subjects of that or any other nation. Wederstrandt would have the freedom to cruise wherever his judgment dictated, but he was firmly encouraged to touch at St. Marys every eight to ten days for updated orders. The *Argus* was to be one-third of a squadron commanded by Capt. Stephen Decatur Jr., but for the next few weeks Wederstrandt would cruise the southern coast alone.[18]

Blakeley wanted to get to sea as soon as possible. Several of his older midshipmen were frequenting gambling houses, inspired no doubt by the antics of the brig's purser, John Lyon. Commodore Decatur had recently removed Lyon from his flagship, the *Chesapeake,* to the purserless *Argus* for the very same vice. Decatur had strictly prohibited such practices and had, on several occasions, "pointed out to Mr. Lyon the impropriety of any person entrusted with publick money visiting such places." Lyon was frequently intoxicated, and Decatur considered him "extremely loose and negligent" in his accounts. He returned to his old habits after only a few days' time and, had there been a replacement purser available, Decatur would have arrested and court-martialed Lyon. Lyon had received only minimal funds with which to run the brig, and Wederstrandt was strictly cautioned against placing further sums within his grasp.[19]

By 15 June 1808 the *Argus* was well within the southernmost limit of its assigned hunting grounds, closely following the movements of an American brig on the Spanish side of the river. Under the cover of darkness, the suspected smuggler finally got under way, its hold crammed with valuable contraband. The sly captain was completely unaware that he was being quietly shadowed by the *Argus*'s armed boats under the command of Lieutenant Blakeley. With muffled oars they traced the wake of the dark, silent brig for several hours until there was absolutely no doubt in Blakeley's mind that all parties concerned were "without Spanish jurisdiction." At Blakeley's command, the heavily armed band suddenly stretched out at their oars, boarded, and then took possession of their incredulous prize. It proved to be the brig *Charles* of Savannah, bound to Havana loaded with flour, cotton, and lumber. While the cargo was Spanish property and would eventually be liberated, the brig itself was a legitimate prize.[20] Just as in time of war, the condemned prize would be sold at auction and half of the proceeds from its sale would be divided up among the captor's crew. Blakeley's share alone might eventually amount to several hundred badly needed dollars, possibly as much as a year's pay.

The following day, Wederstrandt ordered the *Charles* dispatched to its home port for adjudication under Blakeley's spirited direction. "Suffer me to assure you," proclaimed a proud Wederstrandt to Secretary Smith, "that no exertion on my part will be wanting to enforce the embargo law to its utmost extent."[21] Blakeley must have thought it odd, as he sailed his first independent command into Savannah, that he should achieve a greater success by preying upon American commerce than he had done in protecting it. Immediately upon his arrival, he forwarded all papers relative to the brig's capture to the state's attorney, William Bulloch. In spite of "the most gross lies" deposed by the *Charles*'s late master, there seemed no doubt in Bulloch's mind as to the validity of the seizure.[22] The *Argus* would not rejoin its first lieutenant for nearly two weeks, giving Blakeley—the young, amiable southern gentleman—ample time to reacquaint himself with Savannah's social scene. In a delightfully written letter to his godmother, Mary Jones, Blakeley described his cruise up to this point:

Dear Madam, Fanny was right, where the silver locks predominate over the black, if any color can be assigned, it must be light. But although time may whiten my hairs, it will never alter the heart which beats in my bosom, and while it throbs, its pulsations will ever be directed to her and her little sisters. How rapidly time flies! Next May she will be eleven years of age, and five short years more will bring her to that time of life in which I was when she was born and then her parents were the friends dearest to me on earth. How fortunate; how truly so, was my choice; even when the gray hairs themselves shall have fallen from my head, my heart shall retain the conviction. Our cruise has been a various one; our course was first to the river St. Mary, where the summer season rendered the climate intolerably warm, and the state of society made no return for the heat of the weather. I spent ten days in Savannah; Julia I did not see; she had quitted town the day after my arrival. Her husband returned before our departure, but as I had not the pleasure of his acquaintance, I did not wait upon him.[23]

When Wederstrandt returned, he found a revised set of orders awaiting him. When he deemed the Georgia coast sufficiently safe from gross infractions, he was to proceed on without fanfare to the Passamaquoddy Bay on the Maine coast, stopping first at New York for resupply if needed. For several days he was to do everything in his power to make his presence known there, and then quickly, and above all quietly, return to the southward. Meanwhile the *Wasp*, which had initially been cruising these colder waters, would then exchange places with Wederstrandt off the St. Marys. In theory then, the inhabitants of both communities would be led to believe that their respective blockaders were twice their actual, budget-limited size. It was a clever plan, as neither coast would be left without a sloop of war for any great length of time.[24] "Your crews will be better exercised," added Smith, anticipating Wederstrandt's grumbling protests, "and kept in better health and spirits." This last point was well taken. "Exclusive of the Petty Officers," admitted Wederstrandt, "we have not more than ten men that can be called Saylors. . . . The vessel manned as she is now, is by no means safe."[25]

On the last day of June, the *Argus* descended the Savannah River and headed south once again. Wederstrandt was increasingly concerned that his crew, in spite of being "generally very healthy," was more than twenty men short of full complement as well as being vastly inexperienced. Rumor had it that a private armed ship (presumably British) of greatly superior force to the *Argus* would soon appear to intercede on behalf of the blockade runners. But nothing ever came of it.[26] They instead spent the next two weeks "wind bound," simmering beneath the sweltering sun, all alone in the backwater St. Marys. The ever-adaptive locals were now smuggling their contraband cotton a considerable distance upriver, well out of reach of the brig's deep draft, and then crossing over to the Spanish side. "Provided that they continue to adopt the above measure," wrote the brig's frustrated commander, "no vigilance on our side will be possible to prevent their produce from crossing the river." The landlocked civil authorities could perform this thankless job all by themselves, he reported; there was no longer any need for him to remain on the station.[27]

After retracing the coast without success, the *Argus* headed north for resupply. But on the morning of 1 August, with Cape Henry bearing northwest by west some eighty miles distant, the lookout observed a strange schooner on the leeward horizon. After a mere three-hour chase the nimble *Argus* drew to within gunshot, its half-ports knocked clear and the great guns run out, prepared for action. Wederstrandt hoisted an English ensign, a common ruse, but "perceiving she was determined not to be spoke," he replaced them at the mainmast head with its true colors, firing a leeward gun as he did so. The chase echoed this switch of heraldry but continued its flight in great earnest. The *Argus*'s larboard chase gun tossed several additional shot just ahead of the ship, but they too had no effect. When Wederstrandt gave the nod, the *Argus* erupted in a full broadside, sending eight 24-pound balls through the smuggler's top-hamper. However, three carronade slides, long exposed to the southern climate and subsequently quite rotten under their bright paint, gave way on the second broadside. Amid the smoke and confusion came a startled cry from the men in the foretop. Instantly turning their eyes from their upset ordnance, Wederstrandt and Blakeley witnessed the parted fore-topmast backstay slowly whipping about in the breeze. Fortunately the *Argus* bore up in time, only just preventing its unsupported fore-topmast from plunging into the sea. The schooner, which had just begun to haul down its colors in submission, instead rehoisted them and sailed easily away, the stunned master laughing at his miraculous good luck.[28]

A detailed New York survey reported that every one of the brig's gun carriages needed replacing. Perhaps, pleaded the anxious secretary, eight to ten guns alone, fixed upon sound carriages, might be sufficient for cruising during time of peace. There was no need for Wederstrandt to wait for all sixteen because that would take up too much valuable time.[29] The brig's purser was equally rotten and useless. Neither the officers nor the crew could now be paid for the foreseeable future. It seems that Lyon had forgotten all his accounts at Norfolk, and without them it was impossible to discharge those members of the crew whose enlistments had expired, or even to pay those men electing to remain. He had made himself the enemy of all on board, and tempers were short. Secretary Smith ordered Lyon to proceed to Washington immediately and explain his conduct in person.[30] Before departing the city, however, Wederstrandt was once again handed a revised set of cruising orders. The evasions of the embargo had become "so general and of so serious a nature" off the New England coast, the secretary reported, that all three ships of Decatur's squadron were to concentrate there until further notice. The waters north of Cape Cod required the most attention.[31] There would be some frigid cruising ahead for these southern officers.

The *Argus* was not again at sea until early September. At least there had been time enough to properly remount all sixteen carronades. Although the *Argus* cruised off Cape Cod as ordered, it was unable to find Decatur's ship. On the fifth, while rounding Cape Ann, the *Argus* fell in with the schooner *Betsey* of Manchester. As it carried what appeared to be "defective papers," Wederstrandt ordered Midshipman John T. Shubrick to sail into Boston. Shubrick's triumph was bittersweet. His cold and unhappy four-man prize crew deserted at the first opportunity. Winter came very early to New England in 1808, and thanks to Mr. Lyon the *Argus* could not yet provide its people with even minimal cold-weather clothes. The brig *Jefferson* of Plymouth followed the *Betsey* in the following day, its hold deeply laden with dried fish. Wederstrandt had determined from the logbook and other sundry papers that it too had violated its bonds. Although the brig had lawfully set out from the Straits of Belle Isle, it had illegally touched at the Canadian port of Malacash, just east of Halifax. It was now Blakeley's turn to play the prize master once again.[32] Although his crew didn't desert him, his health did. The tired, cold lieutenant continued his letter to Mrs. Jones:

> From Savannah it was expected that we would return to Norfolk, and again be employed—I mean in cruising—but this embargo (I could almost swear at it to you, who never heard me do so), ordered us to this place to prepare for another cruise, which has kept us for the last three months off the coast of New England, where, by way of compensation for the burning sun of Georgia, we have been refreshed with bleak northeasters and cooling showers of snow. This has afforded considerable amusement, in keeping up the circulation of our blood, by blowing our fingers to communicate, if possible, a little heat. It is only since our arrival here, four days ago, that I have been able, with the aid of a good warm fire, to restore them to their former feeling and appearance. Early in September we were clad in our warmest apparel.[33]

Two days later, the *Argus* dropped anchor in Boston's outer roads and its proud commander pulled triumphantly ashore to the district attorney's office. The unwelcome reception Wederstrandt received took him totally by surprise. Although he had gone out of his way to receive the two detained masters "with politeness and [all the] respect that may be due them," he couldn't understand why the local mariners and, in particular, the overwhelmingly Federalist Boston press were attacking him so severely.[34] He was simply doing his duty, enforcing the law. The embargo, he quickly learned, was extremely unpopular in New England. The *Wasp* had made some spectacular catches off this unhappy coast during the same period. In just one night's work off Maine the ship had taken no fewer than fourteen barges loaded to their gunwales with contraband flour, while two anxious British sloops of war hovered in nearby neutral waters ready to receive them. One of the *Wasp*'s prize masters, Lt. John Downes, would learn firsthand just how dangerous Massachusetts mariners could be when their livelihoods are threatened. Contrary winds had prevented him from bringing the *Liberty*, one of his corvette's many prizes, into Boston. While the ship was sheltered in the calm lee of the high-duned Truro shoreline, an armed mob of some thirty men boarded the captured fishing schooner during the night without warning. Many were dressed as Indians and loudly proclaimed themselves to be the true descendants of the 1774 Boston Tea Party–goers. Quickly overpowered, the naively unarmed prize-crew were thrown ashore at Provincetown after a moderate roughing up. The commander of the single cannonless revenue cutter in port refused to go out after them and retrieve the stolen prize. He feared that his eight muskets were insufficient for such a dangerous undertaking.[35]

Returning to sea within days, the nimble *Argus* quickly snatched up three more valuable blockade runners. They nabbed the first on 11 September, a small boat named the *Wolf* that was running east without a clearance, packed with flour, tea, and Indian meal. The *Argus* caught the remaining two on the thirteenth, the schooners *Charles* of Duxbury and *Hero* of Boston. These fishermen, like those aboard the unlucky *Betsey*, had also lawfully worked the Straits of Belle Isle, but, like so many others, had detoured into British ports on their return. The Embargo Act foolishly contained a generous loophole, which was often put to good use in such cases. Vessels in "distress" could lawfully enter English ports for repair or, as did the *Charles* and the *Hero*, for emergency resupply. Ships bound to New Orleans from Savannah often put into Havana, Cuba, on account of some unverifiable mishap. They would then quietly swap their cargoes of cotton for dry goods and continue on their way.[36]

The intrepid *Argus* returned to its Boston anchorage on the sixteenth, retrieved its three prize masters, and then set out once again. This time there was little to capture their attention but the bitterly cold weather. Lyon's loss of his financial accounts had placed both Wederstrandt and the new replacement purser in "a very disagreeable situation." There were still no funds available with which to buy the requisite foul-weather gear.[37] "The weather is verry [*sic*] cold and the winds high," wrote the *Wasp*'s captain, "which produce such a quantity of ice around the ship when at sea to render the situation of the crew truly uncomfortable."[38] At least the *Wasp* had been issued warm clothing. Barely outrunning a severe mid-October gale, the *Argus* put into Portsmouth, New Hampshire, for water and provisions. This was Blakeley's first view of this small yet vitally important naval installation. He would later choose this sheltered haven to complete the fitting out of his final command in 1814. In November, the crew of the *Argus* was back in New York, very much the worse for the weather. Blakeley concluded his letter to his godmother:

> We are here waiting for further orders, and it is much to be feared, we shall be employed all winter in attempting to check the spirit of Yankee enterprise, as the general opinion here is that the embargo will be continued. As to myself, I must try to get myself on shore, as I am told my liver is affected, and nothing but a course of medicine for two or three months can afford a relief. If ordered to sea, I shall endeavor to negotiate an exchange with some officer on this station, being the only means by which a separation from the Brig can be [effected]. This arrangement will enable me to attend to my complaint, and at the same time spare me the mortification of a refusal on application for a leave of absence; besides, it will be easier to obtain a furlough, when my health will permit it, from a station on shore than from a cruising vessel. I shall leave the Brig with reluctance, as I am pleasantly situated on board, and New York—from the prejudice of its citizens against officers—a disagreeable place for us; however, my constitution demands my attention, and as it may enable me to visit you, I shall be a great gainer on the whole. . . . The celebrated Counselor Emmet, from Ireland, I also sat and listened to until late last night. Your determination to remain at Rock Rest gives me inexpressible pleasure; that the other idea may never again revive is my sincere wish. Write without fear, as I have friends here instructed to take care of my letters, should I be absent. Your caution with respect to the two sisters happened too late; a cruise in Boston Bay, in the month of October, would cool a passion of more fervor than mine. I was an ass between two bundles of hay, and had I been willing, neither were disposed to let me bite them. Remember me to Mr. Jones, and give my love to the girls. I beg to continue Your Friend, J. Blakeley.[39]

Blakeley's pessimism was well founded. American unwillingness to withstand the embargo's privations and, as James Madison acknowledged, the unpatriotic interference of the opposition Federalists, doomed the act to certain failure. By the end of 1808, New England and New York were nearly in open revolt. Petitions flooded Congress from angry merchants willing to try their odds against the Royal Navy's threat of seizure. Boston newspapers labeled those officials, like the men of the *Argus* who enforced the embargo, "enemies to the Constitution . . . and hostile to the liberties of this people." The British still obtained most of what they needed through smuggling, albeit at a higher price. Law-abiding merchants went broke watching their more daring compatriots grow rich. On 2 February 1809, the Federalists joined forces with New England Republicans and repealed the embargo, effective 4 March.[40] The newly arrived Lt. Thomas K. Swift left the *Argus* on 11 November "too unwell to proceed to sea." With Blakeley's own health declining daily, Wederstrandt reluctantly informed the secretary that his indispensable first lieutenant would also have to be left behind at New York. The brig's surgeon confirmed Blakeley's illness:

> This may certify that Lieut. J. Blakeley has an infirmity to a degree that renders him unfit to discharge the duty of his office and it is necessary that he should go on a course of Mercury to remove his complaint which cannot be done with safety on board of this brig on her station at this season of the year. I therefore recommend his going to sick quarters on shore for the recovery of his health.[41]

Returning to the frigid New England waters by December, Wederstrandt himself had to join his two former lieutenants ashore.[42] With his health "still much impaired" one full year later, Wederstrandt resigned, with no small regret, from his country's service.[43] Blakeley was also slow to recover. In February 1809 an order was sent to him at New York directing him to the brig *Syren*, but this was soon revoked. So too was his next order, addressed to him at Washington and instructing him to join the frigate *Essex*.[44] Blakeley was permitted to postpone going on board his third assignment, the corvette *John Adams*, until June "because of poor health." He would need the rest. His next eighteen months would be extremely active.

5. Some Refractory Characters on Board

January 1809–December 1810

*T*he year 1809 brought about a profound change in American naval policy. When President Thomas Jefferson left office, he took with him not only his factious program of commercial restriction and retaliation but his much-maligned gunboat program as well. By early spring, senior navy clerk Charles W. Goldsborough, now temporarily the acting secretary, had ordered all the gunboats except those at New Orleans to be laid up and their crews transferred over to the deep-draft, oceangoing men-of-war then readying for sea. The broadly applied embargo had failed, and now the tamer Non-Intercourse Act did not appear to be producing the desired effects either. The enforcement of this new policy made few demands on the navy, however. But the dismal failure of Jefferson's plans, the still unsettled relations with warring Europeans, and the continuing attacks on American shipping forced the new administration to place almost the entire oceangoing navy in commission. Within months, three thousand seamen had enlisted in the service and eleven cruising ships had been prepared for sea. By midsummer of 1809, when foreign affairs at last began to look somewhat peaceful, the navy nevertheless decided upon a policy of keeping ships and crews in active commission. For the next three years, the larger part of the navy was engaged in cruising off the Atlantic coast, reclaiming the sovereignty and the dignity of the flag, and carrying

State Department dispatches abroad. It was to this latter task that the North Carolina midshipman was assigned in late March.[1]

The ship *John Adams,* Johnston Blakeley's new home, no longer bore much resemblance to that proud old frigate that had so persistently graced the entrance to Tripoli only a few years earlier. Although a splendid sailer, naval constructor Josiah Fox had ordered it cut down to a flush-decked corvette, the next class of fighting ship below a frigate. In 1799 Charleston builders had been forced to alter the original, Fox-designed plan to reduce its draft of water and thus ensure a safe passage across that port's notorious bar, lengthening the keel five feet and remolding it with flatter floors. This necessary conversion, however, had made it a poor gun platform. The excessive lateral roll, unintentionally brought about by the modifications, prohibited the navy from placing the firepower worthy of a true frigate on the spar deck. Gone too was William Rush's carefully crafted figurehead of the young nation's last Federalist president. Immediately following the razeeing of the *John Adams,* the navy replaced the conservative Bostonian with the classic involuted "scroll head," an understated and apolitical tribute to the strength and glory of oak and laurel.[2] During its shaving, Fox had perceived that, even with its stores and ballast out, the ship listed noticeably to starboard. To his astonishment, he discovered that the costly live oak frame had actually been built several inches wider on the port side than on the starboard. "I am inclined to believe," he reported to the secretary, "[that] she will be considerably stiffer on the starboard tack than the larboard." This incurable peculiarity aside, the ship was well worth retaining in the service.[3] Its new battery of 42-pounder carronades had transformed the navy's lightest frigate into one of the heaviest corvettes afloat.[4]

When Lieutenant Blakeley, his health now much improved, finally set foot back on board his beloved old frigate-turned-corvette, it was fast approaching July. At this stage in his career, Blakeley had become a highly valued first officer, and his newest commander, Mstr. Comdt. Samuel Evans, was heartily relieved to see him. The strict, no-nonsense Evans had been John Rodgers's first lieutenant in the old *Congress* back in 1804, when Blakeley had acted as the frigate's third. A commanding figure at five feet, eight inches tall, Evans towered over the compact Blakeley. The thirty-two-year-old Evans had slightly graying, sandy blond hair, and he possessed an unusually pale complexion for a sailor so long exposed to the elements. His steel-gray "imperfect" eyes could cut through a subordinate like a scythe. Evans was glad to receive Blakeley aboard, not so much for his considerable abilities as a sea officer but to relieve the physical stresses of his command.

Some years earlier, in the Mediterranean, Evans had received a painful facial wound. The sight in his left eye was materially diminished by what he himself diagnosed as the severing of the "small nerves." Sometimes this old wound would flair up so severely, he would later report, that he could barely distinguish the outlines of large, bright objects. Exposure to cold weather often inflamed and irritated his condition to the point of near blindness. An injured leg also curtailed his activity.[5] As was customary, he probably concealed these debilities from the secretary or at least minimized them. Evans was resigned to one sobering fact: Should his health fail again, his first lieutenant would be required to run the entire show alone. This was the same situation that Blakeley had endured in the *Argus* the previous year; he only held a lieutenant's commission but served unofficially as the acting master commandant. Acting Lieutenants John Pettigrew and Jesse Duncan Elliott, although talented and eager to please, were mere reefers, and the other gentlemen of the steerage were not yet responsible enough to be entrusted with a watch.[6] The looming burdens of this cruise were great, and necessity dictated that Blakeley's newly recovered health must be maintained.

Blakeley's most pressing concern would be finding enough skilled seamen to work the corvette. The *John Adams* had been sent to Maryland specifically to find a crew, but Evans found the recruitment there "extremely dull."[7] Even worse, there was a real possibility that he would lose four of his precious and few able seamen to the British. The corvette's local recruiting officer, Midshipman Josiah Shaw, had signed these men on the books in Washington. Although they had sworn that they were all American citizens, they were in fact English deserters—pressed American sailors—or so they had explained to Evans. They had first run from HMS *Salvadore del Mundo* in Plymouth, England, and had then signed on board a departing merchantman, the *Jarret*. When their unsuspecting civilian master put into Baltimore, they quickly ran away.[8]

British consul William Woods, acting on behalf of the *Jarret*'s distressed master, had sent a letter to Captain Evans politely but firmly requesting their prompt repatriation. Evans's equally civil refusal had one critical complication: The necessary documentation establishing the four men's true nationality, required upon their signing on, could not now be found. The men pleaded that they were drunk when Mr. Shaw recruited them and claimed that they had not been asked to produce such papers in the first place. Nevertheless, Evans told Woods that his most trusted and reliable recruiting officer (who was now in deep trouble) had been instructed to "enter none but native citizens of the U States,"[9] and that he, his captain, held an unwavering faith that Mr. Shaw had adhered strictly to orders. Competition for seamen was great, and Evans was not about to lose four of his most valuable men. "I believe there are but Americans on board," he steadfastly declared to Woods, "and it appears to me necessary that proof be exhibited to the contrary before I, in any manner, can act on your letter."

Two days later, the *Jarret*'s master, now justifiably quite furious, wrote directly to Evans demanding a final answer and "complain[ing] loudly of his detention." He simply could not set sail for home without them, for few Americans wished to sign on board in their place. A Baltimore notary public, retained by the British consul, came on board and requested a final answer, strongly suggesting that a suit would be brought against Evans for substantial financial damages if the men were not returned.[10] With nervous confidence, Evans wrote Secretary Hamilton: "I think you will direct me how to act." But as no satisfactory proof had yet been exhibited against three of the four men (each, by coincidence or private joke, calling himself William), the secretary strongly advised Evans to retain them in the service.[11]

Captain Evans would, however, lose at least one crew member. Midshipman Shaw had enlisted young Jim Rodgers as an "ordinary seaman." Underage and having never before been to sea, he was pursued up the *John Adams*'s gangplank several days later by his anxious father. Although such a neophyte was no great loss, the sum of nine dollars and fifty cents worth of slops that Rodgers had consumed during his brief stay was. Midshipman Shaw was not endearing himself to his new captain.[12]

A much anticipated last-minute draft of men from the *Chesapeake* was unusually dismal. Capt. Isaac Hull had sworn that even though the men were rated only as "ordinary," they were in fact "nearly equal to able seamen." But they were not. Of the seventeen men rated as seamen already on board the *John Adams*, only eleven were actually familiar with the ways of a ship-rigged vessel. It appears that they too had deliberately deceived their recruiting officer, the ever fallible Midshipman Shaw. "Able" seamen, those most skilled and subsequently most valued, earned both a higher wage and a larger signing bonus. Had they not been so difficult to replace, Evans would have reduced them to mere "ordinary" status, or even to landsmen. Of the fifty-five classed as ordinary, only twenty-one had ever been to sea before, and most of those only briefly.[13]

At about this same time, Midshipman Shaw began to feel a growing displeasure over naval life. It had not been the frolicking sea adventure that he had supposed. The tedium of port duty was relieved only by the incessant barking of his overly harsh superiors. Evans seemed particularly displeased with him for what he perceived as only honest mistakes. Entrusted with the role of naval recruiter, he was the honored representative of his country's martial sea service. But so far, his messmates teased, he had succeeded in persuading only underage boys, English deserters, and intoxicated landsmen to sign on. Without close friends, family, or conscience to guide him, and with frivolous habits ashore having reduced him to a debt-laden pauper, he decided to make a change, both in vocation and venue. With equal outrage and surprise, Evans reported to Washington the circumstances of Shaw's abrupt and early retirement:

> Sir, I am under the necessity of stating to you that Midshipman Shaw has deserted from this ship, carrying with him a hundred dollars which I ordered placed in his hands on Thursday last for the purpose of making advances to two or three seamen who he informed me who promised to enter with him. He has also contracted debts here with all who would credit him amounting, I am informed, to upwards of two hundred dollars and he has taken with him a horse which he hired on Friday about noon on the pretext of going a few miles from town to dinner. Mr. Pettegrew [*sic*] returned last evening from pursuing him. He tracked him about seven or eight and twenty miles up the Frederickstown Road, but as he was not able to ascertain what road Shaw took until Saturday morning he found out going the distance above mentioned that he had nearly twenty four hours start of him and considered it was useless to pursue him further.[14]

Shaw stopped briefly at the Frederick County, Maryland, post office, mailed in his formal letter of resignation, and then vanished forever.

Evans requested that the *John Adams* might proceed on a short cruise to fill out the vacancies in its quarter bill. "Charleston, from the circumstance of the ship having been built there," he wrote the secretary, "can perhaps be visited with the most success." If the frigate *Constitution* could always find a reliable crew in Boston, then local southern pride might possibly be called upon to complete the *John Adams*'s muster. A short training cruise would certainly be of great advantage to those numerous neophytes already on board.[15] The secretary at first agreed but then changed his mind. By the end of October, the *John Adams* had instead left Baltimore for New York. The ship sailed very well, Evans observed, much better than before. He was fully satisfied that had the ship been bound out to sea and had it "carried sail" it could have made a record passage from Baltimore in something less than eighteen hours.[16] But the crew's collective skill was still "very bad." At New York there "was not a seaman in the yard," indeed, not "five men in it who had been beyond Sandy Hook."[17] Within a week, however, they were watered, adequately manned, and prepared for foreign service. Exposed to the forbidding northern climate, Blakeley's frail constitution once again began to deteriorate. "I could wish very much, as the ship is to proceed on foreign service, an acting Lieutenant," Evans wrote the secretary. "My reasons for this are the state of Lieut. Blakeley's health, which frequently renders it impossible for him to attend to duty in bad weather."[18]

Evans knew few particulars about his upcoming cruise. He was aware only of his general destination, Europe, and his probable function, that of diplomatic courier. Clues began to reach him well ahead of his formal written instructions in the form of correspondence with the secretary concerning possible passengers. Pierre Samuel Dupont de Nemours of Paris, with whom "the President obtains sentiments very favorable," was to be accommodated on board during the return leg of their journey from France.[19] In addition, wrote Paul Hamilton, the ship was to accommodate Thomas Butler of Philadelphia and his sister, both bound to France for reasons of health.[20] The Frenchman he could handle, but the last thing Evans needed to see on board was one or more sick civilians. He and Blakeley were themselves somewhat indisposed, and the corvette was still without a surgeon. Anticipating Evans's objections, Hamilton continued: "I need add no more than the respectability and objects of Mr. and Miss Butler, make me very solicitous that you should accommodate them."

Evans's instructions were written on 5 December 1809, and arrived in New York soon afterward.[21] The corvette was to proceed directly to France, dropping anchor either in L'Orient or Le Havre. Once there, Evans was to land the State Department's dispatches under the care of one of his more reliable officers and then disembark the ailing Butlers. This same officer was to transport the dispatches overland to General Armstrong in Paris and then proceed on to Amsterdam to await the arrival of the *John Adams*. Captain Evans was immediately to depart the French coast for Portsmouth, presumably after embarking Mr. Dupont de Nemours into the Butler cabin. Evans was then to dispatch another equally reputable officer with similar documents for Mr. Pinckney in London. Without waiting for his return, Evans was required to proceed to Amsterdam and deliver, according to separate Treasury Department instructions, a large, unspecified amount of public specie. Retrieving his first officer, who should then be bearing fresh Paris dispatches, Evans was to backtrack to England, recover his second officer with the latest official London correspondence, and return "with all possible dispatch" to the United States. On the face of it, the mission seemed easy enough. "Should you want officers, apply to Commr Rodgers, who will give you one or two if necessary of experience, indeed two spare officers would not be amiss," Hamilton added ominously, "as you have special service to perform and may expect to encounter severe weather." It is doubtful, however, that Evans ever received his spares. At the last minute, Hamilton ordered Capt. James Fenwick of the Marine Corps to go aboard and carry the State Department dispatches to Paris instead. Likewise, he was to take the specie ashore in Amsterdam after rejoining the ship.[22] Evans no doubt wondered if this last-minute alteration might have represented a lack of confidence on the part of the secretary in his wardroom following the Shaw incident.

American trade was at a standstill during the latter half of the Napoleonic Wars. Both sides in this latest European struggle were seizing American vessels, impounding their cargoes, and imprisoning their crews. President Madison's strategy was to play one side off against the other. He hoped to persuade the British to lift their Orders in Council and encourage Napoleon to rescind his decrees against American trade. If he could convince one side to drop their oppressive policies, he would grant them special privileges, forcing the other to follow suit; in theory this would reopen the seas to Americans. He wrote identical letters to his ambassador in London, William Pinckney, and to his Parisian counterpart, Gen. John Armstrong. He instructed them both to remain firm in their resolve and "not to acquiesce in the edicts of either [belligerent]."

On 15 December the *John Adams* set its topsails, discharged the pilot off Sandy Hook, and ventured out into the eastern sea.[23] Nineteen uneventful days later the corvette struck soundings off the coast of England, and after an additional four sea days, or "meridians," it dispatched Captain Fenwick at La Hogue. Evans sailed for the Downs the following day. He was unable to depart for Holland with the next tide because he was suffering "from indisposition to stand the deck in the tempestuous weather," which "we almost daily experienced." The burdens of command soon fell entirely upon Blakeley. The acting second lieutenant, Midshipmen Pettigrew,[24] although attentive was inexperienced, and Midshipman Elliott, his otherwise capable acting third, was in London. The ordinary midshipmen, Blakeley had reported, were at best "very indifferent." Adverse winds confined them to the English coast for another eight storm-tossed days, but finally, on 19 January 1810, they arrived in Den Helder. Evans sent the purser off to Amsterdam with both the State Department dispatches and the public specie because Fenwick did not appear.

The returning purser brought revised instructions from General Armstrong. The corvette was not to await the arrival of Fenwick, as initially planned. Instead, they were required to return to England at once, to complete their duties there, and only then to retrieve their marine courier at Le Havre. Blakeley brought the *John Adams* safely into Portsmouth on 16 February, but he would have to wait several more weeks for Pinckney to conclude his business and subsequently release young Elliott from his diplomatic bondage. Evans used this time for some much needed rest. He penned a brief note to the secretary: "But just recovering from a severe indisposition that has confined me for upwards of two months, I have scarcely strength to inform you that I have executed your orders."[25]

The *John Adams* was back off the French coast on 28 March, only three days after Elliott's return. "The harbor of Havre is not a fit place for the ship," wrote Evans to Armstrong, announcing his arrival, "and the Roads too much exposed to remain in them with safety in that season." He would stand off Le Havre until his letter, in which were enclosed several dispatches from Pinckney, was answered. He wished to proceed, with the general's consent, to the harbor of Cherbourg, a much safer port at this time of year. Evans did not send his dispatches in the company of an officer, he explained in his cover letter to Armstrong, since Pinckney did not think his correspondence worth the extra expense. But Evans's letter vanished en route. As the days flew quickly by with the ship standing to and fro off Le Havre without receiving any acknowledgment, Evans began to suspect the worst. But he could do nothing until he heard from Armstrong. The general, in turn, was furious when he learned that the corvette had been so long in French waters without his knowledge. As the cruise wore tediously on, Blakeley's health continued to worsen, but he was forced by necessity to remain active at his post. If Blakeley too succumbed to his ills, there would be only midshipmen left to command the corvette. The constant bad weather was the reason for both officers' illness, and the great gale that slammed them on 4 April taxed what little remained of their strength.

The northeast winds first struck the anchored corvette with their full fury at 4:00 A.M., and by the following evening the sea had risen with such a ferocity that "it made a breach over the ship at every pitch." Water poured into the officers' cabins through the gun deck planking, worn thin with age and use, while the currents dragged the anchors ever closer to the fatal French shoals. Blakeley knew that if the corvette was to survive, immediate and decisive action must be taken. There were only three options. They might let go all the anchors and attempt to ride it out. Although the stout hempen cables might be expected to hold the ship in place under normal circumstances, both Blakeley and Evans felt "not the greatest confidence in those furnished at Washington." If the cables parted, the ship and all aboard would perish. Perhaps they might try tacking laboriously off and on a leeward shore, just as John Paul Jones had done with the corvette *Ariel* in these same waters a generation before. But this second alternative was equally risky. They might, too, attempt a bold dash into Le Havre. In spite of heavy seas and shifting winds, they decided to run for the harbor. Failure would be equally catastrophic, but at least the issue would be settled quickly. The *John Adams* slipped its cables the following morning and made a desperate dash through the rock-lined gauntlet:

> On luffing round the entrance, we were . . . running on one side of it, owing to the pilot not giving her sufficient room. In fact we grazed the wall but the ship received no injury, and by his further bad management, in directing the anchor to be let go too soon, we were obliged to cut the cable, to enable us to get within the gates, before the tide left us. Soon however, we were within the gates, without further accident, and moored alongside two French Frigates.

Once they were anchored safely in the harbor, Evans's official business went swiftly and easily. General Armstrong's ruffled feathers were soon smoothed, and Captain Fenwick returned on board with his charges. Evans's final problem remained getting out. His initial fear of being trapped in Le Havre proved well founded. Indeed, Armstrong strongly disapproved of the ship's having entered the harbor in the first place, and he let Evans know it in no uncertain terms.

Vessels drawing more than twelve feet of water could safely leave or enter the shelter of Le Havre only one or two days each month. Complicating matters further, the channel itself was so narrow that it was absolutely necessary to have a fair wind to get out. Anxiously awaiting the next full moon, Evans hauled his ship to the harbor gates and waited. Lieutenant Pettigrew sounded the channel daily. After running hard aground several times, the corvette finally made its way out, but only just. With the vessel's coppered keel gliding mere inches above the channel's ancient sediment, the Yankee mariners sailed free of their confinement on 20 April 1810 and headed for home.

Blakeley spent most of the uneventful passage to the United States confined to his cabin, very ill and probably questioning his choice of vocation.

He disembarked in Baltimore "in consequence of indisposition" and traveled on to Washington.[26] Sufficiently recovered by the first week of July, the secretary issued new orders directing him south to Charleston.[27] Captain Evans lasted only until the second week of July, when he too was carried ashore.[28] And so there the *John Adams* sat: repaired, reprovisioned, readied for sea, fully manned, and lacking only a commander. Secretary Paul Hamilton, however, needed the *John Adams* cruising immediately.

Having once again recovered the greater part of his strength, Blakeley had planned an overland route to his new assignment. Even though he was detached from the *John Adams,* he and the ship were independently bound to the same place. There seemed but one logical solution. The words of the secretary's latest orders jumped out at him from the page:

> Sir, The order which you received to repair to Charleston is for the present revoked. You will immediately take command of the Ship John Adams, in which you will continue until Capt. Evans resumes his station. You are to use every exertion in fitting the ship for service and be careful in preventing desertions and the most minute departure from discipline, in anyone under your command.[29]

By all accounts, the corvette's captain was not expected to recover for some time. Hamilton, no doubt encouraged by Evans, who had every confidence in his former first lieutenant, desired Blakeley to take the corvette to Charleston. The *John Adams* was no ordinary ship. It was the very pride of the southern maritime community, built by the patriotic merchants of Charleston. Blakeley's opportunity to sail it triumphantly home as its commander (albeit only a temporary, acting one) was the greatest honor yet bestowed on him during his ten years afloat.

Then there was that ominous note about discipline. The *John Adams's* crew was not about to cooperate with Blakeley's ambitions. The terms of service for many of them had long since expired, and they had left vowing never to return. Still others, borrowed from Captain Hull in New York, had already been refunded. Daily, both officers and enlisted men alike bombarded the otherwise preoccupied secretary with impertinent demands. The worst by far were the midshipmen. They wanted to be transferred out of what was increasingly becoming an unhappy ship. Evans was known to be overly harsh, and his indisposition may have made him unusually snappish. These problems, whatever their cause, arose during Blakeley's brief furlough ashore, but that made no difference to Hamilton. A weakened Lieutenant Blakeley had been unable to keep his men under control. After a month, the secretary had had enough. He sent Blakeley an official reprimand:

> I cannot omit remarking that, since the arrival of the John Adams, the officers of that ship have given me more trouble than all the rest of the Navy in the same time have, and that I shall not easily forget the disposition towards insubordination, which has manifested itself in too many instances, amongst them. I repeat to you the necessity of strict discipline, and that you are to report to me those, who refuse to submit to it. You will have these sentiments made publicly known.[30]

The Treasury Department required the immediate services of the *John Adams* off the southern coast, but Captain Evans was still unable to command. While Blakeley was more than capable under normal circumstances, the secretary believed that he was still not up to full strength, and his junior officers were apparently getting the better of him. It became clear that an experienced, full-fledged captain was required to take charge of this increasingly unruly ship. Hamilton reluctantly chose Blakeley's successor. "You are to proceed with your ship without delay to Hampton Roads," the secretary wrote him, "and there wait for the arrival of Capt. Dent, who is ordered to take command." Blakeley was then to continue on to Charleston by some unspecified, independent means. Feeling that he had perhaps overreacted in his admonition of Blakeley's wardroom, and fearing quite correctly that Blakeley would take this change of commanders personally, he concluded: "I have nothing to add excepting that you have the confidence of the Department and my best wishes for your prosperity." Blakeley was allowed to leave the moment his replacement appeared.[31]

Hamilton, however, had no intention of letting Blakeley go. "It is necessary that I should inform you, that the John Adams needs that discipline, in which you will be well seconded by Lieut. Blakeley," Hamilton had written that same day to Dent, "[for] there are some refractory characters on board."[32] Hamilton then countermanded his previous instructions, ordering Blakeley to remain on board as Dent's first officer, at least until they reached Charleston. Dent had dumped Blakeley ashore in 1805 from the *Hornet*, yet Blakeley faithfully brought his command into Norfolk and duly surrendered his authority on 16 September 1810. Dent lost no time in giving Hamilton his detailed assessment of the ship's condition and its officers' qualifications.[33] He was particularly unhappy with the latter. On the whole, he thought them "indifferent." He clearly wanted Blakeley gone, although he did not come right out and say it. He preferred instead to bring John

Downes of the frigate *Essex* over in his place.[34] Fearing trouble, Hamilton was forced to lie to Blakeley: "Capt. Dent has made a report relative to the condition of the John Adams, which reflected much credit upon you & which afforded me great satisfaction."[35] Three days later, Blakeley's long-standing orders to the Charleston Station were permanently revoked, and once again he was officially ordained the *John Adams's* first officer.[36] Blakeley was still ailing, however, and he wanted out of the ship as much as Dent wanted him out. Hamilton's denial of Blakeley's second furlough request is probably the best surviving contemporary assessment of his abilities as an officer:

> At this time the public service does not permit your leaving the John Adams: As soon however as I can with propriety, I will grant you the indulgence you desire. If your service were less valuable, you might soon be spared, but if you were permitted to leave the John Adams at this time, I know not where I would conveniently find a competent first lieutenant in your place.[37]

The *John Adams* arrived in Charleston Harbor on 29 September, after a quiet passage of only four days.[38] John Herbert Dent was one of the navy's most controversial officers.[39] While Commo. John Rodgers acknowledged Dent's professional skill, he thought the twenty-nine-year-old Marylander "lacked stability of character."[40] A few years down the road, Capt. David Porter would go so far as to designate him a coward because Dent had resigned his command at the moment that war seemed all but sure. He did not seek sea service again, Porter noted, until very late in the war, when "it was notorious [that] there was no command left for him."[41] Soon after arriving in Charleston, Dent ran afoul of Capt. Hugh G. Campbell, the senior naval officer in the city. Blakeley had drawn up a detailed survey upon their arrival showing what wear the *John Adams* had sustained over the past two years, and he presented it with his recommendations to Campbell. But Dent was far too busy with private dealings ashore to effect any timely repairs. He thus evoked the wrath of Campbell, a strict officer who did things exclusively by the book. Dent took umbrage at this rebuff and, reported Campbell, "we have not exchanged civilities since that day."

Dent continued to irritate Campbell even further. He proceeded to "promulgate" through every stage house within two hundred miles of the city that he, not Campbell, had been appointed to command all naval activities from Cape Fear to Georgia. Furious, Campbell took off his gloves: "This [Dent] has asserted not in the style or manner of the officer or the gentleman, nor with that consideration due to his own character or the feelings of others, but more in the style of a prattling child, pleased with a rattle or some other like bauble."[42]

Dent purchased a small plantation upriver from the city. When the *John Adams* was ordered to Newport, Rhode Island, he threatened to resign the service. "He left home with great reluctance," wrote Campbell, "nor do I believe any service would please him, but that of sailing in and out of Charleston at pleasure."[43] Before retiring Dent made one more brief cruise, patrolling the Georgia coastline in late October. He sent his weakened first lieutenant away in the open launch to gather information up the St. Marys. Blakeley found everything quiet, except perhaps for the pounding of the torrential rains. Even the local customs inspector reported no recent infractions.[44] When he returned aboard, soaked to the bone and coughing convulsively, Dent once again ordered him to survey the ship. The foremast had been weakened in the hounds by the uninterrupted bad weather of the English Channel, and Blakeley had noted that he could actually observe it twisting at times.[45] Furthermore, the bends and the waterways had begun to open up and admit great quantities of seawater, "owing to the pitch being not properly boiled, when caulked at Washington." But the ship sailed well, and a recent alteration to its rudder had produced a noticeable improvement to the steering.

Blakeley served on two courts-martial in early December while still awaiting his long-promised furlough. Dent had brought charges against the ship's chaplain, Garret Barry, for absenting himself without leave for nearly three days. Dent had clashed with Barry, "a desperate character," several times since their initial introduction in Hampton Roads.[46] Barry was returning to the corvette one afternoon after purchasing a quantity of snuff ashore when the sudden cries of "fire," emanating from hundreds of persons "expressed in a tone of distress that put refusal at defiance," arrested his attention. He instantly ran "to the place where it raged" and assisted those fighting the blaze.[47] Exhausted from his heroic deeds, and in severe pain with both arms "considerably burnt," Barry retired to a room in the Planters Hotel, forgoing his official duties. Finding himself "extremely unwell" the next morning, he sent off a message to Blakeley describing his painful plight and pleading for medical aid from the ship. But the civilian courier delivered the letter to the wrong officer. Three days later, when Barry finally returned aboard with both arms buried within thick bandages, Dent placed him under arrest. Although the court found that his absence was both unintentional and unpremeditated, they did "adjudge him to be slightly reprimanded by his commanding officer." What probably upset Dent the most was Barry's initial statement. He claimed that his letter was instantly sent off "to the commander of the John Adams," whom he subsequently and repeatedly identified as Lieutenant Blakeley!

Seaman John Clear also stood trial. He was arrested for breaking into a messmate's sea chest and stealing twenty-seven dollars. The prisoner at first pleaded not guilty, but later, in the face of mounting evidence, he admitted his wrongdoing. According to Clear, the stolen money, wrapped in a handkerchief, had fallen from his pants pocket into Charleston Harbor while he was relieving himself atop the seat of ease. He proclaimed his sorrow and threw himself upon the mercy of the court. Unmoved, the tribunal sentenced him to receive thirty-nine lashes with a "cat o' nine tails on the bare back," the customary twelve strokes for theft plus one additional lash for each dollar taken and not returned.[48]

Attending the second court-martial was Blakeley's newly arrived replacement, Lt. William Burrows.[49] Blakeley's furlough would soon begin. His orders, dated 21 November, required him to wait until he had been "relieved of command" before departing on his long-awaited furlough;[50] inspired perhaps by the frequent reports of Dent's dawdlings ashore, some in Washington still thought of Blakeley as the corvette's captain. From the moment that the John Adams had first put to sea during the summer of 1809 to these final days of 1810, Johnston Blakeley was for all practical purposes the corvette's commander. This had first been occasioned by the indisposition of the respected and capable Evans, and then repeated a year later by the wantonness and ineptitude of Dent. Blakeley departed on or about Christmas Day 1810 for a well-deserved, three-month respite with his adoptive family at Rock Rest, amid the peaceful, gently rolling hills of North Carolina. This would be his final trip home.

6. Delay, Disappointment, and Disaster

January 1811–December 1812

Within days, Johnston Blakeley was back home at the Jones's country seat, a rambling estate nestled deep within the peaceful heart of Chatham County, North Carolina. The endemic fevers that had stolen the first three of the Jones children did not reach here, so the latest additions to the family were all strong, healthy, and thriving. Even while enjoying the wholesome country solitude at Rock Rest, Solicitor General Edward Jones was still relatively close to the hub of tarheel politics in Raleigh. Johnston's final homecoming was producing goodwill from all quarters. He had always been close to Mary Jones, and now even the normally reserved Edward had become unusually paternalistic. Any possible ill feelings between them regarding career paths not taken were soon forgotten. In the evenings, warmed by the snug fire and safe from the winter winds, Edward regaled his godson with tales of their native Ireland. He spoke of the closeness of their two families in the old country, of Johnston's mother, and of the Blakeley clan's unfulfilled hopes for life in the New World. All around him, Johnston saw the Jones children romp and play in youthful innocence. The Jones girls, particularly young Frances (Fanny), had especially primped for and fussed over their handsome hero ever since he first appeared at the portico in all his indigo splendor. The family attended to him with all the love usually reserved only for true relations. However, a sadness began to well up inside him. His parents and his younger brother were dead. He knew of no single living blood relative with whom he might share the joys and triumphs of his life. He was the last of his line.

Still, Johnston enjoyed the great outdoors. While this part of the country shared many of the beauties of New England, the winters here were much milder. One crisp day, while strolling down by the banks of the Haw River bordering the estate, Johnston paused briefly to carve his name in an old beech tree. His future deeds would later transform this stoic old trunk into a cherished local monument. Johnston also sat for a local artist who painted what was then described as an "indifferent" miniature. The picture hung for many years in the Joneses' house, and although it is sadly lost today it served as the basis for a larger oil painting that now graces the halls of the University of North Carolina at Chapel Hill.[1] It bears little resemblance to the frequently reproduced portrait belonging to the Naval Academy, created some years later from a handsome 1816 engraving. But this print, first published in *Analectic Magazine*,[2] was thought to have been a good likeness by all those who knew Captain Blakeley—or at least it was "tolerably correct in the outlines." Some complained, however, that he looked a bit too serious, being somewhat "deficient in expression."[3] Little Fanny Jones, although quite young at the time, recalled in later years her impressions of Johnston's final visit:

> My own recollections of Johnston Blakeley are very indistinct, but the bright and at the same time benevolent expression of his countenance made an indelible impression on my memory. From these recollections I think he must have been very handsome, and the exceeding whiteness of his teeth, and brightness of his eyes, I shall never forget. My mother has often described him to us as rather small, but well made, with very black hair and eyes; grave and gentlemanly in his deportment, but at the same time cheerful and easy when at home. Among strangers, rather reserved, and when very young rather avoiding than seeking young society, he would sit for hours reading and talking with my mother, while the other young people were amusing themselves without. It was remarked of him, both when a boy and a man, that he commanded the respect and affection of all with whom he associated.[4]

A long-overdue affair of honor required Johnston to return briefly to his almost alma mater. "In the year 1810, during his last visit to our family," according to Frances, "he called upon Dr. Caldwell, President of Chapel Hill College, to make, as he said, an apology." Presiding Professor Caldwell was, of course, the very same man whom Blakeley had threatened to throw bodily out his dormitory window a dozen years before. The incident had reportedly left no unfavorable impression with Dr. Caldwell, who was himself very young at the time, and had reflected that he might have done Blakeley an injustice with his initial accusations. "With mutual concessions," concluded Frances, "they were cordially reconciled."

Secretary Hamilton sent off a curious note that arrived at Rock Rest close on the heels of Lieutenant Blakeley. Captain Dent had not kept Washington accurately apprised of his former first lieutenant's status. Blakeley promptly responded that he was indeed on a properly granted furlough and that, as accorded with the letter of his instructions and with the concurrence of Dent, he had first waited to be "relieved by Lieutenant Burrows." Annoyed, he could not help but add to his response a bit of sarcasm: "Permit me to express my thanks to the department for this indulgence."[5] His health fully restored and his heart likewise rejuvenated, Blakeley returned to the rigors of naval life. Another letter, its length in inverse proportion to its worth, awaited his return at Washington: "Sir, you will assume command of the Schooner Enterprize."[6] Even though he was still only a lieutenant, Johnston could at long last be addressed as "Captain Blakeley." He was now formally in command of a vessel of war. This courteous title would later follow him into the *Wasp*, where he served as master commandant. The next step up on the promotion ladder, the rank of captain, would become official only posthumously.

When Blakeley completed his schooner's fitting out, he was to transport a detachment of four dozen marines to Cumberland Island, Georgia. He was then to place his schooner under the orders of the commander of the St. Marys station, Commo. Hugh G. Campbell. As soon as his chest was sent below to his cupboard-sized quarters, Captain Blakeley ordered his schooner downriver to water and provision at Hampton Roads. At two o'clock the following afternoon the crew of the *Enterprize* gazed with reverence at the heavily wooded, western bank of the Potomac River. There they beheld the temple called Mount Vernon. A visit to George Washington's great shrine was considered a sacred pilgrimage, even if made only in passing. With its colors snapping at half-mast in the freshening breeze, the *Enterprize* thundered out a salute of seventeen guns. Captain Blakeley had witnessed this honored ritual many times before, but now things were entirely different. The single gilt epaulet on the coat of his dress uniform no longer adorned his left shoulder. It now sat gleaming on his right side, the prestigious and unmistakable sign of a lieutenant in command. He was in all his glory on this day, but the moment was truly bittersweet. If only John Blakeley could see him here today, he lamented, at the proudest moment yet of his naval career. On 9 May 1811, amid "fresh gales and rain," the *Enterprize* at last put to sea, alongside Gunboat *No. 10*. Captain Blakeley's first official day of command at sea had ended just as it had begun, with melancholy reflections. By the light of the lantern swinging on the beam overhead, he wrote that very evening to Edward Jones: "It would afford me great gratification to hear from you all the information you possess respecting my relations. This trouble your goodness will excuse, when I inform you that for fourteen years I have not beheld one being to whom I was bound by any tie of consanguinity."[7]

A warm and frequent exchange of thoughts and feelings with his godparents began. Johnston wrote to Edward again, "soon after":

> The affection manifested by [Mrs. Jones] is truly grateful to my heart. Indeed, I begin already to feel her filial regard, and the more so, as it was my lot to lose my mother before I was sensible to a mother's tenderness. . . . Should I be fortunate enough to acquire any fame, my good old friend will make me debtor for more than half. With her prayers for my success, can I doubt it? I hope the last Blakeley who exists will lay down his life ere he tarnish the reputation of those who have gone before him. My father's memory is very dear to me, and I trust his son will never cast a reproach upon it.[8]

Blakeley's maiden voyage of command traversing Cape Hatteras would not be a smooth one. The following day's intermittent squalls soon intensified into a full-fledged storm. In spite of all precautions, his consort vanished. When Sailing Master George Williams, the gunboat's commander, first lost sight of the *Enterprize,* he charted an independent course to the St. Marys, prematurely supposing that the schooner had foundered. But along the way, he was grabbed by a strong flood tide setting into "Jakyl Sound" that quickly drove his command hard against the St. Simon's Breakers, unshipping his rudder and depriving him of his best anchor. With great ingenuity and fortitude, however, Williams managed to rally what he described as "the worst crew ever collected" and to bring his seasick passengers safely to their encampment. Blakeley's initial relief soon turned to anger: "I cannot refrain from expressing an opinion [that] the separation must have been produced by one of two causes, neglect, or intention so to do," he reported, "nor do I believe any one else ever experienced on this part of the coast, the six knot tide he speakes [*sic*] of."[9] To Williams's credit, not one life was lost, and he did manage to salvage his wayward helm. Ingeniously fashioning new pintles from the gangway's iron hammock stanchions, he reshipped his heavy rudder and had somehow aligned it with the heaving sternpost, all amid a pounding sea.[10] Displacing less than half the tonnage of the *Enterprize,* the gunboat should not have attempted to round the treacherous cape, especially when it was crammed with passengers. Blakeley overreacted because he wanted his very first independent cruise to go without a hitch. Washington would be closely watching his every move, he believed (with the paranoia inherent to all first-time commanders), and he would be blamed for all things that went awry.

On 16 May the *Guerriere* appeared across the approaches to the St. Marys, arrogantly flaunting the Union Jack. This notorious English frigate had been harassing the coastal trade for well over a year, earning for itself an "obnoxious" reputation. Just two weeks before, the *Guerriere* had pressed an American national within full view of Sandy Hook. This incident caused such an intense public outcry that President Madison ordered Commodore Rodgers to sea with orders to repatriate the kidnapped sailor by force. A nocturnal and violent case of mistaken identity with a much smaller British corvette, however, precipitated the *President–Little Belt* affair. Blakeley was probably unaware of the latest *Guerriere* incident; too little time had elapsed for the news to have reached him. Although impossibly overmatched against such an indomitable foe, Captain Blakeley was nevertheless determined to give the big Englishman trouble if the issue was forced. However, the *Guerriere* "merely inquired our name and how long out but did not board us." The English officers proved "all very polite," reported Blakeley, and the *Guerriere* quietly sailed off.[11] Later that evening, Blakeley got in the final word for the day. He overhauled and briefly detained the British three-masted schooner *Juniper.* Not catching Captain Campbell in the St. Marys where he had hoped to find him, Blakeley sailed north to Charleston.

One July day the searing sun beat mercilessly down upon Dr. Bailey Washington, the schooner's surgeon, as he paced along the dry, sandy shoreline, enjoying a bit of light conversation with his amiable captain. As they passed the station's laid-up gunboats, something peculiar caught Johnston Blakeley's eye. Several of his men from the *Enterprize* were there, toiling against the summer heat to fill the schooner's freshwater casks. But these dutiful men were unattended by any officer. Blakeley had placed this particular party under the command of Midshipman Robert Ward earlier in the morning, but now he was nowhere to be seen. Owing only to their commander's timely approach did the wayward Ward avoid having to deal with a mass desertion, a common problem on the southern station. The *Enterprize's* former commander had frequently reprimanded Ward both for disrespect and for unofficerlike conduct. While his present behavior had been at best only "tolerable" since their departure from Washington, Blakeley had been assured that this would not last. Ward at length appeared from the shade of a white clapboard shop about a hundred yards down the beach. He strode casually out into the furnacelike sun and stood face to face with an officer even hotter. Blakeley ordered him to report himself directly to the officer of the watch, and then to beg to be supplanted with "someone with whom confidence could be placed." Ward, in a fit of stupidity, openly questioned his captain's direct order, offering feeble explanations. In his fury, Blakeley called Ward a "dirty little rascal" and then repeated his order with even greater volume and conviction. Insulted and humiliated, Ward quietly returned to the schooner, but he failed to mention any of these proceedings to anyone. Instead, he dressed in his finest uniform, stowed his pistols under his jacket, and then returned ashore with the second watering party. Commenting on the unusually hot weather, Ward deliberately unbuttoned his coat, revealing his weapons. "I did not wish to see what he had on his bosom," recalled the officer of the launch, "and [I] turned my head away." Even Blakeley was surprised when he read the note that Ward had left for him: "I intend to come on board the schooner no more." However, he also desired his captain to "call on him" at the Planters Hotel. The display of weaponry and the invitation meant that Ward was either seeking a duel, or pretending to do so, to save face. With Campbell's blessings, Blakeley court-martialed him. Ward offered no defense and was duly convicted of "neglect of duty, disobedience of orders, scandalous conduct and mutinous language" and dismissed from the service.[12]

On 5 August, while out cruising the Georgia coast for felonious traders bound to Amelia Island and all points south, Blakeley once again encountered units of the Royal Navy. Four strange vessels appeared late that afternoon, and the *Enterprize* quickly bore away to investigate. The first sail, the brig-sloop *Emulous*, reported that two of the three other vessels were its prizes. But the fourth vessel, a much larger quarter-decked ship-sloop, was seen to be in pursuit of them:

> At 6 hove out the Schooner's distinguishing colors, which she not being able to answer, [she] hoisted English colors. . . . At 10 bore away *for* the Frigate and made all sail, piped to quarters and prepared for action. . . . At meridian hove to and was boarded by H.B.M. Ship Goree on a cruise. . . . At 1 filled away.[13]

Blakeley went right at the ship. Both national honor and his own personal reputation were on the line, so he could not run, not even from what appeared to be a frigate. The *Goree* was in fact a corvette mounting twenty-six heavy carronades upon two decks. During the previous year it had detained the American schooner *Revenge,* demanding that its commander, Lt. Oliver Hazard Perry, come aboard with his papers.[14] Perry had rightly refused, boldly declaring that he was "not obliged to answer any questions put to him by the Royal Navy."[15] Perry was quite well received at home for his bravado. Details of Blakeley's conversation with quite possibly the very same English captain have not been found but the schooner's logbook failed to report the customary "all polite" or an equivalent. Eight days later, these same two players performed an encore further down the coast, but once the *Gorce* recognized the *Enterprize* it bore quietly away.[16]

The substantial repairs completed on the *Enterprize* earlier in the year had been performed on what was essentially a worn-out and increasingly rotten hull. The upper works in particular leaked badly. More extensive refurbishments were needed to keep the ship seaworthy.[17] Back in the nation's capital by early October, the twelve-year-old *Enterprize* was "hauled out, cut down, and stripped to its 'floor timbers'" and then "entirely rebuilt, coppered, launched and re-rigged as a brig . . . having her hull much improved in rebuilding."[18] It was also rearmed with heavier guns and more of them. This was not the first major rebuild that the schooner had received. Mstr. Comdt. Thomas Robinson Jr. had brought the *Enterprize* into the Arsenal of Trieste in 1804, with the intention of giving it a thorough repair in a professionally run yard. When the Venetian artisans ripped it open, they found the ship in a most deplorable condition. Given free access to the best timbers in the yard, Robinson created almost an entirely new schooner, with many improvements:

> I was obliged to put in a new stem and stern post, in doing the latter, I have taken out the square tuck and have also altered in a small degree the fashion of her topsides, by not giving her so much tumblehome aloft, which will afford a better deck and more room to manage her guns, but in every instance I have been particular in preserving her model below.[19]

When it arrived home from the Mediterranean, the *Enterprize* was recorded as having nine gun ports on each side, exclusive of its bow and stern chase ports. Every third broadside port was empty because it never carried more than twelve guns prior to its rebuilding at Washington.[20] The ship's 6-pounders would be of little use against a heavy or distant foe, so the resourceful Robinson prescribed a cure: "I am preparing for a heavy gun," he wrote his commander, "and in such a way that the arrangement will answer for any other deck & shall carry all in the hold to the place of action."[21] He detailed his inspiration to the secretary: "I have almost completed the machinery for the 24-pounder on the schooner's deck, having experienced the inactive situation this description of vessel was in last summer, I calculated her hatches and beams amidships for this mode of armament."[22] By this time the fighting was over, and Robinson's clever scheme was never tested. The machinery was dismantled, struck down in the schooner's hold, and for a while forgotten, only to await Lieutenant Blakeley's eager attention seven years later.

Blakeley explained the squaring and thickening of the *Enterprize*'s top-hamper to Secretary Hamilton:

> The Enterprize being at this time under repairs I would beg leave to suggest the propriety of altering her present rig into that of a brig. Her size renders her present arrangement awkward and inconvenient and as her expenses will be diminished her sailing in all probability increased and her properties [as a] vessel of war greatly improved, I would certainly solicit your permission to carry into effect the proposed alteration. Nothing [of her] present equipment will be lost, her masts, sails, spars, rigging all being susceptible of a change at a very small expense.[23]

Not only did the *Enterprize* now look more imposing under two vast, squared pyramids of canvas, rimmed by lofty sky-sails and edged with taut stun'sails, but it was also a far more stable gun platform. And it would be much harder to dismast in a naval engagement. The secretary scribbled "Agreed to P.H." in the margin, and it was done. Many in the navy had always thought the *Enterprize* far too grand for a mere schooner rig. "Oh how I wish I had got permission to give her a few feet more keel and opened her a little," the innovative Commander Robinson had written to the secretary a half-dozen years before. "What a sweet brig I could have made her, and with no apparent expense." But feeling that he had perhaps overstepped his bounds, he added: "But sir, it is dangerous for officers young in rank to take liberties."[24]

The wardroom crew also was altered while the conversion to a brig was occurring. Midshipman Edward R. McCall, a native of Beaufort, South Carolina, and a headstrong yet capable sailing master, was advanced to acting lieutenant, while his twenty-one-year-old messmate, Thomas G. Tillinghast Jr., replaced him on the vacated lower rung. A graduate of the state's university in his hometown of Columbia, Tillinghast was undoubtedly the best-educated man on board.[25] His family had only recently emigrated from Greenwich, Rhode Island, but his father, a medical doctor, had died not long afterward. His mother soon remarried, to another prominent local physician. Thomas had a brother, Daniel, who lived in Greenville, and another, John, "of the firm of Pierce and Tillinghast," who had died suddenly a few years before of the "malignant fever then raging" in Charleston. "The doctor's solicitude about the young man is very great," wrote family friend and House Representative Wade Hampton, in recommending young Thomas for a naval appointment. He "has it in his power to do nothing more for his relation than to leave him to the success of his own merits and exertions."[26] Tillinghast had spent the first months of his naval service rotting away alongside the laid-up Charleston gunboats until he joined the *John Adams* in late 1810.[27] During one of his very first days aboard Blakeley's corvette Tillinghast was tested.

> One of the young officers wishing to try him, or make him ridiculous, told him that the captain had ordered him to unstep the mainmast and have the foot of it scrubbed. Young Tillinghast immediately discovered the trick, and sent a challenge to the offender; an apology ensued; the parties were good friends after it, and no more tricks were played.[28]

The coming war with Great Britain was brewing. It was created by the Napoleonic Wars, which were themselves the final stage of three centuries of nearly constant conflict among the major imperial European powers. In an effort to solve the problems of social injustice, and inspired in no small way by the success of the recently liberated Americans, France underwent a bloody revolution in 1789 under the watchwords "Liberty, Equality, Fraternity." In 1799, however, Napoleon Bonaparte came to power, stealing away the democratic ideals and creating instead a dictatorship. England had begun its war against the French Republic in 1793, protective of its monarchy and deeply fearful of the effects that any further democratic revolutions might inspire at home. With Bonaparte in power, Britain ironically became the champion of freedom, going to war to preserve all that it held dear. The glorious British victory at Trafalgar in 1805 left England the true ruler of the waves, but the French victory at Austerlitz during the same year left Napoleon in control of the continent. The war was now at a bloody standstill.

America was happy to supply both sides with food, cotton, and other raw materials. In an attempt to starve each other out, both Britain and France equally oppressed neutral trade. Britain continued to issue Orders in Council, allowing seizure of American vessels and their cargoes, while Bonaparte effected the same with his Imperial Decrees. The harassment was deeply galling to Americans, but trade continued to prosper; those ships that could get through made enormous profits. The abortive Embargo Act of 1807 and later similar legislation represented America's futile attempt at a retaliatory, yet peaceful, solution to the problem. While these acts caused a severe economic depression at home, both Britain and France still received their merchandise, albeit at greater cost. Smugglers made fortunes while America's custom house coffers ran dry. The most significant result of these misguided attempts at gunless diplomacy was the ascendancy of Henry Clay and his congressional "War Hawks," an unruly group of southerners and westerners bent upon expelling Great Britain from all of North America. They also set their sights on Spanish Florida, as well as the bountiful Indian territories. Since Great Britain controlled the sea lanes during this period, France was only a minor antagonist. Henry Clay, in league with the reluctant President Madison, prevailed early in that year's congressional term. With the real aim of snatching up Canada while England was preoccupied with Napoleon, the War Hawks declared war on 18 June 1812.

The United States could not have been less prepared for a war. In 1812 there were fewer than seven thousand men in the regular army. These troops were officered mainly by impotent political appointees such as the ancient Gen. William Hull, the corpulent Gen. Henry Dearborn, and the incompetent General Van Rensselaer, New York's largest landowner; the only military qualification any of these men had was that they were good Republicans. Most of the Revolutionary War veterans were either dead or unable to serve because of advanced age. However, America did possess two formidable military assets: the state militias and the fledgling navy. As for the former, the best equipped and best led units were in states that were overwhelmingly Federalist, such as Massachusetts and New Hampshire. Their governors, their citizens, and in some cases even their state constitutions, however, forbade these powerful armies from participating in the war unless their own boundaries were violated. The British were thus wise to leave most of New England alone, which for the most part they did. The navy, having proven itself against the French and the pirates of Barbary, was nonetheless minuscule. America possessed not a single ship of the line, and only a handful of frigates were strong enough to meet their modern European equivalents. The American navy was thought to be of greatest utility in a defensive mode, using its frigates, for example, as harbor block ships. But those few ships that had been able to put to sea in the days before the upcoming war had so upset the balance of world opinion by their series of victories that the myth of the Royal Navy's invincibility was irrevocably shattered.

The little schooner-turned-brig remained safely moored in the "River Powtomack" for the first, peaceful half of 1812. Initially, the *Enterprize* had been ordered to proceed away to New Orleans with its hold crammed full of military stores. Blakeley felt that it would be entirely unsafe to put to sea carrying such a great cargo. "Anxious as I have ever been to render implicit obedience to every order of the Navy Department," Blakeley wrote the secretary, "it is with regret I have to state the total incapacity of the Enterprize to carry those arms." The country was spiraling downhill toward war with Great Britain, as he well knew, and those essential munitions had to be delivered. But the safety of his command must come first. "I do not believe she could possibly stow them below her decks, and if that were even practicable," he continued, "it would load her as to disqualify her in every sense of the word as a vessel of war."[29] The *Enterprize* had to be able to defend not only itself but also the honor of its flag, should any provocation arise en route.

The New Orleans station had little to offer any naval officer aside from heat, humidity, and the dreaded yellow fever. These gloomy prospects no doubt influenced Blakeley's protests as well. If there was to be war, and every one was sure that there would be, Blakeley wanted to be where the fighting was, cruising the deep, blue waters of the North Atlantic, not the gray-brown mud of some turbid frontier backwater. The secretary finally acquiesced on the question of the cargo, but the *Enterprize* was still Louisiana-bound.

Blakeley was instructed to transport Maj. Gen. James Wilkinson, along with his full suite and baggage, to New Orleans.[30] Acquitted by a court-martial for his role in the Aaron Burr conspiracy, this highly controversial general was ordered to resume his former command over all the military forces in the city. In addition, Blakeley received a miniature wooden model of the French frigate *L'Ambuscade*. He was to return it to its rightful owners, the New Orleans Public Library, with his department's sincerest compliments. Furthermore, Blakeley was to beg permission to borrow it once again should the need arise.[31]

During the brief journey down to the mouth of the Patuxent River to collect the unwanted supernumeraries, Blakeley's *Enterprize* passed Mount Vernon, outbound, for a second time.[32] One gun less than the number required to honor a dead president saluted the arrival of their live general and his charges on 29 May. The logbook noted solemnly, "Received on board, belonging to Genl. Wilkinson, 4 Negroes."[33] Some of the *Enterprize*'s crew may have been black, and Wilkinson's "baggage" might have distressed some of the crew. While Blakeley's own thoughts on the subject of slavery are unknown, his values probably paralleled those of his godfather, who favored abolition.[34]

The crowded, nearly month-long passage to New Orleans was entirely uneventful. "It gives me much pleasure to be able to announce," wrote the brig's proud commander, "the gratification we felt in the performance of the Enterprize."[35] Blakeley's new rig was a complete success. They arrived in the Balize on 29 June and wound their way upriver to the city a few days later.

The New Orleans of 1812 was a tightly packed community containing over twenty thousand people, nearly all of them clinging tenaciously to the left bank of a small portion of the Mississippi River.[36] The great river was kept both within its bed and out of the city streets by a long series of levees and dams. This was a considerable feat of engineering because New Orleans was on average about three feet below water level during the rainy season. Health was of great concern to the naval officers in this low, tropical town. The collective filth deposited by hundreds of frail "Kentucky boats," or houseboats, combined with the unregulated dumping into the river of "excrementitious animal matter," contributed notably to the generally un-healthful quality of the city. An eddy in the current running the entire breadth of the city detained the whole of this "baneful matter" along the battery, and Blakeley's first sensation of New Orleans was olfactory. The city's topsoil, a light layer of river mud and decomposing vegetation, was submersible after only a single day's rain, which rendered most of the roads impassable. Frequently the water rose in the wells to within only a few inches of the surface, communicating quickly with the levees and then on out to the open sewers. This created a sort of "stagnant soup," one observer noted, the optimum breeding ground for mosquitoes, still unrecognized as the carriers of the yellow fever.[37] It was the height of the rainy season when Blakeley kedged his little brig into the battery, and his crew began to feel the effects almost immediately.

Any ambitious officer felt hopelessly stranded here, snared tight against the possibility of escape from this unpopular station, unlikely ever to receive new orders. If Capt. John Shaw, the senior naval officer commanding this backwater, thought him valuable enough, Blakeley might well become a per-manent fixture on the Mississippi. Blakeley worried that war was imminent, if it had not already been declared. Glory, promotion, and above all, prize money, lay not here in this tropical purgatory but far out on the open ocean.[38] The *Enterprize*, although small by deep-sea standards, displaced far too much water to be of any use in this shallow filth. He prayed that when war finally came, the secretary might be of the same opinion:

> Situated as I am here, I am unable to refrain from soliciting your permission to return to the Atlantic states in the Enterprize. In making this request, a request known and assented to by Captain Shaw, I am actuated by a conviction of the little utility which would attend her operations on *this station*. The coast of this country affords no encouragement to a vessel drawing as much water as ours; but its dangers and difficulties, it appears we will not be allowed an opportunity to test. Therefore I pray to you, should this meet your approbation, to order the Enterprize to any Atlantic port you may think proper.[39]

It is doubtful that Captain Shaw had any intention of letting the *Enterprize* escape his grasp, however, in spite of what Blakeley reported to Washington. Already the yellow fever was beginning to sweep his decks as effectively as grapeshot. Four of his officers, including Thomas Tillinghast and his valued captain's clerk, already lay prostrate in the naval hospital alongside twenty-two others by the time Blakeley penned his plea. "A number," admitted Shaw in a separate correspondence, "which although great, is liable to be daily augmented from the same vessel." News of the declaration of war against Great Britain arrived six weeks late. On 28 July 1812 Blakeley called his thinning ranks to muster on the gun deck and read out the articles of war for the first time. Those members of the crew who considered themselves subjects of the British crown were asked to report to him later that day for a formal discharge. Over the next week the log recorded the many departures.

The focus of Capt. John Shaw's thoughts shifted from the viral enemy to the English. HBM ship *Brazen,* a frigate-built corvette, had just recently appeared at the mouth of the Balize, and Shaw had nothing at hand of sufficient strength with which to oppose it. Even worse, his largest cruiser, the brig *Syren,* was due in from a routine cruise. Heavily outgunned by the *Brazen,* it would be sailing home into a trap, particularly if its commander was unaware of the declaration of war.

Blakeley was determined to assist the *Syren* in attacking the *Brazen* "should an opportunity be afforded."[40] Shaw immediately sent on board the brig all available able-bodied men to make up the deficiencies in the crew. Several crewmen from the *Enterprize* who had not entirely recovered staggered back on board from the hospital, determined not to miss the fight.

DELAY, DISAPPOINTMENT, AND DISASTER ⌐⤴

The exact plan of attack is not known, but tantalizing clues are revealed in the *Enterprize*'s logbook.[41] On 15 August a long 24-pounder was hoisted aboard, supplied with 187 round-shot and fifty stand of grape in this exclusive caliber, and mounted on Robinson's long-neglected portable pivot carriage. This ponderous piece, described both as a "cannonade" and a "columbiad," was a new type of weapon falling somewhere between a conventional long gun and a carronade in weight, range, and striking power. It was an extremely heavy but nevertheless highly valuable addition to the *Enterprize*'s already overcrowded gun deck. The great number of shot taken on board testifies that Blakeley planned to make as much use of it as the situation would allow. This gun could well outrange anything on board the predominantly carronade-armed *Brazen*, and so, in theory, the nimble *Enterprize* could dart easily about through the shallows and harass the deep-draft Briton with impunity—and perhaps even drive it away. Shaw also sent on board thirty additional cutlasses and fifty extra boarding pikes. If Blakeley found himself alone and stranded within the range of the *Brazen*'s main deck battery of 32-pounder smashers his only hope for survival would be to board. Blakeley's only realistic chance for success, however, was a united action with the heavier *Syren*, where their combined broadsides of 18- and 24-pounder carronades just about equaled the *Brazen*'s weight of metal.

Whether the plan of attack was the brainchild of Shaw or Blakeley is unclear. Shaw wrote that "she goes immediately to the Balize" without explicitly stating that the brig was sailing under his orders. Had it been Shaw's plan, he might well have accompanied it, for just such a successful outcome would have propelled him to fame, promotion, and above all, a change of venue. The War of 1812 is commemorated today primarily for the spectacular successes of the American navy. At the time of the *Enterprize*'s gallant descent downriver, the news of the destruction of the *Guerriere*—the first victory—had not yet reached New Orleans to boost morale.[42]

Blakeley, however, was destined to fight yet another enemy, one infinitely more formidable and insidious. On 17 August Tillinghast had observed in the log the presence of "flying clouds and moderate winds" cantering overhead, not wholly unusual in these latitudes, replacing the previous day's "pleasant" airs. By evening the galloping breeze had intensified audibly, and the low racing clouds had thickened, turning ominously in a broad and turbulent arc. By nine the next morning, the *Enterprize*, fully manned "by considerable exertion," began the twisting journey downstream. By 11:00 A.M. the winds were gusting with such tremendous conviction that Blakeley was obliged to order both topgallant masts struck down on deck, along with all

85

the upper yards. The ship anchored abreast of Fort Charles in the afternoon, pitching violently under the press of the wind, the heaving river, and the added strain of the great 24-pounder amidships.[43]

When at midnight "it blew a hurricane," the brig parted its cables. Without these lifelines, it instantly ran aground and lay over on its beam ends, snapping off its larboard fish-davit under the first heave of the hull. As it beat atop the riverbank, the unrelenting waves smashed every boat to kindling and carried away their fractured remains, along with the sweeps and the gratings. Water flooded in through the exposed hatchways, while the hold's increasing weight pushed the brig even deeper into the mud. At 2:00 A.M. a dark shape loomed out of the driving spray, pushed before the shrieking wind. Lurching through the blackness, the merchant ship *Juno* drove straight into the *Enterprize*'s defenseless, uplifted starboard side, snapping away its mainchains and crushing in its starboard bulwarks. But the *Enterprize*'s live-oak frame held solidly together, and its guns, double breached and double lashed, stuck tight to their assigned stations. The rise of the next wave carried the *Juno* away into the darkness.

The tempest began to moderate when daylight finally peeked through the outermost feeder bands. The faint sunlight saw the brig buried deep in the gray mud, well above the high water mark, and covered with debris. The hold was awash, the provisions spoiled, and the carpenter reported serious injuries to the bilge. How badly the brig was damaged, Blakeley couldn't tell until the hold was drained and cleared. At least the mud had softened the effects of constant pounding. But this created yet another problem. "The relaunching of her," wrote Shaw, "the bottom being a soft mud, will, I am apprehensive, be attended with considerable difficulty and consumption of time." Although one lieutenant and one midshipman, as well as many of the crew, had been seriously injured, no one was killed. And the masts still stood. With daylight at last fully upon him, Lieutenant Blakeley set his people hard at work striking down the topmasts, unbending the sails, and lightening the ship.

"Sir, I greatly deplore the necessity I am under of communicating to you, of the calamitous condition of the small naval force attached to this station," began John Shaw in his official disaster dispatch.[44] This nearly total devastation had been produced by a storm, he continued, "which, both in violence and duration, exceeded anything of the kind, within the recollection of the oldest inhabitant of the country." The brig *Viper* was completely unrigged, losing even the bowsprit and lower mainmast after four large merchantmen had been driven into it. Rammed from its moorings by several castaway merchantmen, the laid-up bomb ketch *Aetna* sank in the channel. The main naval hospital building had been blown completely away, along with the sail loft, the joiners shed, the kitchen, and nearly all of the outbuildings of the yard. There was some good news, however. The *Syren* had made it safely in. Blakeley's people continued lightening ship, and they struck the heavy guns directly on shore; no vessel large enough to transport them remained serviceable. It took a week to heave the *Enterprize* over and inspect the hull. "[We] found the brig's bilge was injured and righted her," wrote Tillinghast in the log. That very day in Washington, Secretary Hamilton penned his response to Blakeley's earlier plea: "I am extremely sorry to hear, as I have done through Capt. Shaw of the unhealthiness of your crew; in consequence of their sickness, and the reasons urged in your letter, I have to direct that you proceed with all possible dispatch to St. Marys."[45]

But it would be quite some time before Blakeley received this overdue bit of good news. Anticipating Shaw's objection, Hamilton added: "P.S. Show this letter to Capt. Shaw & inform him of its contents." The brig's recovery and repairs took nearly seven weeks to complete.[46] The columbiad was carted back to the yard, and Robinson's ad hoc pivot mount was returned to the lightless orlop, never to be tried again. Near the end of October, Shaw reported the brig once again rigged and ready for sea, although acutely short of hands.[47] He added, "I most sincerely regret that the *Enterprize* has been ordered from this station, her services being much wanted here." What was worse, the *Viper* was ordered away, too. Anchored safely at the mouth of the Mississippi on 29 November, Blakeley finally crafted his response to the secretary. The joyous news of his liberation had been received somewhat earlier, while he was still up to his knees in muck, laboriously inching his command back into the unusually opaque element. Since Shaw had kept Hamilton informed of Blakeley's progress, the brig's captain did not think it proper to respond until he could do so with certainty: "Permit me to express to you, how grateful I feel for your attention to my application. How rejoiced I am to be relieved from a station where I have experienced nothing but delay, disappointment and disaster."[48]

Both the wind and the tide at last appeared favorable for departure at 4:00 A.M. on 8 December, but the river was not done playing its torturous games with the North Carolina captain just yet. Within half an hour of making sail, the brig once again struck fast on a mud bank, only two miles from the freedom of the Gulf of Mexico. The *Enterprize* refused to budge. After pumping tons of fresh water over the side, Blakeley sent the bulk of his shot, spare spars, rigging, and even all his bread on board the *Viper*. A nearby military blockhouse provided two lighters for unloading of every movable item. As the hands pressed hard against the capstan bars that refused to turn, the first lighter, crammed with sea-stores, wallowed off to the safety of the blockhouse. And once again, the weather turned against them.[49] "It coming on to blow fresh," recorded the master, "the crew hove the barrels overboard to prevent the lighter from sinking." By 8:00 A.M., with the brig still stubbornly clutching the ooze, Blakeley sent the guns ashore. Twelve hours later, the *Enterprize,* now an unarmed empty shell, was at last hove off. Blakeley now had to suffer the embarrassment of sending his boats back up to New Orleans for resupply. Replacement stores in a backwater city that had just been leveled by a hurricane in wartime would not be easy to come by. Shaw would not be happy. The reprovisioned gunboats returned several days later carrying what few meager items could be scrounged, but there still remained the matter of negotiating the bar. At least no enemy had appeared during the whole debacle. Keeping much of his shifted provisions aboard the two gunboats that had come downriver to protect him, Blakeley ordered the *Enterprize* towed over the bar into deep water. This time he succeeded. His brig repaired, his hold restocked, and his spirits renewed, the North Carolinian finally set sail for home.

7. Chained to the Moorings

Captain Blakeley's two-week circumnavigation of Florida earned him neither laurels nor prizes. Twice, a strange sail teased him from the distant horizon, but in each case neither he nor his loyal consort were able to close with the elusive windward foe. Blakeley landed first at the St. Marys River, while the *Viper* proceeded independently on up to Charleston. With all sail gloriously set, the *Enterprize* tried to stand upriver to speak with the gunboat flotilla, but unceremoniously grounded one last time. Fortunately, the veteran crew of the *Enterprize* easily kedged the ship off. "Captain Campbell is at this time absent at Savannah, but is expected here soon," Blakeley reported to the secretary. "I trust we will now have an opportunity to cruise[, for] our misfortune on the Mississippi and the nature of the station have hitherto deprived us from doing so."[1] On 10 February 1813, the brig was at last visited by Commodore Campbell. Blakeley thoughtfully "drew the shot out of the guns" before he "saluted him with 13." A native South Carolinian of Irish stock, Hugh G. Campbell, or "Old Cork" as he was affectionately known, was a devout believer in rigid discipline.[2] He had commanded the *Adams* during Blakeley's rollicking days off Tripoli in 1803 and, for a short while, the North Carolinian had served under him when the promoted Commodore Rodgers had vacated the *John Adams*. He had turned this formerly lax southern backwater on its head when he assumed command not long afterward. A firm, no-nonsense officer, Campbell was very much like Blakeley's former commanders: Truxtun, Dale, Rodgers, and Evans. So it is likely that these two southern-bred Irish gentlemen shared not only a mutual respect but also a complete understanding, if not an actual friendship. Campbell was an old Revolutionary War-horse who, by this late stage in his life, was rather tired and set in his ways. Still, he was expressly happy to have two relatively strong vessels under his direction (the *Viper* was also under his orders) in addition to the mere handful of gunboats and barges assigned to his vast station. He was especially pleased with the *Enterprize,* commanded by so able and promising an officer.

The *Enterprize* made sail ten days later, standing away to the north against contrary winds with the private sloop *Fellowship* in company. Four wet, uneventful days later, the crew of the *Enterprize* let go their best bower in Five Fathom Hole in the Savannah River. There was not much for the *Enterprize* to do here but defend its anchorage. There was little in the way of an enemy to cruise against, even if Blakeley had been allowed to set his royals in earnest. Campbell showed no inclination to permit the North Carolinian out of his sight, potential prizes or not. Blakeley had by now fully caught up on the thrilling news of the war. Five times the U.S. Navy had met single, comparable ships of the Royal Navy on the open ocean, and on each of these glorious occasions the overgunned but underrated Yankees had emerged victorious. Johnston reflected privately to his godmother, Mary Mallet Todd-Jones, later that April:

> Independent of my personal feeling, I rejoice at the good fortune of the navy, believing it to be that description of force best adapted to the defense of this country. I confess the success of our sailors has been much greater than I had any reason to expect, taking into view the many difficulties they had to encounter. The charm which seemed to have once circled the British navy, and rendered its very name formidable, appears to be fast dispelling. . . . It is true that in the war in which we are engaged, we have to contend under great disadvantages; but this should stimulate [us] to greater exertions, and we have already seen that our enemy is not invincible.[3]

The news of the war had an alarming but predictable effect on all of his officers. Lt. Lawrence Kearney was the first of several who wrote directly to the secretary, begging leave to go on board any other active warship. He had been in the brig for three years, he explained, and he thought himself due the "equal advantages" afforded his brother officers of which fate alone had deprived him.⁴ Midshipmen R. M. Potter and J. P. Wails were arrested on 28 March for "misconduct on shore," while the otherwise reliable Midshipman Claxton was apparently conniving a transfer out of the brig under false pretexts. Claxton had requested and received a furlough "for the restoration of his health" from the honorable secretary, but as far as Dr. Washington was concerned, this officer had daily been performing his full duty and appeared to suffer from no observable malady. "It excited my surprise," he wrote to Blakeley, "as I have not seen him on the sick report since our leaving the Mississippi."⁵ The brig's medical officer had his own bone to pick with the department, for he was still only an acting surgeon. Dr. Washington had originally sailed down the Potomac in 1811 firm in the conviction that Paul Hamilton would provide him with a surgeon's commission before the next session of Congress had convened. "I can vouch in the fullest manner for his unremitting attention and humane treatment towards the sick," Blakeley wrote to the secretary in March, attempting to grease the wheels, "and of the unusually healthy state of the crew of this vessel, with the exception of our stay in New Orleans."⁶

By April 1813 morale was at an all-time low, and Blakeley was once again forced to beg for a new set of orders from Washington. Since he had been extremely lucky to be allowed to get out of New Orleans in the first place, he now ran the real risk of looking like an ungrateful whiner. The problem, as he perceived it, was that Hugh Campbell and the newest secretary of the navy, William Jones, had been the closest of friends for some twenty years. Campbell, like Shaw before him, coveted the presence of Blakeley's brig, even if he had nothing for it to do. But Campbell had another motive as well. The secretary had approved a court-martial to be held in Savannah against a troublesome junior officer, and, without his knowledge, Lieutenant Blakeley had been slated to be the president of the tribunal. Not yet aware of the true reason for the delay or, for that matter, the midstream departmental change of leadership, Blakeley again wrote Paul Hamilton in earnest:

With no feigned reluctance and much real regret do I intrude upon your attention at this time, a period of almost 10 months of war without this vessel being able to cruise. While on the Mississippi the opportunity to do so was withheld until an application in consequence of that refusal was made to the Navy Department and we were ordered to this station. On the 18th January we arrived, since which I have repeatedly applied for application to make a cruise[.] Although I expected any day to receive orders to that effect, no such orders were obtained. I have been too long in the habit of subordination to question the propriety of those placed over me in command, but when it is considered that I have already lost rank and am likely to lose more and when the means of obtaining reputation is not only denied but the certain consequence will be the diminution of any little I might possess, I trust will plead my apology for troubling you. Thirteen years I have been in service; almost the whole of which I have been actively employed and now only ask to enjoy in common with the rest of the Navy, an opportunity to go against the enemy. While every vessel of the United States, every revenue cutter, every privateer are or have been engaged in cruising, this one alone being chained to its moorings. To the magnanimity and justice of the honorable the Secretary of the Navy I look, in fullest confidence, that I may no further be a sufferer in rank and reputation: tho the former is only desirable, and may tend to increase the latter.[7]

One particularly successful Charleston-based cruiser soon appeared in the offing, intent upon taunting poor Blakeley. On the evening of 8 April Lieutenant Tillinghast was out reconnoitering the bar in the first cutter when he observed two white, moonlit flecks several miles out. His oarsmen pulled arduously against both wind and tide to rejoin their brig and herald the approach of the strangers. By 6:00 A.M. the following day the first sail at last came up and made its friendly number. It proved to be the U.S. Revenue Schooner *Nonsuch*, which, with no small display of triumph, "came to astern of us" and dropped anchor. Its brief cruise had been unusually fruitful. The second sail, one of three valuable prizes that had just recently been taken, rejoined it within a few hours. This was the richly laden British privateer sloop *Caledonia*, captured off Amelia Island after a brief but sharp action.[8]

Since the new secretary was continually being bombarded with demands from southern merchants for protection, he ordered all vessels to remain close inshore, at the constant ready to protect the coastline. The commander of the Charleston naval establishment and Blakeley's longtime nemesis, Capt. John Herbert Dent, had received a severe rebuke for allowing the *Nonsuch* out in the first place. Every day reports had been coming in concerning the depredations committed by two notorious British privateers— one, an 8-gun cutter, and the other, a 10-gun schooner. They had sailed together out of New Providence in company with the 32-gun frigate *Aeolus*, and now they were independently raiding the coast. The *Nonsuch* itself had been chased by the *Aeolus* early the previous February, but it had easily "escaped by her superior sailing." The two privateers, cruising together and being very well manned, "principally with Negroes," would have been a close match for the *Enterprize*.[9] Black privateersmen, many of whom were escaped slaves with old scores to settle, were thought by some to be less than cordial in battle, reportedly beating and even killing prisoners who resisted. They were justifiably feared all along the southern coast, and Blakeley desperately wanted to get at them. As the *Caledonia* was described as cutter-rigged, it may well have been half of this notorious privateering pair. Cross-tied at his moorings during these long and desolate weeks, Blakeley could only champ resentfully upon his hempen bit.

Blakeley handed Campbell a formal letter of protest. Politely, but firmly, he requested that it should be forwarded along with the next official stack of Washington-bound correspondence. "You will observe, Sir," began Campbell that very day in his cover letter, "his anxiety to be indulged in the privilege of a cruise."[10] He would have liked to have indulged Blakeley, because, he explained, his enlistments were soon to expire en masse anyway. Had Campbell not received the secretary's specific instructions, ordering him to convene a court of inquiry to look into the latest shenanigans of one of his more troublesome sailing masters, then Lieutenant Blakeley would have most certainly been at sea long since. "The presence of Lieut. Blakeley is essentially necessary in consequence of the scarcity of commissioned officers in this station," he explained, "in which situation I thought proper to detain him." Since there was, at this time, a want of officers to compose the court, the inquiry had been postponed out of fairness to the accused. At least one additional body was needed to sit in judgment. In this peculiar case, nearly every available officer of sufficient rank was either a material witness or the bearer of one of the four formal charges. The timely arrival of Lt. Horace Walpole at last enabled Campbell to proceed with the case. "That having [been] accomplished," he assured the secretary, "I shall send the Enterprize on a cruise." Blakeley no doubt cursed to himself as he read Campbell's letter: "I hereby desire that a court of inquiry to consist of yourself [as] President, Lieut[enant]s Walpole and McCall, members . . . to examine and enquire into the conduct of Mr. Charles F. Grandison, on charges exhibited to him by Capt. Dent."[11] The embarrassing trial took several weeks and all four charges were substantially proven, the most serious being "pusillanimous buffoonery." A complex and controversial character, Grandison, the illegitimate son of the famed and flamboyant British Adm. Sir Sydney Smith, offered little or no defense for his conduct but was merely pronounced guilty of "conduct unbecoming of an officer and a gentleman." Poor

Blakeley had been detained for nearly three months without being allowed to make a cruise, solely to officiate a court-martial against a relatively unimportant acting lieutenant who had been slated for eventual dismissal anyway for an earlier, unrelated act.

"When you have decided in the case of Mr. Grandison," began Commodore Campbell in his confidential orders, "you will proceed in the U.S. Brig Enterprize on a cruise for six weeks (unless good fortune should render necessary a sooner return to port)." Because Campbell provided no further specifics other than this, Blakeley was free to cruise wherever his wisdom and experience dictated. At the expiration of that time, he was to return either to Savannah or to the St. Marys and then prepare for a second cruise. This latest foray would be specifically targeted against the vast Jamaica fleet, thought to be departing for England about mid-May. Campbell was sincerely sorry that he had hindered Blakeley's ambitions for as long as he had, and to so little purpose; thus this unusual latitude granted in his cruising instructions was meant to be a sincere compliment, and no doubt it was received as such. Campbell concluded his brief note "with best wishes for your success and glory," an uncommon endorsement.[12] Blakeley left no official report, probably because his cruise was so uneventful, but clues can be gleaned from the brig's surviving logbook. The weather was apparently both hostile and unrelenting during this period, for rarely did the racing clouds and "black squalls" part long enough for a celestial observation.

Blakeley made his departure from the Tybee Lighthouse at 1:00 P.M. on 3 May. The following day he chased and briefly detained the Russian ship *Hashaw*, bound into Savannah from Charleston. Nine days later the *Enterprize* was prowling through the Bahamas when it spied a strange sail at 9:30 A.M. off the starboard beam. At 11:00 A.M. Blakeley piped all hands to quarters, cleared for action, and then hoisted English colors as he swooped down upon a small schooner. But it was only the neutral Spanish *Louisa*, wallowing away toward Havana, last from New York. One week later Blakeley was back off the Georgia coast, but this time he was several hundred miles out into the Gulf Stream. No luck there. Blakeley was in South Carolina latitudes once again on the twenty-third, but still well out into the desolate eastern longitudes. Here he overhauled only the neutral Spanish schooner *St. Joseph*, bound from Havana to New York. Deeply discouraged by this time, Blakeley was heading home when the lookout "discovered a sail on the starboard beam." By 6:00 A.M., Tillinghast noted, the sail appeared to be "in chase of us," and by 10:00 A.M. he at last made it out to be an enemy's heavy sloop of war. Blakeley easily outweathered the ship to safety and dropped anchor in the St. Marys on 26 May.

Blakeley was destined never to meet the Jamaica fleet. Northern New England, normally a reasonably safe haven for the coastal trade and fisheries, had recently come under the depredations of several shallow-draft British privateers operating out of Nova Scotia. A brig of the *Enterprize*'s light displacement could prove to be of great utility in these waters, thought the commander of the Portsmouth Navy Yard, Capt. Isaac Hull. He was a man who apparently carried greater clout than did Hugh Campbell; when he specifically requested the *Enterprize,* Secretary William Jones unhesitatingly complied. Blakeley was thus ordered to proceed "without delay direct to Portsmouth."[13] The *Enterprize* departed Cumberland Island after only a three-day refit and arrived in Portsmouth on 13 June.[14] The only incident of note was the interception of the blockade runner *Active* "of North Carolina," bound out to Cadiz. Blakeley received its captain aboard with full hospitality, eager to learn the recent affairs of his home state.

Two days after its uneventful week-long passage, a bevy of British blockaders appeared across the entrance of New Hampshire's sole harbor. All but one, however, the heavy corvette *Rattler,* soon retired over the eastern horizon. But now Hull was having a change of heart. "I find the enemy's cruisers so much stronger than we are," he wrote, "that we can hardly promise security to the trade if we undertake to convoy it." The merchants of these lightly guarded ports were nervous. Not only were they incapable of protecting themselves, but if the vastly superior English forces decide to cut out one of the U.S. Navy "protectors," such as the little *Enterprize* or even the recently requested *Syren,* severe collateral damage might occur or possibly even complete retaliatory destruction. The old-timers had not forgotten the wholesale torching of entire coastal communities during the Revolution. The prevailing attitudes were based solely upon survival. If they openly refused to contribute to the war effort, the town fathers rationalized, the British might leave them alone—especially if they quietly traded with the enemy. Hull couldn't fault them because they were, after all, totally defenseless.

Hull instead proposed sending both of his small brigs away on a potentially lucrative cruise ranging from the southern edge of the Grand Banks all the way up to the entrance of the Gulf of St. Lawrence. They would thus be out of the way of the coast-hugging British cruisers and might, with luck, intercept captured American vessels bound into Halifax, or even one or two valuable merchantmen bound out. But the *Rattler,* which had briefly vanished, reappeared with a companion on 24 June. The *Enterprize* was not going to go anywhere for the foreseeable future. Blakeley's acting sailing master, Midshipman John Newell, did not find these northern waters much to his liking. He had written to both Secretary Jones and Captain Hull, requesting permission to leave. Newell wished to rejoin any southern station, politely suggesting to Hull that he might remain in command of one of the harbor's many gunboats until an answer came from Washington. It just so happened that Sailing Master William Harper, the commander of one of these unpopular vessels, was desirous to go aboard a larger, deep-sea cruiser. Reluctantly, Hull agreed to the swap, "not from any wish to indulge Mr. Newell," he wrote the secretary, but "believing that the service would be benefited from doing so."[15]

While the *Syren* would have some blue-water cruising in store for it, the *Enterprize* would not. The first week of July saw Blakeley's brig anchored peacefully in Portland, Maine. Its grumbling officers were all ashore, recruiting seamen for the *Syren* as well as for the *Constitution*, then fitting out in Boston. After he had delivered the men up to Hull, Blakeley was then to proceed back up to Bath and Wiscasset, where "seamen are very plenty." However, after three long, stifling weeks in Portland, he had managed to procure only a small handful of qualified seamen. The smallest British cruiser on the Halifax station, HBM brig *Boxer*, was a tolerable match for his own little *Enterprize*, the latter now armed with fourteen 18-pounder carronades and two long nines. Carrying just one pair of carronades less than his own brig, the *Boxer* was reported to be just offshore, and now there seemed to be the very real possibility of capturing a few laurels before the war ended. Blakeley had drilled his crew incessantly at the great guns ever since Congress had declared war well over a year before, and now he was working them harder than ever. But the two enemy cruisers that suddenly appeared off Portland Harbor effectively kept him bottled up for the next ten days. On 29 July he sent the following disparaging note overland to Hull:

Sir, I almost begin to be afraid we are really blockaded here. The day before yesterday the fog cleared up for a moment when an armed ship and a brig were distinctly to be seen, in the evening of the same day they were close in with Cape Elizabeth, so much so that the men could be seen on their decks with the naked eye; conjectured to be the Rattler and the Boxer. Yesterday the fog was quite thick which continued until noon today. At half past 2 P.M., the Rattler and Boxer were discovered to the Westward of this close in with the land, they now (5 P.M.) bear S. East, standing to the Eastward. It was the Boxer I mistook for the Isabella. She is sometimes rigged as a ship, always, (since her appearance off here) with a white bottom. I cannot but feel surprised they should think it necessary to watch so small a vessel as this with such force. The Boxer alone is equal and would have twelve months ago disdained of the company of the Rattler. I much fear I shall not be able to get to you unless permitted to go off and make a small circuit. I might then get in the same way as when I had the honor first to report myself to you. The winds at this season, and particularly since we have been here, appear to be light and variable attended frequently with fog. We have not had a wind that would carry us to you for a fortnight past, you will oblige me by answering this when your leisure will permit.[16]

The two men-of-war did not reappear the following morning, and so on the second day of their absence, the *Enterprize* sailed home without incident. Since Captain Hull was preoccupied with the construction of the 74-gun ship *Washington*, he sent Lieutenant Blakeley off to the mouth of Portsmouth Harbor to post temporary guard. Hull transferred part of the brig's crew into one of the vacated gunboats, and, sailing together, they awaited the arrival of the expected English privateers. In this way, Hull was able to free up his own crews to work as laborers on the 74, yet they could be ready "at a moment's warning to go on board the remaining gunboats should they be wanting." During Blakeley's absence in Portland, a small yet bold English privateer had taken two coasters within clear sight of the town. But as the light winds were then contrary and as the tide was flowing in, the dispatched gunboats were unable to get to within gunshot.[17]

But on 19 August this same armed schooner made its unfortunate reappearance. During the predawn hours, it had easily snatched up the Portland to Boston packet and had sent it off to Halifax. By afternoon it was clearly visible and well to leeward; Blakeley set off in earnest chase with the gunboat laboring to keep up. Blakeley's official report to Hull is tantalizingly short of details: "Sir, I have the honor to report to you the capture of the British Privateer Schooner, the Fly," he proclaimed. "She was captured yesterday afternoon off Cape Porpoise, after a chase of 8 hours."[18] The capture was bloodless, probably one shot only being fired to bring it to. It mounted three guns and was manned only by fifteen unhappy Canadians. It was no *Boxer*, but it represented several hundred badly needed prize dollars in Blakeley's pocket. The effect of this capture improved morale. "There is now on the coast several small privateers of the enemy that annoy the coasting trade very much," Hull wrote soon after, "[but] they have left this part of the coast since the Enterprize had the good fortune to take the Fly."[19] Many a Maine mariner no doubt toasted Johnston Blakeley's success.

Hull stood on shore, quietly watching the *Enterprize* beat into the harbor with its new acquisition. He clasped an official letter in his hand from Washington addressed to the brig's commander. Today would prove to be doubly lucky for Lieutenant Blakeley. His long seniority had finally endowed him with the rank of master commandant.[20] By his side stood Lt. William Burrows, Blakeley's successor. The tarheel captain was now required to turn the *Enterprize* over to Burrows; his new rank was far too lofty for him to remain in command of a mere gun-brig. Blakeley was instructed to proceed down the coast to Newburyport, Massachusetts, to take command of the new, and as yet unnamed, 22-gun corvette then in the final stages of construction. By some strange twist of fate, this was the second time that Burrows was called upon to fill Blakeley's shoes. The future of both officers would prove to be bright with the flames of glory and immortality that each so desperately craved. For both, however, their new commands would prove to be their last.

PART TWO
The Corvette

8. The *Argus* Accurately Extended

February–September 1813

The secretary of the navy, William Jones, wrote to Burwell Bassett, the chairman of the House Naval Affairs Committee, on 2 February 1813, in an attempt to solicit still further shipbuilding funds from the nation's cash-starved coffers. The legislative branch, in an "Act for Increasing the Navy," had already approved and funded six 44-gun frigates and four 74-gun ships of the line. For the "better organization" of the service, as Jones phrased it, there was another species of naval force ideally suited for the purposes of annoying and distracting the enemy. Jones was referring to "corvettes such as the Hornet or larger," of which the department, with that lone exception, was now destitute. On the previous 18 October the *Hornet*'s sister sloop, the 18-gun *Wasp*, had won a stunning victory against an equally matched and obstinate foe. But before its commander could effect repairs to his ship and to his prize, HBM brig *Frolic*, an ill-placed English ship of the line happened on the scene and took possession of both. Despite the unavoidable loss, it was a creditable victory. The *Wasp* would be replaced. "I think six vessels of this class would be desirable," he advised cautiously. The new corvettes could be built by contract in private yards on what he believed to be reasonable terms. Furthermore, they could be manned by those officers and men currently employed in the now-stagnant gunboat service.[1]

On 3 March 1813 the otherwise penniless Congress graciously approved "an act supplementary for increasing the navy," and thus granted Jones his extravagant wish. The current naval constructor, William Doughty, immediately set about preparing his design for the six newly authorized sloops of war. Doughty's single most pressing design parameter was America's then tightly restricted sphere of influence. An English sloop of war of the *Cruiser* class, hunting for prizes in North American waters, could choose to reprovision in Halifax, Bermuda, Nassau, or a multitude of other safe havens; it did not have to return to England for supplies. An American vessel that set forth upon the same mission, however, might be expected to circumnavigate the entire Atlantic and cruise alone in the Caribbean or the Irish Sea, unaided by any friendly port or even a neutral one if it was strong enough to defend its own sovereignty. Any new ship would have to be fast enough to outrun any man-of-war of greater force than itself. Not only must it be strong enough to contend with enemy vessels of its same class but it also had to be able to survive any potentially destructive victory, effect its own repairs, and then return safely home, even from the remotest reaches. This called for a sloop of war that was not only fast and constructed of the most exceptionally stout scantlings but also for one large enough to carry all the requisite fresh water and provisions required for such a prolonged cruise. The new design would have to be ship-rigged, of course, and flush-decked for speed, as the older corvettes had been. But the vessels must necessarily be larger, for the earlier sloops of war were designed for service in the Barbary Wars, and this time there would not be any well-stocked English naval bases at their disposal. Even though they were to carry twenty-two broadside guns, they were going to be rated only as 18-gun ships. This had less to do with deliberately understating their force to confound the enemy, as has often been asserted, than it did with complying with existing law. Any ship rated at twenty guns or more was required by the current naval regulations to be commanded by a full captain. These six sloops were to be commanded exclusively by the young and impassioned masters commandant.

Understanding naval nomenclature in use was an important consideration. The *Wasp*, its siblings, and its opponents were categorized together, under the collective term "sloop of war." This had nothing whatsoever to do with the single-masted "sloop" rig; it referred only to the class of fighting ship immediately below the frigate. Simply put, a sloop of war could be, like the *Wasp* and its sisters, ship-rigged, meaning that they were built with three masts, a fore, a main, and a mizzen, all of which suspended their sails from yards set "square," or athwartships, at right angles to the masts. But a sloop of war could be brig-rigged as well, similar to a ship with only two masts, a fore and a main only. Blakeley's old *Argus* and most of the prolific British *Cruiser*s were so rigged. Another name used interchangeably with "sloop of war" during this period was its French equivalent, the "corvette." This somewhat ambiguous term was used for both ships and brigs, but more often than not it described a small and by then obsolete class of frigate mounting thirty guns or fewer. They were known throughout the English-speaking world as "frigate-built ships" or "quarter-decked ship-sloops," of which the Royal Navy's *Rattler, Brazen,* and *Goree* were familiar examples. The ship-rigged *Wasp* and its sisters were built without the distinct quarterdecks and forecastles normally found on most British ships of the same tonnage and were thus described as being "flush-decked." Therefore the *Wasp* was a flush-decked, ship-rigged sloop of war, or corvette. It was often simply referred to as a "sloop."

The most common sloop of war design class belonging to the enemy was the *Cruiser* class. Eighty-odd British *Cruiser*s were built over a twenty-year period, seven of which would see single-ship action against the Americans during the War of 1812–15. At just under four hundred tons, they were considered very large for brigs, and in fact, six were rigged as ships. The *Cruiser*s were specifically designed with the carronade in mind. With sixteen 32-pounder carronades, they were a lethal overmatch for any other European sloop of war. They were the Royal Navy's most efficient mode of putting a battery of these devastating "smashers" to sea, and they fully met every expectation. The Admiralty produced so many copies of this design because they had complete confidence in their strength and effectiveness. Nearly every historian since 1815 has derided them shamefully. Modern writers, at best, label them "ubiquitous."

Two illustrations, out of a history filled with countless others, show the respectability of these vessels prior to 1812. In March 1806, the 18-gun *Reindeer,* while cruising off the southeast quarter of Puerto Rico, spotted two French brig corvettes, *La Phaeton* and *La Voltigeur,* "speaking each other," some sixteen leagues from land. In point of force, each individual Frenchman was the equal of the *Reindeer* in tonnage and in the number of guns and seamen aboard. Despite the two-to-one odds against it, the *Reindeer* stood confidently toward its foes. It had one great advantage: Its 32-pounder carronades would be far more devastating at short range than the lighter caliber long-guns employed by the French. From 2:00 P.M. until the onset of darkness, the *Reindeer* engaged both brigs simultaneously. The *Reindeer*'s shattered spars and torn sails rendered it completely unmanageable when the weather turned ugly not long afterward. Although it had clearly gotten the better of its adversaries, the *Reindeer* was unable to pursue them.[2]

In February 1810, the brig *Avon* had been cruising off Basseterre when it spied, far off to leeward, the 22-gun British corvette *Rainbow* in chase of the 44-gun French frigate *La Nereide*. Later that afternoon, fearing the possible English union, the frigate turned suddenly about and attacked the out-ranged *Rainbow,* mauling it severely with its long 18-pounders before the *Avon* could come up and assist. The undamaged Frenchman then turned its guns on the smaller brig, which it had foolishly allowed to close to within carronade range. For nearly an hour the *Avon* alone bore the brunt of its massive foe's fury, but it returned the Frenchman's broadsides with even greater effect. Although the *Avon* was badly used, the crushing fire of its carronades persuaded the frigate to haul off and disengage.[3]

The new Yankee sloops needed to be thick-skinned. Protection from an enemy's shot in battle depended not only on the thickness of the timbers beneath the bulwark's sides but to an even greater extent upon their width. At a distance much beyond point-blank range, an individual round or grapeshot was more likely to be stopped, or even deflected, if it struck the hull's side dead onto a frame timber than if it hit the doubly planked-over space beside it. The *Wasp* and its sisters would have nine-inch-wide timbers, spaced on average only about four inches apart above the waterline. At any given point along its length, an incoming projectile would have a better than two to one chance of striking solidly backed wood than of smashing through salted air-space. The common *Cruiser*-class sloops of war of the Royal Navy, two of whom the new *Wasp* was destined to meet in deadly earnest, offered their gun crews timbers only seven-and-a-half inches wide between the ports, with, in some places, as much as seven inches of space in between. The chances of those timbers inhibiting a nearly spent shot were thus only slightly better than even. But at "pistol shot" distance, or at point-blank range, all bets were off. The carronade's heavy charges usually smashed right on through undaunted.

William Doughty had designed and built many merchant vessels on the Chesapeake Bay, and he was familiar with the sharp-hulled models currently used in those waters. The surviving draft for his sloop of war shows that he had been an ardent supporter, as might be expected, of the "Baltimore clip-per" type of hull. His model was considered an "extreme" design for a sloop of war of such large proportions.[4] The active and influential naval officers, however, had a different idea of what went into the lines of a successful sloop of war. The opposition felt that Blakeley's former brig, the *Argus,* although somewhat on the small side, was the perfect model. Any officer fortunate enough to have served aboard wholeheartedly agreed. Properly enlarged, they believed, its design would best suit the navy's needs. In the world of naval architecture, the "last successful ship design" was almost always the starting point for any new model. At length, Doughty reached a compromise with the secretary and his cadre of captains. Three of the new sloops would be built according to Doughty's own ideas, and three would be appropriately enlarged *Argus*es.

All six ships were originally to be built in private yards. Perhaps as a carrot, however, Doughty was allowed to build one, later named the *Argus,* of his trio under his own direct supervision in the Washington Navy Yard; the other two, later named the *Erie* and the *Ontario,* were constructed in nearby Baltimore.[5] The three *Argus*es, however, were built in yards farther away from his influence: in New York (the *Peacock*) and in Massachusetts (the *Frolic* and the *Wasp*).

On 22 April 1813 Secretary Jones wrote to the navy agent in Boston, Col. Amos Binney, detailing the contracts to be drawn up in that quarter. He included with his letter a detailed, technical set of specifications compiled by the builders of the two Maryland ships. From this, an accurate estimate might be formed when calculating the terms upon which the two Massachusetts sloops were to be built. After making a careful study, with one eye always clearly focused upon economy, Binney was then authorized to contract on the best possible terms with suitable builders on the Merrimack River for one sloop, and at "some other convenient place secure from the enemy" for the other. Either building site must, however, be safe from any attack. If either ship were destroyed by the British while still on the stocks, the government would bear none of the financial responsibility. The communities where they would be built must also be capable of fitting out all the requisite stores, exclusive of the batteries. In addition, there must be a sufficient depth of water for each sloop to proceed to sea with all hands, guns, and provisions on board. Above all, the workmanship of each must be equal to the highest standards set in Boston, Salem, or Portsmouth. "The eastern section of the Union claims superiority in the art and economy of ship building and certainly ought to build cheaper than at Baltimore," he concluded. "I shall furnish you with the draught as soon as the contracts are completed; those two sloops will be *precisely on the model of the Argus accurately extended.*"[6]

Doughty drew up the second plan, as agreed, and his assistant/draftsman, Henry Allen, hurriedly made two relatively crude copies, each one containing very little in concrete detail. One copy was sent to the private yard of Adam and Noah Brown at New York and the other was sent to Commo. William Bainbridge at the Boston Navy Yard.[7] While William Spotswood, Doughty's second assistant, drew up a separate plan of the decks and inboard works, dated 27 July 1813, the draft that Bainbridge examined in early June was of the lines only. As the final armament had yet to be determined in Washington, the spartan profile view was even devoid of any gun ports. The gun deck was represented by a single line only, and the all-important lines indicating the forward cant frames and even the fashion piece were notably absent. The band of shipbuilders surrounding Bainbridge shook their heads with deep disapproval.

Amos Binney selected Josiah Barker to build the second of the two sloops in the latter's private yard in Charlestown, Massachusetts. This fifty-year-old Revolutionary War veteran had constructed no fewer than thirty-nine large merchant vessels in Boston before and during the war. He was held in such high esteem that the navy would eventually hire him as the Boston Navy Yard's master shipwright not long after the hostilities ceased.[8] Chief among the other shipbuilders present were Edmund Hartt and his two sons, Edward and Samuel. The Hartt family had already been selected to construct one of the newly authorized 74-gun ships. Edmund had been the master carpenter during the earlier construction of the famed frigates *Constitution* and *Boston,* and, more important, Edmund had built the brig *Argus* in 1803 to his brother Joseph's drafts. The manner in which Constructor Doughty had extended "their" *Argus,* not surprisingly, did not gain their approval. The Hartt/Barker team, with Bainbridge's blessings, immediately set about redrawing the corvette. After all, when the war began, the Navy Department did not possess a single copy of the *Argus*'s lines. Edward Hartt made a copy from the original draft and carried it to Washington at his own expense. Hartt's design changes to the new corvette were considerable. He lengthened it nearly a foot and a half on the gun deck and thus moved the midship frame back about the same distance. He next enlarged the projection, or "flam," of the stem and cutwater, raised the height of the bulwarks, and sharpened the run of the underwater lines. Despite the secretary's direct orders "*strictly to adhere*" to the plan,[9] he altered the positions of the masts. On 16 June Amos Binney sent Josiah Barker the latest specifications from on high:

Sir, the Honorable Secretary of the Navy has determined that the force of the Sloop of War building by you on contract for the United States shall be twenty 32 pound Carronades and two long 18 or 24 pounders. It is necessary therefore to give her eleven ports on each side, and their stations will be as here stated. . . . Ports in the clear, as before, three feet fore and aft. I have given you the earliest information upon the subject in order that the corrections may be made upon the draught, and that the timbers which come under the ports may be cut to their proper lengths.[10]

Colonel Binney included in this letter the precise position of each gun port, exact to a fraction of an inch, as measured from the forward perpendicular line. Because the location of this vertical datum had been shifted farther forward on the new draft, not to mention the unauthorized shifting of all three masts, along with their dependent shrouds and channels, Binney's list became irrelevant and subsequently it was not used. When Barker, Bainbridge, and the elder Hartt were satisfied with the proper design alterations, which would be used in building the *Frolic*, they assigned young Samuel Hartt to make an exact copy for Cross and Merrill, the contractors on the Merrimack River in Newburyport, Massachusetts. He completed his task on 21 June and was paid twenty dollars, no small sum, for his labor.[11] The draft that master shipbuilder Orlando B. Merrill used for building the *Wasp* was followed "quite closely."[12] Therefore, the *Frolic* and the *Wasp* were nearly identical ships.[13]

The firm of Cross and Merrill was a partnership between William Cross and Orlando Merrill. Cross, a resident of Newburyport, ran the business end of the firm; he had successfully bid on the navy contract to build the *Wasp*. One of the twelve children of Ralph Cross, the Revolutionary War shipbuilder who had constructed, among other notable vessels, the Continental frigates *Hancock* and *Boston*, William had collaborated with Merrill on the construction of the sloop of war *Merrimack* during the Quasi-War with France. Merrill, of adjacent Newbury, was a noted designer in his own right; he is credited for having invented the "lift" half-model method of hull design.[14] The articles of agreement were signed by Cross, Merrill, and Binney on 6 May 1813, in the city of Boston.[15] The price agreed upon was fifty dollars per ton, and as the yet unnamed sloop was to displace 509 $^{21}/_{95}$ tons, as calculated by the dimensions of the contract, the firm would receive in all $25,461.05 for the work. Cross and Merrill would be paid in monthly portions, as certain unspecified stages were completed. No more than three-quarters of the money, however, was to be paid out before the complete planking over of the gun deck. It was to be afloat and ready for armament on or before 16 September. No deviation was to be made "in the smallest matter or manner" without the prior written consent of the secretary.

It would be William Bainbridge and not William Jones, however, who would make the frequent and costly alterations to the ship. "Said vessel is to be built," began the detailed contract, "at such proper and suitable place on the Merrimack River as the said builders may fix upon." The acceptable ground upon which the keel was laid in early June was Merrill's Yard on Moggaridge's Point, in the town of Newbury, not in Newburyport proper.[16] The job of supervising the construction of the Newbury ship, prior to Johnston Blakeley's arrival in late August 1813, fell to Lt. George Parker. It was his job to inspect the progress of the work, to see to it that the contract's precise specifications were completely adhered to, and to deliver the latest alterations to the grumbling and increasingly unhappy contractors. Parker had been William Bainbridge's first lieutenant on board the frigate *Constitution* during its epic battle on 29 December 1812 against the British frigate *Java*. Because Bainbridge was obsessed with building the liner *Independence*, Parker oversaw the Charlestown sloop, the as yet unnamed *Frolic*, as well. In chronic ill health but daily expecting his own master-commandancy, Parker cheerfully spent much of the summer of 1813 riding between the two port cities, confident that the fair-minded secretary would surely reward him with the command of one of the new sloops. He was disheartened when Secretary Jones instead gave him the rotten and irrelevant old *Syren*. He clearly deserved better.

As the summer wound slowly down, Commodore Bainbridge soon began to think about masting and sparring his two sloops of war. He had sent Secretary Jones a detailed set of spar dimensions showing his preferences, purely as a recommendation, of course. Jones had earlier told him, "I recollect our ideas are in perfect consonance as to the quality and lightness of the rigging."[17] When the official dimensions arrived from Washington, Bainbridge inspected each item carefully to spot any variation with his list. Two spars caught his eye. The mizzen topsail yard was far too large, and the crossjack yard was much too small. "I am induced to ask you whether a mistake has not been made," he wrote the secretary.[18] Jones acknowledged that the "error you suggest had crept in," but feeling perhaps that Bainbridge had been somewhat condescending, he allowed the reduction of the topsail yard only and he ordered the crossjack yard's length to stand. Having thus firmly established that he too knew the intricacies of masting and sparring ships of war, the former shipmaster turned secretary of the navy added, "One of the sloops of war building under your direction is to be called the Wasp and the other, the Frolic."[19] Without explaining his reasoning, Bainbridge chose the former name for the ship being built on the Merrimack and the latter for its Charlestown twin. The old, embargo-enforcing *Wasp* had used Newburyport as a frequent base for recruitment and reprovision back in 1808, so perhaps Bainbridge wanted to remind the locals of the new ship's swift and successful lineage. By the end of August, both sloops were nearly ready for launching.

9. The Autumn of Discontent

September–October 1813

$\mathcal{I}$t was late in the afternoon on Saturday, 18 September 1813, when the crowd began to assemble for the grand event. Ship launchings, although commonplace especially before the war, still drew thousands down to the waterfront. Rarely, however, did such a powerful vessel grace the launching ways of a Merrimack shipyard, and the denser than normal audience lining the grounds and the adjacent stone jetty confirmed this. Unemployed shipmasters, elected officials, and many of the region's most prestigious citizens mingled strangely with the destitute, the common folk, and the shipyard laborers. Large gatherings of the curious could plainly be seen across the river, blackening the Salisbury shore. Mstr. Cmdt. Johnston Blakeley stood at the center of the small congregation of officials cloistered high above the fray atop the new ship's topgallant forecastle deck.[1] His finest gilt-laced uniform coat remained relatively unchanged since the days prior to his promotion. From the tightly packed grounds nearly thirty feet below him, the single epaulet glittering upon his right shoulder might have identified its proud wearer as being either a master commandant or merely a lieutenant in command. With an all's-ready nod from the yard's foreman, Blakeley proclaimed: "From the rocks and sands and enemy's hands, God save the Wasp!" and then smashed the traditional bottle of Madiera against the broad heel of the corvette's bowsprit.[2] As the newly liberated corvette slid backwards into the Merrimack the crowds cheered. Even the town's Federalist paper glowed:

> LAUNCH. On Saturday last was launched from Merrill's shipyard the U. States Sloop of War WASP. She moved into her destined element in majestic style. She is pierced for 22 guns and is rated as a 20 gun ship. In point of model and workmanship, we presume she will not suffer by comparison with either of the others of her class built or building in pursuance of the late act of Congress. We understand she is to be fitted for sea with all possible dispatch.[3]

As Blakeley rode back toward his new lodgings at Locke's Hotel, the town's premier lodgings dominating the busy intersection of State and High Streets, he probably reflected upon recent events. Although he had arrived in town some four weeks earlier, he had contributed little to the *Wasp*'s construction. The hull was by then fairly complete, and so the laurels of that ceremonious day should rightfully have gone to George Parker. Worse still was the subject of the recent celebrations back at Portsmouth. Lieutenant William Burrows had taken his former ship, the *Enterprize,* out on a cruise and had managed on the very first day at sea to stumble into the only British cruiser on the station equal to him in force. Forty-five brutal minutes later, Blakeley's old nemesis, the gun-brig *Boxer,* surrendered. Blakeley was probably the only man in New England not euphoric over the news. It was as much Blakeley's victory as it was Burrows's. It was he, after all, who had custom-fitted the *Enterprize* as a brig, and had rearmed and retrained its southern crew. Fortunately for him, however, it was Burrows who had taken the canister shot in the groin and had died in agony several hours later. Kindly sensitive of Blakeley's feelings, the *Herald* had earlier reported:

> Captain Blakeley, who enlisted and drilled the crew of the Enterprize, and to his great regret was not in the late action with the Boxer, left her but thirteen days before the engagement; having been promoted and assigned to the sloop of war Wasp building at Newburyport. To the honor of Captain Blakeley, when war was declared, he turned over to gunboat service, every foreigner, except one Dutch sailor, which was on board her. This battle therefore was fought exclusively by Americans.[4]

The death of William Burrows was not the sole solemnity in the naval life of New England of late. The capture of the fine frigate *Chesapeake* in Boston Harbor on 1 June had also resulted in the deaths of Capt. James Lawrence and his trusted first lieutenant, Augustus C. Ludlow. "Don't give up the ship!" repeatedly cried the mortally wounded Lawrence as he was carried below to the surgeon. But the newly formed ship's company took no heed, and so gave the ship up after no more than fifteen minutes of what was admittedly some of the bloodiest fighting on record. Their broken bodies arrived in Salem during the middle of August, and it was there on the twenty-third that the official funeral services had been held. Every officer of rank that could be spared from duty attended the "solemn and impressive" affair, including Mstr. Cmdt. Johnston Blakeley, who had just posted down from Portsmouth.

The Newburyport Herald of 3 September 1813 described the ceremonies in detail. Business throughout Salem was entirely suspended on that somber August day. The citizenry crowded down to the waterfront, either to participate in or to observe the elaborate tribute offered to the nation's fallen heroes. As the rakish *Rattlesnake* thundered out minute guns from the inner harbor, a pristine score of grieving sailors, "rowing minute strokes" on their slow passage, brought the twin caskets ashore. At one o'clock that afternoon, the landward procession began its two-hour march toward the waiting church. The first to lead the caravan were officers belonging to the various military branches and local militias, whose prominent ranks included Maj. Gen. Henry Dearborn and Brig. Gen. Thomas H. Cushing of the U.S. Army. Clergymen of all denominations came after them, along with officials of differing corporate, Masonic, and marine societies. The sable casket of Captain Lawrence, borne upon a "funeral car" and flanked by his equals, followed next. [5] Captains Isaac Hull, William Bainbridge, and John Orde Creighton paced to larboard of Lawrence's eleven-guinea casket, while Charles Stewart, Johnston Blakeley, and George Parker walked abreast of them to starboard. Behind the bereaved captains rolled the body of poor Ludlow, mortally wounded by a saber slash to the face. He was equally supported by his own saddened and ranking peers, Lieutenants Edward J. Ballard, Beekman V. Hoffman, James Reilly, Jesse Wilkinson, John B. Nicholson, and Otho Norris. George Crowinshield, who had paid for the cartel out of his own deep pockets, followed up the caskets alongside the ten other Salem merchant captains who had accompanied the bodies home. Then came the many friends, relatives, and finally the "elegant" gray-coated Salem Company of Light Infantry. The intense August sun beat down upon the Halifax coffins and their awful contents of these past ten weeks, reminding the uncomfortably clad but still breathing escorts of the severe price to be paid for failure in time of war.

Captain Peabody's Light Artillerymen continued the salute once the bodies had been brought safely to land, booming out their plumed respects every minute from their station in Washington Square. The sidewalks were packed with multitudes from all over New England. The windows and even the rooftops of many of the more accessible houses were lined with patriotic and curious observers. When the train at last arrived at the Episcopal meeting house, the men of the *Rattlesnake* carried Lawrence and Ludlow indoors. The church was shrouded "in the sable habiliments of woe," while the names of the two deceased officers were spelled out in large letters of gold and "encircled by festoons of evergreen" on the face of the high pulpit. The Hon. Judge Story gave the eulogy to the close-packed crowd, while the crew of the *Rattlesnake* "stood during the whole of the performance, leaning upon [the coffins] in an attitude of mourning."[6] Then it was over. Before heading off to Newburyport, Johnston Blakeley spent some time commiserating with his brother officers, the largest collection yet assembled in one place during the war. This group included a young and newly promoted lieutenant, James Reilly. He and Captain Blakeley would soon meet again.

The outlet of the Merrimack River lies along the northern coast of Massachusetts, some twenty miles southwest of Portsmouth, New Hampshire, and nearly forty miles to the northeast of Boston. The river's mouth is bordered to the north by Salisbury and on the south by Plum Island, both mere sand dunes in 1813.[7] Projecting out to sea at the river's terminus was the notorious Newbury Bar, several miles of shallow, sandy shoal water. However, a narrow yet relatively deep channel, restricted by the dry north and south breakers, permitted careful access to the sea by deep-draft merchantmen. Moving inland on the south side of the river past Plum Island lies the town of Newbury (or Olde New Bury), where Orlando Merrill constructed the navy's newest corvette. Several miles inward along the same bank lies Newburyport, where the *Wasp* was towed after its launch for its fitting out and for the recruitment of its crew. Upriver to the eastward lay the then-rural towns of Amesbury, Haverhill, Lawrence, and Lowell, from whose forests the *Wasp*'s timber had been hewn. Teams of oxen had dragged the impermeable white oak, cut when free of sap, from this wilderness to construct the ship's keel, deadwood, lower plank, knees, stem, and stern posts, along with the majority of its frames. Durable, rot-resistant locust and cedar went into the upper frame, the part most prone to decay. The best New England white pine was felled for its spars, beams, and the majority of the planking. Rafted slowly downriver to Mr. Merrill's yard, this native, organic stock was slowly molded, then used in building a strong, fast, and lethal sloop of war.

Newburyport, once called the "golden village at the river's mouth," had long developed a unique character for both independence and prosperity.[8]

By the War of 1812, although the former quality was waning, the latter was not. The town maintained its roots in shipbuilding, fishing, and trade with Europe and the East Indies. To a greater extent than any other New England town, Newburyport amassed an extraordinary self-sufficiency. A remote sea-city, dependent upon itself for food, clothing, material necessities, and luxuries, Federalist Newburyport had been, since the seventeenth century, nearly independent economically. The town produced iron from its own local blacksmiths, fine table settings from its silversmiths, and earthenware pottery and clothing from its numerous homestead merchants. Local artisans produced jewelry, watches, wigs, fine cloths, and carpets. Bowditch's celebrated *Navigator* and Furlong's *American Coast Pilot* were printed and bound within the city. Newburyport, with its numerous artists and artisans, was likened to a walled Aegean city-state.[9] The most attractive aspect of this town's independence, as far as the U.S. Navy was concerned at the beginning of the War of 1812, was the idle yet intact shipbuilding infrastructure. Master carpenters, blockmakers, sailmakers, riggers, coopers, and seaside tradesmen of all kinds were well versed in the ways of Yankee economy and hungry for work. Counteracting Newburyport's favorable construction climate, however, was the political scene. The town was overwhelmingly Federalist: "At the outbreak of the war in June 1812, the merchants in Newburyport in effect suspended their allegiance to the national government and, as hostilities dragged on, acted as though they were totally independent of the Washington authorities."[10]

First the embargo and now the war with Britain had fueled these sentiments. To the Federalists, the war was a pocketbook issue. Believing in the sacred right of the individual states to their own self-determination, they thought both the administration's embargo and its war were not only unjust but also unconstitutional. The Merrimack merchants had made a fortune trading with both sides during the French Revolution and Napoleonic Wars, prior to and during the embargo. They understood and accepted the risks of such trade, and while they might not have liked it, they were willing to live with seizure and impressment. The most vocal of the town's Federalists, the Reverend Elijah Parrish, openly decried the Republican president, James Madison, calling him a "Virginia vassal" in cahoots with Napoleon, a man intent on destroying the prosperity of New England. The real enemy, Parrish preached, came from the southern and western states, not from Great Britain.[11] As Johnston Blakeley, the newly commissioned master commandant from North Carolina, was preparing to depart Portsmouth for the Merrimack, this hellfire Federalist preacher warned his congregation: "Will you admit southern troops into your borders?" Newburyport's citizens would commit neither money nor troops to the war effort, although, relatively speaking, they had large quantities of both. They were delighted to read of the latest American military fiascoes by land, and they brazenly furnished foodstuffs to the Canadians.

For the most part, however, when it came to matters of the sea, they were still loyal Americans. When the *Constitution* captured the *Guerriere* in 1812, Newburyport's Federalists and Republicans rejoiced in harmony. The former group, calling themselves "The Disciples of Washington," ceased their stinging rhetoric against "Mr. Madison's War" long enough to publicly honor and express their admiration for the conduct of Capt. Isaac Hull. Blakeley's only hope for successful cooperation with the citizenry lay within this naval patriotism. The powerful Federalist paper, *The Newburyport Herald and Country Gazette,* remarked that "all the wrongs we have ever sustained have been of a maritime nature [and] a maritime force will redress them."[12] Blakeley hoped that enough mariners shared this view to man his ship.

Few farmers possessed ready cash, so produce from the countryside was both plentiful and cheap. Blakeley would have little difficulty feeding his crew. Money was also used as an encouragement for enlistment. Indeed, one of the first to sign on board was the ship's cook, Richard Jones. Having wandered into town from his native landlocked Woburn, Jones had four reasons for signing up with the U.S. Navy: his wife of fourteen years, Abigail, and his three daughters.[13] Well into his thirties by now, Jones may have been a sailor in his youth but was now too old to effectively withstand the rigors of the sea above decks. Jones did not become the first enlistee merely out of a sense of patriotism—he was there to feed his family. The earliest surviving bill for the *Wasp*'s equipment was for the purchase of a stove, a "large patent camboose [galley] with furniture,"[14] the latter consisting of one each ladle, tormenter (fork), coal shovel and poker, two each iron pots and frying pans, four baker's pans, an iron tea kettle, a tin lantern, and an ax.[15] This galley should have been furnished by the builder, but the navy agent in Boston had purchased it instead for $250. He also paid the $16 delivery charge to Newburyport.

Master Commandant Blakeley was justifiably anxious to get to sea. Three weeks before the corvette's launch, the *Newburyport Herald and Country Gazette* had described one particularly profitable naval encounter.[16] The *Snap Dragon,* an exceptionally fine privateer sailing out of his home state of North Carolina, was said to have cut a merchant brig out of a convoy off the Grand Banks of Newfoundland—not that very far away—to find that it was carrying a cargo of dry goods worth over half a million dollars. This New

Bern raider had previously taken nine other vessels; the aggregate worth had already approached one-and-a-half million dollars. Blakeley probably imagined what he might do with a captain's 15 percent share of such a prize. His two cruises this year in the *Enterprize* off Florida and the western Gulf Stream had produced not a single penny.

From the day he arrived in Newburyport, Blakeley noted the great vulnerability of his ship, and of the port in general. "There is neither a gun mounted nor a soldier stationed for the defense of this place," he informed the secretary.[17] With his present crew of four and without any weapons, he still had to keep things secure from any seaborne menace. Merrill had earlier paid two armed men a total of twenty dollars to stand watch for as many nights prior to the launch, but now even they were gone.[18] Because the ship was scheduled to be rigged and ready before month's end, Blakeley promptly had begun looking for a crew. Commodore Bainbridge had already ordered a rendezvous to be opened for the *Frolic* and had begrudgingly done so for the *Wasp* as well. As things now stood, nobody expected either sloop to be ready for sea until mid-November at the very earliest. But there was another problem. The popular frigate *Constitution* was also fitting out at this time. Even though, as Bainbridge reported, "the sloops built in this quarter are exceedingly fine vessels," they paled in the sailor's eye when compared with "Old Ironsides." Bainbridge openly wished that the two corvettes might have been recruited for earlier, because, as he put it, "sailors are whimsical and often enter for one ship when they will not for another."[19] The secretary subsequently ordered that the first fifty men retained specifically for the new sloops were to go instead directly to the *Constitution*. Time was now precious, and every day that the frigate was delayed in port was a source of anxious regret for the secretary. "I pray therefore you will dispatch that ship in the first instance," Secretary Jones wrote to Commodore Bainbridge, "*in preference to any other object.*"[20]

Bainbridge was nevertheless determined to get at least one of his new ship-sloops to sea this year, if he couldn't manage both. Two brig-sloops, the *Syren* and the *Rattlesnake*, would also be competing for Boston's limited resources. The commodore thus chose to sacrifice the Merrimack ship in favor of its Charlestown sister, the *Frolic,* then fitting out under Mstr. Comdt. Joseph Bainbridge, his younger brother. A fierce competition was raging between Bainbridge and the builders in New York, Baltimore, and Washington. All wanted the honor of getting their respective corvettes to sea first. The *Frolic* had already been the first launched, having slid into the Charles River on 11 September. Unaware of the circumstances against him,

Blakeley confidently placed the first of several advertisements in the *New-buryport Herald* on 24 September:

> To Men of Patriotism and Promoters of a NAVY: All able bodied sea-men who are desirous of entering into the Navy of the United States, may now have an opportunity by repairing to the Rendezvous which is now open at Mr. Samuel Wheeler's Union Hall, for the U.S. Ship of War called the WASP, now laying at Newburyport, JOHNSTON BLAKE-LEY, Esq., Commander. All able bodied seamen will receive two months pay in advance.[21]

On that same day, the first of Blakeley's commissioned officers, Sailing Master James E. Carr, "made his appearance on board."[22] More accurately, he reported to the front desk at Locke's Hotel. James B. Wright, who was acting temporarily in that capacity, greeted Carr at the front door and then departed directly for Boston, since the commodore had particularly desired him for service on board the favored *Frolic*. Like so many others of the *Wasp*'s officers, there is little information on James Carr. Appointed seven years earlier in New York City, Carr had so impressed his superiors that after only two years John Rodgers had brought him on board the *Constitution*.[23] But Carr did not feel himself up to the task.[24] He simply had no ex-perience in such deep-draft ships and the *Constitution* was one of the largest vessels yet produced in the United States. With no smaller vessels available, he quietly submitted his resignation, citing "pecuniary concerns," likely believing that by admitting his insecurities and thereby displaying a weakness of character, he would effectively put an end to his naval career anyway. But Rodgers didn't believe a word of it. He had a knack for recog-nizing quality in a junior officer: "He is none the less a man of correct habits and extremely indefatigable in his attentions to his duty." His resig-nation was not accepted.[25]

The *Wasp* was only about one-third the tonnage of the *Constitution*, so Carr was no doubt pleased with his new assignment. Second only to the captain, the sailing master was the most important man on board, as well as being one of the busiest. His duties involved not only navigation and sail handling; they also required him to note every official transaction in the log-book, to be mindful of both wind and weather, to receive and inspect all the public stores, and to see to it that everything was properly stowed away. Being also the *Wasp*'s chief sailor, he took an especially keen interest in the ship's rigging, now being set up for the first time. Carr's most pressing prob-lem was finding the multitudinous items required by his department. The

Wasp needed, for example, eight compasses: three of brass, three of wood, one "azimuth," and one "amplitude." He also had to scrounge up two brass hanging lanterns for the binnacle, two spyglasses ("one day, one night"), twelve half-hour glasses, twelve 28-second and twelve 14-second glasses, one case of mathematical instruments, one water and one air thermometer, a sextant, at least one reliable chronometer for determining longitude, six speaking trumpets, fifty pencils, four copper freshwater pumps, six signal lanterns, 150 spermaceti candles, one logbook, one journal, "charts suitable," one *Nautical Almanac,* one *Bowditch Navigator,* and one *Coastal Pilot.* And this was only the tip of the iceberg.[26]

Less is known about Thomas McClaine than of any other officer aboard the *Wasp.* McClaine, or McClain as it was also spelled, had been Blakeley's "captain's clerk" on board the *Enterprize* from the previous 1 April until 25 August. Since the brig was in the St. Marys River on that initial date, it is certainly possible that McClaine maintained southern roots. Perhaps Blakeley had lost his original clerk to the New Orleans yellow fever epidemic. (He was known to have been hospitalized.) Taking this speculation one step further, there is a not too unreasonable chance that young Thomas was related to Archibald McClaine, the famed North Carolina legal scholar who had so successfully taught young Edward Jones his trade twenty years before. The position of captain's clerk was a steppingstone by which those without the necessary age or influence might later obtain a purser's commission or a midshipman's warrant. He would have worn the uniform of a midshipman and would have lived and socialized with the ship's young gentlemen.

Secretary William Jones wanted his New England corvettes not only to be fast and strong but also long-lived. The dense white oak hewn for the majority of their stout frames was far less durable than the traditional southern live oak. But this was war, and the latter was unavailable in Massachusetts. Since dry rot was as destructive as the enemy, Jones had ordered the builders to take all appropriate preservative steps. Pouring salt in between the frames to keep the wood constantly moist was one effective remedy. When he had initially approved the contracts, Secretary Jones had envisioned the salted timbers extending all the way up to the plank sheer, or to the level of the lower gun deck sills. By doing so, the builders would preserve not only every timber but the vulnerable ends of the gun deck beams as well. But Commodore Bainbridge became aware of the full extent of the salting requirements far too late in the building process, and so he regrettably had to inform the secretary that such complete measures were not now possible. Both corvettes were and could only be (without expensive reconstruction) salted as high up as the strake of planking between the berth and gun decks. The original order for salting the sloops had erroneously omitted defining exactly how high up the salt was required to go. Bainbridge explained to the secretary, however, that the contract specifications had gone from William Doughty directly to Col. Amos Binney, the Boston navy agent, and from there straight on to both private contractors. The builders were concerned only that their vessels were "carefully and fully salted," as defined by usual practice, in the absence of anything else concretely specified in the contract. Had he been involved in this important step, Bainbridge explained, he would have instantly discovered the mistake and rectified it. As the secretary was adamant on maintaining the ships' longevity, Bainbridge reluctantly gave the order for both sloops to be so altered, whatever the cost.[27]

Orlando Merrill was not happy either. His hull had been launched only two days behind schedule and he had provided the navy with the very best quality of workmanship available on the Merrimack. He now dreaded the thought of ripping apart his new planking, only to pour in salt of questionable value. He might have even made an initial, half-hearted attempt to stuff the salt in through the air courses, the long gaps normally left in the inner ceiling planking for ventilation purposes, but he thought the whole idea neither feasible nor wise. "I endeavored to salt the Wasp in the manner provided," Blakeley wrote Bainbridge on 11 October, "and now have to inform you that I have not been able to proceed owing to her upper works being so closely timbered."[28] Bainbridge responded firmly: "The instructions of the Secretary of the Navy must be complied with [and] we have done it completely and without difficulty in the Frolic."

But Merrill too was firm in his convictions. All along, Commodore Bainbridge had changed this and altered that, and by now he had had enough. He wanted to wipe his hands clean of this whole government contracting business. Blakeley found himself caught in the middle when Merrill informed him that he could not and would not do the extra work. Lieutenant Parker had promised him prompt payment for all the last-minute changes, but to date the navy had paid not a penny of it. Blakeley wrote again to Bainbridge: "I have in vain called on the builders either to salt the upper works of the Wasp in the manner you directed, or to make a statement to you in writing." Bainbridge exploded:

> [I] am surprised to learn the contractors have refused to complete the salting of the Wasp. . . . This order with the Frolic has been complied with; and so might that for the Wasp, if the builders had been masters

of their business. I regret the order for building these vessels of war ran expressly for one to be built on the Merrimack—The complete salting of the Wasp must be done!

The complete salting of the *Wasp* was eventually done. Bainbridge probably threatened to withhold the final payment (one full fifth of the contracting price) from the builder. With assurances from Blakeley that he would eventually be reimbursed for all his extra labors, Merrill finally complied. He billed the Navy Department eighty dollars for "taking off one streak [of] plank round the waist to put in salt and replacing it with new plank, [including] caulking, painting, and puttying."[29] Orlando Merrill's bill was adding up fast. He and Cross had originally bid for a ship mounting twenty broadside guns. But when orders came increasing its force to twenty-two, he was bound by the carpentry rules of the day to make "one port more than agreed for, comprising two beams and eight knees in each deck and the necessary iron." (The official inboard profile and deck plans were still many months away.) This change alone set him back ninety dollars. Bainbridge had ordered the fore hatch moved aft (five dollars) and the captain's companionway with its stanchions and ladder shifted forward to the wardroom (five dollars). In addition, Merrill was ordered to build an extra platform in the hold (twenty-five dollars), alter the fore channels for shifting the position of the fore shrouds (twelve dollars), and step the mizzenmast on the recessed berth deck platform, instead of lower down on the deadwood. This last job necessitated the reinforcement of the undersized beams on either side of the new step and the fashioning of a broad chock underneath (eighty dollars). Bainbridge even made Merrill cut off a pair of perfectly sound stern davits and replace them with others of a design more to his liking (eight dollars). For the myriad changes, the total bill came to nearly $350. Even though he would have to wait more than a year for his money, he would eventually get paid.[30]

It was not so much a lack of salt on the Merrimack as a lack of patriotism that upset the secretary. He had received information from reliable informants that the merchants of that river town were carrying on a substantial, illegal commerce with the enemy. The vast extent of their blatantly open enterprises was unsurpassed by any other Federalist enclave. The larger craft were trading directly with Bermuda and the Canadian maritimes, while the smaller vessels were almost daily ferrying provisions, livestock, and vegetables to the enemy's blockaders. Jones ordered Bainbridge to send two of his gunboats up to the Merrimack with such orders as he might consider the "most effectual for the detection and suppression of that nefarious and criminal traffic." At the same time, they could act under the partial cover of protecting Blakeley's ship from the enemy and, as a bonus, assist him in fitting out and equipping it.[31] Bainbridge chose two sloop-rigged gunboats, unceremoniously named *No. 81* and *No. 83,* to perform the mission. That both were contract built by Jacob Coffin of Newburyport was probably not coincidental.[32]

Bainbridge's gunboats were not as inactive as the secretary assumed. The log of *No. 81* reveals that on 1 August of that year, for example, it "sent 10 hands on shore to get off the guns of the U.S. Frigate Constitution," and twelve days later it "hauled into the wharf to get up a pair of sheers to raise the stern post of the 74." On 12 September, the day after the Charlestown sloop hit the Charles River, "all hands [were] employed getting the US Ship Frolick through the bridge." [33] Bainbridge was as sorry to lose them as Gun-boat *No. 81's* commander, Sailing Master Ansell Cushman, was happy to finally be free to cruise for contraband. But if the crews—composed largely of former crewmembers of the *Chesapeake* just released from parole and, in many cases, from the naval hospital—thought that their days of menial shipyard labor were over, they were sadly mistaken. Alerted to this new government presence on the river, the *Herald* announced:

> Arrived and anchored abreast the sloop of war Wasp, at Horton's Wharf, Gun-boat 81, Captain Cushman, from Boston, via Portsmouth—Left Boston on Monday Evening, and arrived in Portsmouth on Tuesday—sailed from the latter port Wednesday afternoon. Also arrived below, Gun-boat 83, Capt. Brown came out of Portsmouth and Boston with the above mentioned.—She will come up and anchor alongside her consort next tide. Each of them carry [*sic*] a long 24-pounder and a 12 pound carronade and 16 men. We understand they are to be stationed here until next spring.[34]

Earlier in the month, Blakeley had finally received all the promised powder and shot and even the flints for the small arms, but he had heard nothing about his cannon. The cannon had by this time all been cast and proven, but due to the scarcity of wagons they were presently lying in "Frenchtown" along with vast quantities of other stranded goods. It was now far too dangerous with the tight blockade to ship them by sea, and so they had to travel overland hundreds of miles to New England. An unusually wet winter made turnpike traffic even slower. "Mr. Riddle [the Baltimore navy agent] is riding over the country collecting wagons," explained Secretary Jones to Commodore

Bainbridge, "and no exertion will be wanting to forward the guns with utmost dispatch."[35] Worse still, they had to pass through Boston and past Bainbridge's rival *Frolic* first! By the end of October Blakeley had only fifty-one hands all told, including himself, less than one third his allowed complement. Only on the last day of the month did he receive his first solitary marine. Such as they were, the crew ate well during October; they consumed 9,764 pounds of beef at a cost of $39.50 and $9.27 worth of vegetables, according to financial receipts. Fortunately this small group of hands now included several of his junior officers.

10. Two Connecticut Yankees in Newburyport

November–December 1813

"The elite among the navy's seafarers were those who made a voyage around the world," wrote naval historian Christopher McKee of James Reilly, the *Wasp*'s first lieutenant.[1] This exceptionally able twenty-three-year-old sea officer from Middletown, Connecticut, was a favorite of both Captains Hull and Bainbridge. Those political connections, as well as many others, had helped ensure his swift, four-month transition from a lowly midshipman to the first lieutenant of one of the navy's coveted new corvettes. Six years earlier, when the nearly destitute Reilly had first desired employment as an officer in the U.S. Navy, he had asked his uncle, Thomas English, a prominent Boston merchant of influence, for help. English had written directly to the secretary of the navy at the time, Paul Hamilton, on young Reilly's behalf, requesting a midshipman's warrant and, above all, immediate employment. But he received no timely answer, and, as there was little prospect of instant naval service, Reilly instead embarked upon a voyage in the 26-gun, six-hundred-ton merchant ship *Dromo*. English placed him under the care of his longtime friend, Captain Woodward, "knowing that such a voyage would well qualify him for serving his country should he, on his return home, have the honor of an appointment in her navy." With ninety men, the mighty *Dromo* sailed around Cape Horn to the coasts of Peru, Mexico, and California, and from there across the wide

Pacific to China and "The Islands." Returning to Boston in 1810, Reilly found himself "much improved as a seaman and a navigator." To his satisfaction, Reilly also found a berth reserved for him on board the popular frigate *Constitution,* then under the command of Isaac Hull, a native of nearby Derby, Connecticut. English had, many years before, given Hull his first merchant command at sea. "I have long acquaintance with Capt. Hull," English had written Secretary Hamilton. "I am particularly anxious that [Reilly] should be in his care."[2] Hull was fortunate too, for rare indeed was the captain who obtained a midshipman with a globe circumnavigation under his belt. When, later that same year, the merchant sloop *Income* was found meandering helplessly at sea, deprived by accident of its captain, Hull confidently assigned young Reilly as the temporary master and ordered him to carry the leaderless crew home to safety.[3]

From that point on, Reilly's naval career had paralleled that of the *Constitution.* In the famed 1812 battles against the British frigates *Guerriere* and *Java,* he had commanded the forwardmost pair of main deck 24-pounders, no small honor.[4] He served one of these great guns with particular distinction during the war's opening days, helping to effect the *Constitution's* escape from a five-ship British squadron. Lacking adequate firepower on the spar deck, Captain Hull had ordered Reilly's starboard gun hoisted up and rolled aft. Through a makeshift chase-port hastily cut through the frigate's broad taffrail, Reilly had fired upon His Britannic Majesty's representatives on board the advancing flagship, the crack 38-gun frigate *Shannon.* One of the proudest moments of young Reilly's professional life was the sight of the Honorable Sir Philip Broke and his junior officers scattering like mice under his fire. Captain Blakeley, who received his new first lieutenant aboard on 6 October 1813, may have detected a certain overconfidence in Reilly's countenance; any cockiness would have been justified.[5] Reilly was one of Bainbridge's favorites and a nephew of English. Uncle Thomas had, in fact, successfully bid for the very iron kentledge that was now ballasting the *Wasp's* hold. Because both Bainbridge and English would naturally want to see their best and brightest boy at sea, Blakeley saw his prospects of an expedited fitting-out brighten considerably.

Number thirty on the *Wasp's* muster roll arrived close on the heels of the first lieutenant. Purser Lewis Fairchild presented himself with an eagerness second only to that of Mr. Reilly, since both men were debuting in their new ranks on that pleasant October day.[6] Fairchild's naval career had begun with both controversy and indecisiveness. He had been a merchant of some note in Savannah, Georgia, as early as 1802. With financial difficulties dogging him, he entered the navy as a midshipman four years later, certainly much older than the majority of his peers. Just prior to that he had made one initial merchant run before the mast, departing Savannah for Liverpool, and then on to Fayal, before returning home to New York several months later. Upon his acceptance by the Navy Department, he was ordered to one of the many gunboats stationed at New York's inner harbor.[7]

Fairchild's career almost foundered with his false arrest in 1807. A New York merchant named Andrew Cook,[8] with whom Fairchild had been planning some considerable yet unspecified financial transactions, got wind of a foul rumor from his Savannah agent. Fairchild, it appeared, was actually a clever rake who was preparing to run off with nearly two thousand of Cook's hard-earned dollars. With the assistance of a lieutenant who held no favorable opinion of Fairchild's character or abilities, Cook had the surprised midshipman arrested. So clear, complete, and accurate were Fairchild's account books and ledgers, however, that Cook not only dropped all the charges but in addition wrote the secretary a letter to remove any "unfavorable impressions" that might have fallen upon his new and "respected friend." For the next two years, Fairchild held the temporary post of "chaplain," first on board the *Constitution* (where he briefly served alongside James Carr) and then on board the *President*.[9] The chaplain's two primary tasks in the Federal navy were, in order of importance, the instruction of the midshipmen in all subjects including seamanship, and the preaching of the occasional Sunday sermon. More than likely, Fairchild was simply acting as squadron secretary to Commo. John Rodgers, a rare but not unheard-of role for a flagship's chaplain.

At this point in his life, Fairchild desired better money-making opportunities, but he still wished to retain the security of the public service. Despairing of a midshipman's berth, he sought the refuge of a purser's appointment from Paul Hamilton. "Having a knowledge of mercantile business," he later wrote an influential friend, "I consider myself already competent to the duties of a purser, whereas, to be qualified for those of a lieutenant, or even to be of essential service as a midshipman, I have almost everything relative thereto yet to learn."[10] After another merchant voyage to Europe in 1809, Hamilton gave him command of a gunboat and sent him back down to Georgia to await final confirmation of his appointment. Fairchild had his purser's commission in hand for only two weeks when he reported to Captain Blakeley. Of the 123 pursers appointed during the period between 1798 and 1815, Fairchild was one out of only five men known to have made the lateral transition from midshipman.[11]

Purser Fairchild's duties on board the *Wasp* were fourfold. First and foremost, he was responsible for paying all wages and for maintaining the endless stacks of attendant financial records, including financing any and all upcoming purchases while in foreign ports. Second, he was called upon to store, inventory, and distribute the corvette's considerable clothing stocks, as well as the vast quantities of perishable provisions. Third, the purser was authorized to sell "slops," numerous small everyday necessities, to the crew at a profit. The cost of these items was deducted from the seamen's accrued wages, but only up to the strict limit of one-half of their earnings. The percentage that Fairchild could mark up these items was set by Captain Blakeley, and it tended to be in proportion to their perishability. Fairchild purchased these stores with his own cash and credit, and if they were lost, spoiled, or stolen, the loss came exclusively out of his pocket. The total value of the stores taken on board by Fairchild during this cruise would come to nearly $25,000. It was the considerable profit to be earned from this extremely lucrative business that was the real draw of the job, more than making up for the infinity of paperwork headaches required by the first two purser duties. Fairchild was paid a handsome salary in his position—$570 per year—and as a wardroom officer he was eligible for a larger than average portion of any prize money. If he knew his numbers well enough, however, the profits from his "company store" alone might amount to several times his yearly wage and prize shares.[12] His fourth and final responsibility was at this moment one of the more pressing tasks at hand: maintaining both copies of the ship's growing muster roll.

Blakeley's redoubtable old friend Thomas Tillinghast, now at last a full-blown lieutenant, endeavored to rejoin his former commander in Newburyport at this time. Captain Hull had petitioned the secretary to place the captured *Boxer* into immediate service, and he had hoped to commission the ship with Tillinghast as its first lieutenant. "In my opinion," wrote Hull to Jones, "[he] is a very deserving officer."[13] But the waifish *Boxer* was instead sold to private interests. Hull pushed hard for his victorious lieutenant: "Mr. Tillinghast would make an excellent second to one of the sloops of war and he has expressed a wish to join Captain Blakeley," he wrote the secretary soon after. "If you should think it proper to indulge him, I would be gratified."[14] The two Carolinians were reunited on 23 October, much to the horror of Acting Lt. Frederick Baury, who had hoped to reserve the second lieutenant's berth for himself. Midshipman Baury was, with the arrival of Tillinghast, relegated to the status of acting third lieutenant.

Baury's father was Maj. Louis Baury de Bellerive, a native of Santo Domingo who commanded a corps of French volunteers that had been raised in the island during the American Revolution.[15] At the war's end the major settled in Middletown, Connecticut, where he married and produced three sons and a daughter.[16] The eldest boy, Francis, had entered the U.S. Navy as a midshipman in 1798. When naval hostilities unexpectedly commenced against his beloved France, Major Baury immediately withdrew his eldest boy from the service. In 1801 father and son returned to Santo Domingo and joined General Rochambeau, who was then in command of a considerable army assembled for the subjugation of that island. Francis died the following year while leading his regiment into battle. Young Frederick, the middle son, received his midshipman's warrant in 1809, four years after his father's death, with the backing of William Eustis, a close family friend and then secretary of war.[17]

Baury's first commander, Capt. Isaac Hull—then attached to the naval rendezvous in Boston—had long been a family friend.[18] In one of his earliest letters, dated 11 September 1809, Baury offered a candid and surprisingly negative assessment of one of the navy's greatest champions. "I am attached to the Rendezvous here," he began innocently, "and while . . . my pay is $66 per month, as it is likely that I shall stay in Boston this month, I must beg you to send my baggage on as soon as possible [and] also some sheets and blankets which we are obliged to provide our selves." He continued: "You wrote to tell me to tell Capt. Hull to write you, but you will see him I presume before this letter as he went to Connecticut with Mr. Alsop. The Capt[ain] is not so worshipped here as in Middletown, his officers speak very badly of him." Baury may have expected special treatment from the captain but soon learned his error. Baury cautioned his mother specifically against addressing any further letters to "Midshipman Baury," because, as he explained, they "never do except on business of the government." Besides, he feared that his messmates would severely harass him if they ever again saw a letter so addressed.[19] But his initial plea fell upon deaf ears, and his mother addressed her next correspondence to "Midshipman Baury." That prompted another impassioned plea: "I would beg my dear Mama to direct my letters to Mr F. B. instead of Midship because letters are never directed to officers that way unless a Capt. or Commodore."[20] Six months later, the *Essex,* under the command of Capt. John Smith, sailed only from Norfolk to Washington, and Baury was becoming disenchanted with the navy. His hopes of reproducing his late brother's heroic deeds had by then faded considerably. He wrote directly to William Eustis asking for a transfer to the Marine Corps. In this separate branch of military service, explained the impatient midshipman, a junior officer would start on a higher rung on the status ladder, with the prestigious initial rank of lieutenant, not merely that of lowly midshipman:

> It is twelve months since I have made a trial of a seaman's life, & I find that it does not agree with me. The hope of promotion is so long defer'd, that the most ambitious & useful period of my life, that on which my future fame & support must depend, will be spent in my very subordinate capacity. I am now 19, & promotion rarely takes place before six years.[21]

That same day, he wrote to Secretary Hamilton as well:

> After a sufficient tryal of my present Life, I find it does not agree with me. The prospects of war too which held out the dazzling idea of glory & the chance of speedy promotion, have vanished . . . induce me to appeal to your goodness, to honor [me] with a commission in the Marine Corps, in which I understand there are or will be some vacancies. . . . My father, sir, was a soldier![22]

Hamilton responded only that no marine appointments were to be had at present; Baury was not called onto the carpet for his impatience and ingratitude. After another year of reasonably active service, Baury transferred into the more prestigious *Constitution* and made a diplomatic cruise to Europe. Even though two years had passed since their initial introduction, Baury had still not warmed to Isaac Hull. While at anchorage in the Downs, he wrote, "We shall return to our natural land, which is much wished for by us all, finding Capt Hull not quite so agreeable a command as we supposed." He added a disclaimer, recalling his mother's friendship with and high opinion of Hull: "You may think as Capt Hull is very much liked in Middletown, that I have incurred his displeasure but disconcert yourself, I have not to my knowledge."[23]

During the frigate's glorious first year of cruising against the British, Baury held the important post of signal officer and was thus stationed alongside the captain on the quarterdeck.[24] During "the great chase" off New Jersey in 1812, while Midshipman Reilly was blazing away with his 24-pounder, Baury took charge of one of the ship's cutters, part of a small flotilla laboriously kedging "Old Ironsides" forward through the static sea. At one point, Baury stood up in the sternsheets and shook his fist at the approaching *Shannon*, vowing to defend his cutter to the last with his pistols.[25] Commodore Bainbridge later recommended young Frederick for a lieutenant's commission. When "Old Ironsides" returned safely home after its subsequent South

Atlantic adventure, Bainbridge appointed both Baury and Reilly to acting lieutenant status.[26] Secretary Eustis concurred, describing Baury as "irreproachable" and noting the "correctness and striking military cast in his character." Baury followed Reilly on board the *Wasp* three days later. He addressed a letter to his mother from Newburyport on 7 October:

> I am now settled (until we sail at least). . . . I have been running about from place to place until I am quite worn out. I have been so engaged that it was impossible to write as often as I would wish. . . . Our ship, which is a verry [*sic*] fine one, will be ready for sea in a few weeks. Mr. Reilly tells me that he called to see you and that you was not at home, or rather, you did not wish to see him. For when he first inquired for you, the servant said you were at home, and that she afterward said smiling that you had gone out.[27]

The next principal officer to arrive in town was Midshipman David Geisinger.[28] In terms of both seamanship and professional deportment, he was a valuable addition. The same age as First Lieutenant Reilly, Geisinger would be next in line for an acting lieutenancy if some tragedy befell Reilly, Tillinghast, or Baury.[29] Geisinger's first assignment, for nearly two years, was in the brig *Syren*, under the command of Capt Stephen Cassin. In April 1812, Geisinger accompanied Cassin overland from New Orleans to Washington to report on board the *Constellation*. Because the frigate had not completed its repairs in time to slip out before the British cemented over the entrance to the Chesapeake, this assignment had every appearance of going nowhere. For the next year, the *Constellation*'s anxious officers sat quietly in their static frigate, their boredom broken only by reading the published accounts of their rivals' frequent victories on board other cruising ships. The influential Cassin soon obtained a transfer to greener and, potentially at least, more active pastures. As a parting gesture of generosity toward his young protégé, he granted Geisinger permission to proceed on to Boston in search of better opportunities as well. Cassin innocently wrote to the secretary explaining this action:

> Midshipman Geisinger, a gentleman of high standing, as an officer in the navy, and worthy of attention, is very solicitous of being removed from the Constellation, as there is a change of commanders to take place, he has my permission to proceed to Washington and on his arrival, to report himself to the department. Mr. Geisinger is very desirous of being ordered to some ship to the eastward, where there is a prospect of getting to sea as the situation of the enemy here renders it impossible

for this ship to get out at present, and perhaps not during the war, this officer sailed with me in the Brig Siren [*sic*], in the year 1810 and 1811, his conduct then and since under my command here has been that of a very correct officer, and gentleman, always ready and willing to discharge any duty assigned him.[30]

Cassin's good-natured generosity, however, landed him squarely at odds with the secretary. William Jones shot back angrily:

I consider the practice of permitting the officers to leave the ships on station to which they are attached without the sanction of the Department and *with no public object in view very improper and unauthorized*, and in the case of Midshipman Geisinger I consider it indecorous toward the gentleman who is to command the Constellation to strip that ship of her officers on the eve of his arrival to take command. . . . Your opinion that that ship may not get to sea during the War is premature and the expression of such an opinion calculated to produce a bad effect upon the officers and crew.[31]

Jones was just as unhappy about the strictly blockaded Chesapeake Bay as were his junior officers. But he had to keep an active, cohesive, and relatively enthusiastic naval unit at hand, constantly at the ready to run the blockade should the opportunity present itself. The secretary's irate letter had only just gone off in the mail when three more of the *Constellation*'s unsuspecting midshipmen presented themselves at his door, hats in hand. They had heard about Geisinger's special treatment and they wanted the same. Jones angrily fired off a second broadside later that same day: "I have explicitly to forbid in future your assuming a latitude of discretion so improper, and to request that you confine your authority to cases of actual necessity unless you have the previous approbation of this department."[32] But Geisinger made good his escape.

The wardroom of the *Wasp* was now coming together and regional divisions among the officer corps were apparent. Usually, "the southern element greatly predominated" on board some larger ships-of-the-line and "aristocratic feeling and gentility" were assumed to be the exclusive possession of the southern gentlemen.[33] Southerners on the *Wasp* included Blakeley, Captain's Clerk McClaine, Second Lieutenant Tillinghast, Purser Fairchild, Geisinger, and the Virginia-bred midshipman, William Randolph. Northerners, such as First Lieutenant Reilly and Third Lieutenant Baury, from Connecticut, and Sailing Master Carr, from New York, were usually thought of by their southern betters as merely "plebian" government servants. But they at least had their betters outnumbered on this ship, because Dr. Clarke and Midshipmen House, Langdon, Toscan, Hall, Bonneville, Clough, Burley, Larkin, not to mention nearly all the warrant officers, were staunch Yankees. Also, Reilly and Baury had two great victories apiece under their belts, while the North Carolina captain had none.

Johnston Blakeley's immediate superior was Commo. William Bainbridge. Bainbridge always displayed great pride in the navy and devoted himself to the rearing of the young officers placed under his charge. If an inferior officer was thought to be "low or vulgar" or had lost Bainbridge's "good opinion" by failing to carry out the commodore's exact wishes—for example, a junior commander who declined to salt one of his corvettes properly—he could never hope to regain it. He admired spirit in a young officer, and he was always ready to side with and to promote those of an aggressive, manly nature, promising gentlemen such as Midshipmen Reilly or Baury. All the junior officers stood in great fear of him but as long as they did what they were told, Bainbridge usually reconciled his feelings and treated them well. Bainbridge probably held no personal dislike for Blakeley, for the North Carolinian was an active, energetic, and intelligent officer, but instead recognized him as an efficient competitor against his own designs and ambitions. First and foremost, Bainbridge wanted to enable his younger brother, Joseph, in command of the *Frolic*, to achieve glories similar to those he himself had earlier earned in the *Constitution*. If necessary, he would willingly sacrifice Blakeley's career objectives for what he perceived to be the overall good.

The first days of November were frustrating for Blakeley. The promised guns failed to arrive, and the final details of the sloop's construction would have dragged on endlessly had it not been for the gunboats' timely assistance. There was work aplenty for the newcomers to do. While one gunboat would patrol the river, searching for the more enterprising of the local traders, the other would act as a tender to the *Wasp*. While Sailing Master Cushman sent the bulk of his people aboard the corvette to caulk, paint, and hammer, Blakeley ordered *No. 81* away, far out in midriver, to house those least enthusiastic crewmembers of the *Wasp*. Many of Blakeley's men were contemplating early retirement. Despite *No. 81*'s vigilance, Blakeley lost ten seamen by month's end. Others less fortunate, those who had run but who were later forcibly retrieved, were now imprisoned in *No. 81*'s dank hold.[34] Blakeley's men ran away primarily for two reasons: First, neither the unfinished *Wasp* nor the diminutive gunboats were fit lodgings during the increasingly cold weather. Second, the men of the *Wasp* soon began to catch on that something was seriously amiss. Their ship was being deliberately delayed for some unknown reason. Worst of all, they were not at sea earning their badly needed prize money. If they were going to freeze this winter, they preferred to do it at home with their wives and sweethearts. The few marines that had finally begun to trickle in this month were not of the highest caliber either. Private John Carrick soon had to be discharged into the sheriff's custody.[35] His grave misdeed, whatever its nature, was committed "on horseback," and in doing so he had apparently gone back on what "he had promised" earlier not to do.

The British were coming. Or so thought the panicked populace on the evening of 24 November. The 58-gun British razee *Majestic* was rumored to be on its way in to destroy the American naval presence on the river. Blakeley had little choice but to take this threat seriously. Even though the bar was far too shallow to permit the *Majestic*'s entry into the Merrimack, and although the city was well out of range of its heaviest guns, it was still a great danger to the town. It possessed more than five hundred well-armed sailors and marines. As Blakeley hurriedly uncrated all of his remaining small arms and set his crew to work rolling musket cartridges, *No. 81* prepared for action: "at 10 P.M. fired and scaled the Great Gun, Cannonade & Swivel reloaded the guns and got them in readiness for immediate service."[36] Cushman took on board four of the *Wasp*'s best men and then "dropped further to the eastward" to receive the dreaded attack alongside its twin, *No. 83*. The *Newburyport Herald* summarized the situation the following morning:

Majestic Razee. This 54 gun ship came into our bay Tuesday, and captured a schooner off the Isle of Shoales which she kept with her. On Tuesday night [23 November] about 11 o'clock a lieutenant and about 30 or 40 men landed at Plum Island, the Razee, laying about a league from the bar, came up to Mr. Lowell's house and offered him compensation to pilot them up the town, which he declined. They stated that they had a man belonging to this town who entered on board three years since. Their avowed object was to get at the Gunboats and the Sloop of War Wasp. After getting something to drink (which they paid for) and making some jocose observations, they returned to their ship. She was not in sight yesterday morning. The sch[ooner], her prize lay at anchor back of the beach.[37]

But just before going to press, the editor felt compelled to add:

(Since the forgoing was prepared, we have been assured by gentlemen who have been down to the Island, that there is reason to believe, that no persons landed from the Majestic, but that the whole is a farce got up by some designing individual. The conversation of the pretended Lieutenant favors this idea.)

About this time, Commodore Bainbridge made a quick visit to Washington on official business and then took a rambling return trip home through New York and Maryland in order to check out his shipbuilding competition. Therefore, Blakeley's orders came, for a short while, directly from Secretary William Jones. The first of these, dated 16 November, required Blakeley to inform the department the very moment that his guns had arrived and to give a precise estimate of the time required before the *Wasp* was ready to sail. The secretary concluded: "The carronades have been proved at Baltimore . . . but I wish, for your satisfaction, that they be reproved, observing not to put them to any *unnecessary* test." He added thoughtfully, "They have stood the test of our hottest actions."[38]

Naval Surgeon William Montague Clarke made his rather late appearance in Newburyport on 20 November. Educated at the Phillips-Andover Academy, this eager Bostonian came into the service with a strong recommendation from John Rodgers: "[He is] a very deserving young man [who] is said to possess very considerable professional skill."[39] A surgeon's mate since 1809, Dr. Clarke had already served on board four different ships of war.[40] Frequently, however, Clarke had required lengthy leaves of absence "for recovery of health." Left ashore completely debilitated when the *Argus* sailed the previous summer, the newly appointed surgeon desperately scrambled for any active assignment. The secretary eventually granted Clarke's wish and thus ordered him away to the Merrimack. Like all the officers (except Sailing Master Carr) now on board, Clarke was serving his very first assignment in his present professional capacity.[41]

Commodore Bainbridge returned after about a month, making surprisingly good time for such a journey. He proudly reported to the secretary that all twelve vessels that were currently under construction for the public service, all of which he had taken the trouble to inspect, were of the most judicious classes, of the best models, and that their construction was being executed in the most superior manner.[42] December saw little advancement in the *Wasp*'s readiness for active service. No sooner had Blakeley received his minimum eighteen marines than Bainbridge transferred four of them away to the *Frolic*.[43] If, before this incident, Blakeley did not clearly understand the true reasons for his delay, he certainly did so now. He also tried at this time to obtain two particularly desirable midshipmen, both relations of two influential officers, Purser Thomas Shields and Capt. Charles Stewart, but he was unsuccessful.[44] Midshipman John Larkin,[45] the otherwise capable son of the toll collector on the Boston to Charlestown bridge, had no sooner signed on board when a sudden illness necessitated his resignation from the service.[46] Many more Newburyporters jumped ship. False rumors of peace were then circulating throughout the town. The only reason that many of these fishermen-sailors had signed on board in the first place was in the hope of collecting prize money. The money lay in the merchant trade during times of peace, and few Newburyporters wanted to remain trapped in a two-year peacetime hitch.[47]

At 11:00 A.M. on 10 December Cushman's gunboat departed Horton's Wharf on a brief cruise. Taking advantage of "pleasant weather," *No. 81* worked slowly inland for about two miles. Finding nothing of interest there, it wore round and then stood downstream again, bound out toward the bar. The harbor and most of the Merrimack were then "much encumbered with ice," and Cushman hugged the bank, thinking it "imprudent to lay in the stream." As *No. 81* passed the *Wasp*, gusting winds suddenly pushed him into the wharf, hooking the bill of his starboard bower anchor on a cluster of pilings. The anchor-stock split with a resounding snap, and the starboard chain-plates, to which it had been securely lashed, wrenched free, whipping the main topmast down upon the startled deck. Sullen and red-faced, Cushman "made fast to the wharf again," under the glaring eye of Captain Blakeley.

Blakeley traveled southward on 15 December to attend a court-martial in the Boston Navy Yard. The case was short and simple.[48] The boatswain of the *Frolic*, Thomas Jackson, was alleged to have approached Sailing Master Wright in the rigging loft and boldly declared, "I'll be damned if I go on board the Frolic anymore, I am not dependent on the service in any manner whatever and I be damned if I go." Jackson then promptly stormed out of the building and was not again seen in the yard. Three days later, one of the sloop's midshipmen finally caught up with Jackson in some squalid tavern. He ordered Jackson to report back to the ship at once, but the boatswain loudly refused. Jackson then proceeded to abuse the young gentleman in front of the delighted crowd, using "provoking and reproachful language." A file of marines was somewhat more persuasive. The prisoner offered no defense for his actions, except to explain that he had perhaps drunk "a drop too much" on shore and, he added, if he had made any inappropriate exclamations to the young lad (which he, of course, could not remember), he was deeply sorry for it. Blakeley and the other officers presiding at the court-martial had little tolerance for this type of behavior, and Jackson was dismissed from the service outright. Back in his own relatively spartan ship by 20 December, Blakeley penned his thoughts to the secretary:

> The U.S.S. Wasp under my command has at this time her iron and shingle ballast on board, her water casks stowed and filled. She now draws 13 feet ten inches abaft. Altho there are many articles ready here to go on board, I have refrained from doing so until I had an opportunity of consulting you on the subject and suggesting to you the propriety of removing the ship to some other port. This suggestion originates from the little water on this bar, and I believe there cannot be found a person in this place who will undertake to carry her out drawing more than 15 feet of water. I would also, so far as my judgment and information can have weight, beg leave to recommend her speedy removal and with as light of draught of water as may be; for altho it is possible to carry out fifteen feet water, yet to do this, it is requisite to have a fair wind, smooth sea, and spring tides. Her present draught as before stated is thirteen feet ten inches, but there are many things here which ought to be taken on board previous to her sailing to save the expense of transportation. I would however prefer, if permitted to choose that the ship should not draw more than fourteen feet, six inches at the time of her sailing.[49]

Blakeley's concerns were well founded. The *Wasp* would later require fifteen feet, nine inches of water aft, and fourteen feet, one inch forward, to be in its best, fully provisioned trim and ready to proceed against the enemy.[50] He continued:

> She is now alongside of a wharf in the heart of the town, having been compelled to haul in by the quantity of ice which has been running and continues to run in the Merrimack River. Thus situated it would be impossible even if the bar would permit our going out with everything on board to place this vessel and crew in that complete state of organization before going to sea so desirable in times like the present. The wharf where she now lies, altho the best in the place on account of the ice, is by no means a proper one, as she grounds at every tide. We can run to Boston in 6 hours, and to Portsmouth in two. I would prefer the former if it should be thought advisable to take the increased risk. I should, however, be perfectly satisfied as to place, provided we could once get fairly clear of this.

The year 1813, so full of dashed hopes, nevertheless ended on a positive note. On 27 December Blakeley was back in the city of Boston, surrounded by his brother officers bedecked in their finest plumage. But this time, there was no court-martial. Under the direction of the rector of the Trinity Church of Boston, the eminent Reverend Dr. John S. J. Gardiner, Johnston Blakeley at last took a wife. The *Newburyport Herald*'s "Hymnal Register" describes the enigmatic Mrs. Blakeley as "Miss Jane Anne Hoope, daughter of the late John Hoope, Esq., of the Island of St. Croix."[51]

Blakeley had chosen to wait on marriage until he reached the rank of master commandant. He could not have supported a wife, let alone children, on his navy pay until he had at least reached this rank. Jane Anne Blakeley was rather petite, with dark hair and eyes, and exceptionally pretty.[52] She was both intelligent and reasonably well educated for a woman of her day. Infused with the optimism that only a new marriage and a new year can bring, Johnston and Jane Anne returned to Newburyport for their honeymoon at Locke's Hotel. The coming year would finally provide Johnston the glories he so desperately desired, but at a price that would prove unacceptably severe.

11. A DULL, HARMLESS DRONE

January–February 1814

Printed on the back page of the 4 January 1814, edition of the *Newburyport Herald and Country Gazette,* conveniently placed just beneath the joyous proclamation of the wedding of Johnston and Jane Anne, there appeared the following equally gladdening bit of news: "Memoranda: The guns of the Wasp have arrived." Actually, only three of Blakeley's twenty-two heavy guns had completed their arduous trek. But still, it was an encouraging start to a potentially prosperous new year. Salem philanthropist George Peabody, who was then also bedding down at Locke's Hotel on "a visit which lasted several months," reportedly took time out to greet and toast the newlyweds.[1] "May the Peacock's cruises be as prolific," crowed the *New York Gazette,* "as the wife of her able gunner!"[2] Here at least, Johnston Blakeley would be a successful contender. Before year's end, Jane Anne would bear Johnston a daughter, Udney Maria Blakeley.

While editor Ephriham W. Allen continued on with the eighth part of "The Road To Ruin—The Effects of the War on the Mechanic and the Manufacturer," a series describing, in effect, how these favored citizens of Mr. Madison and his party were prospering by the war at the expense of the noble farmer and mariner, this same edition of the *Herald* gives a remarkable insight into the war pulse of the town. Allen described the "fruits of the embargo." He informed the landlocked mariners of Newburyport that all coasters belonging to their common port now lying in Boston were to be hauled up and stripped, the cold-hearted collector having peremptorily refused to grant a clearance for them to come home. The crews of three such vessels belonging to the District of Maine had only just passed through town on foot the afternoon before on their way north "to their famishing families and friends . . . leaving their all to the care of strangers." It was said that between two and three hundred more sailors were on the march from Boston in the same dire situation.

Captain Blakeley's two most senior midshipmen, Frederick Baury and David Geisinger, were equally eager for promotion. Baury had first petitioned Bainbridge and then the secretary himself for an official lieutenancy, begging Jones to place him on the list of those meritorious souls expected to be commissioned during the next session of Congress, "as high, sir, as respects to rank, as [your] opinion of my capability extends."[3] The otherwise championless Geisinger, then in Boston on furlough, wrote back to his immediate commander with the same urgent request. But Blakeley understood that Geisinger, although extremely capable, was nevertheless entirely without battle experience, endowed with only moderate seniority, and possessed of hardly any influence at all. The prospects for his promotion at this time would be slim at best. Blakeley responded with characteristic sincerity and kindness: "[While] the short period you have been under my command and the situation of the Wasp will prevent me from testifying from your qualifications in a nautical view, I can add with great truth that your conduct and deportment on all other points has been perfectly satisfactory."[4]

While in Boston, Geisinger had paid a visit to his longtime friend, Lt. George Budd, then recovering at the naval hospital. As the senior surviving officer of the late frigate *Chesapeake,* Budd had been horribly wounded in a valiant attempt to regain the spardeck from his station below. The *Shannon's* boarders had repulsed him most savagely, slashing his left shoulder with a bone-shattering saber blow that sent him tumbling back down the companion ladder, fracturing his right hand in the bargain. Geisinger faithfully ministered to his friend, doing everything within his limited power to alleviate the lieutenant's still considerable suffering. As a thank-you gift, Budd gave the midshipman a beautifully bound journal to take with him on his upcoming cruise. On the first blue-bordered page, Budd inscribed: "Presented to David Geisinger by Lt. George Budd of the U. States Navy, Boston April 14th, 1814." In this journal, Geisinger chronicled the *Wasp's* cruise. Budd gave Geisinger a second gift, one of greater immediate value. The *Chesapeake* had fallen to the enemy for a variety of causes, but chief among them was a

momentary lack of leadership from the frigate's officers. Nearly every commissioned officer had been either killed outright or at best horribly wounded
during the opening moments of this whirlwind fight; the crew had at first
hesitated and then collapsed under the admittedly heroic English onslaught.
If in the future it came time to board, Budd cautioned the aspiring leader,
an officer must seize the first opportunity and lead his men, regardless of any
personal danger. This advice was well taken.

Prior to contracting for the Merrimack sloop, Secretary Jones had been
assured by all the parties involved that the finished product of Newburyport's skilled artisans could put safely to sea, fully manned and provisioned,
given of course a sufficiently high tide, favorable winds, and clear weather.
But Blakeley's most recent letter had distressed him deeply. Those individuals financially interested in having the *Wasp* built on the river had been,
Jones now believed, deliberately "incorrect in their representations." If
Bainbridge concurred that the formidable Newbury bar was indeed too
shallow to allow the sloop to proceed to sea directly, then he must order the
Wasp around to Portsmouth to complete its victualing.[5] Blakeley needlessly pressed his case even further in a second letter following a heavy bout
of desertions:

> It is with regret I have to state that desertion of the crew must now form
> one more inducement. This has no doubt been produced by the late
> pacific rumors which have spread aboard, situated as we are alongside a
> wharf with a crew recently got together and junior officers without
> experience, I am totally unable to prevent them in every instance. Every
> caution within my knowledge has been used and although it may have
> restrained, I am sorry to say it has not wholly put a stop to it.[6]

Sailing Master Cushman and his gunboat had been released from the
Wasp's firm grasp by the end of December, and now he set about his long-
anticipated cruising, hoping to repay the snickering Federalists following
his recent embarrassment.[7] He set out the day after Christmas and dropped
anchor in "Black Rock Creek, so call'd," moored head to stern with the
bank. The senior gunboat commander, Capt. Eli Brown of *No. 83* (who had
come along for the fun, as his command was now under Blakeley's immediate direction), gave Cushman strict orders to "board every thing passing up
or down" the Merrimack. After inspecting several coasters carrying legitimate cargoes, Cushman boarded an empty schooner, the *Galen*, whose captain complained bitterly that a British privateer schooner had chased him
into the river and was at that moment hovering just off the bar. He had been

forced to dump his entire cargo overboard in order to effect his escape. Before Cushman could act upon this complaint, he intercepted a suspicious chebacco boat (a small coastal trader), the *Growler,* "said to be from Cape Anne." Since its papers appeared questionable, he sent the boat into town under guard for a more thorough investigation. By the time Cushman made it out to the lighthouse, the enemy schooner had departed. The next four days brought nothing but severe gales and bone-numbing cold, his weary crew "clearing the ice and snow from the deck" watch after watch. They did manage to grab two more suspect coasters the following week, however, and they would have done even further mischief to Canadian-American commerce had not the commodore ordered them back to Boston on temporary assignment. The winds proved unfavorable until the fifteenth, when, issued with a new locally printed *American Coast Pilot,* the gallant gunboat men set boldly away on a violent five-day voyage in the midst of a freezing northeaster. Cushman's worst fears were later confirmed when the *Frolic's* sailing master came aboard in Boston and removed six of *No. 81's* most capable seamen and then handed him orders to return to the Merrimack.

Captain Blakeley's presence was also desired elsewhere. When Tillinghast reported on board the previous autumn, he had quickly informed Blakeley that his beloved little brig *Enterprize* had become an unhappy place after his departure. Blakeley had learned not only of the details of its epic battle but also of the growing hatred his former hands were acquiring for the brig's new sailing master, William Harper, and of the tempest brewing below decks. The court-martial of Harper had been placed on hold since December in order to allow the prosecution's key witness to return to Portsmouth. In the interim, however, nearly all of the court's presiding officers had been sent off on foreign service. When an irate and inconvenienced Edward McCall at last returned to give his firsthand testimony, the floating courtroom was nearly empty. "As there is not officers enough on this station to form the court," wrote Isaac Hull, the assembly's president, to the North Carolina captain, "I am directed to order them from your vessel. . . . You will therefore be pleased to give your attendance as a member of said court."[8] Blakeley attended, but he was not pleased. Now, for the third time in this war and the second while on this station, his cruise would be delayed for administrative judicial duties. Tillinghast had long since filled his mentor in on the court's proceedings thus far. Edward McCall, Blakeley's able but hotheaded former first lieutenant, had brought formal charges against Harper for cowardice, openly accusing him of leaving his station on the quarterdeck during the latter part of the action when the *Boxer* had laid across the *Enterprize's* quarter, half-raking the ship. By allegedly doing so, Harper had set a bad example for the crew, who, if inspired to follow his lead, might have caused a needless surrender, "to the disgrace of the American character." Furthermore, Harper had also reportedly begged McCall to haul down the colors at a time "when the firing of the enemy was so much diminished and when that of the Enterprize could have been continued with unabated effect."[9]

Blakeley's replacement, Lt. William Burrows, had always been viewed "as something of an odd fish in the service."[10] A man with a particular "comic sense" and a "dry humor," Burrows enjoyed disguising himself in the trappings of the common sailor and paying covert visits to the more seedy of the taverns to observe what he called "the haunts of low life." Thrilled at what he saw, he returned to his wardroom and ridiculed the bizarre nocturnal traits of the enlisted men. In one of these brothels he picked up a case of syphilis that was slowly killing him. With subordination difficulties dogging him ashore, Burrows had been furloughed in 1811 to serve on board an Indiaman, but his captain abruptly turned him ashore for drunkenness. He soon sobered up, however, and sailed off to China in another ship, only to be captured by a British cruiser on the return leg of his journey, everyone aboard sadly unaware of the outbreak of the war. When Burrows was at last formally exchanged, he received command of Blakeley's brig. This was a promotion based not only upon seniority but also influence; his father was the Marine Corps's first commandant. His command of the Enterprize was brief but glorious.[11]

William Harper had reported on board the Enterprize immediately following Midshipman John Newell's abrupt resignation.[12] A native of Portland, Maine, Harper had commanded several of the loathsome gunboats on this station since about 1809, and now, finally aboard a real man-of-war, albeit a small one, he was determined to make his presence felt. However, he was a bullying tyrant. "The crew were opposed to me," Harper bragged to the court, "because I flogged them too much." Samuel Drinkwater, the civilian coastal pilot who happened to be stranded on board during the Boxer action, testified about the crew's deep dislike for Harper. They called him "cross and crabbed," and several of the seamen openly stated that if ever they were to go into action, they sincerely hoped that Harper would be among those killed.

According to the testimony of the lively court-martial proceedings, Commander Burrows, it appears, did not initially go boldly into action. He had proceeded cautiously from the very start. Disagreements quickly arose between the officers on the quarterdeck. Harper had asked Lieutenant

Tillinghast during a cross-examination the previous December whether there was not "a debate among the officers . . . on the expediency of engaging, and the probability of conquering." Tillinghast replied that while there had indeed been divergence of opinion on the subject, there had been no "debate." According to the pilot, Harper had correctly identified this now-familiar enemy sloop of war when it first came into view. After giving his captain a detailed assessment of the enemy's force, Harper loudly declared that he would never go out in the *Enterprize* again if they did not engage the enemy that afternoon. But apparently Burrows did not have the greatest confidence in his subordinate's vision. He wished to get a better look before he committed himself to a direct attack. According to more than one eye-witness, Harper became increasingly disrespectful to his captain. "What in the hell are we going round Pumpkin Rock for?" Harper had allegedly cried. "We are going to fight that brig!" Burrows, for his part, rightly worried that any other brig but the *Boxer* must necessarily be an overmatch for the compact *Enterprize*. To the mortification of his officers, however, Burrows next ordered part of the taffrail cut away and ordered one of the bow chasers rolled aft. To Harper, Drinkwater, and many of the others the captain was making every preparation not to engage but to run away.[13] The British held the same view.[14] But it was Burrows's intention to fight.

Lasting approximately one hour, the battle was a straightforward broadside-to-broadside affair, with the heavier weight of the American's metal (one more gun per side), its more numerous crew,[15] and its thicker bulwarks finally tipping the balance. At one point the Briton briefly took up a position across the American's stern, but by that time it was too badly damaged to inflict any lasting harm. When Burrows was mortally wounded during the opening broadsides by a canister shot to the groin, his young clerk, Isaac Bowman, "a poor innocent lad and as little acquainted with the world, as he is with a ship," ran below and hid in the shot locker.[16]

Lieutenant Tillinghast was on the quarterdeck during most of the action, and he had earlier testified that Harper did not remain at his station by the wheel after the captain fell. When the *Boxer* took up its much celebrated half-raking position, Tillinghast heard Harper cry out: "The Boxer is going to rake us!" This outburst had so alarmed the marines and the brace men that they crowded behind the questionable narrow shelter afforded by the two masts. Tillinghast, who now had command of the quarterdeck (McCall being forward with the first division) knew exactly what to do. After ordering the gun crews to man the opposite batteries, he called out to the brace men to "let fall the foresail" and bring it around.

Harper, who was then in the gangways, heard this command and took it upon himself to execute it personally. Under cross-examination, Tillinghast had denied ever having seen Harper screen himself behind the foremast, nor did he recall hearing him beg the first lieutenant to haul down the colors. During the entire engagement, Harper and Tillinghast had spoken to each other only once. The second lieutenant had asked the sailing master if they should consider taking a raking position athwart the bows of the enemy. Harper had replied nervously: "We shall soon be in one." Although justifiably "anxious," Harper appeared, to Tillinghast at least, to be "cool and collected." Tillinghast further reported that he had heard of no complaints against Harper's conduct until some twenty-four hours after the action.

Although the testimony shows that Tillinghast clearly disliked Harper, the second lieutenant was downright friendly toward him in comparison with the other officers. Midshipman John Aulick reported seeing Harper hide behind the foremast when the *Boxer* was just passing under the *Enterprize's* stern. "You did not behave yourself as becoming an officer," Aulick had scolded the grizzled Harper before the open court, "by reason of your having left the quarterdeck and coming forward where there was no apparent duty for you to do." Harper, he added, appeared absolutely terrified. John Ball, the brig's boatswain, testified that it was he, and not Harper, who had personally hauled upon the foresail sheets, and Sergeant of Marines Levi Durbin reported having heard the master call out three times to McCall: "You had better cut away the colors!" But the good sergeant had his own personal ax to grind against the poor master. During the opening moments of the battle, Harper had admonished Durbin harshly in front of his marines, warning him to "take better aim and be sure of your object before you discharge your muskets!" Everything looked bleak indeed for poor Harper. Considering the seriousness of the charges, Captain Hull ordered the trial delayed until Lieutenant McCall, the chief accuser, could be recalled from Baltimore to testify.[17] Harper had only one hope left: the impartiality of Lieutenant Tillinghast.

Captain Blakeley boarded the beautiful frigate *Congress* at its anchorage in the Piscataqua on 17 January 1814, and took his seat with the tribunal. As McCall had not yet returned, the first day was confined to the testimony of two seamen, but little more than name-calling was accomplished. The star witness arrived the following morning, and his testimony was damning. McCall reported that he had indeed been forward with Harper during most of the action, and that he clearly saw him duck behind either the cable bits or the foremast every time the report of an enemy gun was heard. Harper, he explained, would then stoop down and pick up the enemy's spent grape and canister shot and place them in his pockets. Seeing his captain near death, McCall had initially petitioned Harper's advice. "By God, Mr. McCall," replied the allegedly wild-eyed Harper, "haul the colors down or we shall all be killed!" The nearby carpenter, he continued, having heard Harper's exclamation, tapped him on the shoulder and said, "Let the colors fly as long as there shall be six men alive and they will all stand by you!" When the enemy at length passed under the *Enterprize*'s stern, Harper once again cried out: "By God, we shall all be killed!" But McCall did admit that even though Harper appeared alarmed, he did not reprimand him at the time. He had instead ordered Harper to "go aft and look out and keep the vessel in a favorable position." Under further cross-examination, McCall conceded that, yes, he had given Harper command of the prize, a strange assignment for an allegedly terrified coward, but he had only done so after all the dangerous British prisoners had been removed. Harper attacked his accuser directly. Did not McCall get these roles reversed? Was it not he, the first lieutenant, who had begged the prisoner, "Mr. Harper, what in God's name shall we do? Had we not better haul down the colors?" The lieutenant merely replied coldly that he had not. McCall then proceeded skillfully to deflect a battery of similar questions, except the last. Did McCall tell any-one, prior to the charges being filed, that he, Harper, had behaved as well as any man aboard during the action? McCall reluctantly confessed that he had. But, he explained, it was done only to protect Harper's family. The prosecution then closed its case.

The following morning, Harper recalled the civilian pilot to the stand and began his spirited defense. According to Drinkwater's testimony, an enthusi-astic Harper had promised Burrows that if they engaged the *Boxer*, they could surely take the ship in only a quarter of an hour. He also testified that Harper had cheered the men on just before the shooting had started: "Now boys, we have a job to do," Harper had allegedly cried, "and we must stick it to them!" Harper next called Tillinghast to the stand. Recalling that the lat-ter had earlier denied ever having heard him call out for surrender, Harper next asked him, "Do you suppose that it was possible that I could have stood on the wardroom hatch and have said to Lieutenant McCall, 'You had better haul down the colors or we shall all be killed' and you [did] not hear it?" Till-inghast did not suppose that it was possible. "I never heard or knew anything of your bad conduct," recalled Tillinghast, "till after you was arrested." Robert Hiley, a Portland merchant, was the last defense witness called. Since he was

eager to learn the details of the late battle, Hiley had gone on board the
Enterprize very soon after the brigs had dropped anchor in port. The town's
selectmen had all begged him to ask specifically how Mr. Harper, the only
Portland officer aboard, had behaved during the action. McCall had reportedly responded, "He behaved very well." Tillinghast concurred: "Very well,
very well," he too had told Hiley. "It was a new business to most of us." Hiley
thought it strange in consequence of what the two senior surviving officers
had told him when he later learned of the charges.

Blakeley's old crew did indeed have it in for the tyrannical Harper, yet
there appeared to be some element of truth to McCall's charges. Harper did
not need to go forward and haul on the foresail braces personally, although
he would not have technically been deserting his post by doing so. He had
managed to alienate nearly everyone on board, including the new captain, in
only a fortnight's time. Ill feelings were at their very worst when Harper
spoke so disrespectfully to Captain Burrows on the quarterdeck so the
enlisted men may have wished to avenge this rude treatment of their late
captain. Much of their testimony appeared to be an exaggerated form of the
truth. Tillinghast alone was unwilling to participate in the lynching. He told
only what he saw, nothing more. Harper probably did advise McCall to surrender, but not in a terrified fit of panic as McCall and the others had
asserted; rather, it was as serious advice, first openly solicited and then honestly given. Tillinghast simply did not hear that conversation. The proof of
this was in one of the four written depositions submitted by Harper himself
to the court as part of his own defense. The purser, Edward Turner, then far
away on foreign service, had been deposed before a Rockingham County
magistrate before leaving the previous December:

> Mr. McCall told me that, on the fall of Captain Burrows being reported
> to him, he went aft with the intention of taking command, but on find-
> ing Captain Burrows still alive, he was therefore undetermined. While
> deliberating, he saw Mr. Harper, and asked him what he should do, sup-
> posing he possessed more experienced information as to situations of
> that sort, than himself. *Mr. Harper advised him to strike the colors, on
> which he, Mr. McCall left him, and went to his station.*

The next day, Harper read his defense to the court. His lengthy dissertation
praised the sacred virtues of honor and heroism, scorned the evils of cowardice, and finally dissected the testimony of all those who were aligned
against him. The crew's false tales and careless observations were those of
mere seamen, he declared, who by their nature had an inherent "want of

habitude of investigation" of any complex subject independent of their simple, immediate concerns. Harper then summed up the whole affair as nothing more than an attempt of the senior surviving officer to hog all the glory for himself: "For this my name has been given to the winds, to be banded to the tongues of Black guard retailers of slander . . . to be chanted in ballads, to the tune of McCall's victory and hawked by peddlers." Only the honorable Thomas Tillinghast stood bravely against the wretches who had conspired with the vainglorious McCall. It was clear to Blakeley and to his fellow jurists that Harper had indeed acted improperly, both in his treatment of the crew and in his actions on that fateful afternoon. While he was by no means an innocent, he could not be found guilty of anything wholly concrete. The nation needed another naval victory, and an unblemished one at that, in the wake of the *Chesapeake* disaster. A guilty verdict would advance neither the cause of the nation nor that of the service, and it would create much unneeded ill-will with the strategically important Portland community. The tribunal, without leaving any explanations for its reasoning, unanimously declared the defendant "not guilty."

Blakeley returned to Newburyport only to find that the balance of his long-promised guns had not yet arrived and, to no one's surprise, still more of his people had jumped ship. Even worse, a false rumor had been widely circulating claiming that the *Peacock* had already sailed and that the *Frolic* was within hours of joining it. The whole Harper affair had distressed him greatly, but at least his old crew had behaved exceptionally well in battle. That alone gave him solace. The latest *Herald,* however, brought depressing news. The famed New York triplets, safely delivered by the wife of the *Peacock*'s gunner only two short weeks before, were alas "no more." They were reportedly deposited together in a common grave.[18] On 28 January Blakeley wrote to Mrs. Jones at Rock Rest:

> I shall ever view as one of the most unfortunate events of my life having quitted the Enterprize at the moment I did. Had I remained in her a fortnight longer, my name might have been classed with those who stand so high. I cannot but consider it a mortifying circumstance that I left her, but a few days before she fell in with the only enemy on this station with which she could have creditably contended. I confess I felt heartily glad when I received my order to take command of the Wasp, conceiving that there was no hope of doing anything in the Enterprize. But when I heard of the contest of the latter ship, and witnessed the great delay in the equipment of the former, I had no cause to congratu-

late myself. The Peacock has ere this spread her plumage to the winds, and the Frolick will soon take her revels on the ocean, but the Wasp will, I fear, remain for some time a dull, harmless drone in the waters of her own country. Why this is, I am not permitted to enquire.[19]

At long last, Commodore Bainbridge sent Captain Blakeley his sailing orders. Once his guns were aboard, he was to traverse the coast up to Portsmouth. But before doing so, he was to send five more of his marines down to Boston for the *Frolic*. Blakeley now had only one corporal and four privates left of his original eighteen to retain the possession of and maintain the discipline of 173 men and boys, not to mention defending the unprepared sloop from attack.[20] Blakeley gathered his junior officers together and conferred with them concerning the absolute necessity of their removal to another, more suitable port. Above all, secrecy must be maintained regarding their departure. The secret quickly flew throughout the town, however, and the *Herald*'s "Ship News" section reported it on the fourth: "It is said that the Sloop of War Wasp will shortly sail from this port, either for Boston or Portsmouth."[21] This rude announcement was too much for Blakeley to bear. Within days, the British blockaders, no doubt having read this very issue, would assemble sufficient forces to intercept him. His crew at this point had had almost no training. Even if they had all been veterans of the *Constitution*, he still did not have the bulk of his cannon, powder, or shot. Blakeley made his displeasure known to the *Herald* editor, Ephriham Allen, prompting an "apology" in the very next issue:

> The report, that the officers of the Wasp were offended at a paragraph in our last respecting her sailing, is too contemptible for notice. We believe them to be gentlemen, of too much sense and liberality, to take exception at the paragraph which could in no possible way prove injurious to themselves or their ship. We further believe the report originated in Jacobian malignity.[22]

Finally it was time to depart. Still, Captain Blakeley thought it appropriate to thank the town for its support, albeit its lukewarm support, over these past six months. On 4 February, with the enthusiastic encouragement of his wife, he threw an early eighty-second birthday gala for the late president George Washington,[23] who also was the country's supreme Federalist icon. Blakeley's initial recommendations for naval service had come from two Federalist members of Congress and his godfather had the ear of a popular Federalist governor. Blakeley also had said some unkind words about the embargo while aboard the *Argus* in 1808, even though he always faithfully carried out its enforcement. The Federalist Party was sympathetic to the navy's well-being, even though they preferred their country's cannon be aimed at the French rather than the English. As the son of a grocer, the latter deeply dependent upon freely imported goods, especially expensive European liquors belonging to a seaport community, Blakeley probably was opposed to the Republican administration's prewar embargo.

Blakeley may have flirted with the French-inspired Republican doctrines while at Chapel Hill, but not for long. The selection of Blakeley to command the one sloop of war built within the very heart of the most radical opposition to the current Republican administration might not have been an entirely random decision or just a coincidence because he happened to be in nearby Portsmouth at the time of his promotion. Both of the brothers Bainbridge in Boston were firm Federalists, but this fact brought them no amnesty from the city's established political leaders.[24] Similarly, it is probably no coincidence that all but one of Blakeley's eight seagoing commanders hailed from the south, the lone exception being Isaac Chauncey of Connecticut. Four of Blakeley's sea fathers, Thomas Truxtun, John Rodgers, Philemon Wederstrandt, and Samuel Evans, all came from Maryland. John Dent and Hugh Campbell were both South Carolinians, while Richard Dale was a Virginian.

Blakeley expected to be in Portsmouth by the late president's birthday. This farewell celebration would also be a long overdue morale boost to the ship's sullen officers, and he soon set everyone to work detailing the ship for the much-anticipated event. Every piece of brightwork, from the quarterdeck companionway's elaborate brass-stanchioned framework (costing an enormous $179) to Paul Revere and Sons' highly ornamented patent capstan, was honed to a brilliance rarely seen during wartime. Preparing a flushed-decked sloop of war for a grand social engagement was far more difficult than preparing a much larger frigate for a similar ceremony.[25] There was no relatively warm, roomy, and, above all, securely enclosed gun deck, ideal for entertaining. Most of the functions must necessarily be played out on the *Wasp*'s open spardeck. In this case, ample precaution had to be made against February's bitterly cold and damp night airs.

The day began with fresh gales and low clouds flying in from the northwest, but the weather softened toward evening into lighter, but still intensely cold, westerly winds. By evening, the upper, exposed portion of the ship had been magically transformed into a general promenade. Nearly the entire length of the spar deck, from the foremast to the taffrail, was enclosed within spacious canvas awnings.

The center of the ballroom was illuminated by the ornate capstan, with the customary "pyramid of light, arranged with singular effect, and with taste unquestionable." The ship's muskets, by tradition, lashed in a circle about its base, acted as brightly polished candlesticks, their ironwork and brass fittings gleaming like silver and gold beneath the muzzles' flames. The upper portion of this martial chandelier, a deadly corral of bayonets, was intertwined with whatever greenery the winter landscape could provide. Punched-tin battle lanterns and portable stoves radiated both light and heat toward the crowd from wherever they could be placed with relative safety. The curious throngs of the city's best, brightest, and most beautiful were carefully herded down the companion ladders into the officers' wardroom, tastefully cordoned off by still more screens of banners and bunting. Here and there, temporary tables and their borrowed settings served out generous portions of the best bounties of food and the most complete selection of fine wines and spirits that the smugglers' art could deliver. The dignitaries included not only those merchants responsible for the *Wasp*'s fitting out but also some of the city's most influential citizens. Officers from the volunteer "Washington Light Guards" were there, bending low to avoid the beams, as were the leaders of the lesser militia defenders of the approaches to Plum Island. So too were the "Sea-fencibles," those unemployed shipmasters turned militiamen, most of them hardline Federalists who rallied around their separate New England flag, a pentastellar version of Old Glory. The "Silver Grays," another militia company composed of over one hundred elderly "men of wealth and standing," essentially a private army that exercised elaborate defensive maneuvers at least once every week, were also fully represented. The editor of the *Herald* was impressed:

> On Friday evening last an elegant Ball was given by the officers of the U.S. Sloop-of-War Wasp, on board that ship, which for novelty of appearance and elegance of style has seldom been exceeded in this place. The evening was remarkably favorable, and a very large and splendid collection of Ladies added the attractions of Grand and Beauty to the scene. Nothing seemed to interrupt the pleasure and gratification so happily produced by the honorable exertions and liberality of the officers.[26]

After the grand ball, Blakeley reexamined his growing indent of stores, along with their soon to be forwarded stack of receipts.[27] The $8,400 bill for composition metalwork, for example, included: the copper to sheath the underwater portions of the hull and to line the magazine; the brass for the lightning spire, the companionway pillars and railings, the ship's bell, and both fire engines; and the lead to line the bread room (to prevent the rats from gnawing through), to "sheath the gripe" of the cutwater, and to complete the all important pumps. Books, charts, and mathematical instruments alone cost $485, while the skylight gratings cost $118. Rent of the brig *Anne Marie,* hired to carry some of the multifarious stores from Boston, cost $213, and the "use of the crabb for fitting masts and use of the blocks to set masts" cost $61.

After endless delays, Blakeley's heavy guns began to arrive, not all at once but in twos and threes. By 21 February he reported his ship nearly ready to sail. Blakeley privately reflected that he had better get out while he still had a crew. Only forty-eight hours before, five able seamen had vanished forever into the snow-flecked night. "I do not feel warranted in fixing a determinable period which we will be ready for sea, but I trust and hope it will be in a few weeks," he wrote the secretary. "The Wasp will leave this, the moment a fair wind, and water enough on the bar can be obtained."[28]

The favorable conditions did not appear until one week later, however. On Monday morning, 28 February, the *Wasp* at long last proceeded under its own power toward the mouth of the great river, propelled by a snowy northwesterly breeze.[29] The two gunboats wallowed after it, dangerously overloaded with the lightened corvette's stores, including four of its heavy 32-pounder carronades apiece. No vessels of any kind, not even the often-reported British "schooner with a tier of ports," could be seen. Slowly and with great caution, Blakeley eased the vessel over the bar; there was to be no repeat of the embarrassments off the Mississippi and St. Marys rivers on this day. The *Wasp* quickly restowed its guns and provisions on the happier side of the bar. "I have the honor to report to you," Blakeley announced to the secretary later that afternoon from Portsmouth, "the arrival of this ship at this place."[30] But his wait was still far from over.

Sketch of the Old East Building, University of North Carolina at Chapel Hill, drawn by John Pettigrew in 1797. This was Johnston's home for three tumultuous years. One wonders which window junior collegian Blakeley threatened to throw presiding Professor Caldwell through! From Kemp S. Battle, *History of the University of North Carolina,* vol. 1, 1974

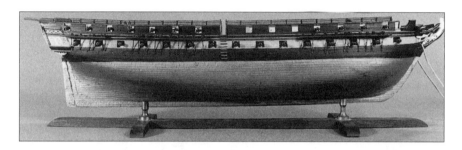

USS *President,* 44 guns, launched at New York in 1800. Naval officers universally believe that their first seagoing assignments are the finest of ships. In the case of Midshipman Blakeley, that assertion is true. Although paling in comparison with the deeds of sister ships *Constitution* and *United States,* the *President* always remained the U.S. Navy's favorite heavy frigate. With the optimal combination of firepower and speed, it was the finest frigate in the world. Shown here in its original configuration, it is a true double-banked, spardecked 60-gun ship. When the *President* was captured by the British in 1815, the nation grieved. (All of the models shown were built in eighth-inch scale by Harold Bosche of Islip, New York.) Courtesy of Harold Bosche

USS *John Adams,* 32 guns, built by subscription at Charleston, South Carolina, in 1799 and considered the belle of the navy's Southern officers. Painstakingly reconstructed from the few surviving naval plans, this model shows both the beauty and complexity of the classical ship rig. This is the ship's pre-razee configuration, as it would have appeared during Blakeley's Mediterranean tenure. Blakeley's *Congress* fell somewhere in between the *John Adams* and the *President* in size and force. Courtesy of Harold Bosche

USS *Hornet*, 18 guns, built in Baltimore, Maryland, was Blakeley's home in 1805 under Cdr. Isaac Chauncey. This model clearly shows the classic brig rig. Considered a bit large for its two-masted rig, *Hornet* was rerigged as a ship in 1811, to the great satisfaction of subsequent commanders. The ubiquitous British *Cruiser*-class brigs, whose prolific ranks included *Reindeer* and *Avon*, would have appeared nearly identical. Courtesy of Harold Bosche

USS *Argus*, 18 guns, built in Boston in 1803, was Blakeley's home during the embargo of 1808–9. Smaller than the *Hornet*, it wore its brig rig very well. Long believed to be the fastest sloop of war in the navy at the time, the *Argus* was a favorite of the masters commandant cadre. Visually sleeker than the *Hornet*, the *Argus* was the obvious design upon which to base the later sloops of war *Wasp*, *Frolic*, and *Peacock*. Courtesy of Harold Bosche

USS *Enterprize,* 12 guns, built privately on Maryland's Eastern Shore in 1798 and bought by the navy. Of the dozens of small armed vessels purchased for service during the Quasi-War with France, it alone was spared the budget ax and retained in the service. Reconstructed here with the schooner rig, this is configuration maintained throughout the early Barbary Wars years and well into Lieutenant Blakeley's tenure as commander. In 1811, however, Blakeley rerigged the *Enterprize* as a brig. The change much improved its character as a steady gun platform, without reducing its considerable sailing abilities. Courtesy of Harold Bosche

USS *Wasp*, 18 guns, built by contract in Newburyport, Massachusetts, in 1813. This model, although under construction, shows the marriage of the best of both worlds: the flush deck design of the *Argus,* suitably enlarged, with the frigate's ship rig. After being razeed down into a corvette in 1808, the *John Adams,* Blakeley's first unofficial command, shared this successful form—albeit to somewhat larger dimensions. Courtesy of Harold Bosche

Midshipman Blakeley's mentor, Commo. John Rodgers, as he appeared circa 1815 before famed artist John Wesley Jarvis. U.S. Naval Academy Museum

This oil portrait of Captain Blakeley has graced the hallowed halls of the University of North Carolina at Chapel Hill since the days of the Monroe administration. Long the possession of the campus Philanthropic Society, this painting was reportedly created from what was then described as an "indifferent" miniature that once hung in the Jones estate at Rock Rest and is now lost. One would be hard-pressed to find much resemblance between this portrait and Gimbrede's work. Courtesy of Dr. Donald Higgenbotham, University of North Carolina at Chapel Hill

This handsome stipple engraving of Johnston Blakeley by Thomas Gimbrede (1781–1832) first appeared in early 1816 as a frontispiece for *Analectic Magazine*. It appears to have served as the basis for several later oil works, including two now residing at the U.S. Naval Academy; one is the work of Elizabeth McClure, the other that of an unknown Chinese artist. (A third copy, painted by R. D. Fairfax, is currently displayed at Independence Historical Park, Philadelphia.) Although those who knew Blakeley thought Gimbrede's version serious and somewhat lacking in expression, they did acknowledge that it was "tolerably correct in its proportions." U.S. Naval Academy Museum

Postwar view of Newburyport Harbor as seen from Ring's Island, off the Salisbury shore of the Merrimack River. From Sarah Anna Emery, *Reminiscences of a Nonagenarian*, 1879

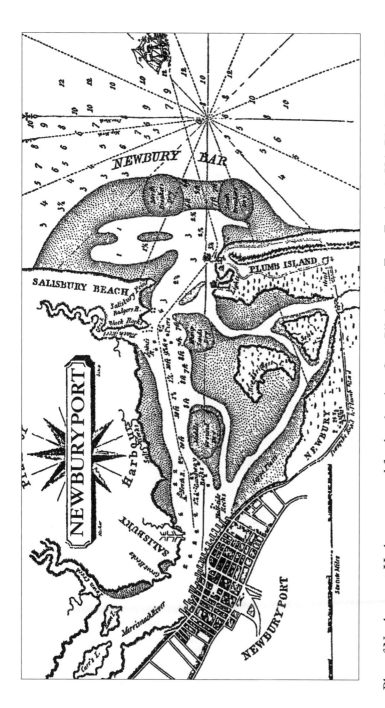

Plan of Newburyport Harbour engraved for the *American Coast Pilot* in 1809. From Euphemia Vale Blake, *History of New–buryport*, 1854

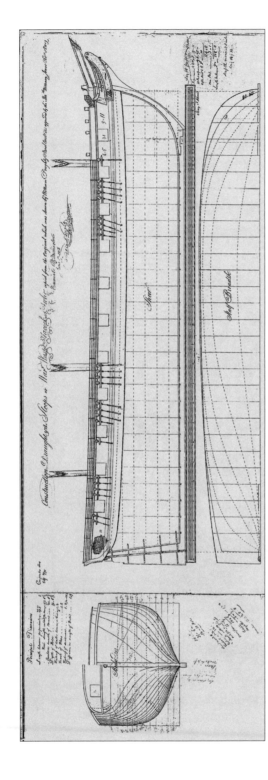

This plan of the *Wasp*, *Peacock*, and *Frolic*, drawn by Henry Allen and dated 1 June 1813, shows the sheer, half-breadth, and body of the three *Argus*-inspired sloops as designed. National Archives CR41-5-6-A

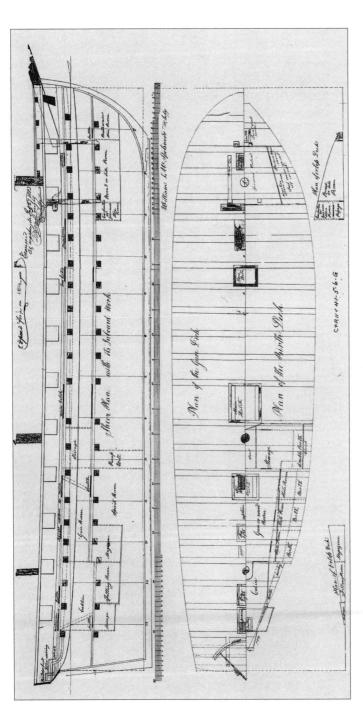

This drawing, done by William Spotswood and signed by William Doughty on 27 July 1813, shows the intended plan of the *Wasp*'s decks before Commodore Bainbridge instituted his many changes. The berth deck was home to all 172 officers, men, and boys. All space aft the mizzenmast belonged exclusively to the captain. National Archives CR41-5-6-G

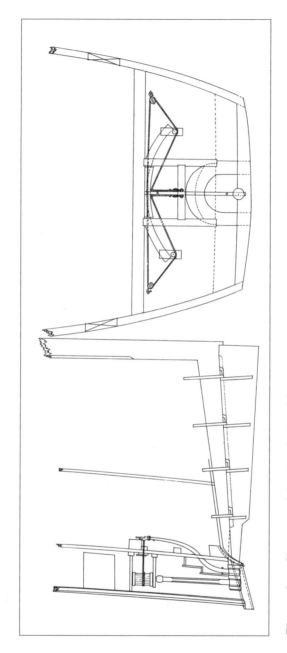

Plan and profile views of the *Frolic's* tiller. The faded original drawing is at the National Maritime Museum, Greenwich. Drawing by the author

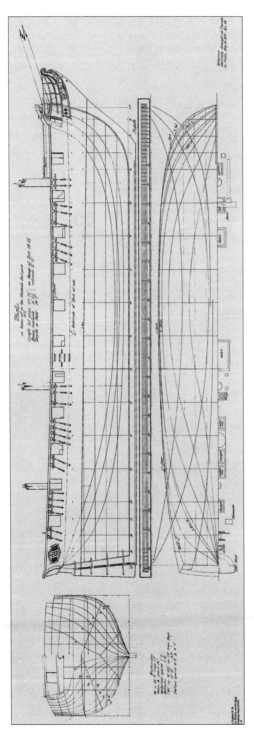

The draft of HMS *Florida*, formerly the USS *Frolic*, as taken off in the Woolwich Yard in 1816. This modern drawing by Howard I. Chapelle details the countless minor changes made to Doughty's original design by Bainbridge, Barker, and Hartt and best portrays the *Wasp* as actually built. The Massachusetts corvettes were probably as identical to one another as any two ships built to the same draft in separate yards could have been. Smithsonian Institution

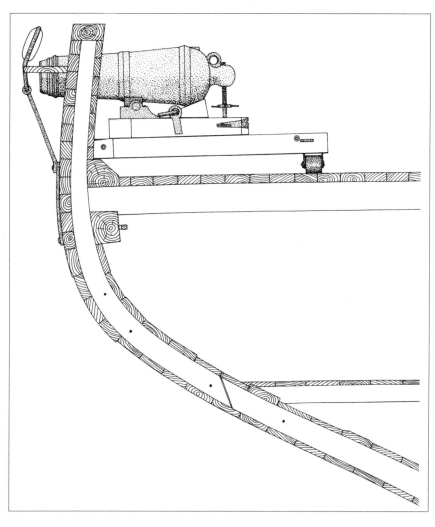

An American carronade and slide carriage of 1814: in this case, a 42-pounder as fitted on board the sloop of war *Jefferson*. The *Wasp*'s nineteen 32-pounders would have been slightly smaller but of identical proportions, and they would have been indistinguishable from their English cousins. Drawing by Dr. Kevin Crisman, Texas A&M University

A bluejacket of the 1830s in full shore-going rig. This portrait of George Brown, bosun's mate of the U.S. sloop of war *Concord,* might aptly describe any one of the *Wasp*'s warrant officers. Brown's right hand rests upon a 12-pounder boat carronade. The gun is mounted atop a shifting carriage identical to the one belonging to the *Reindeer* and subsequently taken aboard the *Wasp.* Author's collection

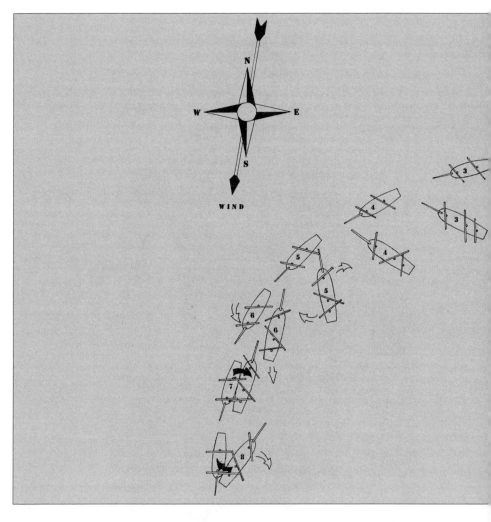

The *Wasp* and the *Reindeer*, 28 June 1814. *(1)* The *Reindeer* opens fire with its shifting boat carronade and larboard bow chaser into the *Wasp*'s starboard quarter. The time is 3:15 P.M., American time. *(2)* The *Wasp* puts its helm up and discharges its first broadside into the *Reindeer*'s larboard bow. Captain Manners is wounded in both legs. The time is 3:24 P.M. *(3)* The sloops exchange probably no more than two or three broadsides. The *Wasp*'s fore rigging is much cut up, and the *Reindeer*'s hull and crew suffer heavily. Wounded seriously in both thighs, Manners is carried to his quarterdeck. *(4)* The *Wasp* inadvertently continues to turn into the wind, enabling the *Reindeer* to rake the starboard bow. Blakeley orders the mainsail hauled around, but damage aloft prevents a timely correction. The time is approximately 3:32 P.M. *(5)* The *Reindeer* continues to rake the *Wasp*, while the latter continues to turn to starboard. Midshipman Langdon is seriously wounded. *(6)* The *Wasp* gathers sternway while the *Reindeer* puts

H.B.M.S. REINDEER

U.S.S. WASP

before the wind in a deliberate attempt to make contact and board. The *Wasp* discharges its fresh larboard battery. *(7)* The sloops collide nose to tail. Manners and his purser are killed leading the boarders across *(arrow)*. The survivors gain the *Wasp's* forecastle and inflict many American casualties. *(8)* The sloops pull apart as the *Wasp* fills on its new tack, but the *Reindeer's* bow anchor hooks on the *Wasp's* mizzen chains. Those English boarders stranded on the *Wasp's* forecastle are trapped and overwhelmed. The remaining crew from the *Reindeer* try to board over their own forecastle but are to a man shot down or piked. Blakeley and Geisinger in turn lead their boarders across *(arrow)* but meet little resistance. At 3:45 P.M., the English colors are hauled down. The *Reindeer's* red ensign, 10 feet by 19.5 feet, was saved, sent home with the dispatches, and may be seen at the U.S. Naval Academy Museum alongside a smaller flag reportedly taken from the *Avon*. Drawing by the author

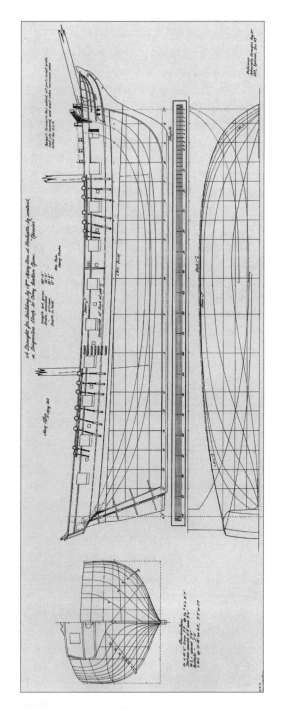

The draft of HMS *Epervier*, which was captured in 1814 by the *Wasp*'s sister sloop the *Peacock*. This drawing by Chapelle is representative of the *Cruiser* class of sloops of war, to which both *Reindeer* and *Avon* belonged. Smithsonian Institution

"The Commencement of Action on the *Reindeer*," one of a series of four prints of the engagement by John Thomas Serres (1759–1825), painted sometime between 1815 and 1825. An Admiralty draftsman as well as an accomplished marine painter, Serres was obviously confused by Blakeley's official dispatches. Since no rake was mentioned, and since no official British version ever appeared in the press, Serres believed Blakeley's report to have been in error. How could the engagement have begun on the *Wasp*'s starboard side and have ended on the larboard quarter? Perhaps Blakeley mistook starboard for larboard. But at which mention? Serres created his own clever but incorrect solution: the sloops attacked each other bow on! Nevertheless, the accuracy of detail of this and the three other prints is striking. Note, for example, the clearly defined square-tuck stern of the *Reindeer*, the mandatory mark of a fir-built ship. Courtesy of the Henry Francis du Pont Winterthur Museum

"The *Wasp* with the Gib Boom in the *Reindeer*'s Lee Rigging." This is the only print of Serres's four that shows the two sloops properly oriented toward each other. It was at this point that Midshipman Langdon was wounded. Note the *Wasp*'s mainsail being hauled around while its jib-boom catches the *Reindeer*'s foreyard. This second print is the most accurate surviving contemporary portrait of the *Wasp*. Serres had been employed in the Royal Navy dockyards as a draftsman and so had access to the captured *Frolic* as well as its draft. Interestingly, the *Wasp* is shown here with a full figurehead extending right arm forward. Courtesy of the Henry Francis du Pont Winterthur Museum

"Vessels Are alongside Each Other." While Serres's exciting view of the boarding melee is highly detailed, it incorrectly shows the sloops facing in the same direction. The disparity in size between the two sloops, while considerable, is somewhat exaggerated here. Note the bodies falling or perhaps leaping over the *Wasp*'s head and taffrail into the sea. The tip of the *Wasp*'s jib-boom is also visible, snapped off yet still dangling in its tackle. Courtesy

"Hull of the *Wasp* in the Act of Sinking the *Reindeer.*" This view shows the true majesty of the ship-rigged corvette. Note the *Wasp*'s enormous jib and spanker, and the more common round-tuck stern. Serres deliberately condensed the postbattle scenes here to tell a story. Unfortunately, the *Reindeer* was burned, not merely scuttled, and the magazines did not explode until well after dark. In addition, the cartel brig *Lisbon Packet (left)* was not overhauled until the following day. Curiously, Blakeley's shattered and discarded stern-boat can just be seen partially submerged in the right foreground. From whom did Serres learn that unique detail? Courtesy of the Henry Francis du Pont Winterthur Museum

HMS *Epervier,* sister brig to the *Reindeer* and *Avon,* was captured off eastern Florida in April 1814 by the *Wasp*'s sister sloop, the *Peacock.* While at first glance this contemporary engraving appears cartoonish, it nevertheless shows an important characteristic that the vessel shared with the *Avon.* Note the unarmed sham port all the way aft in lieu of a quarter badge. This ersatz feature, combined with the normally unarmed bridle port far forward, gives the impression of "eleven ports aside," as related in a widely published although unidentified letter. This false perception of extra length caused Blakeley to proclaim his second antagonist "one of the largest brigs in the British Navy," even though it was just a sister brig to his first. This sketch was made by an unknown artist, reportedly from an original engraving on a gold-headed walking stick belonging to Mstr. Comdt. Lewis Warrington, the brig's captor. Author's collection

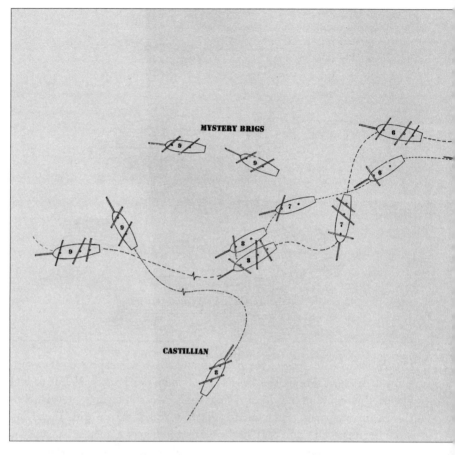

The *Wasp* and the *Avon*, 2 September 1814. (Distances not to scale.) *(1)* The *Wasp* approaches the *Avon* near enough to hail it. Sailing Master Carr fires the *Reindeer*'s boat carronade and begins the bout. The time is approximately 9:00 P.M. *(2)* The sloops haul to port and exchange broadsides. *(3)* *Wasp* tries to rake *Avon*'s stern but is foiled by the latter's nimble and skillful handling. Both crews man their opposite broadsides and the fight begins in earnest. *(4)* Although losing the weather-gauge, the *Wasp* takes up an advantageous position on the fleeing *Avon*'s starboard quarter, and for the most part remains there. *(5)* The *Avon* frequently bears up to rake the *Wasp*'s bow, but without much success. *(6)* The *Avon*'s mainmast has come crashing down, and the crew's fire slackens considerably. The time is approximately 10:00 P.M. *(7)* Blakeley easily recaptures the weather-gauge. Since his last two broadsides have not been returned, Blakeley hails his opponent to ask if

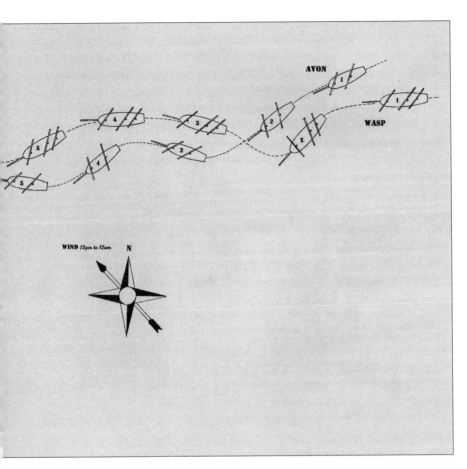

AVON

WASP

WIND *12pm to 12am*   N

he has struck. To this, the *Avon* replies with one gun and a handful of muskets. Blakeley fires a partial broadside into the brig's larboard quarter, ceases
fire, and hails again. This time the answer comes back "in the affirmative."
The time is approximately 10:12 P.M. *(8)* The *Wasp* is alongside the *Avon* and
is in the act of hoisting out the boats when the *Castillian* appears from the
southwest, off Blakeley's larboard bow. Blakeley abandons his prize, puts
before the wind, and prepares for a second engagement. *(9)* At approximately 11:30 P.M., English time, the *Castillian* crosses the *Wasp*'s wake and
fires into the starboard rigging. At this moment Blakeley's lookout reports
the sudden appearance of two more brigs, one off the larboard quarter and
the other astern. The *Castillian* returns to the sinking *Avon* at approximately
11:55 P.M. and takes off the surviving crew. At 1:00 A.M., the *Avon* sinks by the
bow. Drawing by the author

Realistic representations of the *Wasp-Avon* battle are few and far between, as is the case with most nighttime engagements. This 1891 ink drawing by artist J. O. Davidson, entitled "The Wasp Sinking the Avon," is better than most. Even in this sketch, the leeward *Wasp* is fighting its wrong broadside. One might also suppose from this that the Briton was slightly larger than the American, a common error in many a nineteenth-century American naval print. From Edgar S. Maclay, *A History of the United States Navy*, vol. 1, 1906

Silver Congressional Medal awarded posthumously to Captain Blakeley for his capture of the *Reindeer,* voted by Congress on 3 November 1814, but not made by artist Moritz Furst for the U.S. Mint until 1820. U.S. Naval Academy Museum

Silver service awarded to Jane Anne Blakeley by the state of North Carolina in 1816 and presented the following year. Undated photo presented by "Miss Laura E. Smith" of "Jeb Street, Greensboro," presumably the last known possessor of the service. Courtesy of the North Carolina Division of Archives and History

12. PROVISIONING ON THE PISCATAQUA

March–April 1814

M str. Comdt. Johnston Blakeley had every reason to feel proud of his new command. The *Wasp* did its designers and builders great credit, for it was judged by all who came aboard to be one of the most finished specimens of naval architecture ever to float upon the peaceful Piscataqua. Standing on the windward horse-block, the new captain surveyed the vast expanse of his corvette's upper deck. His ship was 119 feet, 6 inches on the gun deck, as measured from the forward edge of the planking rabbet cut in the stempost, or the "forward perpendicular," to the after edge of the corresponding groove adzed in the sternpost at the same level, the "aft perpendicular." The *Wasp*'s maximum molded breadth was 31 feet, 6 inches, frame to frame, and the depth of its hold was 14 feet, 2 inches, from the underside of the berth deck plank to the top of the limber streak abutting the keel. Its calculated displacement was slightly over 509 tons, American measurement.

The ship's stem was the only deliberately ornate region. A thickly vined bas-relief scroll, not unlike the head of a fiddle, unraveled slowly down the trail boards, mingling first with a crossed banner and ax and then winding around a densely starred escutcheon, itself clustered with cannon, spears, and sabers, before meeting its eventual terminus at the cabled hawser holes. The low, thin stern was entirely without ornamentation, except for the raised molding bordering the taffrail, intended originally to resemble an upended, radial section of an apple. Instead, it now wore a revised, somewhat sausage-shaped frown. A carved quarter badge, a meek imitation of a true quarter gallery, projected mere inches from the corvette's side just abaft the eleventh partially hidden carronade. Above the *Wasp*'s stout bulwarks, a lace of hammocks belonging to 175 men billowed upward from their netted burnished-iron stanchions, sweeping fore and aft with an understated sheer.

Although for the moment they remained hidden from view, this corvette could spread an immense span of canvas wings. The *Wasp*'s marginally raking main mast, the largest single spar on board, was exactly 75 feet from its broad heel, resting atop the keelson well below the waterline, to its lofty head, towering some 60 feet above the deck and nearly 26 inches wide at the deck partners. Beneath the broad fighting platform, called the "main top," hung the main yard, with its tightly furled mainsail or "main course," 67 feet, 6 inches long, end to end, with 4-foot arms and measuring 16 inches in diameter in the slings amidships. The main topmast, rising up with the same mild aft-leaning rake, was 45 feet in length with a 6-foot, 9-inch trestle-treed head. It was here, more than 90 feet above the deck, that the lookout would normally be found swaying to and fro, scanning the horizon for distant flecks of sail. Beneath his feet hung the main topsail yard, 50 feet, 6 inches in length. The corvette hoisted no spars higher than this while it remained anchored at the quiet, fluid boundary between Maine and New Hampshire. The 22-foot, 6-inch topgallant mast and the 12-foot, 6-inch royal pole still lay alongside the boats in the waist. So too did the main topgallant yard, the main royal yard, and the main skysail yard, each at present stripped of all canvas and measuring 34 feet; 22 feet, 9 inches; and 13 feet, 9 inches; respectively. The foremast shared the main yard's length exactly, and the mizzenmast was only about 4 feet shorter still. Nearly every yard was equipped with a complete array of studding sails, or stun'sail gear. These athwart-ships extensions of their respective spars ranged from the mainmast's lower swinging boom, over 40 feet in length with its 20-foot paired upper yard, to the mizzen royal's slender adjuncts, measuring just over 13 and 7 feet, respectively.[1]

In time of peace, the *Wasp* and its sisters would have been sparred almost exclusively with Georgia pine, but because of the tightening blockade, Blakeley had to make do with the otherwise select New England white pine, with the occasional piece of straight-grained Yankee spruce thrown in for good measure. The stronger, more flexible southern timber could be made slightly narrower and still retain the same strength. The resultant savings of an inch or two off each stick's diameter would have trimmed away many hundreds of pounds, to the considerable relief of the hard-working standing rigging. For every foot in length of one of the *Wasp*'s yards, for example, the diameter at its greatest thickness in the slings would correspond to exactly twenty-two hundredths of an inch. But if this same spar were instead made of stronger, southern stock, the ratio would drop to twenty hundredths, no insignificant reduction.

The great bowsprit, 32 feet of seasoned New England pine and 2 feet thick at the buffalo rail, jutted forward from beneath the flush, topgallant forecastle deck at an angle of about seventeen degrees to the gun deck. It was joined two-thirds out by the graceful jib-boom, 35 feet, 3 inches long, and it, in turn, would later be mated to the slender flying jib-boom, measuring out at 38 feet, 9 inches. This was the only set of spars on board for which the corresponding lengths increased with the ascending altitude. The *Wasp* probably also sported the dashing double dolphin striker. Fixed beneath the bowsprit cap, this dual spar had adorned the first *Wasp* as well as the *Constitution*. Its purpose was simply to support the flying jib martingale stays and guys. Uniquely American during this early period, the inverted vee made it almost impossible to pass for anything but an American on the high seas. But then again, so too did the spanker mast and the thick white streak bisecting the blackened freeboard.

The *Wasp* and its sisters also carried an auxiliary mast called the spencer, or the aforementioned spanker mast. This short and slender pole (sometimes called a snow sail mast or a try sail mast) was stepped directly into the gun deck and it terminated into the bottom of the mizzen cap, just above the mizzen top. Its function was to provide an axis for the gaffed mizzen sail to pivot about. The lower arm supporting this great sail, 50 feet, 6 inches in length, and at this moment casting a very faint shadow over the bustling quarterdeck, was called the mizzen or spanker "boom." Although the paired upper yard, the 38-foot-long swinging spanker "gaff," was presently devoid of all but firmly brailed-up canvas, it nevertheless displayed Blakeley's proud ensign. By shifting the center of rotation aft, by even a score of inches, the gaff and boom could be made to swing through a greater arc before meeting the mizzen shrouds, and thus improve the ship's performance while tacking or wearing. Furthermore, if the lower portion of the mizzenmast suffered serious battle damage or become sprung above the partners by a storm, it could still be securely splinted without inhibiting the freedom of movement of the jaws of the gaff and the boom. In times of stress, light airs, or both, the *Wasp* could shift a temporary extension of its gaffed mizzen sail, a "ring tail sail," even farther astern. In calm airs a 22-foot, 6-inch "ring tail boom" hooked onto the after-end of the swinging spanker boom, while above it the "ring tail yard," exactly one-half the length of its corresponding lower companion, hung from the spanker's great gaff just aft of the waving ensign. This ring-tailed *Wasp* was built for speed.

The ship was admired for more than its flowing and graceful lines, towering masts, and promised broad eclipses of bright canvas. Its steering gear was one of the designers' proudest innovations. By the limits of the fast, flush-deck design, the ship's tiller necessarily had to protrude from the rudder head at ankle level, just above the wing transom. In the old *Wasp*, the massive wooden helm arced from side to side just inches above the deck, in the English fashion, interfering with and even inhibiting a full and proper gun emplacement abaft the wheel. On the new *Wasp*, however, no sooner did the iron tiller emerge from the rudder's thickly reinforced, metal-banded head just below the level of the cap rail than it arched gracefully downward like a swan's neck into the great cabin below. To keep the water from rushing down into the captain's cabin through this aperture, an intricate combination step-down rudder hood and tiller casing was carefully crafted against the backward-sloping transom, resembling one-half of a two-tiered wedding cake, with a radius of about 4 feet at the lowest level. This left room aplenty, if necessary, to work the chase guns aft. The canvas-ringed rudder head protruded from the top of the cake, however, with a squared void mortised completely through it just below its iron-wrapped peak. If an unlucky ball carried away the wheel during an action, an auxiliary, 10-foot-long pine tiller could instantly be shipped at waist level, allowing the corvette to be steered by hand in the French privateer fashion.

The *Wasp* was steered by a single mahogany wheel, about 4 feet in diameter counting the full reach of the ten spokes in the addition, set into the fore end of a 22-inch-long barrel that was itself 16 inches in diameter and centered about a yard above the deck. The two turns of the tiller rope quickly vanished below deck via a pair of brass sliding boxes set into the bottom of the wheel's frame. The tiller blocks, the sheaves, the tensioning tackle, and all but a small portion of the greased and pampered rope worked through its complex harness below, between the two aftermost beams of Blakeley's cabin ceiling, safe and dry and away from the elements.

The *Wasp*'s eleven broadside ports were spaced about 6 feet, 6 inches apart on average and were exactly 3 feet wide. Their sides, beginning at the lower port sills, the latter raised about 18 inches above the deck, terminated directly into the thick cap rail, the whole bulwark being a bit over 5 feet in height. So stout were these timbers that no upper port sills were required. The twenty-two great guns could be securely tackled into place, run out as far as they could be, and closed in by their respective pairs of half-ports. The lower drop-down piece was hinged, while the removable, interlocking upper lid was buckled or latched in tight, both canvas-lined halves completely encircling the muzzle. The bulwarks between the guns were painted in a contrasting hue, perhaps the apple green of the *Constitution* or possibly the slate gray of the late *Chesapeake*. The rammers, sponges, and assorted implements were securely lashed into racks fastened to the bulwarks just forward of their respective guns, while more than one hundred rounds of 32- and 12-pounder shot, tightly netted into their blackened garlands, encircled every hatchway, companionway, and skylight.

Checking on the progress of the numerous last-minute preparations, Johnston Blakeley many times descended the eight athwartships steps into the dimly lit lair of the gun room. This great partition, 20 feet in length and about 28 feet at its greatest breadth, also served as the wardroom on this small ship, and as such it was the off-duty home to Blakeley's cadre of commissioned officers. A canvas awning spread taut over the companionway's intricate brass frame. Each of Blakeley's six commissioned officers maintained his own private apartment here, each cabin being approximately 6 feet wide by 5 feet deep and opening out into the wardroom on either side. Reilly, Tillinghast, and Baury berthed on one side, their order of seniority increasing with their proximity to the captain, while the purser, master, and surgeon lived humbly together on the other. Beneath the central skylight a great table extended for much of the room's length, abutting the companion ladder on the after-end and the officers' pantry on the forward edge. By the particular order of Commodore Bainbridge, the quarterdeck companionway ran straight down into the officers' accommodations, not directly into Blakeley's cabin as Doughty had originally intended. This meant that his own great room remained relatively secluded, while he, in turn, interrupted his overworked underlings every time he went on deck or came below.

Forward of the gun room lay the steerage, home to the *Wasp*'s young gentlemen. While these midshipmen took only 13 feet of the ship's length, they were forced to share their quarters with the great mainmast, along with the inconvenient series of lockers built up around it, segregating the cramped room into two distinct messes. There were two pairs of open "double berths," or bunk beds, built on either side of the ship's upwardly sloping timbers, with barely enough room for each of the youngsters to stretch out. The warrant officers shared the "forward cabin" under the forecastle, directly beneath the stout cable bits and just ahead of the great galley stove. Here, in this forward-most of livable rooms, the sailmaker, gunner, boatswain, and carpenter slung their hammocks together, surrounded by the storerooms of their respective trades. Between the apartments of these two distinct classes of officers lay the seamen's quarters amidships, 45 feet in length, and at best 30 feet in width. But still it was room enough for about 150 men to call home.

The hold was full beneath them, and the ship's cooper, Benjamin Edwards, was below staving and securing his many charges. The *Wasp* carried 221 oaken casks of various sizes to sea, containing, among other things, many thousands of gallons of the Granite State's finest snow run-off. These casks were the product of Newburyport artisan Johnathon Boardmann, now $1,507.45 the richer. The boatswain's crew awaited the order to attend the anchors atop the topgallant forecastle deck, an unprotected and for the moment unarmed platform built up flush with the cap rail. The *Wasp* carried six anchors: three bowers weighing on average about 3,100 pounds apiece, two kedges of just under 850 pounds each, and a solitary 808-pound kedge. They in turn could be mated to any combination of hempen cables: four 15-inch-diameter serpents; a stream cable 8½ inches wide; and three hawsers of 5½, 5, and 4½ inches in diameter. All eight were of the same great length, 120 fathoms.

Blakeley stepped into, or rather down into, his own private "great cabin" in the aftermost partition on the enclosed berth deck. While the junior officers could expect no more than 5 feet of clearance from the top of the berth deck planking to the underside of the gun deck beam, the diminutive captain was lavished with a further 12 inches of headroom. This was accomplished by dropping the berth deck down the same distance aft of the cabin's forward bulwarks. Although the flush deck design permitted this corvette no grand gallery of stern windows, as normally befitted British sloops of war of the same tonnage, this cabin was the best lit of all those below decks. Blakeley's own private skylight lay just forward of the wheel amidships, shining what light the sun saw fit to offer straight down upon the central chart table. A map of the New England coast usually lay unrolled across its entire length. As space was always at a premium on board a man-of-war, the compact recessed writing desk had been built directly into the forward, larboard corner of his cabin bulkhead alongside his bunk.

Entering his cabin on the afternoon of 2 May 1814, Blakeley stooped beneath an arched deck beam and removed the honorable secretary's confidential cruising orders from the top of the stack. The past few months had been hectic. His crew was at least numerically complete, and they had thus far stowed safely in the hold more than enough victuals for several months of service. The drizzling weather, attended with its thick and dangerous fog, had slowly begun to clear toward afternoon, and although the horizon was still overcast, there was nevertheless an increasing northwesterly breeze blowing over the Piscataqua, inviting him out to sea.[2] Today gave every appearance of being the long-awaited day of reckoning. Blakeley reread the orders he had received in March:

> Steer to the Eastward, pass about a degree to the Southward of the Tail of the Great Bank and then, under easy sail, shape your course for the Azores. Cruise in that position ten or twelve days and then head for a point between Ushant and Scilly. Cruise there for about 30 days. Steer then for Cape Clear and cruise between that point and the English coast for two or three weeks. Then take a wide circuit to the Westward and Southward to bring Cape Finisterre to beam. Cruise near this position 20 or 25 days and then cruise up and down the Portuguese coast for eight or ten days. Head then for the Shetland Isles and try to intercept the British Archangel fleet, homeward bound. If then in need of water and provisions, put into L'Orient on the Northern Shore of the Bay of Biscay. Make all possible speed in refitting there and then leave that coast for another cruise. As the Autumnal season will be advanced, seek a milder climate. Steer therefore for the Island of Madeira and cruise in that area for three or four weeks. After that, head for the Coast of Cayenne, Berbice and Demerara. Cruise along that coast, look into the Bay of Honduras, and then steer for the mouth of the Mississippi, Pensacola, and through the Gulph to St. Mary's, Georgia, touching there for information and refreshments.[3]

Blakeley's successful departure from this latest port depended upon the enemy having the good grace to abandon the coast at the exact moment when the wind and weather turned favorable. There was usually one unidentified large sail in sight from the *Wasp*'s deck at any given time. Only one week before, the frigate *Tenedos* had brazenly sailed into the harbor. "Reconnoitered Portsmouth," recorded the master laconically, "and saw Congress and Wasp at anchor."[4] If the weather had permitted, Blakeley would have gladly teamed up with the *Congress* offshore but the opportunity to repeat the glories of Philip Broke's *Shannon* did not materialize. Prepared for the worst, *Congress*'s Capt. John Smith had taken on board a new weapon, just in case the enemy attacked him in squadron strength: "Rec'd on board, a furnace for heating shot."[5]

Two weeks before the *Tenedos* came boldly in, three large ships had been spotted from the deck of the anchored *Congress*, "in the offing, standing to the eastward."[6] The Yankee frigate then spoke to an inbound schooner, which reported "three large ships off the Isles of Shoals."[7] A second schooner reported being chased by a frigate off Newburyport.[8] The British intent was clear. "The British Frigate Statira . . . [was] in our bay Wednesday last," reported the local paper in early April. "They boarded a fishing boat and informed them that they were to cruise in this bay to blockade the *Congress* and the *Wasp* in Portsmouth Harbor, but [they] would not molest the fishermen."[9]

Portsmouth's normally active gunboats had long since been laid up and their crews put hard at work building the 74-gun ship *Washington* beneath the mammoth new ship-house on Fernald's Island. If the enemy had suddenly send its boats in for a cutting-out or burning expedition, the *Wasp* and *Congress* would have had to fend for themselves. The *Congress* had hauled out its largest boat, a thirty-foot-long schooner-rigged launch, in which it "mounted four swivels and one 12-pounder carronade, [and] rec'd a quantity of cartridges from the magazine." This vigilant sentry had proceeded to ply to and fro across the harbor's shallow waters for several weeks.[10] If the *Wasp* been issued similar light guns, it too would have followed suit. Returning back alongside the frigate after venturing briefly into town one "pleasant" Thursday morning, the armed launch suddenly "ran foul the hawser and carried away all her masts."[11] Positioned as it was in the middle of the stream, the *Congress* was as dangerous to American small craft as it was planned to be for the English. On 22 April tragedy had struck once again. At 11:00 A.M., while "under-running the sheet cable for the purpose of weighing the anchor," the frigate "took a sheer" and swung toward the gondola with such violence that it knocked overboard and severely injured several local men, one of whom drowned.[12] Two days later, in spite of all precautions, disaster struck the *Congress* a third time. The best bower was sitting in the very same gondola when, at the instant that the tide was flowing with its greatest strength, the wind suddenly increased. When the frigate lurched laterally, it tore the anchor straight out through the gondola's bow, sending it instantly to the bottom. Fortunately, the *Congress's* repaired launch and its first cutter were alongside and saved the crew.[13] The gondola's evil luck, however, had not been confined to just the *Congress*. The *Newburyport Herald* had described another melancholy accident: "Killed on Friday evening last by the falling of a stick of timber, in endeavoring to hoist it from a gondola on board the U.S. Sloop of War Wasp, in Portsmouth Harbor, MR. RODGERS, of

Kennebunk, master's mate of said vessel."[14] In the *Wasp's* muster roll, Rodgers was labeled "DD," or "discharged dead," on 7 April, offering by way of explanation only that he had been "killed by a stick."[15]

During March and April the weather had been bitterly cold. Unusually severe winter gales had defined the first two weeks of March, which encouraged several more sailors to jump ship, and Blakeley at that point still had not been able to replace his thirteen stolen marines. Captain Hull, who did everything in his power to assist Captain Blakeley, was finally forced to give the painful though necessary order to enter ordinary seamen to fill the place of the marines. Of the five marines on board on 2 May, Pvt. Henry Richardson was signed on in April. A native Philadelphian, Richardson had enlisted in 1812 without ever uttering a word to his estranged wife of five years or to his three young children. His first assignment was to the frigate *Congress* in June of that year. He was later transferred to the Portsmouth marine barracks when the *Congress* was laid up for repairs in December 1813, following one of the least eventful cruises of the war.[16] Even finding enough seamen to fill this ad hoc service had taken time; the competition for manpower was fierce among naval units, both public and private.[17] "I have been obliged to turn over every man from the yard that was subject to be turned over," confessed Hull to Secretary Jones, adding without enthusiasm, "She will sail with the first wind and will have a tolerable crew."[18] High praise indeed.

The secretary believed that the practice of sending in prizes, unless they were very valuable or within a stone's throw of a friendly port, was "extremely precarious and injurious" to the fighting abilities of the service. Blakeley was therefore ordered to destroy all of his captures and retain his crew intact. What was worse, seamen removed from the prizes were to be brought home to the United States as hostages to secure the quick and safe return of an equal number of captive Americans. While Blakeley expressed great satisfaction at the honorable route assigned to his ship, he questioned the prisoner provision. In March, he had responded to Jones on this and other topics:

> I am at a loss to know your wishes with respect to returning any prisoners we may make on board the Wasp until our return should we take any in the early part of our cruise. This shall be attended with much inconvenience and from their consumption of provisions [this] would compel a return to port sooner than I would wish. . . . I would also be obliged to be permitted to return to New York or the Delaware instead of St. Marys. As the period of our return will be in the winter season, I think

we would have a better chance to avoid superior force in making a port in the middle or southern states.[19]

Jones's response to Blakeley probably mirrored instructions Capt. Charles Stewart received later in the year when Stewart took the *Constitution* to sea. Secretary Jones ordered Stewart to land his prisoners in the Azores. It is likely that Blakeley, ordered to cruise in the same seas, was passed a similar gambit.

Blakeley's full china cabinet, built into the bulkhead by his "bed-place," now provided some satisfaction. He had paid dearly for the nondescript cups, plates, and utensils, stowed carefully within the painted pine frame. So too for the cook stove, the candle holders, and every piece of furniture in the adjacent wardroom. He had earlier written William Bainbridge on the subject of procuring just such cabin "furniture":

> I had hitherto delayed making out an indent, for cabin equipment, waiting for something definitive on that subject. I have with me a list of such articles as yourself and Capt. Morris had allowed to sloops-of-war. Will you have the goodness to say to me if I shall go on with these articles and 500 dollars, or point out any other mode by which my requisition shall be regulated?[20]

Commodore Bainbridge had responded coolly: "As it respects the subject of cabin furniture I refer you to a direct communication with the Secretary of the Navy." Blakeley had been furious. The *Constitution*, the *Frolic*, the *Syren*, and the *Rattlesnake* were all at sea. There was no longer any justification to delay the *Wasp* in port. This seemed like petty spite. Perhaps because Blakeley had failed to expedite the placing of the commodore's precious salt between the corvette's timbers the previous autumn, Bainbridge was not willing to place the same element on his wardroom table this spring. No doubt the respective Captains Stewart, Bainbridge, Parker, and Creighton carried to sea all the candle snuffers and napkin rings their hearts desired. The good commodore was well versed in the art of equipping an officer's mess. Blakeley had responded to the secretary and enclosed a copy of the *Enterprize*'s indent and his estimate of the cost. "Should the amount not meet your approbation, I will most cheerfully reduce it to any sum you may direct," he pleaded to Jones, "and hope and trust that in everything relating to my personal convenience I should not be found unreasonable or entertaining the remotest wish to put the government to any expense not absolutely necessary."

During the three-week interval in March between Blakeley's note and Jones's response, Bainbridge had gotten wind of Blakeley's complaints and had given him a terse reprimand. The *Wasp's* captain therefore felt compelled to write a disclaimer. He did not mean to imply that the commodore had refused to sign an official indent supplied by the honorable secretary, for no "official" document then existed. Furthermore, Blakeley wished only to explain to the secretary that he was entirely "unacquainted with the value of these articles" and would in the future always refer these things to those "better qualified" than himself. A detailed list of all the stores required of a 22-gun sloop of war had already been drawn up in Baltimore in 1813 for the semisister corvettes *Erie* and *Ontario*.[21] While it lists, in great detail, every conceivable item for each department, from cannons down to spare nails, the indent describes the hundreds of items required as part of any well-found ship's cabin furniture with but one word: "discretionary." At this point, no doubt Blakeley would gladly eat off the floor if he could just get the *Wasp* to sea before the hostilities ceased.

By 2 May Blakeley was glad he had received not only his complete set of china but also his full complement of men and all twenty-two of his heavy guns. He glanced again at the last paragraph of Jones's instructions:

The President of the United States, persuaded that the gallantry of our Naval officers resting upon the rock of glory cannot be shaken by the ostentatious vanity of a boasting, but a mortified enemy; and from motives of obvious policy . . . has given it to me in charge, to prohibit, in the strictest manner, the giving or accepting of a challenge, to fight ship to ship; which injunction you will strictly observe.

This condition was, of course, occasioned by the *Chesapeake* disaster the summer before. It was mistakenly believed that Captain Lawrence had taken his frigate out to his own tragic destruction in direct response to a written challenge from Captain Broke. Blakeley was probably aware that this order was not written just expressly for him. An exact copy, dated 16 March, had been delivered to Mstr. Comdt. Charles Ridgely of the *Erie* at Baltimore.[22] When the Royal Navy tightly and irrevocably corked the entrance to the Chesapeake Bay, Ridgely's tactical instructions were forwarded to Newburyport.

By regulation, a copy of the *Wasp's* pay and muster roll was to be sent on shore at the final moment with the local pilot. If any calamity befell Blakeley's command, this list was the only complete record of all the officers and men on board. It too sat buried within the desk's competing clutter awaiting his signature. The very last page of this roll bore a "recapitulation" of the 173 souls under his care. It included the names of the forty-seven men rated "able seamen." They were Blakeley's very best blue-water mariners. The sixty-eight "ordinary seamen," a catch-all phrase describing, at one extreme, the coastal, occasional sailors, on down to the mere farm boys and landsmen, were very rough. But they were at least strong, healthy, and possessed the highest potential.

Blakeley was glad that the triumvirate of trouble, which had been simmering in the *Wasp*'s steerage for months, was finally settled. Three mischievous midshipmen—Clough, Burley, and Bonneville—had caused Blakeley embarrassment both aboard and ashore. Midshipman Ebenezer Clough of Boston was as crude as they came. During the first year of the war, young Clough had managed to make a brief privateering cruise before being captured and imprisoned for three months. Despite this experience, he wrote the secretary that "I like the seas very well" in his request for a midshipman's warrant.[23] But the *Wasp* was not a loose-disciplined privateer, and his drinking, fighting, and terrorizing of the ship's thirteen young boys was not conduct becoming an officer. Isaac Hull summed him up directly: "Midshipman Clough will never make an officer or a gentleman, his manners and habits are coarse and vulgar, and his associates [are] of the lowest class."[24] How such a character could have gained admission to the officer corps is abominable.[25]

Clough's sidekick, Midshipman William Burley of Beverly, Massachusetts, was nearly as troublesome. His vice seems to have been alcohol, along with an overwillingness to tag along after the much younger Clough. Burley had never before been to sea, and, at age twenty-five, he was, with the exception of David Geisinger, much older than his peers. The son of a prominent Republican family, he had acquired his warrant only recently. He had twice been expelled from Harvard for crimes ranging from making "indecent noises" during lectures to assaulting his professors and habitually smashing windows.[26] Their careers effectively ended on 19 April, when Sailing Master Carr reported their latest impropriety to his captain:

> I report Midshipman Ebenezer Clough, who was sent on shore in charge of the 3rd cutter with six men for the officers at Portsmouth. At 8 P.M. or thereabout, I came down to the wharf where the boat lay, and found the officer so drunk that he could not stand. I jumped in the boat and ordered him to follow me, the boat being shoved off. I inquired if the officer was in her? The men answered that he was leaning against a

post on shore, finding him incapable to get in the boat, I sent the men on shore and brought him on board. He fell asleep several times in the boat, while rowing to the ship. Several of the boat's crew appeared to be intoxicated, [and] at the same time, there was a number of citizens on the wharf.[27]

Disgracing the ship in front of the local citizenry was the final straw. Blakeley forwarded Carr's report, along with a second more succinct note written by Lieutenant Baury, to Captain Hull, who in turn forwarded them to the secretary with his own comments: "I would observe that this is not the first offense of a similar kind by Mr. Burley and for which he has been admonished and advised by me and upon his promise of amendment had been permitted to return to duty." Taking the captain's recommendation to heart, the secretary immediately expelled Clough from the service, but not his companion. Burley was sent ashore in disgrace, but, by the kindness of Captain Hull, he was given one final, undeserved chance to redeem himself. It was not long, however, before Burley had again "given himself entirely up to Bacchus" and was expelled.[28] Clough was found dead in Boston one cold evening in February 1815, presumably face down outside some seedy tavern, at the ripe old age of twenty-two.[29] Burley lasted until 1821, when he too departed his own lost life, from probably the very same vice.[30]

Blakeley's third problem child was French-born Midshipman Thomas Nicholas Bonneville of Kings County, New York.[31] Only fourteen years old, Bonneville was far too young to tag along to the taverns ashore, so he was spared the fate of his two older mates. A family friend had written of him, "He has had a common English education, reads, writes etc . . . and he is active and healthy." But, she concluded, "his morals are no way exceptional."[32] Through the influence of Katherine "Kitty" Nicholson Few, in-law to Secretary of the Treasury Albert Gallatin, the lad was admitted into the naval officer corps and directed to "the care of" Marine Lt. E. H. Cummings of New York in June 1812.[33] His father, Nicholas de Bonneville, was the famed "learned philosophical radical," pamphleteer, and ardent promoter of liberty and human rights during the French Revolution. He was an intimate friend of Lafayette, Condorcet, and none other than Blakeley's old nemesis, Thomas Paine. In fact, Paine had lived for five years in the Bonneville's Parisian household and was actually the godfather of his honored namesake, young Thomas N. Bonneville. When Paine came to America in 1802, he had advised the Bonnevilles to follow him over quickly, before the brief Peace of Amiens dissolved. Thomas and his two brothers, Benjamin and Louis, accompanied their "educated and talented" mother, Marguerite Brazier Bonneville, across the Atlantic in August 1803, but Nicholas remained behind. Having incurred the wrath of the Bonaparte regime for his openly contrary views, Nicholas dared not move; he remained alone in France until the Corsican's downfall more than a decade later.

Although increasingly ostracized and in declining health, Paine nevertheless cared for Marguerite, she acting for several years as his housekeeper, and her three sons in New York. Because young Thomas was said to have borne a striking resemblance to the philosopher Paine, this gave rise to no small amount of scandalous conversation. Paine did indeed take an especially close interest in the boy, more so than either of his brothers, often referring to him as "Thomas Paine Bonneville." "It will always give me pleasure to know that he does well," Paine wrote to a family friend on the very eve of his death. The nearly destitute philosopher still offered to pay for any of young Thomas's material needs. But he was constantly admonishing his godson to behave himself: "He shall not want anything if he be a good boy and learns no bad words." Paine sent his little namesake off to Stonington, Connecticut, in 1804, and placed him under the care of a Unitarian minister friend who taught school there.[34] When Paine died in obscurity in 1809 and was buried in the pasture of his New Rochelle farm, few attended the graveside service besides the Bonneville clan and a few neighbors. It can hardly be surprising, therefore, considering Blakeley's later disavowal of Paine's religious principles, that he and the young Bonneville would soon and frequently run afoul of one another. Blakeley was fully aware of the public status of young Thomas.[35] Sensitive to the facts of his lineage, perhaps, this young midshipman had always made a point of signing his full name, "Thomas N. Bonneville," to every single letter and document, as if repeatedly to acknowledge his blood connection with his exiled father, Nicholas.

When Thomas Paine himself was himself a lad, he had run off to enlist on board a British privateer during the Seven Years War (against his own father's will); no one was surprised when the younger Thomas desired to follow his lead. With Paine now dead and Nicholas Bonneville still trapped in Paris, an isolated Marguerite approved the sending of her troublesome, adolescent son to sea under the restrictive but gentlemanly care of their new country's navy. The eager Thomas had written the secretary during the war's earliest days: "Sir, if you would favor me with an order to get on board one of the frigates, so that I may participate in the glory and in the danger of our brave officers, I would be obliged."[36] The secretary could not help but smile. Soon after entering the service, Bonneville realized that his first assignment, New York's sole guardship, the feeble *Alert,* was a dead end: "Sir, as there is no prospect of this ship ever going to sea," he again wrote seeking his glory, "I humbly request the favor of your order for some other ship, I should prefer the [New] York or [the] Constitution."[37] His third request for a cruising ship, even "one of the sloops of war," was finally granted. He had been the second young gentleman assigned to the *Wasp.*[38] Now that Clough and Burley had been dismissed, Blakeley was hopeful that the troubles with Bonneville were over.

The replacements for Clough and Burley reported aboard in late April. Henry Sherburne Langdon Jr. came from one of the finest families of Portsmouth. He was one of fourteen children (including nine boys) created by the joining of Henry Sr. and Anne Langdon. This midshipman's powerful family connections made his naval appointment easy enough. His father, in addition to being Portsmouth's navy agent, was a prominent member of the state legislature and one of the charter members of the New Hampshire Union Bank. Also, Henry's uncle was William Eustis, the former secretary of war. Although Henry Sr. owned many properties around Portsmouth proper and in northern New Hampshire, the Langdon clan lived at this time in the immense "Old Judge Langdon" house, a massive, three-story affair built of brick "so it could not burn like the first wooden one did." Uncle William had recommended Henry Jr. personally, and like so many other aspiring youths caught up in the naval euphoria of 1812, he had specifically requested assignment to the frigate *Constitution.* Henry then traveled to Washington in late 1812 to complete his study of navigation under the renowned Dr. Andrew Hunter.[39] He reported on board the corvette *Adams,* then lying in the Potomac; the line to the victorious *Constitution* was apparently far too long. Like many others, Henry soon fell victim to the dreaded yellow fever epidemic that was then sweeping the Chesapeake. Capt. Charles Morris described Henry Jr.'s condition:

> The health of Mr. Langdon, never having been restored since his illness at Annapolis in August last, has induced me to send him to the city that he may obtain permission from the Department to return to his friends until he shall again be able to perform his duty. His anxiety for service is great, and this step has been taken rather from my advice than his own wishes. His conduct has ever been remarkably correct since he joined the ship and I doubt not he will make an excellent officer.[40]

After returning home, Henry recovered just enough of his strength to report to active service when the *Wasp* unexpectedly sailed into port. Curiously,

Henry's boyhood friend, Frank Toscan, just happened to be the second replacement reefer for the *Wasp*'s steerage. Toscan was the son of Jean Joseph Marie Toscan, a man who had come to Portsmouth as the French Consul in 1782. He was also the grandson of Portsmouth's Capt. John Parrot of Revolutionary War fame.[41] Frank was the eldest of the seven Toscan children, and he had long entertained an attraction to the sea. His father had told him many tales of his close friend, Captain John Paul Jones, who had resided with the vice consul in the Purcel Boarding House. Jones was then in town attending the fitting out of his much celebrated ship, the *Ranger*, under the direction of Henry Jr.'s great uncle, John Langdon.[42] The Toscans stubbornly held on to their French heritage, as is evidenced by the name of their fourth son, Bonaparte Toscan. Frank had made one merchant voyage with a Captain Flagg following the death of his father in 1805. He evidently preferred life before the mast to both of his previous vocations, working the family farm and assisting old Dr. Goddard in his Portsmouth apothecary shop.[43] At the request of Federalist senator Charles Cutts, young Toscan, "a lad of good education and correct manners [and possessing] some experience as a sailor," finally received his warrant during the first year of the war.[44] He sat in port for six long months without assignment, daydreaming no doubt of frigate glories. In May 1813, Hull observed Toscan ashore "doing nothing," so he gave him command of a gunboat.[45] But this was a poor substitute. "Having been some time in the navy, and . . . not in the way of seeing much active service, I have obtained leave of Capt. Hull to apply for orders to go on board the Congress or the Wasp," he later wrote to Jones. "I shall consider it a favor to be order'd to either of the above ships."[46]

A fellow Portsmouthian, Midshipman Ashton Stoodley Hall, met Toscan and Langdon at the gangway. If they had not all been friends in their youth, they would become well acquainted during their time on the *Wasp*. Ashton was the only child of local shipbuilder Elijah Hall.[47] The elder Hall had been John Paul Jones's second lieutenant on board the *Ranger* in 1777, and it was the memory of this patriotic service alone that had won Ashton his warrant.[48] Ashton's official letter of acceptance contained a brief description of his background: "I have never been on a voyage to sea, but I have been engaged in a counting house ever since I have finished my studies."[49] Hall, having come down to Newburyport in February, might have sought Blakeley out as a possible connection, through Blakeley's association with Richard Dale, to John Paul Jones. This was not true, however, for Langdon or Toscan. Blakeley had sought them out as last-minute replacements; they were the only ones left in port. Hall, Langdon, and Toscan soon formed a close bond. As they gazed out across the harbor at Shaefe's Wharf, the site of the old *Ranger*'s fitting-out, each recalled to one another their respective family's personal connection with the great man himself. They each hoped to repeat his glories.

Republican congressman Burwell Bassett and Norfolk's navy agent, Theodore Armistead, had both recommended young Virginian William Byrd Randolph to Paul Hamilton for appointment as a midshipman.[50] William's uncle, Representative John Randolph, the brilliant yet eccentric Jeffersonian conservative from Roanoke, Virginia, most likely put in a good word for him as well. Young Randolph's naval career, through no fault of his own, had gotten off to a very rocky start.[51] He served with Capt. Samuel Evans on board the *Chesapeake* throughout 1812, and he remained on board when James Lawrence took over command in May 1813. Evans had recognized Randolph's leadership and seamanship abilities early on, and had placed him in command of the frigate's elite foretopmen.[52] He retained that lofty position up until the fateful first of June, when the *Chesapeake* was taken by the *Shannon*. Back in Boston on parole, Randolph secured permission from Bainbridge to proceed on to Washington, presumably to utilize his considerable political clout to help expedite his exchange. He first stopped en route in New London to pay his respects to Commo. Stephen Decatur, whose frigate, the *United States*, was then blockaded in port. Randolph dearly wanted to cruise with Decatur, and if he were to be exchanged in time, he told the secretary, the commodore had promised to take him on board his frigate: "Being very desirous to get out immediately in some ship on this station, I have to request . . ." He then crossed out the word "request," but not too heavily, and continued, ". . . I have to beg, Sir, you will gratify my wishes in facilitating my exchange."[53]

What young William conveniently forgot to mention to the honorable secretary was that his older brother, Robert Byrd Randolph, a hot-tempered young man destined to ignominy as the country's first presidential assailant, was also aboard the *United States*, serving as a midshipman.[54] The inherent difficulties, thought Decatur, of having two siblings in the same mess were more than outweighed, first, by the obvious professional competencies of both brothers, and second, by the political advantages gained from pleasing the Republican Randolphs of Roanoke. But, as his exchange was many months in coming, the brothers Randolph were not reunited. Blakeley, Tillinghast, and Geisinger were no doubt as happy to receive another southerner in their midst as were Baury and Bonneville to have gained another first generation Franco-American in the person of Frank Toscan. The final midshipman to come aboard was William House of Philadelphia.[55] In a letter to Secretary Jones, he sounded like Thomas Bonneville, requesting assignment to one of the frigates:

> I shall always regret the misfortune of not participating in the dangers and glory of those victories which have crown'd with luster the honor of our country, you, I hope, Sir, will anticipate my feeling on the occasion and believe that there is no favor which can be confirmed on me, that will contribute more to my wishes than serving my country, my life is of small estimation when put in competency with the safety of my country.[56]

The secretary instead sent him off to the Delaware flotilla. Tiring of mundane gunboat duties, House offered his resignation until he could, as he put it, "be of service to both my country and myself." Surprisingly, it worked. Perhaps the secretary recognized the value of the gambler's instinct in the making of a successful fighting officer. "Order him to the Boxer," scrawled Jones in the margin of House's letter. But then remembering that this small brig was not going to be adopted into the service, he crossed out his previous order and wrote: "Report to Comm. Bainbridge for one of the sloops of war."[57] That will cure him, he probably thought. On board during Blakeley's final "recapitulation" were eight midshipmen:[58] Bonneville, Geisinger, Hall, House, Langdon, Randolph, Toscan, and one unnamed gentleman. Technically, Third Lieutenant Baury was still only a midshipman, but Blakeley listed him separately among the three lieutenants on the muster and pay roll.

At 4:00 P.M. on 2 May 1814, with the northwest wind increasing and the restless lower clouds still screening the ship from those feared, yet not too distant Britons, the cheerful order echoed throughout the crowded ship to the relief of all: "All hands to up anchor, ahoy!" As the *Wasp* crept from its anchorage, its canvas wings expanded majestically as it headed apprehensively, but eagerly, out toward its true element. When they at last departed the protection of the harbor, the men of the *Congress* cheered them with three thunderous huzzahs. There followed soon after similar acclaims in succession from Fort Sullivan, Fort Washington, and the outermost batteries guarding Newcastle Island, Fort Constitution. All the while, flags, hats, and handkerchiefs swayed continuously from both the Maine and New Hampshire banks of the Piscataqua. By 6:00 P.M., the corvette had passed abreast the Portsmouth Light House. "I have the honor to inform you that the Wasp, Johnston Blakeley, Commanding, sailed last evening with a fine wind and every prospect of its continuing," wrote Isaac Hull, viewing the long-delayed departure from Fernald's Island on the Kittery side. "The wind is fair for her this morning, and, as there has been no enemy's vessels off for some days, I hope she will get off the coast without meeting them."[59] At 8:30, Boon Island Light bearing four leagues southwest by south through the thickening darkness, Captain Blakeley ordered his main topsail laid to the mast. Blakeley was back at his now unencumbered pine secretary at exactly 9:00 P.M., and he jotted off the first of his official reports:

> I have the pleasure to inform you, we sailed this day at 4 P.M. from Portsmouth N.H., and have now a fine breeze at the northwest. From the specimen of the sailing of this ship since leaving port, I entertain the most favorable presages of her future performances. I shall keep you informed of my proceedings by every proper opportunity.[60]

With unbounded pleasure, Capt. Johnston Blakeley at long last addressed his official letter, "U.S.S. Wasp—At Sea." He handed it to his clerk, who ran it quickly up on deck. Ascending the companion ladder himself a few moments later, the elated, anxious captain discharged the pilot's cutter and then gave a final, unseen wave to the distant Jane Anne ashore. With the topgallants set, Blakeley's untried corvette at last stood out toward the darkening east, wafted along by the coming night's propitious winds.

PART THREE

The Cruise

13. THE TESTING BEGINS

May 1814

Beginning his cruise on 2 May 1814, Mstr. Comdt. Johnston Blakeley entertained little hope for excitement of any sort during his corvette's slow meander across the Grand Banks, unless, of course, he managed to stumble into an enemy frigate. Barring this last grim possibility happening too soon after sailing, there would be plenty of time to train his 173 incongruous, and for the moment violently ill, subordinates into a cohesive fighting unit. He would also be able to observe the minute intricacies of the *Wasp*'s sailing qualities as well. All the long months of preparation were over. The cruise and Blakeley's chance for glory had finally begun.

Of the six newly built Yankee corvettes, the *Frolic,* under Mstr. Comdt. Joseph Bainbridge's command, had been the first to sea on 18 February 1814. Bainbridge, the lucky captain of Charlestown's heavy new sloop of war, had begun his long naval career during the Quasi-War with France. After earning a degree from Columbia College in 1798, this amiable and intelligent officer had befriended fellow "intellectual" Johnston Blakeley in the crowded midshipmen's berth of his first seagoing assignment, Thomas Truxtun's *President.* Bainbridge's abilities shone the brightest not long after, when, as one of Stephen Decatur's volunteers during the daring raid into the harbor of Tripoli, he helped recapture and then burn the frigate *Philadelphia*. Bainbridge and the then-Lieutenant Decatur soon became close friends; they also served together on board five different warships during the intervening years. In 1803, while on liberty in Malta from the *New York,* Joseph Bainbridge became involved in an affray with James Cochran, a prominent Englishman. Young and hotheaded, Bainbridge shoved Mr. Cochran, then Malta's acting colonial secretary, after a mutual exchange of nationalistic insults got entirely out of hand. With an enthusiastic Decatur acting as his second during the subsequent day's duel, Bainbridge shot the Englishman in the forehead at a range of only four paces.[1] Commodore Morris quickly whisked both officers out of Valetta just ahead of formal murder charges. Brave yet brash, Bainbridge had one great debilitating vice:

> In all candor it must be recognized that Joseph Bainbridge had a reputation for intemperance through most of his naval career. He reached captain's rank during the War of 1812. During the summer of Preble's Mediterranean command, for no visible reason, Bainbridge appears to have fallen out of favor with both Preble and Decatur as the summer progressed. It may well be that his alleged alcohol addiction began at this time.[2]

During Commo. Edward Preble's gallant first attack upon Tripoli in 1804, Joseph Bainbridge was given command of one of the six small gunboats assigned to support the flag-frigate *Constitution*. After receiving a withering fire that completely dismantled his rigging early on in the action, Joseph followed his older brother's lead by running hard aground on a patch of ill-placed rocks, and so sat out the day's many glories. Any rumor of cowardice or a want of zeal against Bainbridge, either real or imagined, for failing to support the attack may have accounted for his sudden alienation from Decatur because Decatur's brother, Lt. James Decatur, was killed commanding an identical gunboat during the same battle. Joseph remained in this mundane service for two more years. Later, while stationed in New Orleans, he served with distinction in the "Burr War" and was employed chasing many a smuggler, privateer, and pirate. Afterward, he was honored with the command of several small, relatively unremarkable vessels, including the worn-out bomb-ketch *Aetna*. While on the New Orleans station, however, Joseph butted heads with his immediate naval superior, Capt. John Shaw, and did so once too often. Shaw brought charges for neglect of duty against Bainbridge in 1812 and then successfully court-martialed him. As punishment for his most scandalous conduct, Shaw ordered him away to Washington, so that he might receive a personal reprimand directly from the mouth of Secretary of the Navy Paul Hamilton. Shaw explained his reasoning:

> I found it morally impossible, with all my exertions to get any duty performed by the Brig Viper then under the command of Lieut. Bainbridge. Under various pretexts, notwithstanding my most pressing representations, of the urgent necessity of activity, he kept that vessel as appears from the Log-book, six months out of seven, lying at anchor, in a state of almost perfect inactivity; nor could I ever prevail on him to *cruise out* along the coast, as was absolutely necessary for the protection of our commerce. These circumstances, and a full persuasion of the perfectly lost state, to which the extravagantly dissipated customs of the country had drawn him, have been the sole cause of my wishing him to be removed from this place.[3]

But Hamilton thought this punishment extreme. Shaw could have reprimanded Lieutenant Bainbridge just as effectively by letter alone. Hamilton knew that Shaw wanted Bainbridge off the gulf station, but such personnel decisions were his alone to make, and not Shaw's. Hamilton instead gave Bainbridge some reflective, "wholesome advice" and then sent him packing, all the way back down to New Orleans "the very day afterwards." The fifteen-hundred-mile return trip overland was made as much to punish Shaw as it was to chastise Bainbridge. But Bainbridge carried with him new orders to take over the command of the sloop of war *Syren*. The wayward lieutenant, already greatly indisposed, was forced to make his arduous trek down the Mississippi and Ohio rivers aboard "open skiffs and Kentucky flatt boats." When he at last arrived in Natchez, Mississippi, after a "long and tedious passage of fifty days," he promptly collapsed and remained prostrate for nearly a week.[4] Before he sailed to Boston in early 1813, he once again grounded his command in the Balize. He freed himself only after heaving the majority of his irreplaceable carronades over the side, losing them forever in the thick, all-concealing mud.

The year 1814 was a clean slate, however, for Joseph Bainbridge. He was promoted to master commandant, with the same men whose deserving ranks included Johnston Blakeley, and no officer in any of the world's navies commanded a finer, better-equipped sloop of war. The blatant nepotism then reigning at Boston's naval establishment ensured him of every necessary article. While Blakeley sat waiting for his ordnance, the *Frolic* was lavished with an extra pair of carronade slides and carriages in the unlikely event that any of his newly mounted twenty should wear out through repeated

use. Blakeley received his only extra set by default: Only nineteen of his carronades ever reached him. The disparity in material support during the construction and outfitting of the two sister-sloops was obvious, even for the
flags and the signal colors. The *Frolic* carried four American ensigns, one
jack, and three pendants, and the *Wasp* received only three, one, and one,
respectively. While the Charles River sloop carried, as a ruse, one naval
ensign and pendant each for England, France, Sweden, Spain, and Portugal,
its Merrimack twin possessed an ensign only for the first four countries,
without any foreign pendants whatsoever, and nothing at all for Portugal.
The *Frolic*'s carefully hand-painted Portuguese ensign alone cost more than
seventy-five dollars.[5]

Captain Bainbridge feared that the 175 men allowed him was far too
small a complement for a ship of the *Frolic*'s prime stature. To completely
and properly fill up his "state bill," he believed that at least 190 souls should
come aboard, and he had informed the secretary that if any of the captured
prizes were to be manned and sent in, the number must necessarily jump to
well over 200.[6] The secretary of the navy, William Jones, did not share his
optimism; when Joseph sailed on 18 February 1814, he left with only the
allotted numbers. Bainbridge was financially strapped with a young wife, a
child "on the stocks," as he put it, and steadily mounting debts. He needed
to bring in as many prizes as he possibly could without weakening his ship.
Joseph was content, however, because, with his older brother William's
enthusiastic assistance, he was the first of the captains of the six new sloops
of war to be set loose upon the ocean. Bainbridge was ordered to cruise southward to the Gulf Stream, staying well to the eastward of Bermuda en route,
touching off the islands of St. Thomas, Puerto Rico, Santo Domingo, and
the western approaches to Cuba and Jamaica. He was then to circumnavigate the Gulf of Mexico in search of fat English West-Indiamen. After
touching first at the now familiar Balize, the *Frolic* was to cruise briefly off
Mobile and Pensacola, trace the entire coastline of Spanish Florida with its
wake, and then proceed as far north as the Carolinas. Bainbridge was either
to await further instructions while off Savannah, or possibly cruise alongside
the *Rattlesnake* and the *Enterprize*, which, he was told in strict confidence,
ought by then to be sharing these same coastal latitudes.[7]

Three sails were observed from the masthead on the first afternoon the
fleet-of-foot *Frolic* took "her revels on the ocean." Bainbridge instantly
tacked in chase of the windward ship, hoping to snatch up the other two
leeward vessels soon afterward. His chase was the largest of the intriguing
trio, but it proved to be the worst possible choice. It was the swift, new

38-gun frigate *Junon,* a powerful, clean-bottomed English blockader. Fortunately, Bainbridge soon recognized that his quarry was a "large man of war" who seemed to be displaying an equally zealous interest in him. Bainbridge tacked ship and stood away from the Briton at 1:00 P.M., setting all sail "to the best advantage" in the freshening breeze, including for the first time even his lofty royals.[8] This alone, however, was not going to be enough to effect an escape; despite everyone's best efforts, the frigate still gained on the *Frolic.* By 2:00 P.M., the men of the *Frolic* were rapidly discharging hundreds of pounds of iron shot in the direction of their pursuer, not with their guns but with their hands. Dozens of barrels of coal and equal quantities of casked provisions soon followed the 32-pound round shot into the shallow recesses of Massachusetts Bay. Bainbridge's best bower anchor next splashed over the starboard side, as the boatswain "came up the lee rigging fore and aft." Even these drastic measures had little noticeable effect. Only when Bainbridge ordered large portions of his valuable freshwater stocks pumped into the sea did the lightened sloop finally pull ahead of the big frigate. By 7:00 P.M., the *Junon* gave up its chase and bore away into the thickening fog.[9]

At 11:00 A.M. on the morning of 24 February, the wind suddenly increased without warning, proving to be just as potentially dangerous to the sloop as the British. Before the staysails and flying jib could be taken in, the fore topmast and the main topgallant mast were carried away with a rending double crack, flinging three of Bainbridge's best foretopmen into the sea, drowning one of them.[10] The meandering southern trek continued. On 12 March, in the midst of their first live-fire exercise, the *Frolic* "struck a dolphin."[11] At 6:00 A.M. on the seventeenth, the officer of the watch observed a phantom light blinking far ahead in the darkness. At daylight, a small sail appeared two points off the starboard bow, in the direction of the mysterious light. Within four hours, Bainbridge took possession of his first prize of the war. The English merchant brig *Little Fox* had sailed out of St. Johns some seventeen days before, carrying a cargo of fish and lumber to the island of Tobago. Bainbridge shifted aboard dried cod, casks of salted beef, and ship's stores of every description, including every precious drop of fresh Newfoundland water. He set the *Little Fox* ablaze at 6:00 P.M., and the cargo of pine and cedar boards burned throughout the night.[12] At 8:30 on the morning of 29 March, with a gentle breeze wafting in from over the lush, easternmost landfall of the island of Cuba, Captain Bainbridge and his officers observed, to their collective astonishment, a large schooner standing out from the coast in earnest pursuit of them. As the stranger neared, the crew of the *Frolic* made out the long tier of gun ports and an upper deck close packed with well-armed black- and brown-skinned men. It was a pirate, and it had mistaken the *Frolic* for a fat Yankee trader. "At 9 received a shot from her [and] called all hands to quarters & cleared ship for action." Keeping his silently grinning men out of sight behind their own tightly shut port lids, Bainbridge eagerly awaited the onslaught. One of his junior officers recalled the morning:

> At [?] past 9 neared us & received her shot several times. At 20 minutes past 10 we opened our fire upon her which was kept up until 11, when they called for quarters being in a sinking condition. Hailed and ordered him under our lee quarter, lowered down the third cutter and sent her along side. She proved to be a privateer under Carthagenian colors, but on examining her papers &c, we were in[clined] to believe her a pirate. At [?] past 11, she filling very [fast], we got a hawser aboard & m[ade] fast, hauled her along s[ide] & in 5 minutes she went d[own]. Fortunately, none of our crew [were] wounded. . . . Between 20 & thirty Carthagenians were killed or wounded, the wounded went down in the schooner. The Com[man]d[er] of her in the action with 5 or 6 men went off in her jolly boat.[13]

The *Frolic* suffered no casualties in the action and, according to its captain, received only "very triffling" damage.[14] The schooner was considerably smaller than the *Frolic* and must therefore have carried much lighter guns, and fewer of them. Realizing his costly error in judgment, the schooner's captain must have made the fight a running one. He also knew that a hangman's noose awaited any captured pirate (at least at the hands of the British), and so he had no choice but to fight on desperately until the bitter end. By definition, a pirate was an armed vessel acting the role of privateersman but without the benefit of an official governmental sanction, the letter of marque. Because broadsides should not have taken forty minutes to subdue the rabble, the *Frolic*'s gunnery probably had performed rather poorly. Either sensitive to potential criticism or unaware of the time it took, Bainbridge reported that the schooner surrendered "after a few minutes."[15] That the pirate captain was able to escape ashore entirely unmolested was amazing. Perhaps the *Frolic*'s rigging was not quite as pristine as its captain had implied. Bainbridge, however, did land thirty-one surviving buccaneers ashore and then sailed calmly away. By the end of the day, he could say with pride that he had sunk a pirate, and the morale of his now battle-hardened crew was higher than ever.

On 2 April Bainbridge observed a brig and a schooner lying suspiciously close to one another to windward. When the *Frolic* set every stitch of canvas to come up with them, the larger schooner abandoned its prize and flew effortlessly away over the windward horizon. The small merchant brig proved to be the *St. Quanifione,* bound out of and presumably belonging to New Orleans. It had been intercepted on its way to its destination, St. Jago de Cuba, by the armed schooner. The irate master reported that he had been detained very much against his will for eight seemingly endless days by this American privateer, the famed *Saucy Jack* of Charleston. During this time, the privateersmen had plundered his brig of two very valuable brass cannon and every bit of his ammunition. He had been released from his illegal confinement only because the *Frolic,* appearing to be a British cruiser, had hauled into view.[16] The next day, the *Frolic* boarded a diminutive English schooner belonging to the Grand Caymans.

It was Bainbridge's turn to play the pirate once again. He plundered it of everything valuable, including the entire cargo of live seaturtles. In addition, his crew broke up the decks for firewood before scuttling the schooner. The crew enjoyed the feast of fresh turtle, cooked hot with the very wood that had delivered them aboard.[17] The light western airs faded to a dead calm on 6 April, just as the *Frolic* was attempting the tricky Yucatan Channel into the Gulf of Mexico. The steadfast current slowly began to set the ship perilously in toward the westernmost tip of Cuba, and only the determined labor of the crew in the little armada of ship's boats kept the corvette away from the deadly shoals of Cape Corrientes. An uneventful three-day northwesterly passage brought the *Frolic* directly into the waters off the Mississippi Delta and Mobile Bay, bypassing the Mexican Gulf Coast entirely. After yet another fruitless week of tacking about in empty seas, the frustrated commander ran south to the Keys and then east through the Straits of Florida toward home.

Three strange sails first appeared in the *Frolic's* wake at just after five in the morning on 18 April 1814. The American corvette was then standing northeast through the Florida Straits with its starboard tacks aboard, working easily against a moderate easterly wind.[18] This cluster of canvas on the northwest horizon, two ships and a schooner, were, in order of importance, the British 36-gun frigate *Orpheus,* the 12-gun schooner *Shelbourne,* its consort, and an unidentified ship-rigged merchantman. The ever-alert Capt. Hugh Pigot of the *Orpheus* had, in turn, spotted the *Frolic* not long after daylight. "The cut of her sails soon shewed her to be a man of war," according to one of the English officers, "and [from] their whiteness, that she was

American."[19] As Bainbridge was deeply inquisitive as well, he tacked his ship to the southwest for a better look, while Master's Mate James Robinson hurried up to the fore-topmast trestle-trees to scrutinize the strangers, then over six miles away and safely to leeward. Satisfied that he had seen all that he was going to see for the immediate future, Robinson climbed back down to the foretop and informed Sailing Master Wright—who was then straining through his own spyglass at the *Orpheus* from his perch atop the foreyard—that the larger stranger was probably an armed letter of marque or a privateer. But at this point, he could not even be sure whether it was lying to or was under way.

Together, they watched the merchantman suddenly wear away to the northward, while the schooner dashed curiously behind the larger vessel as if, they thought, to hide. Both now agreed that the big sail was certainly a "cruiser," probably British, but no one dared to venture a guess at its force. Cautiously optimistic, Bainbridge ordered the *Frolic* to stand off and on for some time, waiting for the broad gap to close. This decision would prove fatal. Bainbridge could not yet tell whether the square-rigged stranger, at this time nearly bow on, was a ship—a vessel necessarily stronger than or, at best, equal to him in force—or a lesser brig, and his private signals, which had been flying all the while, continued to be ignored. Eventually Bainbridge "became suspicious that she was something superior" in force. At 7:30 A.M., when certainty had at last superseded surmise, Wright descended the fore shrouds, walked aft, and to the crew's collective horror, reported the strangers to be "a friggate and schooner in company." Normally, the swift-sailing *Frolic* could have easily out-weathered the slower frigate, but since the broad Florida Reef stood directly to windward, Bainbridge was forced to give up his corvette's greatest sailing advantage, for it was a fine, fast, and, above all, a weatherly ship. He instead stood down for the northern Cuban shore, not yet visible over the horizon, while the Britons tacked directly after him. Slowly and methodically, they began to forereach upon him. The hunter was now the hunted.

Acknowledging his error, Bainbridge endeavored to gain the hypothetical safety of Matanzas Bay. Whether the English captain would respect Spanish "neutrality" was iffy but worth a try. When the land appeared later that morning, Bainbridge saw that he was seven miles too far to the leeward of his destination. The *Orpheus*, a better sailer under the prevailing conditions, was now closing in on his lee, while the *Shelbourne* had already carved its way onto his weather quarter, crossing his wake. The uncooperative wind, shifting now more to the north, had combined with the westerly shore current to oppose an escape. With the frigate less than two miles off, the *Frolic* tacked once again and headed northwest by west. As they passed each other, the *Orpheus*, by now within pistol shot, fired its bow chaser. "There is a shot!" observed the first lieutenant needlessly, as the ball whistled overhead. "Let them fire!" dared the defiant Bainbridge, clearly worried. The *Orpheus* soon obliged him with a second round shot, producing a sudden white plume just twenty yards abreast the starboard main-chains. The wind began to freshen again, but even so, Bainbridge added the main, windward studding sails to the already dangerously overcrowded, drum-taut pyramids of canvas. The lee port sills were soon buried under a turbulent white foam, while the deck listed so steeply that it was becoming increasingly difficult to stand without support. Still the *Orpheus* gained. Bainbridge reluctantly called a council of his subordinates.

The *Frolic*'s officers all agreed that they must now lighten the ship of every item that they could get their hands on. All the unnecessary provisions had earlier gone into Cape Cod Bay, and these past two months of cruising had already consumed much of their remaining supplies. The vote cast that afternoon was unanimous. The eleven larboard guns, their muzzles already underwater, went over the side. They were followed immediately afterward by the four remaining anchors, all the shot on deck, the muskets, pistols, cutlasses, and the few remaining turtles. But even those herculean efforts were not enough. If they could not get away, they might perhaps deny the British possession of their beautiful new corvette. Had the shoreline been less rugged, claimed Bainbridge, for the "rough and craggy" vista was dotted with "perpendicular rocks," the *Frolic* might have been beached broadside on, fought to the last extremity with its remaining windward batteries, and then set afire after the crew had been safely ferried ashore. Lieutenant Armstrong, however, argued that the "the frigate was so near that we could not have got on shore, before we had been all cut to pieces." It appeared that duty called upon Bainbridge to run his command deliberately aground, but he was either unwilling or unable to do so.

The *Orpheus*, having tacked in hot pursuit, and then only slightly better than a quarter-mile astern, slowly squared away and prepared to deliver its full, raking broadside. Bainbridge hurriedly asked his distraught officers for their opinions. Lieutenant Armstrong spoke up first: "As we have tried to get clear by lightening, I think that it is prudent to haul the colors down." All the principal officers, making repeated nervous glances over the taffrail, were in immediate and total agreement. And so, "down went the 'star-spangled banner' and its stripes from the mizzen peak." Anarchy instantly broke out among the crew. Some men fought each other over their few private possessions below decks, while others broke into the spirit room and served themselves aplenty. Still mindful of their duty to deny everything possible to the enemy, several of the clearer-thinking warrant officers smashed the flintlocks of the remaining great guns and tossed over the side everything useful that came to hand, including the ensign that was struck. "The pursers store-room was next sacked; then the men got into the gun-room and the captain's cabin, and pillaged them." The ship "bore the semblance of a town given up to the pillage of soldiery."[20] Even Captain Pigot felt it unsafe to send his boarding party across during this melee. If the American captain could not restore order, he thought, he would. A single, harmless volley of marine musketry, fired well over their heads from the frigate's gangways, instantly checked the ruckus. The ship was then boarded and the prisoners secured.

This disgraceful state of affairs was alluded to only once during the December 1814 court-martial. Lieutenant Armstrong stated, "I thought the men somewhat confused after we commenced lightening, but the orders were all obeyed with as much promptitude by the *officers* as they possibly could be under the circumstances." He felt compelled, however, to amend his statement: "The men scuffled for their things, but there was no disobedience to orders." Armstrong failed to mention whether the enlisted men also obeyed their commands with the same steady promptitude.

Having heard the rumors that Bainbridge was "addicted to intoxication," the court felt compelled, for both the good of the service and for the sake of the good captain's reputation, to take the most unusual step of asking all the officers assembled if they knew anything about his alleged vice. Perhaps fearing professional retribution at the hands of the all-powerful William Bainbridge, every one of them denied, both before the court and in front of each other, not only the alleged vice but even having heard of the widespread rumor. Armstrong added, as an aside, that Bainbridge "would take his glass as other gentlemen." Commo. John Rodgers, then the navy's most senior officer, evaluated Joseph Bainbridge in 1815 for the incoming secretary, Benjamin Crowninshield: "Captain Bainbridge, *the junior,* I do not think qualified for any command, as I have reason to believe him intemperate, and I am induced to mention this that you may be guarded against giving [him] a command *at sea.*"[21] He never received another.

Neither Captain Bainbridge nor any of his junior officers ever reported the exact latitude or longitude of the *Frolic* at the beginning of the chase. Bainbridge described himself as "being in the Florida Passage and being equidistant from Matanzas and Havannah at half past 5 A.M."[22] But this is questionable. The *Orpheus* reported its position at twenty-four degrees, twelve minutes north latitude and eighty-one degrees, twenty-five minutes west longitude at the start of the encounter.[23] It was therefore to the eastward, and thus to the windward, of both of these Cuban ports. Indeed, the *Orpheus* had spotted the *Frolic* even farther to the eastward of itself, a relative position that American accounts later confirmed. Had Bainbridge properly identified the *Orpheus* early on, instead of standing leisurely off to the southwest until the frigate, by one estimate, was within one and a quarter miles of him, he could have easily reached Matanzas in time, it still being then to leeward. How he could have allowed the stodgy old frigate, "who was but an indifferent sailor" and whose copper was foul from over a year of blockading, to outsail one of the quickest corvettes then afloat, and even to permit the Englishmen to wrest the weather-gauge from him, is astounding. At the time of the court-martial, however, not all the facts were known. The court exonerated Bainbridge, of course, and further praised his "cool and collected" demeanor. He had done his utmost to prevent capture, they concluded, and he unquestionably possessed every courage becoming an officer and a gentleman. Needing something to say against the British in order to end the court-martial with some perceived advantage, the officers concluded: "It has been proved by the court that the enemy fired a volley of musketry into the Frolic after the colors were struck."

The British thought the American surrender was not only tame but also disgraceful.[24] Bainbridge was called a coward for not making even a token show of resistance. The *Frolic* still had all of its guns when the *Orpheus* opened its brief fire. Bainbridge's two chase guns, long 18-pounders of considerable range, could have been shifted to fire out of any gun port, and therefore in nearly any direction. Even though the breeze was fresh, the frigate wore its royals and studding sails; a lucky shot could have had dramatic results. For the sake of honor alone, Bainbridge probably should have tried it. He might at least have turned on the frail *Shelbourne*, formerly the *Racer*, a slight-of-frame Baltimore blockade runner cut out of the Chesapeake the year before, from whose popguns he had nothing to fear. Since one well-placed broadside might have put it in a sinking condition (after all, the *Frolic*'s crew had hands-on experience in sinking small schooners), he might have thus effected his escape while the *Orpheus* was forced to heave to and rescue the schooner's crew. The *Orpheus* was of the same force relative to the *Frolic* as the latter was to the sunken pirate. Considering the desperate, even manly, resistance offered by those mere "Carthagenian privateers," even a single, token shot of resistance would have traveled far indeed for the preservation of Joseph Bainbridge's honor and reputation.

Thanks to Joseph Bainbridge, however, a full description of the *Frolic*'s seagoing characteristics, and thus to a great degree the *Wasp*'s also, survives in the British archives.[25] The Royal Navy had always maintained a particular interest in their numerous multinational prizes, and this curiosity had not waned by the time they examined the swift and beautiful *Frolic*. The Charlestown sloop rode passively enough at its anchors, observed the English dockyard officials in their detailed sailing report, and it stood remarkably stiff under sail and behaved unusually "easy" in the trough of a sea. Easy, they noted, but not dry. The Admiralty had always thought the flush-decked ship design inherently unsafe, and the *Frolic* was no exception. It carried its lee ports far too low for English tastes. This damp state of affairs must have been sorely magnified in the *Wasp*, since the *Frolic* was always lightly laden in British service (transport and coast guard assignments only), never carrying more than twelve guns and rarely taking on enough provisions to draw better than fourteen feet of water aft.

The American corvettes pitched "very little" and were, generally speaking, easy ships. They carried their helms well, but generally slacker than most English ships. Furthermore, their "harder than usual" although conversely "easy" steering was attributed to their ingenious goosenecked tillers. The *Frolic* stayed well when in exact trim and behaved "very well" in laying to, but it was considered long in wearing. By the log, with as much wind as it could "safely" bear under single reefed topsails and topgallant sails alone, the *Frolic* had run a respectable eight knots, six fathoms, close-hauled in smooth water. Likewise, under double-reefed topsails, it had run off nine and two, respectively, in a "contrary sea." On one occasion, while running large and under all sail that could "properly" be set, it had dashed a fantastic thirteen-plus knots off the reel. Likewise, it had run a solid eleven directly before the wind. The *Frolic* was never chased, nor in turn did it ever chase anyone during its peaceful English service, so these numbers must be considered conservative. The *Frolic*, and therefore also the *Wasp*, had no single best point of sailing. They were both remarkable "off the wind in any direction." The *Frolic*'s captors observed that it could store only three months' provisions under its hatches with what they termed "convenience." But that was its only drawback. According to its Admiralty report, the *Frolic* beat every ship that challenged it off the wind. They reckoned it was unusually strong, "very well built and finished," and they marveled at the stout materials put into its "fine frame."

Mstr. Comdt. Lewis Warrington had had an opportunity to put another of the *Wasp*'s sister-sloops, the *Peacock*, through its paces earlier in the year

in New York's spacious harbor. His ship had been modified from the original plan in most of the same ways as had its two Massachusetts cousins, and,
because all three were sparred identically, Warrington's comments are also
relevant to the performance of Blakeley's command. In January 1814, Warrington had agreed to try his ship against "a fast sailing privateer schooner,"
the quickest type of vessel that Yankee ingenuity and private enterprise
could produce. He whipped it solidly:

> [The Peacock] works quick and close, is very weatherly, stands stiff on
> her legs, and moves fast through the water. In turning to windward in
> this narrow channel, the schooner necessarily had the advantage, and
> soon gained our wake, but we quickly discovered that we invariably
> forereached her when on the same tack, and beat her also with ease
> going large—we beat to the tail of the west bank, and returned, when
> we anchored some time before the schooner.[26]

Warrington was so very proud of this contest that he would later brag of it to
his British prisoners. While escorting his prize, the *Cruiser*-class brig *Epervier*, into Savannah, Warrington had easily outrun two English frigates, one
of which was Blakeley's old nightmare, the razee *Majestic*.[27] Warrington at
length concluded that his mizzen topsail and topgallant sail were of "no use"
at all to him. He could not make them set upon a wind by any means, for the
main topsail apparently overlapped them far too much. He believed that a
spartan, pole topmast, upon which he could occasionally set a flying mizzen
topgallant sail, would be far more serviceable. In fact, British intelligence
would actually report the *Peacock* cruising off the African coast "bark-rigged"
in the fall of 1814, this being by definition entirely without square sails on the
mizzen.[28] Warrington was an anathema to Commodore Bainbridge, who
preferred oversparring every stick belonging to the aftermost mast. Warrington tested out his theories one last time before he set out in earnest:

> We worked the ship without the mizzen topsail, substituting for it the
> gaff topsail, which is large, and answered so well, that I shall never think
> of using a square sail on the mizzen mast except when the wind is a
> beam [*sic*] or four points free. . . . I have just heard of the sailing of the
> Frolic, which I hoped to have left in port, as my great wish has been to
> be the first sloop out.[29]

Blakeley had his hands full on the *Wasp*. Not only did he have to get his crew
in tip-top shape, he also had to learn the intricacies of how best to maneuver his ship on the ocean seas. He also had to visualize possible scenarios

when ships were sighted and how best to handle these encounters. His years of training were finally being put to the test. The *Wasp*'s lookouts sighted several strange sails soon after leaving Portsmouth. The first, illuminated by the pleasant midafternoon sun on their second day at sea, appeared fine on the larboard bow standing peacefully to the south-southwest. But it was too far aweather for Blakeley to take any serious interest. The second sail, observed one point on the weather bow two hours later, suddenly hauled to the northwest and revealed itself as a ship, in all probability a heavy blockader. Blakeley did not bother with it either. A third suspicious sail, apparently a schooner and therefore most likely a merchantman of unknown nationality, was discovered at 5:00 A.M. on the following day. Blakeley set his broad main course and tacked to the northwest in pursuit. He chased it throughout the day, but by 4:00 P.M., a squall struck the ship and Blakeley was forced to reduce canvas. The heavy sea, the "rain at intervals," the approaching darkness, and the split fore topsail all conspired to conceal any trace of the schooner. At just after sunset, Blakeley wore ship to the southward and reluctantly "gave up the chase." It was a good exercise for the crew, Blakeley consoled himself, for they really had needed it. That brief storm, mild by Blakeley's standards, had already taken its toll. "She has now," recalled Midshipman House, "a complement . . . so green, that is, so unaccustomed to the sea, that they were seasick for a week."[30]

Most of the younger sailors hailed from Newburyport or its immediate environs and their average age was twenty-three. Six of the forty-seven men rated as able seamen were married and came from Massachusetts. Probably older than average, they may have had more experience and traveled farther than the common bachelor sailor in pursuit of a living for themselves and their families. Twelve dollars a month was considered an attractive salary in the blockaded New England of 1814. Two of these hard-working husbands lived their entire lives in nearby Marblehead. Able Seaman Joseph Atkins was getting a little too old to haul upon a rope; he had married Sarah Jones in 1798. Probably in his early to mid-thirties at this time, quite ancient for a mariner before the mast, he had two daughters, Betty, aged eleven, and the infant Ambrose. Between their distant births were twins, Joseph and Thomas, aged five.[31] Fellow Marbleheader David Brindlecomb was probably close in age to Atkins and had six good reasons for going off to sea: his wife, also named Sarah, and his children, David Jr., John, Hannah, Thomas, and little Sarah.[32]

Robert Lowther had married his beloved Hannah in their native Cumberland Island, a small community located near Portland, Maine, in 1798 and had three children, at least two of them girls.[33] Although Able Seaman Joseph Phippen of Salem had married somewhat more recently, in late 1803, he nevertheless managed to rack up a substantial brood. His wife, Nabby, brought forth Abigail, Mary, Rebecca, Joseph, and Margaret, aged nine, eight, six, five, and one, respectively, into the world since that time, and they all needed to be fed. Therefore Joseph went happily off to war. He was an elite among the foremast hands; he was also rated captain's coxswain, a position that meant far more professional prestige, if not additional money.[34] William Stone, an experienced navy seaman, had no children, either with his late wife, Polly, whom he had married in 1802 in the First Church of Christ in his native Ipswich, or from his second wife, Mary, from the same congregation.[35]

Seaman Francis Brown was the newlywed of the bunch. He had married Charlotte Kendall in Boston almost exactly one year before. Concerned that Francis would not be able to provide for his daughter by fishing the heavily blockaded coast, Benjamin Kendall took Francis aside and went over the options. Francis must provide for Charlotte. Period. Apparently Mr. Kendall's vocation as a master "cord wainer," or ropemaker, did not sound too appealing to Francis, nor did that of Charlotte's brother, stone-cutter John Kendall. At length they decided that the best prospects for their son/brother-in-law lay with the navy. There was always the potential financial windfall if the right English prizes were taken. With this in mind, both Benjamin and John escorted Francis to the Newburyport rendezvous, where the elder Kendall "stood his surety," allowing him to receive his advances in pay and slops. Francis signed up under the assumed name of Andrew Passenger, he would later explain to his father-in-law, merely for "personal reasons."[36]

Although many of the warrant officers and their respective mates were acting only in their current professional capacities, the *Wasp* bore the great distinction of being more densely populated with officers—about one in seven—than any other American ship during the war.[37] One such "officer" was Gideon Bartlett, boatswain's mate. Like so many of the others, this middle-aged Newburyport native had signed on board the *Wasp* purely out of financial necessity. Patriotism and a yearning for glory were not upper-most in his mind. His father, Stephen Bartlett, a local shopkeeper of note, had died suddenly in early 1811, leaving his financial affairs in total disarray. Showing great responsibility, Gideon quickly signed the bulk of his wages, a hefty eighteen dollars per month, over to his wife, who was then expecting the birth of their first child. Gideon had married Mary Perkins Anderson during the previous November under the direction of John Giles, the minister of Newburyport's Second Presbyterian Society.[38] The Bartlett name, a proud one dating back to the arrival of the *Mayflower*, was well known to Johnston Blakeley. Local shipmaster Josiah Bartlett, an enterprising uncle to Gideon, had made a substantial fortune smuggling English contraband down from Canada, both during the war and the embargo.[39] Another distant relative, Gideon's great-uncle Enoch Bartlett, was not only a successful shipmaster and an affluent businessman but also a famed amateur horticulturist.[40] Gideon, however, was sharing in none of the family riches, so he went happily off to sea.

Gideon's immediate boss, Boatswain Joseph Martin, was the most valuable man on board. His job was both the management of the complexities of the ship's rigging and the maintenance of discipline over all those required to haul, belay, or climb upon it. Martin had served continuously in the navy since 1799, which was only slightly longer than had Captain Blakeley. Having rounded the Cape of Good Hope to Batavia and back in Capt. Edward Preble's *Essex* during the Quasi-War with France, he had just recently returned to Boston in the frigate *Chesapeake* following Samuel Evans's financially lucky 1812–13 cruise. But the prize monies, including his share of the captured British ship *Volunteer*, whose cargo alone was estimated at several hundred thousand dollars, had yet to be paid out. Therefore his wife, Elizabeth, supported his decision to keep on sailing in the service of his country; she needed his steady twenty dollars per month. They had no children, but were supporting Elizabeth's aged and infirm mother in their Cumberland Island home.[41]

Even though not all of the men came from Newburyport proper, the popular legend of the *Wasp* as a warship manned almost exclusively by New Englanders began. For the most part correct, with the important exception of the bulk of its commissioned officers, the *Wasp* bore a large proportion of its unintentional namesakes, the White Anglo-Saxon Protestants. Victorian historian John Spears wrote an enthusiastic description of their collective qualities:

> And as for the crew they were to a man Americans and almost all of them Yankees—the typical New Englander whose drawling nasal style of speech has for time out of mind served English writers with an abundant source of amusement. That they talked about the "keows" and the "kritters" need not be doubted. They were young hay-makers and wood-choppers—very likely more than half of them were from the farms. . . .

But that some of them had looked through the sights of a rifle at running deer, to the destruction of the deer is also certain, as will appear farther on, and the back that could swing a scythe could lend vigor to the stroke of a cutlass or the lunge of a boarding pike. They were not only good physically but mentally. They were from the "deestrict" schools, on one hand, and from the "teown meetin" on the other—they had common school educations, and they were independent minded voters, while the traditions which their fathers had told them before the wide fireplaces of their log cabin homes were of the deeds done along the shore by British naval officers, beginning with that of the infamous Mowatt when nearby Portland (Falmouth) was burned in winter.[42]

On the afternoon of 4 May, with the New England coast now far astern, Captain Blakeley ordered what would be the first of several critical live-fire exercises.[43] Those few hands not still leaning over the lee bulwarks or lying prostrate in the sick berth were already dutifully employed resetting and repairing the rigging, restowing provisions, and performing the countless other "sundry" tasks required of a new man-of-war. Blakeley confined this first exercise to musketry, utilizing only the marines and topmen, collectively known as the fourth division, under the able direction of the acting marine officer, Corp. James Swetser, and the acting gunner, Andrew Flagg. Commodore Bainbridge had seen to it that the *Wasp* was issued fifty .69 caliber sea-service muskets, all described as "brass mounted" and costing a hefty $12.50 apiece. These maple-stocked muskets, endowed with the more expensive brass furniture, were the very best of naval small arms, normally reserved exclusively for the marines.[44] In this one acquisition, at least, Blakeley was far more fortunate than his competitors. Lewis Warrington was greatly displeased with the *Peacock*'s small arms. He later learned, to his growing indignation, that every one of the iron-fixtured muskets supplied to his sloop at New York had earlier been rejected by the army. After capturing the British *Epervier*, Warrington swapped all sixty of his "standard-issue" small arms for the forty-five good English Tower Muskets found on board the brig.[45] In this case, he thought, less is more. In addition, Bainbridge had issued the crew of the *Wasp* forty pair of boarding pistols from the same Boston vendor at the same price per set.[46] The *Wasp* also carried 100 pounds of lead musket balls, 50 pounds of pistol balls, 112 pounds of buckshot, and one thousand spare flints.[47]

The ninth of May by sea had begun pleasantly enough, but by early the following morning the *Wasp* was forging ahead through deep swells under double-reefed topsails and drum-taut storm staysails alone. Beneath a sky that flashed with incessant lightning and resounded with angry trailing reports, the lookout spied a distant white fleck, far away on the weather beam. But it was rightly ignored, the seas being then far too unpleasant for a chase. The weather the next day grew into "heavy gales and a heavy sea, [with] the gundeck constantly under water, [and] the hatches battened down fore and aft." The worst damage, discovered the following morning, was two parted main shrouds. Having no spare rigging stores on board of appropriate girth, Blakeley reluctantly ordered one of his valuable hawsers (each 120 fathoms long and between four and five inches in diameter) hauled up on deck from the cable tier and cut into makeshift standing rigging.[48]

The nineteenth of May was brilliantly clear, with both the air and the water measuring a balmy 66 degrees. Just after daybreak, the watch on deck shook out the reefs from the topsails, hoping to coax a little more thrust from these calmer, dryer airs. They were followed soon after by the long-neglected topgallants, and even the lofty royals were drawing by the forenoon watch. At the meridian, Captain Blakeley beheld his beautiful new command in all its pristine glory for the first time. Its holystoned decks were now clear of casks and coils, its falls neatly flemished and channels finally free of the unsettled masses. Untold fathoms of Plymouth cordage ran through Boston blocks, reining in the rippling white curtains of Watertown canvas suspended, in turn, from the best Merrimack pine. It was the quintessential Yankee *Wasp*! At long last, his corvette was carrying its engines of destruction with all possible dispatch toward the vulnerable home waters of the enemy. After nearly two years of frustration and delay, Johnston Blakeley was finally in his true element. As there was still much work to be done in the martial line, the acting drummer (the supernumerary drummer and fifer having both quit in Portsmouth) beat the call to quarters. There would be live firing today.

Although rated at a mere eighteen guns, the *Wasp* could actually mount twenty-two heavy broadside cannon. It was not quite as powerful, however, as its designers had intended. Blakeley's pair of long 18-pounders had never arrived from Connecticut and he made do instead with long 12s, shipped up with "carriages and implements complete" from Midshipman Bonneville's old guard-ship, the *Alert*.[49] Even worse, Blakeley had been forced to sail from Portsmouth with only nineteen of his twenty promised carronades, reluctantly taking on board a third long 12-pounder to fill the empty port.[50] He was lucky to get even these. As late as 21 February, a week before his sailing from the Merrimack, ten of his carronades still lay at the Boston wharves.[51] The *Frolic,* as expected, had sailed with its complete battery.[52] The carronade was a lightweight naval howitzer that had revolutionized sea gunnery a generation before. For the weight of a conventional long 9-pounder, a lowly sloop of war might now bear a gun that could heave a 32-pound round shot up to a thousand yards. This English invention, also known as the "smasher," was quickly embraced by the U.S. Navy. These short-range weapons had transformed the small *Wasp* and its English counterparts into the proverbial eggshells armed with hammers.

The transportation bottleneck by land could not alone account for the scarcity of these powerful guns. So flawed with air pockets and internal cracks were the first wartime production carronades cast in Havre de Grace, Maryland, that half of the twenty 32-pounders made for the new sloop of war *Erie* burst when its commander, Charles Ridgely, test-fired them. One gun, proof-charged with five pounds of powder, three wads, and two shot, exploded into thirty jagged components that flew for hundreds of yards in all directions.[53]

The naval establishment of September 1813 had allowed sixty round shot, forty stand of grape (a dozen plum-sized iron balls clustered together), and twenty canister shot for each carronade mounted on board an American sloop of war. For each long gun, the navy provided one hundred, forty, and zero such shot, respectively, in addition to five double-headed or bar shot apiece and generous quantities of specialized "dismantling" shot.[54] The round shot supplied to the *Wasp,* and to most other New England ships and coastal fortifications, came by way of contractor Bartlett Murdock. Before the war, Murdock had allegedly stoked the furnace as a common "illiterate" molder in a Plymouth iron foundry. But "by a little noise and bluster," complained an admittedly biased competitor, this vendor had "raised himself into the favor of similar characters," presumably meaning Bainbridge and Binney. Instead of casting his shot himself, Murdock had purchased inferior quality cannonballs at every less-than-reputable furnace in the region. His cheap shot had reportedly been cast in sand instead of in the proper iron molds. Such unfit projectiles tended to deform when heated and shattered upon impact. They were thus the suspected cause of many a burst cannon. For this reason, the European powers had ceased using sand-cast balls long since. The very first shot fired in anger during the War of 1812 was a 24-pound ball delivered from the USS *President* into the stern of HBM frigate *Belvedera.* It proved to be "of [such] bad quality, [that] it split into about 50 pieces," recalled one of the British lieutenants. The same chase-gun exploded on its third discharge for quite possibly this same reason, killing and wounding scores of men, including, in the latter category, Commo. John Rodgers. Murdock himself admitted that "the shot made are not large enuf" and that even though "they aut to way" 32, 24, and 18 pounds, they in fact weighed, when delivered to the navy, at best 30 3/4, 21 3/4, and 7 1/4, respectively.[55] Blakeley complained that the particular specimens delivered to the *Wasp* were even worse by far. The heaviest example that he could find in his shot locker weighed only 30 1/4 pounds, with the vast majority weighing considerably less.[56]

The American practice of multiple shotting a single discharge worsened the odds of catastrophic failure. "The Constitution fired from her carronades," reported Thomas Tingey, "two round shot [at] each discharge during the entire battle with the Guerriere," in addition to the grape and canister. The initial broadside fired from the main deck guns of the USS *Chesapeake* into the side of HBMS *Shannon* were quadruple-shotted: one each of round, grape, canister, and bar and chain.[57] Although, miraculously, none of the American guns burst, few of the *Chesapeake*'s projectiles managed to pass completely through the Briton's sides. Tingey also made a poignant remark about the wineglass-shaped barshot: "This did great execution aboard the Guerriere, [and] the enemy complained much of their effect," he bragged. "One double headed shot cut her foremast about one third off." The British later reported that, in addition to bar and chain shot, the *Wasp* carried a mysterious item known as "swan shot." This may have been another name for "star shot," five forged bars that expanded in flight about a central ring, meant to dismantle the enemy's rigging. "Chain shot" consisted of these same long bars linked end to end, utilized for the same purpose.

This was Andrew Flagg's first tour as a full-fledged gunner. Even though he was only acting in this capacity—like seemingly everyone else on board—he was nevertheless determined to prove himself before his captain's critical eye. Flagg was now becoming used to new responsibilities. He had just recently wed his young bride, Lucy, in their native Portsmouth, and had received the most precious of New Year's Eve gifts, little Louisa Chase Flagg. The gunner of a sloop of war was responsible for more varied and complex pieces of equipment than any other warrant officer aboard. Aside from the great guns themselves, Andrew Flagg maintained all the small arms, the powder, shot and armorers stores, along with such other miscellaneous items as the ship's thirty fire buckets, twenty blue lights, twelve sky rockets, two boarding grapnels with chains, sixty pair of handcuffs, fifty pair of footcuffs, and the fife and the drum, the latter complete with four spare heads. Flagg's department was even responsible for the one hundred pounds of soap used to clean and lubricate the tiller ropes. His two assistants, Quarter-Gunners John Martin (no relation to Joseph Martin) and James Manley, were native Newburyporters; both were married but neither had children. Martin was probably older, having married in August 1802, while Manley had wed only days before the ship sailed.[58]

While the exercised great guns returned to the tackles of their confinement, the topgallants and royals did not. So calm were the postmeridian hours that Blakeley employed his people staying the masts, including even setting up the fore topgallant shrouds and rigging, with all these lofty sails still gloriously set. Although the early morning was somewhat "squally with rain" and the night watch "made and took in sail occasionally," the royals remained spread majestically throughout, barely drawing upon the breeze. Only the odd speck of canvas spotted on the starboard, weather bow at 8:00 A.M. occasioned their furling. They were followed quickly afterward by the fore course and the trio of topgallants as the *Wasp* stripped down to fighting canvas. The nearing stranger's long tier of ports soon identified it as a large sloop of war of the *Wasp*'s class. Although the tricolor snapped high overhead, Blakeley kept his cannoneers at their batteries. But French it was:

> At 10 hove to & sent our boat on board, she proved to be the French National Brig Olivia from L'Orient bound to New York with dispatches for our government, she gave us the following information, that Bonaparte had abdicated the throne of France at the request of the people and had retired to the Island of Elba in the Mediterranean, that the house of Bourbon was again reinstated that Louis the 18th had left his [exile?] for France and it is the General belief is crowned ere this time, that the King of Prussia, the Emperor of Russia & Crown Prince of Sweden were in Paris that Lords Liverpool & Milne on the part of Great Britain were in Parris [*sic*] engaging in amicable negotiation that British officers in the ports of France visiting on shore [were] amicably treated.[59]

This news presented the very real possibility that no French port would remain open to them in case of emergency. This *Olive* was an unwelcome branch of peace. Recalling that his orders had required him to inform the secretary of his progress at every reasonable opportunity, Blakeley hastily penned off a brief note: "I have the honor to report this ship to you, all [is] well." Conveniently forgetting the four unknown vessels spotted off the Grand Banks, he added: "The French National Brig Olive which carries this is the only vessel we have spotted since our departure from Portsmouth, N.H."[60] But there was indeed something to be proud of. His "tolerable" crew had gained their sea legs and they were now growing intimate with both the handling of the sails and the firing of the great guns. Midshipman Geisinger reported that the crew was in very good health on this day, with one man only on the sick list. He attributed their fine state to the captain's generous practice of allowing two quarts of fresh water to each man every day. On 24 May the masthead sighted the island of Corro, the nearest of the Azores. As these waters were a frequent path not only for England's merchantmen but also for its heavy cruisers, Blakeley ordered the month's remaining days spent exercising the batteries. All the while, he kept a vigilant lookout for the distant topsails of the enemy. He would find them very soon.

The other sloops of war, which had aggressively competed against the *Wasp* for America's scant naval stores, would have their share of troubles during the summer of 1814. Noted builder Thomas Kemp had agreed to launch the two Baltimore corvettes, the *Erie* and *Ontario*, by 15 August and 25 October, respectively. William Doughty was not completely satisfied with his initial clipper draft, however; no sooner was a copy sent to Baltimore than he suffered a change of heart concerning the trio's lines. But Kemp was too far advanced on his first sloop by the time the new drafts were finalized, so Doughty allowed him to proceed on uninterrupted. Doughty's pet *Argus* was built upon the new lines, however, and, in order to expedite the alterations to the second Maryland sloop, Doughty shipped his complete set of molds from the Washington Navy Yard as soon as his own frames were completed, "to save [Mr. Kemp] much trouble and labor."[61] Not that it mattered. Both sloops sat out the war blockaded in Baltimore, destined never to fire a shot in anger, while the new *Argus* suffered a more sanguinary fate. Afloat at the wharf, with all its armament and equipment aboard (minus only sails, provisions, powder, and, of course, crew), Capt. John Orde Creighton lit a heap of oil-soaked combustibles piled high below its decks in September 1814 to prevent its capture by the invading British.[62] Due to its hastily seasoned wartime timbers, the *Erie* lasted only until 1821, when she was broken up and entirely rebuilt to a slightly longer variation on the same theme. The popular *Ontario*, once described as "a light o' keel, rakish rover of a craft," remained in active service until 1856, due in no small part to a last-minute substitution of select Honduran mahogany, part of an English cargo taken by a local privateer, for a major portion of its frame.

It took some time for the still frail and pallid George Parker to clean up his new command after Joseph Bainbridge's tenure. The *Syren* required major repairs before it could become seaworthy once again, and the scarcity of replacement cannon in Boston confounded him. Captain Bainbridge had left behind all but eight or ten of his original 24-pounder carronades somewhere back in the Balize, and now there was none of like caliber to be found anywhere. Commodore Bainbridge thought that perhaps it might mount at least part of the *Alert*'s battery of long 12-pounders as replacements, but soon found that the sharp little brig could not bear them. A half-dozen long-9s were eventually rounded up and successfully mounted, but now it was too weak to defend itself against even a middling foe. At length, two enormous 42-pounder carronades were dredged up and mounted amidships, requiring a considerable amount of reinforcement to the deck and bulwarks.[63] Still, the *Syren* managed to sail from Boston well ahead of the *Wasp*, and at long last, the increasingly ill George Parker was free to prove his own merits. Given the best possible opportunity for cruising, he was bound to the Indian Ocean with orders to capture the obscenely wealthy ships of the British East India and China trades. There was a fortune to be made by an intelligent and energetic officer. Off the coast of Africa, the *Syren* made a few minor captures, but it never made it around the Cape of Good Hope. On 12 July 1814 it was taken by the 74-gun *Medway* after a chase of eleven hours on a wind, during which time all of its hard-won cannon were thrown over the side. Parker was spared the mortification of seeing his colors come down, however; he had died alone in his cabin only days after putting to sea.

The *Rattlesnake*, a beautiful privateer-built brig, privately constructed in Boston on the model of the popular *Argus*, had to scrounge for its mixed bag of cannon as well, but it too followed the *Syren* and *Frolic* into their watery realm well ahead of Blakeley's slighted Newburyport corvette. It cruised for a while in company with the *Enterprize* off the Carolinas, and when the *Frolic* failed to appear, it then proceeded away on its own. It was soon spied by a British frigate, however, and a long chase ensued. Only after throwing overboard all of its guns but two did the *Rattlesnake* effect its escape. Knowing that his lost cannon could not be replaced at home, Cdr. John Orde Creighton instead made a bold dash across the Atlantic, in hopes of refitting in L'Orient. But a passing neutral informed him of the peace and of the requisite French neutrality.[64] Even though there could be no French cannon available to him in L'Orient, Creighton probably should have continued on, which Blakeley did after receiving essentially the same news in midocean. Two guns were enough to confound most merchantmen. Creighton did make a few bold attacks upon at least one armed British convoy, and he had managed to cut one or two unwary fellows out of it before heading home. But just as the *Rattlesnake* came to within sight of its native soil on 22 June

1814, it was set upon in rough weather by the 58-gun frigate *Leander*. After a chase lasting nearly seventeen hours, during which time its two remaining guns and just about everything else that came to hand were thrown into the sea, Commander Creighton struck his colors in proper turn.[65] Of the four sloops of war fitted out in Massachusetts by William Bainbridge, only the intrepid *Wasp*, so long resigned to the proverbial backwater, would remain safely out of British hands by summer's end.

14. The Carnage Was Dreadful

June 1814

The great gale was well on into its third meridian when the strange sail appeared through the flying sheets of tepid rain.[1] Over the course of the previous two days, the *Wasp* had furled most of its square sails tight up against the yards and had once again bent in their place the heavy, fore-and-aft storm staysails. The bundled light weather canvas, normally stowed safely in the tops, had already come down on deck to ease the strain, along with the trio of topgallant masts. All the while, the emergency hawser shrouds strained taut under the pressure from even these close-reefed sails. Although ordinarily mere survival was the accepted goal in such weather, at 9:00 A.M. on 3 June 1814 the impatient captain set the topsails, albeit close-reefed, and wore in chase of the enticing stranger, then visible only on the top of the rise on the east-northeast horizon. Johnston Blakeley had been just over a month at sea, and now it was time to take his first prize, no matter the risk.

By 1:00 P.M. the breeze had abated somewhat, and with the rain mostly gone, Captain Blakeley ordered a solitary reef turned out of the courses and the spanker, while at the same time he adorned the now uppermost standing rigging with still further scraps of canvas, the drum-taut, triangular topmast staysails. Paying no heed to the 12-pounder's rumbling 2:00 P.M. introduction, the chase pressed on to the westward. The American corvette wore once again, set its broad main course, let another reef out of its topsails, and began to race dangerously along after the barque-rigged stranger, at this hour still hull up but progressing farther away on the weather bow. At 5:00 P.M., seeing his quarry continue to pull even farther ahead, Blakeley ordered the three topgallant masts restepped, beginning at the mainmast. With the topmasts swinging dangerously through the gusting rain, and with the lee chains of both vessels now hidden beneath the foam, this was a perilous job for even the ablest of seamen, the slightest mistake promising to be costly indeed. But no sooner were the bare fore and mizzen topgallant poles fidded safely home, when the leading counterpart at the main tore loose under its assigned yard's impetus and carried away. This accident, luckily without human casualties, happened far too late to affect the chase, and by this time the wind had already dropped considerably. By 6:00 P.M. the crew of the *Wasp* had already rigged a replacement. As the corvette was built for speed and the barque was not, the chase at length hove to, briefly hoisting and then lowering its English colors.

In this lonely stretch of disturbed gray ocean, several hundred miles to the southwest of his native Ireland, Johnston Blakeley at long last took his first prize. His prey, the 207-ton barque *Neptune*, belonged to the Liverpool firm of Derryhouse, Henderson, Whitting, and Dawson, and had sailed out of Cork, Ireland, only twelve days before, bound to Halifax, Nova Scotia, under the command of John Mordiew.[2] With its cargo of "sundries" destined for the northern frontiers, the *Neptune* instead became a vast, exploitable storeship, crammed with linens, foodstuffs, spirits, and manufactured goods of every description. Its spare ship's stores, particularly the presently set sails, blocks, and cordage, would provide the lean *Wasp* with nearly every piece of nonmartial material found wanting or deficient since its departure. The *Neptune* turned out to be well worth the investment of a topgallant mast. At 8:00 P.M., Blakeley sent his prize-master, Lt. Frederick Baury, and ten able seamen across to secure the barque. At 5:00 A.M., Blakeley hoisted his remaining ship's boats out off the booms, and for the next twelve overcast hours he employed the men of the *Wasp* in "bringing rigging, canvas and sundry articles from the prize." At 6:15 P.M., Lieutenant Baury set the *Neptune* afire. But it was not until long after Blakeley had resumed his meandering eastward course that the intensity of the blazing hull finally overwhelmed the rain. At 9:00 P.M., wrote Midshipman Geisinger, "the masts of the prize fell, she being completely enveloped in flame." As the *Wasp* stood proudly on, the tangerine glow slowly reddened in the distant fog, diminishing by degrees and then vanishing completely when the charred corpse finally filled and sank just before midnight.

The next eleven days and 750 miles were entirely without note. Repeated depth soundings with the 120-fathom line found no bottom and thus no imminence of landfall. On 9 June, Midshipman Geisinger recorded the most singularly important day of training: "Piped all hands to quarters & exercised the crew at great guns, with small arms, boarding and repelling boarders, &c, &c."[3] After the warm carronades were boused up against the bulwarks, the gunner broke out the three distinctive types of bladed boarding arms: the cutlass, the pike, and the ax. The principal offensive weapon during this period was the heavy, broad-bladed cutlass. Amos Binney had provided the *Wasp* with one hundred of these brass-hilted swords at a cost of $5.00 apiece. The eighty boarding pikes, costing only $1.00 each, were primarily defensive weapons. Stored in circular racks around the base of the fore and the main masts, these pikes, essentially eight-foot-long iron-pointed sticks, were the most basic and primitive of arms. The thirty boarding axes, at $1.12 per specimen, were weapons of last resort only.[4] Their primary purpose was to chop free and drag away fallen, shattered spars and cordage, clearing the deck during and after an action.[5] The *Wasp*'s boarders, unlike their British counterparts, were supplied with double-visored leather helmets called "boarding caps," similar in appearance to the firemen's hats of the day. Reinforced with stout, forged-iron bands that crisscrossed each other in all three planes, they protected the boarder's head from the stroke of an enemy's cutlass. They had a comically girlish silhouette, since the ear-to-ear band was thoughtfully curled up at both ends to catch the deflected enemy blade before it glanced down into the wearer's shoulder.[6] An American seaman belonging to the sloop of war *Syren* recalled that the chin straps of his brig's boarding caps were covered with bearskin strips "serving the purpose of false whiskers." Similar fur adorned the fore-and-aft crest, "causing us to look as fierce as hungry wolves."[7]

On 14 June, amid yet another unpleasant gale, the *Wasp* snatched up its second victim, the British brig *William*. Daniel Rankin, the master and distressed part-owner, had sailed from Limerick six days before, bound via the westerlies to Lisbon.[8] There being no use whatsoever for the cargo of barley in its unmalted form, the *William* was also burned. During the following calm, the leadsman at long last "got soundings with 85 fathom line." The welcome bottom, which indicated the approaches to land, consisted of "fine gray sand." Soon they would be within the path of enemy shipping. At daylight on the seventeenth, the *Wasp* found itself skirting a convoy of nine sail to windward; by late afternoon, it had sufficiently "neared them so as to discover they were under convoy of a frigate." The *Wasp* prudently bore away toward the lone leeward sail, easily catching it by 9:30 P.M. But it was only the neutral Dutch galliot *Dejong Peters,* out of Lisbon fifteen days, bound to Amsterdam, Holland. Earlier in the morning, Blakeley had detained the equally valueless Portuguese brig *Bella D'Eschola,* and so this Dutchman was his third disappointment of that day. But his perseverance would eventually pay off. On the following afternoon, the lookout spotted two lone sail to leeward. The first was yet another innocent, the salt-laden Swede *Swaxsund,* but the second, overhauled just after sunset, was British.[9]

The 130-ton, lightly armed brig *Pallas,* sixteen days out of Mogador, Morocco, and bound to London with its cargo of "goat skins, almonds &c," was an extremely lucrative capture. Blakeley employed his boats "removing sundries" for two hours before destroying it. Putting the ship to the torch was now out of the question, for they were well into the track of enemy shipping. The resultant tall column of smoke would scatter merchantmen away on all points of the horizon and would bring every English cruiser in the channel down upon him. At noon, "all the boats returned having cut away the masts of the prize and scuttled her." For the remainder of that day, and for the better part of the next, the *Wasp* interrupted the peaceful passages of several more neutrals. Not only were these encounters inconvenient, but they were potentially lethal, for word of the American's presence had no doubt by this time been sweeping up and down the channel, and each nonbelligerent became yet another unwelcome conduit of information. As the *Wasp* bore down upon another suspicious yet oddly familiar sail the following day, Blakeley suddenly recognized the grim figure standing cross-armed on the quarterdeck. He was Francathon Osmon, master of the *Swaxsund,* "the Swedish Brig that we boarded yesterday."

Henrietta was the name of Blakeley's fourth captive. A broad, slow cargo carrier, it was rigged in the Dutch fashion as a galliot.[10] Midshipman Geisinger, however, mistook it for a ketch, a type of vessel with only a main and a mizzen mast, or, simply put, a ship without a foremast.[11] By definition, a galliot carried only one mast, exclusive of its bowsprit, which was stayed directly to the stempost. This solitary mast carried a large gaff or spritsail abaft it, staysails and jibs before it, and a square topsail above. The larger galliots, such as the 171-ton *Henrietta,* often carried a small, separate gaffed mast for steering, little larger than a flag staff.[12] Geisinger thought this stick a mizzen and hence raised the *Henrietta*'s lowly status to that of a noble ketch. Belonging to and sailing from Belfast, it was six days out on its journey to Guadaloupe, crammed with cargo tantalizingly described as mere "provisions." Blakeley once again employed his people "discharging the prize" and "bringing sundries from the prize" for the next eleven hours of daylight. Blakeley now had an acute problem. Including his latest additions, there were at present thirty-eight unwanted guests on board. Since this slug of a prize was of no real importance outside of its cargo, Blakeley turned it into a cartel. All of its remaining cargo, "except what was necessary to ballast her," went over the side. Blakeley placed the cartel under the command of the master of the late brig *Pallas*, David Cargill, and discharged it to England with all his prisoners, each parolee having first pledged in writing not to serve against the United States unless formally exchanged. They landed at Dublin on 30 June.

Blakeley, however, was violating his written orders: "It is a great object with the enemy to capture and detain, in prison, our seamen, and this can only be counteracted by capturing and bringing into port an equal number," Secretary of the Navy William Jones had written. "The releasing at sea, on parole, though practiced by all civilized nations, is utterly disregarded by our enemy." The British were right to consider such paroles by sea invalid. To have legally been a cartel ship, the *Henrietta* would have had to sail either from an American port or from a neutral one. If prizes were handled in Blakeley's manner, they would be secure against recapture, while the *Wasp* could remain at sea much longer and with an undiminished crew, since the cartels were always manned by prisoners. More important, the *Wasp*'s provisions could be reserved entirely for its own people. Blakeley was well aware of this, but he felt that the ends justified the means.

On 27 June the *Wasp* made its fifth and most valuable capture to date.[13] At 3:45 P.M., two sails appeared in quick succession on the *Wasp*'s lee beam. As the second appeared to be the more enticing of the two, a large ship-rigged vessel, the *Wasp* spread all available canvas in chase. When Blakeley hoisted his colors and fired a chaser, the stranger spread still more sail and continued its flight in great earnest. By 6:10 P.M., Blakeley was alongside of it, but this time he used his entire 11-gun broadside. The chase, now duly convinced, lowered its colors and hove to. The North Carolinian's newest acquisition was the 325-ton ship *Orange Boven*, a reasonably well armed letter of marque, twenty-nine days out of its home port of Bermuda, stuffed with a rich cargo of coffee and sugar. The crew of seventeen was far too small to work the eight guns, let alone to carry a letter of marque allowing the ship to take prizes. Blakeley again ordered Lieutenant Baury, along with Midshipmen Geisinger and Toscan and ten able seamen, aboard with instructions to keep in close company. Despite its enormous value, Blakeley would reluctantly give the order to scuttle it later that day, after stripping the ship of everything useful, including sufficient quantities of coffee and sugar for all hands, probably enough indeed for several voyages. According to one London paper, Blakeley's people set about their task with a bit too much enthusiasm:

> A seaman captured on the Orange Boven, by the American sloop Wasp, who has since landed at Plymouth, reports, that as nothing could exceed the politeness of Captain Blakeley, so nothing was ever seen surpassing the insolence and brutality of his crew. . . . The prisoners were ordered below, and . . . the bullying and hectoring of the crew of the Wasp rose to the highest pitch. He says that at least two thirds of the desperadoes are Scotch men and Irishmen and are most bitter in their invectives against their native soil. They would have plundered every prisoner, even to his shirt, but for the authority of Capt. Blakeley, who appears to be a brave man, and thoroughly captain of his own ship.[14]

The *Wasp*, with the *Orange Boven* still in company, chased another strange sail during the latter part of the day. But as his consort fell quickly astern in spite of its able handling, Blakeley gave up on any final, feeble hope of preserving the *Orange Boven* and the balance of its considerable cargo. The chase, who was soon after overhauled, spoken, and released, was an insignificant French fishing schooner, bound eastward toward the Grand Banks. The letter of marque was opened to the sea at nine o'clock that evening, and it went down peacefully exactly one hour later. Under a pleasant topsail breeze, the *Wasp* filled away to the northeast, strengthening its progress by setting first the courses and then the jibs just before midnight. The sail discovered at just after 4:00 A.M. on the weather beam was, as the watch on deck had supposed, British. But this time it was not a helpless merchantman but His Britannic Majesty's 18-gun sloop of war *Reindeer*, and it was coming confidently down for a closer look at the *Wasp*.

Thomas Chambers, the senior lieutenant on board the approaching brig-rigged sentry, strained through his spyglass at the ship-rigged intruder far to leeward. From the brilliant pallor of its sails on down to the broad white band bordering the many gun ports, it was immediately recognizable as an American, even in the moonlight. Because the scores of Yankee privateersmen infesting these same waters preferred, almost without exception, the brig or schooner rig, Chambers was confident that this particular specimen was a ship of war. Even though he was the "senior," or first lieutenant belonging to the *Reindeer*, Chambers was also at present the only officer of such rank aboard, acting or otherwise. The brig's second lieutenant and all but one of its passed midshipmen had been left behind "indisposed" at the Plymouth Naval Hospital. Chambers had been sixteen continuous years in His Majesty's Service, nine of them with the West Indies squadron, with, he would often proudly proclaim, never an inactive day on half-pay. As an acting master's mate, Chambers had played a central role in the many cutting-out expeditions of his frigate, the flying *Franchise,* against the enemy's privateers and smaller national vessels. During one such bloody affair in the Bay of Campeche in 1806, he had boarded the brig *Raposa* only to be welcomed aboard by a Spanish saber that slashed open the right side of his face. Still, he rallied his boarders and turned the *Raposa's* own cannon against an adjacent 8-gun Spanish schooner and then upon seven nearby gunboats, winning a very creditable victory on that long-forgotten day.[15] The resultant scar from his wound gave him an appearance of malignity that rivaled that of even the most fiercely bear-skinned of American boarders. Fully recovered six months later, Chambers was once again wounded, this time by a French musket ball in his shoulder. After a four-month stay in a Jamaican hospital, Chambers served with distinction on board the brigs *Diligent* and *Favorite* until his long-overdue formal commission was granted in 1810, transferring him to the *Reindeer* as its first officer. He knew better than anyone else the true value of efficiently executed boarding tactics; for the next four years he had trained his crew incessantly with the pike and the cutlass.[16]

His captain was William Manners, a prominent, yet at present untried, member of one of the oldest and most influential naval families of Great Britain, headed by the esteemed Duke of Rutland. William was the son of the late Lord Robert Manners. Remembered by his peers for being both an "accomplished and elegant gentleman" and for possessing a "daring enterprise and a chivalric courage," William's naval career had been, like that of so many others, completely unremarkable.[17] When war broke out against America two years before, Manners had longed for an opportunity to meet an equally rated Yankee ship-to-ship. Manners had been cruising the waters off southern Ireland searching for two companion sloops of war, each similarly engaged in privateer hunting, when the inviting leeward ship caught the alert eye of the early-morning watch.

Longtime friend William Bowers, a lieutenant on board one of the other sloops, had often discussed with William Manners the proper mode for dealing with their disproportionally heavy American foes. "Yardarm to yardarm," declared one William to the other, "three broadsides double-shotted, and board!" On this day, Manners would get a chance to test his theory.[18] The brig under his able, six-year command was the same *Reindeer* that had bested the two French brig-corvettes off Puerto Rico in 1806. However, unlike the majority of its sisters, the *Reindeer* had been rather hastily put together in the Plymouth Dockyard with Baltic fir, an inexpensive, lightweight substitute timber that tended to splinter horribly when struck by shot. There was little in its appearance, however, beneath the flawless paintwork and the shining brass, to betray its softwood skeleton, save perhaps for the anachronistic square-tuck stern, mandatory on all fir-built vessels. The decade-old *Reindeer* was probably on its last commission, completely worn out after too many years of hard service—too many years, at least, for a softwood sloop.[19] Making matters even worse, it had been caught up in a severe gale on the cruise previous to this, and Manners had been obliged to throw overboard a number of his 32-pounder carronades to avoid foundering. Finding no replacements readily available with the Plymouth storekeeper, Manners had reluctantly received on board a surrogate battery of 24-pounders, the only guns in stock. Regulations forbade him from sailing with either an incomplete or a mixed-caliber carronade battery, so Manners had to forfeit his remaining 32s as well.[20] Although the sloop of war class was generally somewhat "indifferently" manned in the British Navy, Manners's crew of 118 was instead publicly celebrated as "the Pride of Plymouth" and Manners was reported to be "the idol and delight of his ship's company." Under the acute eye of Chambers, they had some of the best pike and cutlass men in the fleet. "Her crew were remarkably fine young men," proclaimed one English paper, "and had sailed together six years and upwards, which is very seldom the case in these small vessels."

These two sloops of war, both bound to the westward, hull down on their respective starboard tacks, and propelled along by the same moderate north-northeast breeze, had been studying one another's topsails since well before sunrise. The *Wasp* bore west-southwest, or just a few points off the *Reindeer*'s larboard bow, while the Briton held the critical weather-gauge. By 10 A.M., satisfied that this "large corvette mounting 22-guns" was indeed an enemy, Manners hoisted the private signal flag, "a blue and yellow diagonally [*sic*]," at the mainmast head and then punctuated his declaration with a gun. As expected, his introduction went unanswered. At just after noon, Manners tried a second signal to be absolutely sure: "a blue and white flag diagonally at the fore." Wishing to close as soon as possible in the dying breeze, Manners next ordered his hands to break out the great ashen sweeps and row their brig down in pursuit. Manners utilized the only advantage possessed by his smaller, softwood sloop: its relatively light weight. At 1:10 P.M., the *Wasp* tacked to the eastward and stood toward the *Reindeer,* hoisting three broad, peppermint-striped ensigns. Manners tacked also, took out the first reefs in his topsails, and then cleared for action.[21] He knew that this mercurial wind might well shift at any moment, costing him his weather-gauge. The *Wasp* appeared much larger than the *Reindeer,* certainly possessed a more numerous crew, and, Manners reflected, American corvettes were known to carry heavier guns and more of them. If he expected to take the approaching ship, he must, above all else, keep his precious weather-gauge. This leverage was now only slight in the northerly backing breeze; if the big American was a more weatherly ship, no great assumption, he might lose his only advantage on this present tack before he was within carronade range. "Finding she would soon pass to windward," recalled one of Manners's men, "by hard sweeping we soon gained a position that would enable us to keep the weather-gauge."[22] Confident of his bearings, Manners "put about" at 2:30 P.M. and once again stood directly toward the corvette. "The enemy," wrote Lieutenant Chambers afterward, "who not being able to weather us, tacked again to the westward." Both sloops were now pursuing the same course and direction that they had held initially, but by midafternoon they were rapidly converging.

Captain Manners held a council of war on the quarterdeck with his officers: one each lieutenant and midshipman, the master, the purser, the gunner, and his own captain's clerk. To ensure victory, he told them, the *Reindeer* must use its windward supremacy to run across either one of the American's vulnerable extremities, rake them repeatedly, and then board in the confusion. The previous summer, William Allen's brig of war, the *Argus,* had immediately submitted under just such an onslaught by a sister-brig, the *Pelican.* Britain's two single-ship victories against the Americans during this present war had ended with the use of English steel. This coming engagement must not turn into a lengthy, broadside-to-broadside contest at the great guns. The Americans had proven that they were capable of delivering their shot with deadly accuracy. Therefore, Manners continued, the superior weight of the American's guns, 32-pounders at least, with all other things being equal, must eventually win out over his 24s. Were he to pass under his enemy's frail stern, its single most assailable point, but fail to cause instant and crippling destruction, then he would lose his weather authority and with it the fight. If he sailed across the ship's bow, the next most vulnerable region, then he would have more time, considering their mutual inertia, to cause the requisite havoc. If he failed on this initial forward attempt, he might still maintain the weather-gauge. To cross the unwilling American's bows, however, he must first brave its broadsides en route for several agonizing minutes of certain butchery. During this time his rigging had to remain intact amid the storm of Yankee dismantling shot. Outmasted two to three, the British brig would be far easier to disable than the American ship, and should any accident befall his gaff or main boom, he would become entirely unmanageable. Manners's choice of extremities depended on what his enemy did. If the American ship decided to luff up into the wind and bring his guns to bear early on, a forward attack was ideal. If not, Manners concluded, he must pass under the stern.

Leaving Chambers in temporary command of the quarterdeck, Manners ascended once again to the topgallant forecastle. There a small team of gunners stood by the brig's boat howitzer, a small, 12-pounder carronade. The enemy ship's stern was nearly bow on at this point, and no broadside gun on either side would yet bear. Unobstructed on its high but exposed perch, this stunted little gun would be the first to sight on the target, and he, the captain, would have the honor of pulling the lanyard. The distance at which both broadsides would now mutually be brought to bear was "half-pistol shot," a range at which any size ball would kill. Rapidity and accuracy must decide the question. If he succeeded, Manners would be the first English commander to take an American of significantly heavier force. But first he would have to survive his glory.

Johnston Blakeley had been paying particularly close attention to the approaching brig throughout the early morning hours. Its familiar profile as a *Cruiser*-class brig had betrayed its martial, English identity since the beginning of the forenoon watch, and its subsequent aggressive posturing, "coming down under a crowd of sail," confirmed his hopes. At noon, the crew of the *Wasp* "cleared up the decks, the men in high spirits, expecting an engagement." At 1:15 P.M., the enemy, "then about two miles astern," at last flaunted its English colors at the gaff's end.[23] Blakeley made his first tack at 1:22 P.M., hoping to work to windward. He was making solid albeit slow progress when, a half-hour later, the chase tacked to the eastward in kind. At 2:00 P.M., Blakeley introduced himself. He hoisted an ensign and a jack at the mizzen peak, a second ensign at the fore, and a streaming, eight-foot star-spangled pennant at the main topgallant masthead. Blakeley fired three guns to windward in slow succession, but only the first was returned. He was not sure if the brig was running eastward, away from him in flight, or just judiciously maintaining its wind. With "the enemy still standing from us," Blakeley next ordered his royals, upper staysails, and flying jib set in pursuit, firing a fourth gun as he did so. Suddenly, the brig spun about and bore back down upon him. It took nearly fifteen minutes for Blakeley to tack successfully back around to the westward, but by then it was too late. The weather-gauge was irretrievably lost. The wind, now due north, had been slowly backing counterclockwise to the westward all day. Perhaps this elemental shift might, given enough time, hand him the advantage by default. Resigning his fate to the wind, Blakeley brailed up his spanker and awaited his skillfully handled foe.[24]

Captain Blakeley stood next to James Carr at the wheel, intent upon his nearing adversary. His almost fifteen years of hard service was now rapidly approaching either its apex or its destruction. He had seen combat before, distant cannonading at disreputable Barbary corsairs, but nothing like this. The lives of 172 men and boys now depended on his knowledge, his skill, and his bravery. Did his accumulation of Merrimack fishermen and smugglers yet amount to a fighting crew? Would they fight like the men of the *Constitution* and the *Enterprize,* or would they recoil in horror as did those of the *Chesapeake* and the *Argus?* Lawrence's men on the *Chesapeake* had been cruising together for at best only eight hours, while he had commanded his people at sea for as many weeks. But Allen had had his crew on the *Argus* for even longer. Would the coming British fight more skillfully now that they were defending home waters? They needed only to disable him, while he, on the other hand, was required not only to defeat his foe but also to survive his success reasonably intact and escape the multitude of heavy cruisers thought to be loitering within earshot just over the horizon.

At 3:15 P.M., American time, Captain William Manners sprung the flintlock of his double-shotted 12-pounder and commenced the bout. Midshipman Henry S. Langdon Jr., commanding the foretop's small-arms men, heard the distant, hollow report of a gun, followed closely by the hammer blows of iron striking oak beneath him, the tearing sound of canvas below and abaft, and a few startled cries farther astern. Tomorrow being the day he would officially pass into manhood, his eighteenth birthday, Langdon was determined to do all he could to ensure a victorious outcome for the *Wasp.*[25] He had been told that the enemy was on the weather quarter and that they were at this very moment only sixty yards away, but he could see nothing apart from his ship's own billowing main topsail. At 3:18 P.M., confident that his recharged, repositioned little gun was again sighted true, Manners sent a second ball and stand of grape scattering into the corvette's stern, while at that same instant, the chase-gun went off beneath him. The *Wasp's* crew stood impatiently at their own silent batteries while these double loads of six- and twelve-pound shot flew above and about them. At 3:21 Manners fired a third time. "From a gun placed on the forecastle," recalled a survivor, "Captain Manners galled the enemy considerably, killing and wounding several of his men. . . . This advantage was however but temporary: they were silently preparing a deadly return."[26] Round and grapeshot had already splintered Blakeley's stern boat, embedded themselves within the transom, chewed up the mizzenmast and boom, and perforated his canvas, but his people did not flinch. In his official report to the secretary, he praised their "cool and patient conduct . . . while exposed to the fire of the shifting gun . . . without an opportunity of returning it."

One such stoic soul was Q.M. Henry Flanders, who stood with a subdued rigidity, clutching the smooth spokes of his mahogany wheel. During what seemed like the longest five minutes of his life, Flanders's thoughts must have raced back to his native Arundel, where his wife and his three children were at this hour just finishing their breakfast.[27] Sr. Q.M. Jonathan Dick, Flanders's mirror image across the highly polished wheel, suddenly jerked forward with a cry of astonishment and incredulity, struck to the deck by a splinter, a ball, or both. Q.M. John Mullen instantly took his place. Another acting quartermaster, Masters Mate John Swett, whose duty it would have been to relieve either Mullen or Flanders as next in line, was himself hit, but much less seriously. While Dick and Swett were carried down the after hatchway to see Dr. Clarke, Sailing Master Carr nervously set things back to rights, straining his professional composure to the utmost to appear unaffected. By the fourth such provocation, Johnston Blakeley had had enough. It was 3:24 P.M.

The *Reindeer* was now less than a ship's length away. "Finding that the enemy did not get sufficiently on the beam," dutifully recorded Blakeley's clerk, Thomas McClaine, "[we] put the helm alee and . . . commenced the action with the after carronade on the starboard side, and fired in succession." Musketry from the *Wasp's* twenty-six topmen added their ragged volleys to the din, while round, grape, "langrage, swan shot and other unfair pieces of missile instruments" took flight far down below.[28] "Luffing athwart our bows," recalled an English sailor, "he poured in a deadly broadside, which mowed down our people like grass." Manners, presumably having just come down off the forecastle ladder, was grazed by a 32-pound ball, 6 1/4 inches in diameter, that scooped away both of his calves. No sooner had he collapsed to his knees than a grapeshot passed though both thighs, flinging him forward onto the deck.[29] "The two vessels were now nearly alongside each other," continued the more fortunate sailor, "[and] the carnage was dreadful."[30] Despite his severe wounds, Manners was carried to his quarter-deck. He could see that his men were delivering his proposed three double-shotted broadsides, and although his brig was being hit very hard, the American's billet-head was slowly turning into view. They were going to rake the American's bow, just as he had planned.

Pacing the quarterdeck, sword in hand and shouting words of praise and encouragement, Johnston Blakeley was exhilarated by his own gunners' performance during these first five seemingly endless minutes of the cannonade. The enemy's fire, although quite brisk, appeared, whether by accident or intent, to be directed over his men's heads—but only barely so. Most of his starboard hammocks, including their cloths, nettings, ridge-ropes, and iron stanchions, had already been blasted inboard. The dense plumes from twenty active carriage guns, piling up over his head to leeward, obscured the *Wasp*'s crippled tophamper from his view until it was nearly too late. The sloops of war converged like two intruding cloudbursts on this beautifully clear, sunlit afternoon. The gun crews on both sides of the fray served their pieces like heroes: loading, running-out, training, firing, and then repeating.

Just before Blakeley brought his starboard batteries to bear, he had instructed his quartermaster to put the helm hard alee. This was the first stage of a normal maneuver where, in more peaceful surroundings, the *Wasp* might tack and thus alter its course, passing first through the eye of the wind. Blakeley had no intention of actually tacking, of course; he wanted only to respond to Manners's provocation. But his last-minute luff went horribly wrong. There was no time to trim the yards more favorably to this new track, a few points closer to the northerly wind. This circumstance, combined with Mullen's abrupt leeward turn of the helm, created a critical drag against the *Wasp*'s momentum, slowing it down considerably. For several minutes the windward brig completely blanketed whatever light winds remained, and so it shot slowly ahead of the *Wasp*. The American's mizzen topsail was the first to catch the returning breeze on the brig's passing, and it slowly spun the decelerating ship clockwise about its center of gravity, directly into the wind. Damage to the foremast's sheets, tacks, and braces, combined with the general confusion inherent in a green crew's first battle, prevented a timely correction. Only eight minutes into the action, the *Wasp* was hanging due north "in stays," with a determined enemy athwart its bow raking it mercilessly. This was Blakeley's worst nightmare. At 3:34 P.M., he ordered the mainsail hauled around to the larboard tack,[31] hoping to fall off and swing the port guns into action when the enemy passed his bow. For the next few minutes, however, he knew he was going to be hammered hard.

"The enemy," Chambers told his superiors, "hove in stays, we passing under her bows raking her; her jib boom just clearing our main rigging."[32] The nine larboard English cannon delivered their smoking iron directly into the *Wasp*'s prow at point-blank range. They tore a pair of Blakeley's forward guns violently from their carriages,[33] and stamped the shank of the *Wasp*'s best bower anchor, lashed securely atop the fore chains, back in upon itself with a resounding clang.[34] The best laid shot of the day was a 24-pound ball that punched a jagged hole, five and a half inches wide, straight through the center of the *Wasp*'s foremast, about seven feet above the deck. At the same time, two brass 4-pounder howitzers dumped canister and grape from the Britisher's fighting-tops down upon the exposed American forecastle. But the English gunners had underestimated the strength of Mr. Merrill's stout cant frames and hawser pieces. The whole assembly was hewn from three pieces of seasoned oaken stock, each eighteen inches wide and spiked flush, side by side. The crew of the *Reindeer* had triple-shotted their guns anticipating the rake, vastly diminishing their carronades' penetrating power. "The *Wasp*'s bow is composed of solid oak," lamented a survivor in a London paper, "which proved impenetrable to the *Reindeer*'s shot."[35] Had the guns not been quite so overcharged, the brig's round and grape might well have passed straight on through, killing scores and instantly deciding the contest. But their loads, nearly six hundred pounds of spherical iron from each overstuffed broadside, instead embedded themselves in the impermeable white oak.

Midshipman Langdon heard many shot strike far below him, but he could see little of the enemy from behind the becalmed fore-topsail. Below him, the men of the *Wasp*'s first division were embracing whatever cover they could find. "About the middle of the action," recalled Midshipman Hall in a letter reprinted in the Portsmouth papers, "the Reindeer shot athwart the Wasp's bows, so that the foresail . . . was in the way of [Langdon's] men and prevented the effect of their fire." Langdon instantly jumped out onto the foreyard, followed by several of his men, and together, balanced precariously over the deck and supported only by frail foot-ropes, they poured a "deadly and destructive fire" down onto the *Reindeer* from under the fore-topsail. "In this hazardous situation," continued Hall, Langdon "received a musket ball in the breast." Although seriously wounded, Langdon nevertheless refused to be taken on deck or to quit his post. "With a veteran composure to the last" of the battle, concluded Hall, "he kept encouraging his men to keep cool and take good aim."[36]

Captain Manners was distressed to see his enemy reuniting with the breeze and begin to slowly gather sternway. Soon the *Wasp* would fall off with its larboard tacks aboard, revealing its fresh port batteries. He must board now, while the smoke was still thick and before the surviving Americans, most certainly devastated by his raking fire, regained their wits. Manners ordered his helm put up before the wind and "laid onto her, our small bower anchor hooking her larboard quarter."[37] The *Wasp* had not yet paid off when the *Reindeer* ground into it, but lay facing just east of north and now drifting perceptively backward, with its shivering sails just beginning to catch the returning breeze. The two sloops now embraced each other, broadside to broadside, nose to tail. The *Wasp*'s newly manned port carronades, themselves treble-shotted, emptied close to half a ton of Bartlett Murdock's finest sand-cast into the shattered Englishman, blasting in entire sections of bulwark, along with a good many of the hearts of oak behind them. All across the hundred-foot-long, hammock-topped bastions, the men of two nations thrust and hacked at one other through the open ports with axes, pikes, and cutlasses, and they wrestled rammers and sponges from opposing hands. "Our men falling fast," wrote Chambers "[we] endeavored to board." Manners pulled himself slowly up, tottering on his nearly hollow legs, with "his left elbow on the larboard roundhouse, and waving his sword in his right to encourage his men."[38] The American's bow, cruelly raked by his able gunners, would be their weakest point, he thought. Here they must capitulate under the focused weight of his men. "Follow me boys," he reportedly cried, raising his sword, "we must board!"[39] Midshipman Langdon's foretopmen now had a clear target for their vengeance. With a superhuman effort, Manners had somehow pulled himself into the *Reindeer*'s main shrouds when the two musket balls crashed down into his forehead. Placing his left hand over what remained of his face, he was heard to cry out, "Oh God!" before falling backward onto his own men, his right hand still "convulsively brandishing his own sword." Twelve additional shot reportedly struck his body before he hit the quarterdeck.[40]

Behind him, Lieutenant Chambers fell with a dangerous wound to the hip ("which did not prevent my remaining on deck, until from the loss of blood, I fainted") and beyond him, the master collapsed "with severe wounds in the thigh and arm." The purser and the quartermaster in turn sank to the deck abaft him, "covered with wounds."[41] But Manners's enraged and inspired Britons, although leaderless, poured determinedly down upon the unprepared Newburyporters and scythed them aside. Midshipman Frank Toscan, assigned to the forward division, fell violently backward onto the deck, seriously wounded. A British pistol ball, made of soft copper, had flattened deep within his chest.[42] Before the *Wasp*'s boarders and marines could rally, the outnumbered men of the *Reindeer* nearly cleared the forecastle. While ramming home his musket charge, one American small-arms man was caught completely off guard by an English boarder appearing suddenly through the smoke atop the bulwarks. The American fell backward in surprise, firing his piece wild at the threat above. The ramrod passed through the boarder's head, flinging him backward onto his own deck. His companions begged him to go below to the surgeon and have it removed, but he refused—as his late captain had done. He instead staggered back to his gun. "If all the wounded of the *Reindeer* were as able to fight as I am," he said, "we should make the American strike!"[43] One of the *Wasp*'s few boarders who recovered his wits in time was Boatswain's Mate William Thompson. He had been leading the American boarders forward when the same invisible hand pressed him forcefully to the planks mere yards away from Midshipman Toscan, his left shoulder pierced by an English ball.[44] With most of the single-shot weapons now discharged, the seamen and marines of both nations brutally savaged each other with their blades. Beneath crackling topsails and snapping jibs, dozens of barefoot boarders slashed out with sharpened swords and speared ahead with sapling-sized pikes and extended bayonets.

The balance of the men of the *Wasp* soon recovered from their collective shock, and, at a considerable cost to both sides, they corralled the last of the invaders back across the twin hammock-topped barricades. The *Wasp*'s fore and main sails at long last filled, and they pulled it clockwise, to starboard. And now, helped along by the concussions of the last few loaded guns, the sloops parted. But the English anchor still held fast, while the surviving boarders of both navies raced back toward the convergence of the ever-widening vee. The formerly inactive American main and mizzen topmen, grasping their freshly charged muskets, had at long last a clearly defined target. About two dozen men of the *Reindeer* could now be seen bottle-necking at their own forecastle ladders, preparing to pour over and then down upon the *Wasp*'s quarterdeck in one last desperate lunge. As the shirtless boarders drove once again over the *Wasp*'s bulwarks alongside the remaining red-coated marines, the American topmen, "cool and deliberate" to a man, released their volley. "The execution of our musketry at this time was terrible," recalled Geisinger in his private journal. "Every man without exception was either shot down or piked as they showed their heads above their topgallant forecastle."[45] The time was 3:44 P.M., and Blakeley now gave the order to board.

Recalling every word of advice that the poor crippled George Budd had given him, David Geisinger instantly scrambled over the cap-rail, the first to challenge the British on their own planks.[46] "Her decks presented an awful and shocking spectacle," he noted. "She was literally cut to pieces [and] her foremast almost shot in two, but it being calm kept it from going overboard." Blakeley, close on Geisinger's heels, later marveled at the damage that his men had inflicted: "The *Reindeer* was literally cut to pieces in a line with her ports—her upper works, boats and spare spars were one complete wreck." The *Reindeer*'s gunner, Henry Saunders, was now the senior officer left standing. But he was busy at his station, far below in the magazine. Richard Collins, the late captain's clerk, stood over the twisted, crimson mass that had been, only a half-hour before, his confident captain of these past six years. Thundering straight for him and his quarterdeck was a blade-brandishing mob, halloaing like the animals whose fur now adorned their iron-strapped heads. A brief glance to the right at the empty after companionway told him that he was, at this instant, the brig's acting commander. At 3:45 P.M., young Collins formally surrendered the *Reindeer*. Gunner Saunders found the hatchway ringed with marine muskets when he at last presented his squinting eyes to the blinding sunlight. The smoke had by then dissipated. The warm air, the sea, and the sky were just as peaceful now as he had seen them thirty minutes before. But everything else had changed.

The *Reindeer* had opened fire on the *Wasp*'s starboard quarter hulling its little gig, exchanged near-crippling broadsides with it on the starboard beam, raked it across the bow, boarded it first on the larboard bow and then again on the larboard quarter, with the brig's bowsprit crushing the *Wasp*'s stern boat beyond all repair at the finale. In just twenty-four minutes of battle (nineteen after his first reciprocated shot) Blakeley and his *Wasp* had been completely circumnavigated, no small feat in such light airs. Aside from its wounded foremast, the *Wasp* had sustained no grave or crippling injury. Its shredded sails and dangling rigging would soon be repaired, and the cosmetics could wait until later. In fact, neither sloop had lost a spar. "Six round shot struck our hull and many grape," wrote Blakeley, "which did not penetrate far." But his crew was hard hit. Eleven men had either been killed outright or were mortally wounded, and at least eighteen others were more or less seriously injured, approximately one man in six. Many others, bruised and bumped about to various minor degrees, unofficially suffering "small hurts," probably never made the list. But the crew of the *Reindeer*, by comparison, had been slaughtered. Thirty-three wounds eventually proved mortal, if they had not done so immediately, while thirty-four other men survived their shocking, and in many cases permanently debilitating, wounds—totaling more than half of Manners's courageous crew.

The reaction of the American newspapers to this battle was euphoric. The country was still in shocked mourning over the loss of the fine frigate *Chesapeake,* taken just over a year before. On a bright summer day, the *Shannon* had sailed right up to Boston harbor, daring the authorities to send a frigate out and accept its obvious challenge. James Lawrence, commanding a ship of equal force, had obliged. Even though he possessed the weather-gauge, Lawrence had been completely beaten in fifteen minutes, with his men fleeing before English steel. The heroic American captain lay dying with his decks a splintered slaughter-house. But now here was the *Wasp,* "rated" equally at 18 guns, just like the *Reindeer,* and, after having similarly challenged the latter in the Briton's own backyard, they had beaten their foe in just nineteen minutes and topped off the whole affair with a brilliant, cutlass-wielding finale. The death of Lawrence was now avenged with Manners's blood. The myth of the invincible British boarder was forever dispelled, and American national pride was fully restored. Of course, Blakeley failed to mention in his report that he had been raked, a professional humiliation of the first order. He also implied a parity of material force where there was none. Counting the *Reindeer*'s two tiny yet effective swivel howitzers in its tops along with the 12-pounder boat carronade, Blakeley thus elevated the *Reindeer* into a 21-gun sloop of war, while forgetting to reveal his "18-gun" ship's true status. This was not entirely deceit for glory's sake, however. If an enemy of equal or greater force were captured, the entire proceeds, either the purchase price, should the vessel be somehow brought home and taken into the service, or any cash reward earned for its destruction, would be bestowed entirely upon the officers and crew. Otherwise, the money would be split equally with the naval pension fund. After all, Blakeley now had a family to support.

Blakeley treated the whole affair in his official report as though there was but a mere cannonade, broadside to broadside for a quarter of an hour, that had ended most manfully with the clashing of the sword. He gave no details at all, failing to explain how the action could have opened on his starboard, windward quarter and could have concluded with the *Reindeer*'s larboard bow colliding into his larboard quarter.[47]

As victorious commanders tend to do, Blakeley described his glory in the rosiest of terms. He gave official praise for "the promptitude and firmness with which every attempt to board was met and successfully *repelled*," and declared that "our loss in men has been severe . . . chiefly in *repelling* boarders." This was a strange way to praise his crew's fighting skills. These touchy statements imply that the British might have actually come close to pulling off the first boarding surge. Perhaps they had been prematurely stranded, isolated, and then overwhelmed by numbers only after the sloops had pulled apart. Chambers, Blakeley, and all later historians describe the boarding affair as one long, diminishing melee at the bulwarks. An anonymous published letter from an English officer, however, confirms the fight's true structure; the officer admits that his companions, "having been repulsed in *two* attempts to board, [were] under the painful necessity of lowering the British colors."[48] Blakeley did not have to be so sensitive, considering what small-arms men he was given to work with: four marine privates and a corporal. His crew, although numerous, were mere sweepings. They were unemployed fishermen, smugglers, and a few blackguarded men from the *Chesapeake,* last-minute bones tossed to him by preoccupied commanders with wholly different priorities.

The British papers treated the whole affair as David being slain by Goliath. They concentrated on the incredible performance of the dying William Manners, and they lamented Manners's forced switch to the lighter caliber guns. Of the seven single-ship sloop of war actions of the War of 1812 (from which the Americans emerged victorious six times), the *Wasp-Reindeer* fight had the greatest disparity of force between any of the rivals. In 1910 historian Theodore Roosevelt carefully calculated the broadside force and declared the difference to be about three to two.[49] Still, these two combatants' respective ratios in men and metal were exactly the same as those of all three American frigate victories of 1812. But in this battle, as well as in all the other sloop of war engagements, the range was point-blank, a distance where carronade shot of any size, if efficiently plied, would penetrate wooden bulwarks and kill men. Considering the *Reindeer*'s slightly high firing and multiple charging, it is questionable whether its original 32-pounders would necessarily have tipped the balance. The *Wasp*'s thick foremast would still have stood in the light weather even if just such a heavier shot had hit it, while the rigging would have been equally cut with either size ball. On the other hand, the heavier shot would have penetrated the *Wasp*'s bow at such a close range, even if triple-shotted, and would have maimed proportionally more men. Had the *Reindeer* been literally inches closer during its skillful rake, it might have lashed onto the *Wasp*'s jib-boom and hung on, blazing away until the helpless American surrendered.

"Never was there a braver crew than the *Reindeer*'s," wrote historian William James, "never a ship more ably fought . . . [and] never an officer that better deserved a monument in Westminster Abbey, than the gallant heroic Manners."[50] Neither side did anything to be ashamed of in the least on this bloody day, even though the Right Honorable Lords of the Admiralty felt inclined to suppress all official reports and letters from the anxious public. A formal court-martial was held the following August. Manners and Chambers were both acquitted of any wrongdoing.[51] Recriminations are not necessary. "It is difficult to say which ship behaved the best in this short but gallant combat," wrote former Midshipman James Fenimore Cooper in his naval history. "I doubt the war produced two better single ship commanders," Roosevelt also concluded.[52] Simply put, one heavy sloop of war with a green crew and sailing far from home met, by mutual consent, another of the same class, although not quite so strong, in the latter's home waters. The second belonged to the world's greatest maritime power, possessing one of the best trained and most experienced crews in its navy. This action was about quantity versus quality and youth versus experience. With the intervention of luck and with the realization that all things are rarely equal, youthful quantity prevailed.

15. L'ORIENT

July–August 1814

*T*he following morning, the painfully wounded Lt. Thomas Chambers addressed an equally agonizing letter to his conqueror, Capt. Johnston Blakeley, Esquire. "Chances of war having placed you in possession of His Majesty's Late Sloop Reindeer, whose crew having been nearly all killed and wounded," he began, "I am impelled by virtues of humanity to request that you will take into consideration the deplorable condition of the latter." Because they were at present so near the coast of His Britannic Majesty, Chambers reasoned, and because the *Reindeer*'s wounded could not possibly receive the attention they so rightfully deserved while at sea, might his distinguished captor, as a concerned gentleman operating under the same beneficent motives, consider sending the battered brig into the nearest port as a cartel? As the ranking representative of the Honorable Lords Commissioners of the Admiralty now on board, he would give his ironclad guarantee upon their behalf that both the *Reindeer*'s emergency cartel status and the parole of its men would be completely honored. And if the Lords Commissioners did not immediately allow the *Reindeer* to return to the United States, fully manned with a crew of exchanged American seamen, then he could at least guarantee that his late brig would never again put to sea under English colors.[1] At any rate, everyone aboard knew that the *Reindeer* was too seriously knocked about to cruise effectively alongside the *Wasp* without first receiving major dockyard repair.

Chambers thought the *Wasp* was critically injured as well. Perhaps by overestimating the damage that his brig had wrought, he was firmly convinced that the wounded ship must certainly be headed home. While it was sadly true that his *Reindeer* had been beaten, horribly beaten, into four hundred tons of bloodstained kindling, Chambers consoled himself that he had, at least, stopped a bullet aimed at the very heart of the English maritime. Blakeley had no such course in mind, but he probably spoon-fed this whole idea into Chambers's head. "She has in all probability proceeded for America," sighed a London paper, "where she was launched only seven months since at Portsmouth, in New Hampshire."[2] If Blakeley's answer was not an initial, unequivocal "no," it instantly became one when the strengthening afternoon breeze brought the shroudless foremast and the equally spartan main topmast, the *Reindeer*'s two great antlers, crashing down on deck.

Blakeley employed his exhausted crew in the dual role of repairing the *Wasp*'s damages as best they could ("knotting and splicing the lower rigging" was the most pressing, immediate task), and stripping the splintered *Reindeer* clean of any warlike stores. Blakeley also took on board Manners's shifting carronade. The *Wasp* possessed a stout topgallant forecastle deck ready to receive it, and because it fired a caliber already on board in great quantity, its acquisition would present no great confusion to the gunner's department. It would be a good replacement for one of the two dismounted guns, especially if one of their irreparable barrels had been shattered. This lifeless English sloop of war was now the most complete storeship imaginable. The finest British blocks, cordage, and sailcloth would propel this commerce-killing New Englander against the land of their own origin. American sailors would consume English beef and bread, and, should there be another engagement, the boom of British powder would echo back at His Britannic Majesty's servants.

The remains of William Manners, now becoming unpleasant after lying nearly twenty-eight hours on deck, were finally committed to the deep, "having been previously sewn up in his cot." After Blakeley read the appropriate service to the combined ships' companies, Captain Manners's mortal coil slid silently overboard at sunset, alongside that of his late purser, both men weighted down by clusters of 24-pound shot placed at their feet. American marine muskets, the very instruments of their death, volleyed out an abrupt tribute, and then it was done. The remains of the others—the quartermaster, the armorer, the rope-maker, the captain of the foremast, the ten seamen (five able, five ordinary), the three landsmen, the four marines, and the quartet of young boys—had been thrown over the side not long after the brig's guns had cooled. At 9:00 P.M. on 30 June 1814, Blakeley's prize crew set the brig on fire. The American captain's gig, now lying wrecked in the waist with the others, was deemed beyond repair by the wholly preoccupied carpenter. At 11:00 P.M., the *Wasp* laid its main topsail, now glowing a somber orange, sharply to the mast, momentarily checking its way. "Hoisted out the small boat," reported Midshipman Geisinger in his journal, "and took the *Reindeer*'s in." The pyre blazed defiantly on until 2:00 A.M., when the magazines finally erupted. What little that remained descended slowly into the dark abyss, in loyal pursuit of its late captain. At this very same instant, deep below the waterline in the *Wasp*'s cockpit, Robert Caldwell, a dangerously wounded English seaman, breathed his last.[3]

The brig-sloops *Helicon* and *Achates* happened on the scene not long after. Lt. William Bowers of the former was beginning to grow more than a bit concerned at the lengthening absence of the *Reindeer*, his overdue companion, when the lookout spotted debris half-submerged in the swells. On closer examination, they discovered the wreckage of a large mast, bound hopelessly with fresh cordage. This caused no initial alarm because all on board reasoned that it belonged to some unfortunate coaster. Many such small merchant craft plied continuously across these seas, and they had so frequently wrecked along the coast that floating spars were a sadly common menace to navigation. The boat sent to examine the wreckage, however, was startled to find grapeshot sticking into the wood and that the blackened mainmast had been burned off by the copper in the wake of the boom. They soon discovered the *Reindeer*'s unique markings. "Everything denoted that the strife had been sanguinary and the catastrophe recent." With stoic consolation, Bowers added truthfully, "Whoever had been the antagonist, he had found tough work." The duo steered away toward the setting sun, in an anxious search for the enemy, "fervently praying for an opportunity of avenging our unfortunate companions." The American intruder would in all probability, they thought, be limping home to the westward. They joined up with the *Scylla* of 18 guns, "not long after," but their combined endeavors, Bowers admitted, proved "impotent." Ironically, they did come upon Blakeley's first command, the corvette *John Adams*. This Yankee cartel was sailing home from Holland under a properly sanctioned diplomatic immunity, so they begrudgingly allowed it to proceed unmolested.[4] Returning to the site of the wreckage one week later, the *Helicon* found the shot-laden tangle of the *Reindeer*'s foremast.[5]

Burdened with more than one hundred prisoners, many of them horribly wounded, and weighted down still further by their combined baggage, the *Wasp* crept along under moderate sail up the channel, knotting and splicing all the way. Two more crewmembers of the *Reindeer* "departed this life" at 2:00 P.M. on the following day. At 4:15, a large sail revealed herself through the dissipating drizzle, one point off the weather bow. A second, more accessible sail appeared on the lee beam fifteen minutes later. Try as it might, the *Wasp* could not under these present conditions weather the first vessel, a large ship sailing alone, quite possibly a rich, homeward-bound Indiaman. After an unsuccessful hour of trying to come up with her, they tacked regretfully down upon the second, much smaller craft. It proved to be the Portuguese brig *Lisbon Packet*, out four days from its namesake port, bound to Havre de Grace.[6] To his relief and utter astonishment, Blakeley learned from the amiable Portuguese captain, with whom the first sail had spoken earlier in the morning, that their initial target had actually been His Majesty's ship *Hibernia*, a massive, three-decked line-of-battle ship rated at 110 guns. One of the largest such vessels then afloat, the *Hibernia* was returning home from the Mediterranean under the able command of Adm. Sir Sidney Smith.[7] Often on board the old *Hornet* and again just recently in Charleston, Blakeley had heard Sailing Master Charles F. Grandison, or Charles Smith as he was known abroad, drone on and on about the admiral, his alleged, but as far as anyone could tell, unacknowledged father.

Blakeley's selection was doubly fortunate. Here was an opportunity, with the paid cooperation of the Portuguese captain, of course, for the *Wasp* to unload some unwanted guests. He could not resume anything like a real cruise, nor could he even return safely to America crammed so perilously with prisoners, especially with those so obviously in need of hospitalization. Through "motives of humanity," Blakeley selected twenty-three of the most seriously wounded, placed them on board the *Lisbon Packet*, and instructed its captain to repair directly to the nearest English port under a strict parole. "The means of assistance now in my power," wrote the *Reindeer*'s surgeon in a later justification, "being so inadequate as hardly enables me to afford them the slightest relief."[8] Lieutenant Chambers was not included in the list. Whether the senior British officer was not considered to be sufficiently endangered to warrant sending him off to hospital, or conversely, was thought too badly hurt to risk a transshipping, his omission was unacceptable to him. He wrote Captain Blakeley a heartfelt plea:

> I beg leave to request you will take my situation being severely wounded into consideration and permit me to be one of that number, under such

obligations as you may think necessary to effectuate my being exchanged for an officer of equal rank, or failure thereof on recovery of my wounds, to return to the United States of America as a prisoner of war. I have no hesitation in saying I feel satisfaction the Lords Commissioners of the Admiralty will satisfy any arrangement you may require of me.[9]

Perhaps Blakeley thought Chambers necessary as a hostage to ensure compliance with their unorthodox and somewhat questionable parole. At any rate, he gave in. "Your situation and the pledge offered there said has induced my consent," replied Blakeley.[10] The "parole of honor," signed by all the remaining officers, pledged them not to serve against the United States until regularly exchanged.[11] Feeling especially generous (or perhaps opportunistic), Blakeley also allowed the master, the surgeon, the servants and clerks, and the entire, almost forgotten crew of the *Orange Boven* leave to go home as well. The cartel dropped anchor in Cowsand Bay on the seventh, and Chambers set immediately to work. "My logs and records having been captured," dispatched the lieutenant to his admiral in London, "I have to request you will be pleased to move their Lordships to grant me a dispensing order, to enable me to pass my accounts." Feeling somewhat emboldened by his latest tribulations under fire, he then wrote directly to "The Right Honorable the Lords Commissioners of the Admiralty," recapping his career and recommending that "I may be deemed an object not unworthy [of] your lordships notice for promotion."[12] But Blakeley's generosity went for naught. "This parole is null and void," scribbled Admiral Crocker angrily in the margin of his letter-book one week later. "The Lt. and men . . . are released from parole which they ought not have given!"[13] Crocker's reasons for rejection were sound. Chambers had unwittingly enabled the now less encumbered *Wasp* to continue cruising against His Majesty's valuable commerce, should the American captain choose to do so. It was of only secondary importance that the lieutenant may have, admittedly, saved a few equally valuable English lives. But Blakeley did not choose to continue cruising right away. While his damaged fore and mizzen masts still caused him much apprehension, he was gravely concerned about the worsening condition of his two young gentlemen, Midshipmen Langdon and Toscan. They needed first-class French surgeons ashore if they were to survive. Blakeley explained his actions to the secretary:

> After the capture of . . . the Reindeer, it was my wish to have continued the cruise as directed by you. I was however necessitated to relinquish this desire after a few days for the consideration of the wounded of our

crew, whose wounds at this season had become offensive, and aggra-
vated by the number of prisoners on board at the time, being seventy-
seven in number. Fearing from the crowded state of the Wasp that some
valuable lives might be lost if retained on board, I was compelled, with
some reluctance, to make the first neutral port.[14]

As fate is oftentimes kind, Blakeley was allowed to sail into the now neutral L'Orient entirely unmolested, while gobbling up an additional pair of
Englishmen en route. The first victim was snatched up at 6:00 P.M. on 5 July.
One lone musket shot was sufficient to convince the British brig *Regulator*
to haul in its studding sails and cease its useless flight. This very wealthy
prize was twelve days out of Oporto bound to London with 144 pipes of
port wine and a large quantity of cork wood. The crew of eight included
the Liverpool master, Robert Fields, and his wife. Blakeley at length came
to the painful decision to destroy the ship. The brig was incinerated two
hours later, and the volatile cargo lit up the sky until sunrise, when Midshipman Geisinger noted laconically, "At $1/2$ past six, lost sight of the
prize." A French schooner, the *Diana,* and a Swedish brig, the *Speculator,*
occupied their attention for most of the following day. Persistence paid off
toward evening, however, in the form of the *Jenny,* a small, slow, Plymouth
schooner, loaded with "sweet-oil, etc.," out a leisurely thirty days from
Leghorn, Italy, bound to St. Petersburg. Blakeley scuttled it at sunset. The
seventh was taken up with the successful pursuit of no fewer than five
strange sail, no small feat for such a damaged and overcrowded ship.
Unfortunately, they were all neutrals, four Frenchmen and a Swede. These
disappointing chases led Blakeley to within sight of the menacing Pen-
mark Rocks by the following morning. Ghosting along with the moderate
westerly breeze, gliding beneath a brilliant cloud of canvas crowned by the
imperial royals, the *Wasp* picked up the L'Orient pilot just before noon. It
then stood proudly in for Port Louis, adorned with star-spangled bunting
and enveloped with hard-won laurels.

"I have the honor to announce to you the arrival of this ship at this
place," Blakeley wrote the secretary. "From the time of our sailing, I continued to follow the route pointed out in your instructions, until our arrival
at this place." He had been instructed, however, and in no uncertain terms,
to focus his concentration exclusively upon the merchantmen of the enemy.
He continued uneasily: "I found it impossible to maintain anything like a
station and was led farther up the English Channel than was intended."
As a result, Blakeley now had his long-sought glory. He could very well

have declined Manners's invitation to duel, if he had chosen to do so, because the *Wasp* was the swifter of the two sloops of war. Had he lost to the *Reindeer,* as he had at one point come perilously close to doing, Blakeley would have felt the full weight of the secretary's wrath, just as Lawrence of the *Chesapeake* would have, had he survived his disastrous bout with the *Shannon.* Blakeley's job was to hit the enemy where he would do the most damage, in their pocketbooks, and where it would give the greatest impetus to future negotiations. The *Wasp* was to be a naval irritant of the first order, sent deep inside English home waters to help seed, as it were, the pearl of peace. Sparse naval resources must not at this critical time be squandered for the pursuit of personal fame, and although he was at this moment basking in the glory of his very creditable victory, he was now out of commission for the foreseeable future. When they were once again back in the channel, the element of surprise would be entirely lost. Furthermore, two promising young gentlemen-sons of very prominent Portsmouth families lay dangerously, perhaps mortally, wounded in the cockpit. The future resumption of his war on commerce would require the cooperation of the French authorities, and with England and France now at peace, any assumptions held by the secretary on the feasibility of French assistance were now invalid. Might the French allow him to remove his foremast and carry it ashore for repair, and then grant him return to the field? Before this letter joined the growing stack of unforwarded reports atop his writing desk, he amended his present thoughts with an upbeat assessment:

> It gives me much pleasure to state to you the very healthy condition of the crew of the Wasp during the cruise. Sometimes [we were] without one [man] on the sick list and at no time [were there] any that remained there more than a few days. Great praise is due to Dr. Clarke for his skill and attention at all times, but particularly after the action with the Reindeer. The ship is at present under quarantine, but we expect to be released from it tomorrow, when the wounded will be sent to the hospital and every exertion made to prepare the Wasp for sea.[15]

The king's pilot came aboard at 3:30 A.M. and shepherded them safely into St. Louis Roads on the incoming tide. They had already lashed the royal masts and yards securely on deck by the time the best bower anchor plunged into eleven fathoms of water at the "man-of-war's moorings" in the estuary of the Blauvet River one hour later. Fort Louis bore three-quarters of a mile astern to the southwest, and the island of St. Michaels, "in one with the

Tower of L'Orient," rose ahead of them to the northeast. By midmorning all the ship's cutters had left the waist and were bobbing expectantly alongside in the ebbing gray roads. The light clouds, led inshore by westerly winds, began to clear when the "health physician" at last boarded the *Wasp*. He briefly examined the crew, declared them fit, and gave Blakeley his official written *pratique*. Very soon afterward, Midshipmen Langdon and Toscan were rowed ashore, along with eleven other pale and broken bodies.[16] Dr. Clarke sat alongside the motionless forms of the two young officers, each one now only barely clinging to life. Midshipman Ashton Hall, the only fit Portsmouthian, could not help but be distracted from his grief by the many sights and sounds of this busy port, the very same base of operations of his father's service with John Paul Jones during the late Revolution. The scenes that played upon his eyes were little changed from the days of Lt. Elijah Hall's triumphant return in the *Ranger*. The *Wasp* followed them into the inner harbor the following morning and anchored with two fifty-fathom cables in the shallow water.

To his utter surprise, the French officials showed Blakeley not only complete cooperation but even goodwill. "Since our arrival at this place," he wrote Jones, "we have experienced every civility from the public authorities." His polite quarantine had lasted only a few hours, and his dangerously wounded men had been received most compassionately and were now "very comfortably situated" in the naval hospital. "Our foremast, although very badly wounded, can be repaired and will be taken on shore as soon as possible," he continued, "[and] all the other damages sustained can be repaired by ourselves."[17] After a day spent clearing the ship's decks, the *Wasp* hauled up to the "frigates mooring" a half-mile from shore, no small honor for a sloop of war. Blakeley hired the *Marie Louise*, a small lugger or *chase marée*, to act as a cartel, and then generously provided his ship's own stores for the brief voyage home. "It having been the first instance of prisoners brought into France since the change of its relations," Blakeley explained in a third letter to the secretary six weeks later, "I was induced to try the experiment as it would have a tendency to settle the practice for future occasions."[18]

Blakeley accorded his English prisoners an immediate, although temporary, leave to go about on shore until the proper cartel arrangements could be finalized. While the crew of the *Reindeer* were "but indifferently received" by the local population, the wide-eyed men of the *Wasp* were "hailed as victors, tapped on the back, shaken by the hand and complimented for their superior prowess." Blakeley need not have worried about his own reception, either. The *Plymouth Dock Telegraph* recorded a rare, although somewhat angry, glimpse of the prevailing French attitudes:

> The Wasp . . . was put under quarantine until the following morning, when a number of French officers came off to remedy her defects. Every possible attention was paid to her wants, and she was regularly provided with fresh beef. . . . The American crew received every civility, while the British were treated with contempt and insults. A deputy American consul (a Frenchman) struck the master of an English schooner, for merely asking him a simple question. The treatment of the British on board the Wasp was very indulgent in every respect, except that the men were shackled both hands and feet. The crew of the Wasp confessed that their complement in the late action amounted to 210, among whom were several Englishmen, some of which were perfectly known to the people of the Reindeer. . . . Our blood boils with indignation at narrating the shameful conduct of the French.[19]

Because the French long had a history of being uncordial to American seafarers, Blakeley began to wonder if he would have been as warmly received had he not won such a great victory. It was common knowledge that the American successes of this war had had a profound effect on the demoralized French navy. In 1813, as one example, the otherwise crack British frigate *Amelia* had been unable to take the French *Arethusa*, a frigate of equal force, and what was even more shocking, the French ship had been horribly mauled in the attempt. The French had not fought with such purpose and zeal in a generation. All of continental Europe was amazed and secretly amused at the naval humiliations being inflicted upon England by the fledgling American navy. "The French government, even under a Bourbon king, was not ill disposed toward a nation which was deflating the overweening pride of the mistress of the seas," wrote C. S. Forester.[20] Even though France was now a neutral power, new regulations forbade any belligerent from arming in any French port. The sale of prizes was also prohibited. It was most likely in anticipation of the latter restriction that Blakeley had destroyed the valuable *Regulator* and *Jenny* so close to L'Orient. The courtesies afforded to American men-of-war by their professional French counterparts were not extended to mere Yankee merchantmen, however. Not long after the peace, the *Decatur*, an American letter of marque, had been seized, treated shabbily, and held under these restrictions for nearly two months. But during this very same period, three British letters of marque had entered French ports and were allowed to proceed back out to sea unmolested. This uneven application of the French regulations caused no small volume of work for the American minister in Paris, William Harris Crawford.

"News traveled slowly along the roads from Brittany to Paris. Instructions traveled slowly back and had to be reinterpreted."[21] The British government protested loudly in deaf French ears when the *Wasp* was granted permission to stay until repairs could be properly effected. The delay was certainly as much diplomatic as it was due to the extent of the ship's injuries. The ambassador, "a giant of a man" at six foot, three inches, and weighing over two hundred pounds, would have towered over the compact North Carolinian, yet the two men shared much in common. Both were southerners (Crawford had been, until very recently, a Georgia senator), both had grown up in legal and legislative home environments, and sadly, both had lost their fathers well before they had achieved their professional reputations. Crawford was very active physically; he had grown up in the wilds of northern Georgia, then but a rugged frontier, a place where the weak generally withered and died. Crawford had come over the year before in the commerce-killing *Argus* under the able command of William Henry Allen. The new minister had unexpectedly earned a practical appreciation of the navy's world; his storm-tossed, month-long passage was especially gut-wrenching.

Senator Crawford had voted against the prewar naval expansion legislation, believing, as most did at that early time, that the Royal Navy was unconquerable. Since the bill's margin of defeat was narrow, the United States might well have begun the war with thirteen additional frigates had the influential Crawford been an early believer in the importance of naval power. Even as late as December 1812, Senator Crawford had opposed funding for six 74-gun ships of the line. Why build ships that must certainly be taken in the event of war? But now the U.S. Navy had lifted the British spell of invincibility from the minds of the penny-pinching Congress, as well as from the French. Crawford was satisfied but generally amazed at this newly found goodwill, and he could not help but contrast it with the cool reception that he and the as-yet-unproven crew of the *Argus* had received in the same port only a year before. Crawford's enthusiasm for his country's little navy had strengthened considerably. "The brilliant achievements of the navy in the conflict," wrote Charles Mooney, his biographer, "changed his attitude, and he heartily approved the large appropriations for the navy in the postwar years."[22] Crawford needed a swift and strong route home for his State Department dispatches and the *Wasp* was his perfect Hermes. Although he knew that in the present ministry "there exists no feelings friendly to the United States," France might present an act "of justice or apparent friendship" toward Washington if their national interests required it. And they might yet help the United States fend off the terrible military machinery of Great Britain. He wrote optimistically to Secretary of State James Monroe: "The dispatches of Capt. Blakeley to the Navy Department, which I enclose, will show you how difficult it will be for this government to preserve its neutrality, and avoid another war with England."[23]

Repairs to the *Wasp* progressed slowly but methodically throughout the remainder of July and well into August. Although Blakeley had spliced and patched his ship all the way into port, these bandages were only temporary. On 14 July, Bastille Day, the real work began. "At 11 A.M.," wrote Midshipman Geisinger in his journal, "[we] sent on shore one of our Bower anchors, it being broke in the shank by a shot in the late action." At one that afternoon, a hired schooner crept alongside and began to receive the bulk of the *Wasp*'s "provisions, sails and lumber." Much of this unloading was in preparation for taking out the massive foremast, no simple task even in port. The *Wasp*'s built-up foremast, 67½ feet from heel to head, was pulled out the following morning and sent ashore to be patched, recaulked, and fished. It was back between its rightful partners thirteen days later, securely shrouded and stayed. Much hard work had been done on board during its absence. The dawn of the twentieth found the "carpenter and crew repairing shot holes," and the "armorer repairing hammocks, stanchions, etc." The twentieth of July was a typically busy day:

> Commences with light Breezes from the Westwd & Pleasant Weather, got up the Miz T.G. Mast & Rigg'd it, employ'd overhauling the Rigging, blacked the Cross Jack & Miz T. Gt. Yards, Sail Maker & Crew Repairing a F. Sail, Carpenter & Crew Repairing Shot holes forwd, Gunner & Crew on the Main Rigging & Gun tackle blocks—Armorer repairing damages in the Iron Work, some hands employ'd hoisting provisions out of the Schooner & stowing it away in the Hold, Rattled down the Miz. & Miz. T. M. Rigging, Ends fresh Breezes & Cloudy Weather.[24]

In his journal, Geisinger recorded many minor instances of "the sail maker repairing sails" well into the month of August, yet it is not clear whether they referred to battle damage or to normal maintenance. The last specifically referenced instance of the mending of war wounds was recorded 30 July: "The carpenter and crew repairing damages sustained in the action." This was well over a month after the slaying of the *Reindeer*. Midshipman Geisinger also recorded a few valuable details of the *Wasp*'s appearance:

"The carpenter painting the white streak"; the crew "blacking the guns"; "blacking the cross-jack yard"; and "white-washing the berth-deck." One afternoon the crew "scraped down the T. Gt. masts and top masts and gave them a coat of hogs lard." An ingenious, newfangled French machine soon caught this midshipman's fancy: "Rec'd on board 4,000 galls by a watering *tank*." Geisinger recorded events of note as well. On 4 August, "General Soult visited this place and was rec'd with great eclats"; and "this day [25 August] a Grand fete of Louis the 18th [arrived] & the town of L'Orient Illuminated in a most brilliant style." On the day of Soult's arrival, two of the five remaining members of the original eighteen-man marine detachment set a fine example for their sailor brethren to follow: "Wm. Miller, a Marine, stabb'd Henry Richardson, a Marine, in the arm."

Personnel changes also grace this journal's blue-bordered pages, the most serious being the deaths of two of the wounded. On the very day that they extracted the foremast, Geisinger noted: "Died on shore at the French Naval Hospital in L'Orient, Midshipman F. Toscan." The following morning at 10 A.M., "the officers and men left the ship to attend to Mr. Frank Toscan's Funeral, at ½ past noon the men returned." Valiantly clinging to life for as long as he could, Midshipman Henry S. Langdon Jr. finally lost his own struggle at 3:30 A.M. on 1 August to the great despair of the *Wasp*'s wardroom. "Both were buried in the Cemetery at L'Orient . . . and a handsome tablet to their memory was placed above their graves."[25] In his final landlocked report to the secretary, Blakeley remarked:

> It is with sincere sorrow I have to announce to you the decease of Midshipmen Henry S. Langdon and Frank Toscan. They were wounded in the severe [action] with the Rein Deer and all our efforts to save them after our arrival were unavailing. It was their first essay, and altho wounded remained at their posts until the contest terminated. The constancy and courage with which they [bore] their sufferings leaves to their country the melancholy, though proud reflection of what they might have been, had providence ordained otherwise. Every [respect] due to worth, was shown to their memory.[26]

During July and early August fifteen new men joined the ship at L'Orient to replace those killed and incapacitated.[27] All were rated able seamen except John Mede, "wardroom steward." According to Geisinger's journal, of the other thirteen total men hospitalized in L'Orient, one had died on 20 July,[28] and only five of the hospitalized men returned on board as they became able.[29] Seven would be left behind gravely wounded. One of these was Boatswain's Mate William Thompson, because his painful shoulder wound did not heal quickly. The French naval hospital demanded payment for their services, so the 160-plus remaining men of the *Wasp* made a collective contribution of $2.21 per man to help defray the bill for the wounded sailors' care.

Thompson's future care and his eventual transportation back home after the war was going to be mostly his own responsibility. On 23 August Purser Lewis Fairchild paid Thompson the remainder of his accrued pay.[30] During the War of 1812, a highly skilled boatswain's mate earned $19.00 per month, and since he had signed on board the *Wasp* almost exactly eleven months before, Thompson had earned a respectable $209.63. He had run up a considerable tab, however. The recruiting officer had long ago advanced him $38.00, while Fairchild had paid him $89.06 in cash and $21.73 worth of slops. Given his own contribution to the hospital fund, Thompson was left with only $53.60 in his pocket when the *Wasp* sailed. Blakeley instructed the American consular agent at L'Orient, Aaron B. Sail, to provide Thompson with his half-pay, amounting to 49.87 French francs every month, and to help pay his expenses for as long as he remained stranded in this port. Another man left behind was Seaman Francis Brown, who was using the alias Andrew Passenger. Never returning home to his new wife, as evidenced by Charlotte's pension application, Andrew either died of his wounds after the *Wasp* departed L'Orient or he elected to return quietly to his native England following the peace, hoping perhaps to make a clean slate of it.[31]

Two unhappy crewmen from the *Wasp* deserted on 1 August, but one was retrieved by the local authorities on the eve of the corvette's departure three weeks later: "Came on board Berent Johnson, a deserter, from the gaol [prison] on shore, having been taken last Thursday."[32] On 6 August Geisinger observed: "Discharged Wm. Simmons & John Bennet, Seamen, they being Frenchmen." Was this dismissal of these two new men in compliance with France's strict neutrality regulations against fitting out belligerents, or was something more impolitic at work? The New England papers had crowed loudly that the *Enterprize*'s victory over the *Boxer* had been an exclusively American achievement. They had also credited Blakeley with removing all "foreigners" but one from the brig at the war's onset.[33] Was he now doing the same thing again? Just such motives, however justified, probably had an unsettling effect upon his French, ultra-nationalist third lieutenant, Frederick Baury. Preparing to soon continue his cruise, Blakeley took account of his personnel. As a result of the encounter with the *Reindeer,* Blakeley had lost eighteen men: five were killed outright, six were mortally wounded, and seven were so badly knocked about that they were unable to resume their duties. He had been able to retain thirteen new hands, but one original sailor had successfully deserted. Therefore the *Wasp* set out with a total of 167 officers, men, and boys from L'Orient.

The fifteenth of August 1814 commenced with "clear and pleasant weather." Blakeley, his three lieutenants, and the coastal pilot, Michael Drews, concentrated their full attention on the slight ocean-borne breeze. It had been three days since Blakeley had "sent the schooner to the place we received her from," cleared at last of all remaining American property. "The wind [was] so far to the westward," lamented Midshipman Geisinger, "[that] we could not get under weigh." Nor could they the next day. Nor the next. Every morning the pilot came on board, gazed at the heavens, and promptly returned ashore at noon. Clearing the scuppers, coiling the cables, scaling the guns, loosening the sails to air and dry, and at one time shifting one hundred stand of grapeshot aft to the spirit room to trim the corvette down by the stern constituted some of the "sundry" employment of the increasingly edgy crew. For twelve endless days, they sat languishing at the "King's moorings," baking in the sun, waiting for a favorable wind.

Johnston Blakeley had spent nearly the entire war stranded alone in one port or another. John Shaw and the great hurricane had kept him occupied in New Orleans for much of 1812. Dent, Campbell, and Grandison had greedily conspired to husband his attentions in Savannah for the early part of 1813. Hull had detained him in Portsmouth the previous summer, two suspected blockaders had sealed him briefly into Portland during the ensuing August, and William Bainbridge had chained him up for six months on the Merrimack. Finally, national poverty had moored him on the Piscataqua until May 1814. First diplomacy and now the natural elements threatened to do the very same this autumn in France. "It is with regret that I have to inform you of the delays . . . at this place," wrote Blakeley to the secretary, "but had they been of shorter duration, we could not have sailed, as one continued westerly wind has prevented [us] from the hour of our arrival to the present day."[34] Everything changed on 27 August. At sunrise, the freshening breeze had backed slowly around to the northeast, and within the hour the confident pilot rejoined the crowded quarterdeck. This appeared to be it, the long-awaited moment of reckoning. "*All ready for sea,*" emphasized an elated Geisinger, "at 11:30 . . . cast off the moorings and made sail out of port." Blakeley finished his third letter while anxiously hove to just north of "the fort off the Isle of Groa," waiting for the pilot's boat to come up:

> The cruise pointed out in your instructions having been interrupted, I shall endeavor [to continue] until your *further* instructions, as far as may possibly be in my power. With great satisfaction, I add that every aid and information in the power of Mr. Crawford has been promptly afforded, and that I feel under obligation to him for his attention and assistance. We are now off this place with a fair wind and a favorable sea.[35]

Blakeley at long last said good-bye to this last landfall and stood boldly out into the sparkling sea. The day of 27 August lasted only twelve hours, ending abruptly at noon to "commence the sea log." Blakeley's hard-won freedom was now ripe with activity. The *Wasp* chased every sail that appeared within its horizon. The first, boarded at just after dinner, was a Portuguese brig called the *St. Peter.* After annoying a wine-laden Frenchman later that evening, they proceeded to bring to another *St. Peter* the following morning, this time an Antwerp-bound Dutch galliot. Spreading royals and studding sails aloft and alow against the azure autumn sky, the crew of the *Wasp* paid a visit the ensuing day to the *Two Friends,* yet another disappointing French neutral. The thirty-first brought two more Frenchmen, two Swedes, a Dutchman, and at long last, an unlucky Briton within the fatigued crew's grasp. The British brig *Lattice,* the fourth acquaintance of the day, was taken at 10:30 P.M. Lieutenant Baury, Midshipman Geisinger, the newly recovered Master's Mate John Swett, and six able seamen temporarily exchanged their lodgings with the master, Henry Cockburn, and his six-man crew. Not finding much of immediate use either in its hold or storerooms, Baury scuttled the little *Lattice* at 2:00 A.M. The British brig *Bonacord,* deeply laden with wool, wine, and fruit, bound to London twenty-one days out of Seville, was captured and destroyed early in the first afternoon of September. The following morning would prove to be not only extremely active but also exhilarating:

> At ³/4 past 8 discov'd 2 sail bearing West & 2 bearing W by N by N made the 2 last to be a ship and brig by the wind upon the Starboard Tack, at 9 called all hands to quarters and cleared for action, discov'd a fleet of ten or twelve sail to leeward of the ship and brig five or six miles. At 9 the ship and brig hoisted English colours, Observed that the ship had the Brig in tow, [at ?] past 9 observing the ship and brig standing from us towards the fleet. Hoisted American colours and opened a fire upon

the ship. 40 minutes after 9 the Ship cast the brig off & set her studding sails, continued our fire upon the ship as long as the guns would reach, run in between the brig and fleet, when the Brig hauled down her colours, ordered her to heave to which was done, hove main topsail to the mast, and sent a boat on board, she proved to be a British Transport Brig *Mary*, John L. Allen master, laden with Guns, Military and Commissary stores, from Gibraltar to Plymouth (Engl) under convoy of the *Armada* 74 and a Bomb Ship.[36]

The *Armada* had itself been engaged in towing on this day, not very glamorous work for a line-of-battle ship. It had been dragging that ignoble ketch, the bombship *Strombolo*, in its wake all throughout the previous night. But by 7:30 A.M., it finally cast off its fellow sentry and sent a boat out trailing the well-worn hawser to assist an even slower vessel, the transport *Connoly*. The dispersing convoy soon began to outpace the encumbered *Armada*, and by 9:30 A.M., most had moved well on to leeward. The signal midshipman had been kept quite busy all morning, relaying a myriad of nagging messages, such as: "Connoly heave to and keep within hail"; "Beresford make more sail"; and "Convoy to windward to shorten sail." Ten minutes later, however, he observed the *Strombolo* begin to fire signal guns. Slowly, the convoy then began to condense about their thundering bombship, bearing up into the wind en masse and altering their courses back toward the *Armada*. The 74's officers were at first somewhat perplexed at the bombship's noisy antics. There did not appear to be any danger visible from their perspective, but by 10 A.M. they were at last able to discern the *Strombolo's* signal describing "an enemy eastward." True enough, they had seen a ship and a brig lying to in that general direction, but those who had bothered to notice it at all had assumed the pair to be the ship *Prince* and its companion in tow, the wallowing *Mary*. Upon closer inspection, they saw that the ship was indeed a stranger evidently up to no good, and that the *Prince*, having long since abandoned the *Mary*, was fleeing under a great press of canvas, now almost hull down to the northward. The noise of their brief engagement had drifted off to leeward along with the smoke and had gone entirely unnoticed. The *Armada* had just cast off the *Connoly* by the time the first tongues of flame appeared dancing their way up through the *Mary's* abandoned hatchways. The vengeful two-decker soon set every stitch of canvas that it could possibly bear, but by noon found itself "separating from the convoy fast." It shortened sail and very reluctantly wore round to rejoin its charges. Pursuing this strange ship, quite obviously a Yankee privateer, was not worth endangering the balance of the convoy with just the slug *Strombolo*, an aged and lightly armed converted merchantman. As the horizon hazed closer, the *Wasp* began to disappear by imperceptible degrees from their southern perspective, vanishing entirely by 12:30 P.M., "when last seen under all sail." As they let go the deep-sea lead, unsuccessfully trying to find bottom with 117-fathom line, they sadly observed "the *Mary*, burnt to the water's edge, go down."[37]

The poor *Mary* had required its tow not because it had been damaged in any way. It had simply been so deeply laden with military stores that it had lagged behind from the very start. Stacked and gleaming within its hold, alongside an arsenal of munitions from the Gibraltar garrison, were valuable brass cannon taken many years before from the Spaniards. Within half an hour of its capture, the *Mary* was ablaze from stem to stern, while the *Wasp* stood to the northwest, bound in toward the remaining convoy. Abandoning its scattered namesake, the *Armada* had tacked around and was observed "under a press of sail," coming down to intercept them. Not liking the insurmountable odds of a possible meeting, Blakeley rightly hauled his wind to the west-southwest. At noon the *Armada* gave up the chase, because, as Geisinger gloated: "they finding we out sailed her." Blakeley's audacious attack ended here. The *Wasp* did not, as Theodore Roosevelt claimed, hover "like a hawk" around the merchantmen. He was not "chased off again and again by the line of battleship, always returning the instant the pursuit stopped."[38] This single brave attack was daring enough in its own right, requiring no additional late-nineteenth-century embellishments.

Seeing the 74 haul off in apparent failure, Blakeley ordered his own sail reduced. At just past noon on 2 September, the *Wasp*'s crew hauled in the staysails and jib and the ship turned more into the wind, now blowing fresh from the southeast. At 1:45 they furled the main and mizzen sails and hauled the jibs back down. As the outer elements of the *Armada*'s convoy vanished completely into the leeward haze at about 4:00 P.M., Blakeley put confidently before the wind once more, heading west-northwest at a steady six knots. The breeze was now on his best point of sailing, just abaft the larboard quarter. What might have been the quiet, restful end of an active and exhilarating day would prove to be the exact opposite. This first day of September, for the date was as yet unchanged by land, was to be one of the greatest in America's early naval history. Before the day was done, Blakeley would achieve his greatest professional triumph and stand on the very pinnacle of his fame. What he would do that evening would set him apart from every other victorious American commander of the War of 1812. At 6:30 P.M., three sail ghosted along into view through the fine mist, one on the weather bow to the westward, and two additional far forward on the lee. Only fifteen minutes had passed when a fourth vessel revealed herself on the leeward beam. "At 7," recalled Midshipman Geisinger, "discovered the sail to windward to be a large Brig of War, having a signal flying at her Royal Mast Head." Piping his confident Yankee mariners to quarters, Blakeley prepared his little ship for battle and unprecedented glory. Tonight, they would find both.

16. The *Wasp*, To Be Sure

2 September 1814

H is Britannic Majesty's sloop of war *Tartarus*, the leewardmost of the four sails spotted late that hazy Thursday afternoon by Midshipman Geisinger, was caught in the very act of discharging prisoners from its prize, a small recaptured English merchant brig. Capt. John Pasco had been cruising about Cape Clear, off the southern coast of Ireland, under strict orders to search for and to destroy any of the large numbers of American privateers then harassing the coastal trade. Pasco had earlier been Lord Horatio Nelson's signal lieutenant on board the flagship *Victory* during the battle of Trafalgar, nearly a decade before. He had personally hoisted the most famous of all naval signals during the age of sail: "England expects every man to do his duty."[1] Pasco entertained little hope of catching any of these pesky new antagonists from across the Atlantic, however. Although only a few years off the stocks, the ship-rigged *Tartarus* was designed primarily as a fireship, but in the interim had been armed, fitted, and commissioned as a heavy sloop of war, at least until such time as a phoenixlike role might be called upon. Rated at twenty guns, the *Tartarus* actually carried thirty-two cannon upon two closely packed decks, almost all of them carronades.[2] Sailing under conditions calculated for easy speed in any average vessel, this high-bulwarked, frigate-built fireship was barely able to sustain six knots. Under a dangerous press of sail, the foremast had sprung just moments before taking possession of its prize. Prior to this mishap, the *Tartarus* had been closely watching the movements of the homeward-bound Lisbon convoy, under the official protection of the 18-gun brig-sloop *Kangaroo*,[3] when at sunrise the lookout spied the large schooner hovering ominously nearby. While the *Kangaroo* gathered its charges in closer, the top-heavy *Tartarus* bore away in chase of the suspected privateer.[4]

Captain Pasco was cut short, however, when the nimble 18-gun sister brigs *Avon* and *Castillian*, appearing seemingly out of nowhere, left him signaling in their wakes as they tore jauntily off after their common enemy. He might well have missed this rich little merchant brig, because it resembled any one of the loosely formed convoy, if the American prize crew had not panicked at the ship's approach and dashed away toward the perceived safety of a schooner now racing away to windward and well ahead of the two brig-sloops. From his new prisoners Pasco learned that it was the privateer *Tiger* of Baltimore and coincidentally, it was reportedly "last from Newberyport." Although the *Tiger*'s crew had boarded the brig at 9:00 A.M., it was not its captor. "The brig . . . proved to be a prize of the Chasseur American Privateer," wrote Pasco triumphantly in his log, beautifully scribing the name of this infamous Yankee within the mundane, roughly written entries. Depending upon when this brig had been taken by the Americans, it might well represent a small windfall to the *Tartarus*'s captain and crew in the form of "salvage," a percentage of its overall worth paid out by the insurers. Since it appeared to all on board that the brig had been taken more than twenty-four hours before, the minimum allowed time, it was thought to be a legitimate prize. This was the closest Captain Pasco could ever hope to get to the pride of Baltimore and the bane of Britain. He, at least, might owe the *Chasseur* a debt of gratitude. Nursing the wounded forward spar, the *Tartarus* and its little companion next altered their courses to the northeast, exiting the stage at the end of the first act.

The acting commander of the *Castillian*, Lt. George Lloyd, was no doubt in high spirits. When his former commander, Capt. David Braimer, abruptly left the service at Cork, the temporary command of the *Castillian* fell upon his able shoulders. Lloyd had been cruising in company with the *Avon* for the past three weeks. Specifically ordered to work together as a team, they were scouring the sea-lanes for privateers. The 14-gun American schooner *York* had been particularly active about the Cork station during the past few days. It had, in fact, recently nabbed and sent off to America the *Coromandel*, a richly laden coffee trader bound in from Batavia.[5] But the *Chasseur*, against whom the *York* and lesser brethren paled in comparison, was also known to be in these very waters. In an attempt to cut off the unknown schooner, Capt. James Arbuthnot of the *Avon,* the senior commander in Lloyd's little squadron, had signaled the *Castillian* to dash off to the leeward of the flying enemy. The *Avon* would at the same time work up to windward, and between the two of them they would be able to pinch off the privateer from its desired escape sometime within the next few hours. For all that Arbuthnot and Lloyd knew, the flying *Tiger* might well have been the *Chasseur,* this most infamous of Yankee privateers.[6] Under the spirited command of Thomas Boyle, the *Chasseur* was cruising in these same seas from the end of August on through the first weeks of September.[7]

Slowly, from "the Castillian's superiority of sailing free," the brig-sloops began to part company, while the *Tartarus* had by this time already given up the chase. "Captain Pasco afterward communicated by signal," Lloyd reported, "that his masts were wounded, and I subsequently supposed her to be unable to carry sail, if hard pressed." The *Castillian,* racing along at nine knots to the south-southwest with larboard tacks aboard, was increasingly alone as the afternoon wore down. By 6:00 P.M., the *Avon* was nearly six miles distant and the *Tartarus* was but a distant memory. A half-hour later, Lloyd's companion vanished completely in the hazy northeast as well. But he was gaining fast on the *Tiger,* now just three miles away and racing into the setting sun. Lloyd had noticed a strange sail, far off on his weather beam just before dusk, but as there were many merchantmen about, he took no further notice.

"About 8, I lost sight of the chase," Lloyd recalled, "but as I knew the moon would rise a short time after, I did not despair of seeing her again." The eastern illumination appeared much farther north than Lloyd had expected. Instead of glowing silver on the rim of the horizon, the light flashed out a violent gold, well below the blurred starline. The muffled booms that lagged their flashes by several seconds telegraphed their urgent message. "I immediately wore and made all possible sail, firing rockets and burning blue lights to denote our approach," Lloyd reported. Such tactics, well calculated "to intimidate the enemy," were all that Lloyd could do. He stood by his anxious gun crews for well over one seemingly endless hour, staring with horror at the staccato light show that showed no sign of fading. From the very start, Lloyd admitted, "I conceived the Avon to be engaged," but with whom, he could not tell.[8]

The *Avon* was another member of the "ubiquitous" 18-gun *Cruiser* class and was therefore a sister brig to both the *Castillian* and the *Kangaroo* as well as to the late and valiant *Reindeer.* Built in Mr. Symonds's private yard at Falmouth in 1805, the *Avon* did not labor under the three severe handicaps endured by William Manners. First, its frame was constructed of the traditional, solid English oak, not the cheaper Baltic fir used during the crisis of 1803–4. Second, the *Avon* retained its original battery of 32-pounder carronades, the same guns used against the French frigate *Nereide* in 1810. And last, while the *Reindeer* had been destined for the dockyard, or perhaps even for the breaker's yard when it was taken, the *Avon* had just received a substantial "middling" repair at the Portsmouth Naval Yard during the previous November. Having been issued refurnished masts, yards, and rigging, and racing atop brand new copper sheathing,[9] "the Avon was a very fine brig sloop," admitted London's *Naval Chronicle,* "and had a large complement of men."[10]

While in the dockyard, the *Avon* had also received a significant visual alteration. The carved quarter gallery badges, normally placed at the after end of each side, were removed, and thus the broad ocher streak continued on back toward the transom unimpeded. A black square was next painted where the badge once stood, mimicking an additional gun port at the stern end. Normally, because of the tiller ropes riding exposed just inches above the decking, as well as the presence of two essential roundhouses or officers' privies, no gun protruded from the after six feet or so of the gun deck bulwarks. But the artificers further fashioned a sham wooden muzzle and nailed it atop the newly painted square.[11] The overall effect gave a lengthened, more intimidating appearance and it worked. Captain Blakeley proclaimed that his adversary was "one of the largest brigs in the British Navy." Despite its perceived "great length," the *Avon* was the same size as the undergunned *Reindeer.* But it did indeed carry an extra pair of guns, quite possibly private brass pieces acting as standing stern chasers. Probably only long 6-pounders, they could not bear in the true broadside position, being imprisoned behind the tiller's tackle and deprived of any vacant broadside ports. Excluding the standard boat carronade and the traditional swivel guns in its tops, the *Avon* mounted twenty carriage guns, sixteen of them 32-pounder carronades. It was a most formidable sloop of war. While the name *Avon* was held in very high esteem in the Royal Navy for the severe thrashing that it had given to the *Nereide,* the very same name was held in contempt on the other side of the Atlantic. This pariah brig had been involved in one of the countless petty impressment affairs in American territorial waters before the war. Its name graced a dubious list that included the infamous *Leopard, Leander,* and *Guerriere.* The editor of the influential *Niles' Weekly Register* commented upon this when news of the proceedings on 2 September 1814 crossed the ocean:

> The Avon was the same vessel that had behaved so impudently in the Delaware in 1810, while British vessels were interdicted from our waters in consequence of the insolence of their officers. She then carried 18 thirty-two pound carronades, besides bow and stern guns. . . . It would be well if the impertinent fellow who commanded the Avon in 1810 should also have had the command when Blakeley put her pride in the cellar.[12]

If the name *Avon* possessed notoriety in the United States, then so too did the family name of the brig's latest commander, the Hon. Capt. James Arbuthnot. Sir James was the son of Adm. Mariot Arbuthnot, the naval officer who had commanded the British fleet at the siege and eventual capture of Charleston, South Carolina, during the War of Independence. Blakeley had an odd knack for colliding with the sons of the English nobility. Any patriotic boy growing up in the Carolina maritimes would have instantly recognized the Arbuthnot name. Most likely, however, Blakeley never learned the identity of the man he was about to fight. James Arbuthnot had been a master and commander for not quite a year now. His former commanding officer, the Hon. Capt. Sir George Ralph Collier, had recommended his promotion in honor of his most gallant service when, as second lieutenant on board the 38-gun frigate *Surveillante,* he led landing parties of seamen and marines on two rollicking but bloody cutting-out expeditions on the coasts of France and Spain.[13] The *Avon* was thus his reward, and an exceptionally fine one at that.[14]

Blakeley's ominous ship made its silent appearance at about 4:00 P.M. off the *Avon*'s larboard, windward beam, and appeared to be standing down directly for them. The *Castillian* was then about eight miles ahead, somewhere off the leeward bow, while the *Tartarus* had only just vanished into the graying northeast a quarter of an hour before. "She appeared considerably larger than we were," recalled 2d Lt. John Harvey, "higher out of the water, and I should think from her length [that] she mounted four more guns than ourselves." The *Wasp*'s aggressive posturing left no doubt of its nature or intentions. Both British brigs had been ordered to sea in haste; the *Castillian* sailed under the command of the former first lieutenant and the *Avon* had left behind its valuable sailing master (the coastal pilot, who was unexpectedly detained, was given an acting order in his place), along with the surgeon's mate and all but one of the midshipmen. Arbuthnot had been instructed to stick close to the *Castillian*. The recent humiliations surrounding the losses of the *Epervier* and the *Reindeer* probably played a part in this forced union. The Lords Commissioners undoubtedly wanted any American intruders captured quickly and cleanly to avoid any further embarrassments.

Sir James made the private signals and then enforced them with cannon, in the vain hope that the rapidly closing ship was friendly. But, as he had feared, his warning went unheeded. Clearing his sloop of war for action, Arbuthnot made the recall signal to his ship's far distant companion, augmenting the *Avon's* brightly colored flags with still more powder. But they too went unappreciated. "As it came on to dark, we made repeated signals with rockets and blue lights," recalled Lieutenant Harvey. "I had no doubt of her being an enemy's corvette," admitted Captain Arbuthnot, as he bore away into the orange-streaked, violet haze. Even though the wind had now freshened, Arbuthnot nevertheless decided to set his fore topmast studding sail. He was already straining his masts under drum-taut courses, topsails, and jib, "as much sail as we could carry," but he did not want to fight this determined enemy alone.[15]

The American captain carefully studied the large brig on his starboard bow. Stark black against the dimming purple horizon, it now flew signal flags from its silhouetted fore topgallant masthead, which, Blakeley noted, "could not be distinguished for want of light." The stranger next hoisted lanterns aloft, and then fired a leeward gun and signal rockets. Was this Englishman, quite obviously a man-of-war, warning the convoy of Blakeley's presence, or was he requesting assistance from additional cruisers? Who were those three other vessels now lost to the misting darkness? Even under the worst scenario, for now at least, this brig appeared to be reasonably isolated, and its captain did not possess the same bold inclination to fight as did the late William Manners. At 7:45 P.M., Blakeley set the main course and hoisted his country's ensign at the mizzen peak. So that there could be no mistaking his identity, he also ordered a bright signal lantern hoisted right up alongside, so that the snapping Stars and Stripes could be clearly discerned through the still moonless twilight. The chase next hauled down its lights for good, and Blakeley followed suit. As the American captain offered his brailed-up spanker to the reviving breeze and sheeted his flying jib home, he burned a blue light on the forecastle to announce his intentions. At 8:30 P.M., Arbuthnot yielded to the inevitable and fired the first angry shot of the evening from his starboard stern chaser.[16] Lieutenant Harvey observed that they were sailing nine knots when the strange ship at long last came up to within hailing distance on his larboard, weather quarter.

Evening engagements were at best tricky affairs. Commodore Truxtun's moonlit match against *La Vengeance* had been a prolonged, expensive, and bloody business that had ended in a crippling stalemate. Blakeley doubtless thought back to his own experiences under just such conditions. His night-time bombardment of the Tripolitan shore batteries a decade before had not exactly brought honor and accolades down upon Commodore Morris. At least on those two occasions, the extent of the enemy's force was generally known. What was the nature of those three other sails now hidden behind the opaque horizon? "What ship is that?" interrupted an officer on the *Avon*'s quarter-deck. "What brig is that?" Blakeley shot back defiantly against the race of black air. The wind stole away the answer. "His Majesty's Brig . . . ," was all that he heard. Once again, the Englishman hailed the *Wasp*, posing the same question. If they heaved to, Blakeley retorted, he would be happy to enlighten them. Fearing that none of his answers had survived the intervening gusts, Blakeley sent Sailing Master Carr forward to the topgallant forecastle to relay the message through his speaking trumpet. The Briton addressed the American one last time: "What ship is that?" Blakeley's answer came much clearer now. "He told us to heave to," recalled Lieutenant Harvey, "and he would send his boat on board and let us know who he was." His captain's message at last delivered, Carr stepped back out of the way while the attendant quarter gunner tripped the lock of the *Reindeer*'s veteran 12-pounder.

Before Carr's eyes could accustom themselves to the darkness, the *Avon* suddenly hauled to port and vanished in nine rippling white flashes. But this half-raking broadside whistled harmlessly through the *Wasp*'s cordage. The American's eleven starboard guns instantly returned the salute, and the bout began in earnest. Blakeley suddenly bore up in an attempt to rake the brig across its stern. But the nimble *Avon*, spinning about, delivered its parry by bearing up as well. Both crews now ran to their opposite batteries, the crew of the *Wasp* manning the larboard side and that of the *Avon* the starboard. Blakeley had lost this first round, for Arbuthnot now possessed the weather-gauge, such as it was. He did, however, put an interesting twist on his faux pas: "[We] ran under his lee bow to prevent his escaping." The *Avon* soon ate his wind, however, and forged ahead, leaving the *Wasp* on its starboard quarter. "The action then became general on the starboard side and within half-pistol shot," Harvey would later testify, "both of us yawing about to prevent each other from being raked."[17]

Arbuthnot suffered a tragic loss almost at the very start. First Lieutenant Pendergrast "fell by a grapeshot while nobly cheering the crew."[18] But the

Avon's gunners plied their trade with both bravery and zeal. Lieutenant Harvey later boasted that his guns were both "quick and well worked," while the gunner, Charles Helliken, testified that his ammunition was in "plenty and well supplied." The crew of the *Avon*, unlike that of many of its sister-brigs, had practiced with their great-guns quite frequently: "We exercised them every evening," stated Harvey, "from the time we first left Plymouth," some ten months before. The British gunners fired intentionally high, in hopes of dismantling and thus delaying the *Wasp*.

Yardarm to yardarm, with their larboard tacks aboard, the combatants sailed off with their austere billet heads racing into the west-southwest, exchanging iron 32-pound spheres amid deafening booms and blinding flashes. Even though the smoke carried effortlessly away after each discharge, the two teams of gun crews could scarcely see one another. The blackened airs would just barely permit an obscure image of their racing target, when a flash of infinite brightness would momentarily blind both sides. Just as their dilated pupils would once again readjust to the darkness, the white thunder would appear once more, in ones and twos or the occasional rolling partial broadside. The British gunners aimed at the long white streak on the *Wasp*'s pitching side, while the Americans focused on the *Avon*'s broad band of ocher, which was altogether shorter, lower, and dimmer. Not surprisingly, many shots from both sides flew harmlessly into the sea.

As the clock ticked slowly down toward 10:00 P.M., Commander Arbuthnot assessed his mounting losses. Over one-third of his company had been struck down already, his brig was in shambles, and the enemy fire was still pouring in unabated. Like Captain Manners before him, he too had been wounded seriously in both legs, but he was still able to stand. Besides the loss of his sole midshipman, fourteen of his eighteen marines had already gone below to the surgeon. There was no longer any hope of boarding. Marine Pvt. John Weir had an arm carried away while serving his musket, while Pvts. George Jones and Thomas Loader each lost a leg below the knee. An imperfectly cast 32-pound ball still managed to graze Pvt. William Baxter's right thigh, pressing it into a horrific pulp, necessitating an immediate and nearly lethal amputation at the hip.

When the unsupported mainmast finally crashed over the side at just before ten o'clock, the issue was settled. Up until that point, the shattered brig continued to forge on ahead at a good six knots. The entirety of the running rigging and all but two shrouds of the foremast's standing rigging had been shot away, and there was neither a brace nor a bowline left to work the remaining yards. Both the wheel and its relieving tackle were gone, so now the brig had to be steered manually by the tiller. Even then, the bulky stern chasers on either side were in the way. The carpenter, George Handly, reported seven feet of water in the hold, lapping just inches below the lower deck hatches. Handly had found seven shot holes beneath the waterline, all but one of them aft. Lieutenant Harvey had by this time already started to pull his men away from the great-guns to man the pumps and bail at the hatchways. While standing in water up to his knees, the gunner nevertheless continued to serve out the remaining dry powder until the very moment of surrender, when he heroically snatched up all the signal cartridges that he could carry and then climbed out of his flooding magazine. "Do you think the brig could have been defended longer?" Boatswain John Brack was asked at the court-martial. Perhaps, responded the warrant officer coolly, "provided she could have swam."

After at least an hour of intense combat, Blakeley observed that the enemy's fire had now slackened considerably. At 10:00 P.M., he ordered his men to cease their firing altogether, at the same time hailing the brig to ask if it had surrendered. "To this inquiry, no answer was given," recalled one of the *Wasp*'s officers, "but [he] fired a gun and a few muskets from his tops." The *Wasp* resumed its fire for several additional minutes and then easily recaptured the weather-gauge athwart the *Avon*'s larboard quarter. By this time, however, the wind had abated significantly, and the glowing moon had risen into full view through the thickening fog bank. "She must have suffered a great deal, as we could distinctly hear the groans and screams of the wounded."[19] At 10:10 P.M., Blakeley ordered the starboard guns remanned. Only "three or four" of them had discharged by the time Blakeley again ordered his batteries to cease their well-directed fire. At 10:12 P.M., observing that the enemy had made no return to the *Wasp*'s last two larboard broadsides, and none since he had regained the weather-gauge, Blakeley again hailed the brig: "Have you surrendered?" This time, the response came back "in the affirmative." Both sides agreed on the time of surrender, but on little else. During the next few minutes, someone on board the *Avon* called out across the intervening water: "What ship is that?" One of the elated Americans, quite possibly Blakeley himself, as it would have been his right, replied triumphantly: "The Wasp to be sure!"[20]

The *Wasp*'s sails were in tatters, perforated by hundreds of English spheres of various radii; the yards were hanging in their preventive chains without a brace or bowline remaining; and the renewed foremast was deeply embedded with countless grape and canister shot. Yet Blakeley was extremely fortunate. Only four 32-pounder round shot had struck the hull, and none of these had passed completely through. Only two of his people lay dead, but one of them was his indispensable veteran boatswain, Joseph Martin, and the other, an equally valuable quarter gunner, Henry Staples. Three other men had been slightly wounded, the most serious a sailor whose collarbone had been snapped in two by a spent British wad. The *Avon* had suffered ten killed and thirty-two wounded. Blakeley was in his glory. A shout from the masthead soon diverted his attention. What had at first been taken for a merchantman turned out to be another brig-rigged sloop of war, "a little distance astern."[21] The crew of the *Wasp* abandoned their boats and ran hurriedly back to their guns. Unable to yet brace up his yards against the abating although still considerable breeze, Blakeley instead put before the wind toward the northwest, his riggers working feverishly in the moonlight. Before the *Wasp* abandoned him, Arbuthnot thought that he heard an American cry out, "I am off to attack the other brig" or, as he would relate to Captain Pasco, "words to that purpose."[22] Blakeley, in turn, thought that he heard someone call out that the brig was sinking, although he wasn't at all sure. He couldn't even identify the name of his late adversary with any certainty. In the confusion of the moment, perhaps, the lookout thought that he saw two more sail bearing down upon them, "one astern and the other one point on our lee quarter."

Lieutenant Lloyd had observed the action "for upwards of an hour" when at last he came close enough to make out the situation clearly. The men of the *Castillian* could by then recognize the *Avon*, "a totally dismantled and ungovernable wreck," and to the leeward of her, "a large ship corvette." The enemy appeared in flight, "having neither light nor ensign at the peak at this time." Still, it took Lloyd the better part of an hour to catch up to the crippled ship. Shortening sail for action, he hailed it several times without receiving any response, observing "the confusion which evidently prevailed on board the enemy." All the while, his dying companion fired frequent signal guns of distress, and Lloyd was forced to make the single most difficult choice of his suddenly endangered career:

> I had the gratification to be within half a cables [*sic*] length [away] on her weather quarter, but I lament to state, at this anxious crisis the Avon's situation became most alarming—she had commenced firing minute guns and making every signal of distress, and of being in want of immediate assistance. . . . The damage she [the *Wasp*] had sustained and her bad steerage, together with the cool and steady conduct of the officers and men I have the honor to command, I had no doubt of her

falling an easy prey could we have persisted in attacking her—but which was not to be done without sacrificing the lives of the surviving gallant crew of our consort. . . . I resolved (with the opinion of the officers) to return to their assistance, and was obliged (contrary to the wishes of all, except under so urgent a circumstance) to leave the flying enemy to escape.[23]

However, hoping to deliver the coup de grâce, finishing off any last hope the American captain might have of escaping, at about 11:30 P.M., Lloyd took up a half-raking position on the *Wasp*'s weather quarter and fired his full larboard battery into her. "I feel somewhat gratified," he proclaimed to his superiors, "[that] the situation . . . enabled me to give him a raking, and I doubt not, from the closeness of the two vessels, a most destructive broadside." As proof of his gunnery skills, Lloyd noted that the enemy did not return even a single gun: "A circumstance," he added disingenuously, "that I trust cannot fail to prove how destructive the Avon's fire must have been." Perhaps if Lloyd had placed his brig in a more accessible position—for no American gun could possibly bear upon him from abaft their larboard, windward quarter—he might have received an appropriate reply. At such a range, Lloyd's double-shotted broadside might have been devastating, and perhaps even fatal, had it been well aimed. Instead, his shot flew even higher than the *Avon*'s, cutting away the *Wasp*'s main topmast backstay, splintering a large section of the maintop, and blasting off part of the lower main cross trees. Apart from giving Blakeley's carpenter a lot of additional work to do, Lloyd's gunners injured no one, not even in the slightest.[24] Blakeley kept off his wind, he reported, not only to repair his cut braces but also in hopes of drawing the *Castillian* away from what he perceived to be two additional consorts. "The second brig could have engaged us if he thought proper," Blakeley recalled, "as he neared us fast." But the *Wasp* continued on into the misty northwest; the weary crew was busy knotting and splicing well past dawn.

When Lloyd finally rejoined his battered companion at 11:55 P.M., the situation proved dire indeed. "Although the after guns were hove overboard, the anchors cut away, [along with] everything else that could be got at," wrote Lieutenant Harvey, the water still gained fast on the pumps. At 1:00 A.M., when the last of the *Castillian*'s boats had just pulled away from the *Avon*, the waterlogged brig went down by the head. Now crammed with more than 230 men, the *Castillian* made all possible sail "after the beaten and flying enemy." Lloyd and Arbuthnot pooled their collective wisdom and concluded that the *Wasp*, although last seen sailing free into the northwestern haze, would have instead altered course to the northeast just as soon as the rigging was put to right. The American captain would most certainly be attempting to make the nearest accessible naval dockyard, presumably L'Orient, before his ship foundered. Their combined fire could have produced no lesser effect upon the hopelessly shattered American, they assured each other. But much to their dismay, Blakeley instead continued on his original course.

Twenty-four hours later, the *Castillian* greeted its old companion, the *Tartarus*, still sailing in company with its valuable little prize. Captain Pasco, now the senior officer present, took on board forty volunteers from the *Avon*'s crew and appropriated part of the *Castillian*'s gunnery stores, primarily "pole axes" and cutlasses, along with additional quantities of fresh water. He ordered Lloyd and Arbuthnot to take the wounded crewmembers of the *Avon* back to Cork, while at the same time escorting his valuable prize brig safely in. Pasco, his foremast now securely splinted, then bore away after the *Wasp*, this time in the proper direction, but by then it was too late. Far too many miles of intervening sea lay between them.

James Arbuthnot and his men stood trial on 1 October. Without recording the reasons for their decision, the court found that "no blame whatever is imputable to the captain . . . his officers and sloops company for their conduct." They were all honorably acquitted.[25] No mention is made of superior forces in men or metal, poor gunnery, the drawing of breech or fighting bolts, or of any early catastrophic loss of masts, sails, or rigging. The court, however, accepted Arbuthnot's testimony, which stated that the battle lasted two-and-a-half-hours.[26] It was Lloyd alone who repeatedly brought up the issue of the great disparity between the two forces. The English newspapers, lacking other sources, picked it up, and British historian William James ran with it, so the battle deserves further discussion. Excluding, for simplicity's sake, the bow and stern chase guns, the shifting boat-guns and swivel-howitzers that were by now plentiful on both sides, any historical argument must rest upon the main batteries of the two sloops. The *Avon* mounted sixteen 32-pounder carronades and the *Wasp* nineteen. This assumes, of course, that Blakeley had not lost the permanent use of either of the two carriage guns reportedly dismounted during the *Reindeer*'s action. This makes the disparity of broadside force, at best, about ten to eight against the English, much closer than in any of the celebrated frigate actions of 1812. The *Wasp* was greater in length by about one full fifth, and its sides were proportionally higher out of the water. But this should have served to make its hull an easier target to hit. True enough, the ship-rigged American, having by definition three masts (and much stouter ones, too), would have taken longer to cripple than the two-masted brig. But the *Avon* should at least have been able to slow its heavier antagonist down long enough to allow its consorts to come up. The point is this: The *Avon* did not have to win to protect its nation's commerce. It need only have made the *Wasp* pay an unacceptably high price for its victory. A bold, aggressive stroke in the spirit of William Manners might have brought James Arbuthnot limitless glory. Instead, he fought only a running, defensive battle. It is important to remember that the French frigate *Nereide*, so badly mauled by this same brig back in 1810, had mounted forty-four guns and carried 350 men, exactly double the number of each then on board the *Wasp*. However, it is difficult to criticize the actions of an undeniably brave man who kept on fighting until his vessel literally sank beneath him.

Arbuthnot never completely recovered from his leg wounds. He retired from the navy "a year or two later," after briefly commanding the sloop of war *Martin*. He then removed to the island of Madeira, where his wounds reportedly developed some unspecified complication, and he died "soon after."[27]

The unsuccessful tactic of flight, or rather of endeavoring to close with its consort as per orders, combined with high firing deliberately calculated to disable the pursuer, were the two factors that effectively did in the *Avon*. The *Wasp* did not win simply because it carried one or two extra carronades a side, or because it was somewhat larger. Counteracting this advantage was the certain knowledge that help for the *Avon* was only a few miles away and that native soil lay just over the northern horizon. The *Wasp*, for its part, was completely isolated and thousands of miles away from home. Furthermore, the crew of the *Wasp* had already had a very busy day of it. Prior to that evening's battle, Blakeley's men had chased a large convoy, shot it out with the *Prince* and the *Mary*, secured and burned the latter, and then won a chase in earnest against the mighty *Armada*.

The most critical point of contention surrounding this battle is time. While Arbuthnot, Lloyd, and Blakeley all agreed that the shooting ceased at about 10:15 P.M., plus or minus a couple of minutes, they disagreed radically on the moment of commencement. Their opening times are 8:00, 9:00, and 9:30 P.M., respectively. Excluding the last one-sided, fifteen-minute interval (the time after which Blakeley had first hailed to ask if the British had surrendered), the fight lasted either one-half hour (Blakeley), one hour (Lloyd), or two hours (Arbuthnot). Lloyd, it turns out, was the only one telling the truth. He was the "disinterested" third party. Lloyd reported having heard the heavy gunfire begin at exactly 9:00 P.M. Had the shooting begun earlier he would certainly have heard it because he would have been at that time much closer. Both the captain's and the master's log of the *Castillian* concur with his statement.[28] Two anonymous letters, both published in an American newspaper, also state that the fight began at "about 9."[29] What seems to have happened is this: The fight, as defined as a mutual exchange of gunnery, actually lasted one hour, from 9:00 P.M. to 10:00 P.M., which does not count the final, one-sided fifteen-minute phase. Blakeley cut this duration in half, while Arbuthnot, in turn, doubled it. Having taken the *Reindeer* in a mere nineteen minutes, Blakeley probably thought that seventy-five minutes would appear a bit too long. He might even have feared professional criticism for not having taking possession of his vanquished foe earlier, before the arrival of the second brig. The quicker the victory, the greater the glory.

Arbuthnot's version began at 8:00 P.M., presumably when he fired the first signal gun.[30] James, giving his countryman every benefit of the doubt, suggested that if these "signals" were all aimed at the approaching American, then Arbuthnot would technically have been correct.[31] Arbuthnot needed to show that he had bravely withstood the onslaught "for two and one half hours, broadside to broadside," against a vastly superior foe. This embellishment, however, would later backfire on him. For the first week or so after the battle, everyone truly believed that the *Wasp* had been severely punished as well. "The Wasp was supposed to have sunk also," wrote an unidentified British officer in a Cork newspaper, "as she was waterlogged and not afterwards seen." However, he reassured the readers, "if she was still above water," the multitude of cruisers off the coast would soon deal with her. Arbuthnot had initially received great accolades for his brave defeat. "This action will forever rank among the most brilliant achievements recorded in the naval annals of this eventful war," crowed one Plymouth paper.[32] But then a neutral cartel put quietly into the Downs, carrying the masters of the *Lattice,* the *Bonacord,* and the *Mary.* Because they had all been witnesses to the action, they astonished the local ministry when they related how little damaged the American ship actually had been. What was even worse, not only was it still afloat, but the *Wasp* was once again plying its trade, a situation the *Naval Chronicle* could only describe as "incredible." The cartel also allegedly contained a bold challenge, reportedly given by Captain Blakeley, "to engage any two brigs in his majesty's service!"[33] Arbuthnot was now in the uncomfortable position of having to explain how he could have fired his guns at point-blank range for so long without having done any significant harm to his adversary.

Despite Johnston Blakeley's statement to the contrary, no other brig-sloops approached him that September evening. While he might have mistaken two nearby merchantmen for cruisers, it is very doubtful that any civilian vessel would have sailed directly toward the sights and sounds of heavy, protracted gunfire. Perhaps Blakeley just believed the reports of an overimaginative lookout. Many historians have blindly accepted Blakeley's statement as accurate, believing that the *Tartarus* and its prize were the two other sail that he reported seeing. "They [the *Castillian* and *Tartarus*] had seen what the Wasp's guns had done to their consort," boasted one modern American writer, "and neither quite cared to follow that terrible raider into the dark alone."[34] Remembering that the *Avon* was just one of four vessels that he had seen sailing in company that afternoon, and observing that the second sail was also a man-of-war, Blakeley had to acknowledge the very real possibility that all four were hostile. Although he could have seen neither the *Tartarus* nor its prize at that late hour, they being at the time too far away, he had to believe that they might come up out of the growing mist at any moment. Then again, considering the report of the cartel's challenge to be true, Blakeley would have needed more than the approach of just two brigs to justify his retiring from the field. Nevertheless, because official British reports were suppressed and the newspaper accounts were muddled, Blakeley got away with this presumably unintentional little tale.

The deeply Federalist, antiwar newspapers, the *Newburyport Herald* and Portsmouth's *New Hampshire Gazette*, dutifully reported all of Blakeley's official letters, but without much boastful comment. The editors were clearly happy, but they dared not cross the line and give the impression of supporting "Mr. Madison's war."[35] The former paper even printed up a special, two-column supplemental insert when Blakeley's official *Reindeer* action report at last became available. It shared double billing with the glorious account of a failed cutting-out action attempted by the boats of the British frigate *Endymion* against the American privateer *Prince de Neufchatel*. Like the *Wasp*'s first action, this gruesome cutlass contest off the Nantucket coast had been decided in the Yankees' favor in only twenty minutes. The *Chesapeake*'s hand-to-hand humiliation had now been doubly avenged. New England's maritime manhood had twice been vindicated. The national paper, *The Niles' Weekly Register*, was jubilant: "If Captain Blakeley should return to France . . . what will the Frenchmen think of him and us?"[36] The newspapers from the pro-Republican southern states were even more euphoric.

"Well Done Wasp!" proclaimed the headlines of the 17 November *Savannah Republican and Evening Ledger,* when the second victory became known:

> Captain Blakeley, his officers and crew have earned a garland of praise. Twice have they challenged the would be mistress of the ocean to combat, and twice have they compelled her to lower her ensign of sovereignty submissively to the conclusive logic of American cannon. Too much praise cannot be stowed [*sic*] on these daring sons of the ocean, on that cool collected bravery that dauntless enterprise that superior skill that they have uniformly displayed—honors and rewards to the men who have rendered honor to their country! Praise and glory be on their heads!

The editor of the Republican *New York Columbian* wrote a lengthy dissertation on the unprecedented glories of the *Wasp's* commander; the leading Republican weekly in Raleigh, *The Star,* reprinted this glowing tribute to their hometown boy in its entirety:

> Equaled only in gunnery by that with which the immortal Lawrence literally reduced to a wreck, the British Peacock, the gallant capt. of the Wasp stands preeminently entitled to the richest marks of distinction and the sincerest applause of a grateful people. . . . When he returns to the United States, then we must hail him not merely as a companion of [Lewis] Warrington, but as a fit yoke fellow even for the illustrious [Isaac] Hull, and the equally illustrious victors of the Java [William Bainbridge] and Macedonian [Stephen Decatur]. We must greet him as a hero who first explored a new field of glory; and once more as a nation, pour forth strains of gratitude to him who returns from the deep with twin laurels on his brow. We must unite with one voice to afford the noble tar a magnificent welcome and as he advances through the land of his birth, give him that suitable testimony of his exalted virtues which the hearts of enlightened millions are ever ready to bestow.[37]

The best-read histories of any war are more often than not written by the winning side. In the case of the War of 1812, the authors were also the victors. They tended to paint a picture with so heavy-handed a brush that the results are barely believable. Many modern works are merely watered-down copies of their predecessors, their authors unwilling to dig into the archives and come up with new insights or original conclusions. This is especially evident in the study of this particular conflict. Perhaps the most meaningful expression of praise for Johnston Blakeley comes from none other than the Anglophile (and Ameriphobe), William James:

> To the merit justly due the captain of the Wasp, for his conduct in his two successful actions, America must be contented to divide her claim; as Captain Blakeley was a native of Dublin, and, with some English and Scotch, did not it may be certain, neglect to have in his crew a great many Irish. The construction of so fine a ship as the Wasp, and the equipment of her as an efficient man of war, is that part of the merit, and no small part either, which belongs exclusively to the United States.[38]

The accomplishments of the *Wasp* and its gallant commander were not only unprecedented, they were never again repeated in the postconstitutional American sailing navy. Only four sail-powered American naval ships ever triumphed over more than one comparably classed single-ship opponent during any war. The glorious quartet included the frigates *Constitution* and *Constellation,* and the sloops of war *Hornet* and *Wasp.* But only in the last case were the dual glories achieved while out on a single cruise. Three commanders alone fought more than one such action during the War of 1812: James Lawrence, Stephen Decatur, and Johnston Blakeley. Both Lawrence and Decatur, however, had lost their second actions along with their respective frigates, and, in the case of the former, his life as well. There were only two doubly victorious single-war, single-ship captains in the history of this nation's sailing navy: Thomas Truxtun of the *Constellation* during the Quasi-War, and Johnston Blakeley. But Blakeley alone, it cannot be overstressed, achieved his glories while out on a single cruise, sailing under one set of orders, and without returning home to revel in his fame and properly repair his ship. Lawrence, Decatur, and Truxtun were all full-fledged, double-epauletted captains, and in the case of the latter two, honorary commodores, when they fought their second battles. "Captain" Blakeley was still only a mere master commandant when he achieved his dual glories.

Of all the much-heralded victories achieved by the U.S. Navy during this incredible war, Blakeley's two battles occurred in waters closer to the enemy's sacred soil than any of the others. This was especially meaningful to Blakeley because his glories were earned within a half-day's sailing of his native Ireland. Blakeley had attacked a convoy guarded by no fewer than four enemy sloops of war, the *Avon, Castillian, Tartarus,* and *Kangaroo;* destroyed the one closest to his own force; and then made his complete getaway. (There were actually five sloops of war; the British sloop *Cephalus,* yet another

18-gun *Cruiser*-class bruiser, was hull down on the southwestern horizon at the start of the engagement.) Blakeley's aggressive attack upon Arbuthnot's squadron might be considered excessively bold and perhaps even a bit rash, while the same brave and resourceful British officer who had behaved so gallantly upon the enemy's shores seemed to have been at a loss as to what to do by sea. Indeed, the battle between the *Wasp* and the *Avon* might be described as a contest between temerity and timidity. While the Royal Navy could easily replace their two lost brig-corvettes, the loss of face they suffered was incalculably great. Politically, Blakeley's backyard victories caused his enemy nearly as much embarrassment as all the others combined. From the study of its martial accomplishments alone, therefore, it becomes increasingly clear that the *Wasp* was the most effective cruiser ever to fly the Stars and Stripes under sail. Ton for ton and gun for gun, the gallant little *Wasp* achieved far more in this war than did even the mighty *Constitution*.

In making a fair judgment of the qualities of Johnston Blakeley as an officer, one must examine, and similarly place into proper perspective, not only his dual achievements but also the human resources at his disposal beforehand, and the time that he had available to mold them into proper shape. Commodore Decatur had the crew of his *United States* together as a cohesive fighting unit for nearly two years when he met, whipped, and captured the *Macedonian*. Similarly, Captain Hull had retained his men for nearly the same period when he slew the *Guerriere* during the summer of 1812, and the hearty men of the *Constitution* were still virtually unchanged by the time Commodore Bainbridge took Old Ironsides into action again five months later against the *Java*. Mstrs. Comdt. James Lawrence and Jacob Jones had each commanded their ship sloops, the *Hornet* and the first *Wasp*, for about eighteen months when they crippled their respective English cruisers, the *Peacock* and the *Frolic*. And lest we forget, Lieutenant Blakeley had had nearly two and a half years to work his southern *Enterprize* crew into fighting fitness before they knocked out the *Boxer*. Later in the war, when Charles Stewart simultaneously defeated the heavy corvettes *Cyane* and *Levant* in Old Ironsides's third celebrated triumph, he had preserved his people together for nearly two years. This was also the case for James Biddle, when he took the *Hornet*, its second victory of the conflict, against the British brig *Penguin*. On the other side of the glory equation, Philip Broke had kept his crew of the *Shannon* for about six years when they killed James Lawrence, and John Maples's men of the *Pelican* had served together for not quite a year when they did the same to the *Argus*'s William Allen.

The *Wasp*'s men had been together at sea for only two months before they encountered the *Reindeer*. The only other victorious American commander during this war laboring under similar constraints was Lewis Warrington, who had been at sea for nearly as many days when he plucked the brig *Epervier*. But his *Peacock* was New York City's sole sloop of war, and this major port was not, for whatever reason, selected to construct either a single frigate or a ship of the line, and so Warrington had his pick of the plentiful bluewater mariners, not to mention provisions. Each of the six other American ships of war had enjoyed the bounty of peace from which to select the choicest cut of America's maritime manhood, and each had similarly participated in one or more shakedown cruises beforehand to fine-tune their seamanship. But such was not the case in Newburyport in 1814. Blakeley had received only those meager table scraps that Bainbridge and others had tossed to him; Bainbridge had sent his best people and nearly all of his marines south to his brother Joseph. The captain from North Carolina had molded his crew into an efficient fighting force in about one-tenth the time, on average, available to his winning rivals. If one considers the *Boxer* to have been as much Blakeley's prize as Burrow's—the latter had fallen on the very first British broadside, and the Blakeley-trained officers and crew had fought the vast majority of the action alone—then one must admit that Johnston Blakeley has as much claim to the title of America's "Nelson" as do Stephen Decatur, Isaac Hull, James Lawrence, or even John Paul Jones. The accomplishments of this North Carolina "Nelson" were just as important, if not more so. Johnston Blakeley must rightfully be considered America's most accomplished naval commander during the age of sail.[39]

17. ADIEU

September–October 1814

$\mathcal{K}$notting and splicing was once again the supreme order of the day on board the *Wasp* for at least the next seventy-two hours. Although he had left a page blank in his journal for the date, David Geisinger never wrote any entries for 2 September 1814. He leaves the reader on the first, "clearing [the] ship for action." Perhaps the conflicting versions left him somewhat perplexed, for he was duty-bound both to record his own personal reflections as well as to support his captain's official dispatches. Equally likely, he might simply have forgotten in the haste and intense labor of the moment. Geisinger continued his account on the third, noting that the entirety of the day was spent bending new courses and topsails to the grape-laden yards and "repairing damages sustained in the late action." It was most fortuitous indeed that the weather had moderated at the exact moment that it did, and had then continued to remain relatively mild over the next few days. By the fifth, the rerigged *Wasp* easily overhauled the neutral Swedish *Eolus,* and Captain Blakeley persuaded the master of this Gothenburg-bound brig to become yet another paid cartel.

On the tenth, the *Wasp* "spoke" a Swedish ship that had, coincidentally, been one of the several neutral merchantmen detained by this same corvette back on 31 August. The Swedish captain's patience was sorely tried the following day, when the eager North Carolinian captain interrupted his voyage to Amelia Island for a third time. During this brief respite, Blakeley at long last had time to catch up on his paperwork. He wrote Secretary Jones on 11 September, beginning with a brief account of the fight with the "mystery brig," including a separate "minutes of the action," and concluding with praise for his junior officers:

> It is with real satisfaction I have the pleasure of bearing testimony to the merits of Lieutenants Reilly, Tillinghast, Baury, and Sailing Master Carr; and to the good conduct of every officer and man aboard the Wasp. Their divisions and departments were attended and supplied with the utmost regularity and abundance, which, with the good order maintained, together with the vivacity and precision of their fire, reflects on them the greatest credit.[1]

Blakeley had every reason to be proud of them. Reilly had now achieved the honorable distinction of having placed more victories under his belt than any other U.S. Navy lieutenant during the war. Acting Third Lieutenant Baury, whose wartime career exactly paralleled that of his longtime friend Reilly, held the same distinction and total for the rank of midshipman. Both men had also participated in more battles during this war, win or lose, than any other naval officers. Tillinghast came in second with three laurels. Blakeley continued:

> The hull received four round-shot and the fore-mast many grape-shot. Our rigging and sails suffered a great deal. Every damage has been repaired the day after, with the exception of our sails. . . . Of the vessel with whom we were engaged, nothing positive can be said with regard to her name or force. While hailing him, previous to his being fired into, it was blowing fresh, (then going 10 knots,) and the name was not distinctly understood. Of her force, the four shot that struck us are all 32 pounds in weight, being a pound and three quarters heavier than any belonging to this vessel. From this circumstance, the number of men in her tops, her general appearance, and great length, she is believed to be one of the largest brigs in the British navy.

The *Avon*'s force was still further aggrandized by an unidentified midshipman. "She appeared larger and more lofty than we and had 11 ports upon her side," bragged the enthusiastic youth in a widely published letter, "and I am confident with our present commander and crew we could beat a 28-gun frigate."[2] As there were nine filled gun ports per side, plus an unarmed bridle-port and the sham port far aft, he was technically correct. Indeed, there is every probability that the *Wasp* could have successfully challenged just such a formidable foe. After all, back in 1812 Blakeley had attempted to do exactly that against the 28-gun *Brazen* with his little 16-gun *Enterprize*.

At 4:00 P.M. on 13 September, the "pleasant breezes" urged the *Wasp* easily down upon a deeply laden English brig, the *Three Brothers*, bound to London out of Lanzarote sixteen days, with an exceptionally valuable cargo of wine and dry goods aboard. Blakeley off-loaded as much of its cargo as he could accommodate into his own increasingly crowded hold. Before his crew scuttled it at 1:00 P.M. the following day, nearly everything of value and utility that was not nailed down had been removed. Later in his life, David Geisinger, then a captain himself, described to Blakeley's biographer, Dr. James Johnson, some details of the *Wasp*'s method of plunder. Johnson wrote in 1854:

> Capt. Geisinger informs us that while he was on board the Wasp, they were in the habit of taking from the captured vessels, whatever was considered most valuable before they were destroyed. The ship was soon filled with packages of broad cloths, linens, silks, etc. . . . When the next prize was examined, other articles would be found more valuable than these, and dry goods were thrown overboard without hesitation to make room for laces, cashmeres, watches jewelry and ready money. Chronometers and other nautical instruments were very plenty and cheap on board the Wasp. We may even imagine one of her sprightly midshipmen, sporting a gold watch or two, and with gold rings on his fingers, throwing his bed and blanket out of a port hole, that he might sleep on broad clothes [*sic*], covered with silks and cashmeres, and resting his head on a pillow of laces.[3]

The Newfoundland brig *Bacchus* fell victim on the following day. Amid light showers, the *Wasp*'s boats took invaluable quantities of fresh Canadian water into the *Wasp*'s thirsty hold, alongside generous portions of dried codfish and still more crates of nondescript "sundries." At just after 2:00 P.M., like nearly all the others, the woeful *Bacchus* was sent gliding quietly down to the Atlantic seabed. At just before noon on 21 September, a large sail appeared on the *Wasp*'s weather beam, some thirty-six miles due west of Porto Santo, Madeira, bearing away from it to the northeast. Distinctly American, the ship was long and low, sporting two sharply raking, square-rigged masts and a full tier of gun ports. By 3:00 P.M., Blakeley was close alongside, cleared for action and making nine and a half knots through the growing swells, conditions that always tended to favor the larger vessel in just such a contest. The brig at length lowered its Union Jack. It was the merchant brig *Atalanta*, having recently sailed from Bordeaux bound to Pensacola, Spanish Florida, with an unusually rich cargo of wine, brandy, fruits, silks, cambrics, and crate after crate of manufactured goods of the finest quality.

This was the richest prize that Blakeley had yet taken. The *Atalanta* had originally been a hermaphrodite-rigged letter of marque schooner, the *Siro* of Baltimore. Displacing a healthy 253 tons, mounting eight 9-pounders (six of them carronades) and "coppered to the bends," this unusually fine Baltimore clipper had easily run the tight blockade into Savannah during the winter of 1813, carrying a profitable cargo of fish, brandy, soap, and candles to the embargoed continent. The adaptable *Siro* was one of only two known Baltimore brigs ever to have made both a letter-of-marque, blockade-running voyage as well as a privateering cruise while operating under the same wartime commission.[4] Loaded with Georgia cotton, it had been bound out on its second expedition to France in January 1814 when a lucky English cruiser had snatched it up in the Bay of Biscay.[5] But now, under private British ownership, it was partially disarmed, conservatively square-rigged, deeply laden, and, with only nineteen men, grossly undermanned. This explains how a leeward and still somewhat damaged ship-rigged corvette was able to come up on it so quickly. These beautiful clippers could normally escape almost straight into the eye of the wind. If the *Atalanta* had been well manned and in proper privateer trim, few men-of-war could have even approached it.

The Liverpool master, as expected, was entirely uncooperative. While admitting the brig's nationality, he nevertheless declared his entire cargo to be French property. If the *Atalanta* was burned, he told Blakeley, the French owners would have a just and legal claim against him for damages. The cargo had been purchased in France for more than forty-eight thousand francs, but it was worth considerably more in the empty-shelved United States.[6] To avoid this impending catastrophic financial loss, the master reasoned, Blakeley must therefore allow him either to proceed home under a ransom bond, or to load all the cargo aboard the *Wasp* before destroying the brig. The first option, as Blakeley well knew, was illegal and was therefore considered null and void in England's eyes. The second, if indeed physically possible, would be cumbersome and impractical. There was a third option, however. He might attempt to send it home for adjudication, but the voyage across the broad Atlantic would be long, and the prospect of recapture by the numerous blockaders was far from remote. Blakeley delayed his decision one full day, until he had had time enough to digest all the brig's manifests. It contained ninety-nine oaken casks and eighteen hundred bottles of fine claret wine. These alone were worth a sizable fortune back in the United States. The *Atalanta* also carried ten pipes of brandy and fifteen large boxes of assorted liquors. Captain Blakeley and Purser Fairchild carefully inspected the hundreds of meticulously stowed hogsheads, boxes, and crates, each filled with fruit, capers, prunes, olives, anchovies, almonds, cream of tartar, and cologne water.[7] Blakeley had not seen such a rich collection of merchandise since the days when, as a boy, he had visited his father's warehouses. What would his father think, he might well have pondered, if he knew that his only heir was considering putting such wealth to the torch! He had done it before and it must surely have sickened him. Besides, even if the cargo was not condemnable, the market would certainly be receptive to a large, Maryland-built, copper-sheathed privateer brig—especially one constructed of live oak. Indeed, this fine brig was known as the most expensive clipper to have been built in Baltimore during the war. Most of this cost was attributed to the "fine materials" put into its frame, and it was reputedly very fast, even for its breed. *Siro* had been the talk of the Chesapeake Bay when launched, and many of the *Wasp*'s officers were aware of its considerable charms. Blakeley made his decision:

> I have the honor to inform you that I yesterday captured the brig Atalanta with a cargo said and appearing to be French Property, altho there is not a doubt in my own mind of the cargo being really English property. Yet possessing only presumptive proof, I did not feel authorized to destroy the vessel and cargo, the course pursued with all others. I therefore am constrained to send her to the United States. The Atalanta was formerly the privateer schooner Siro and sails remarkably fast and with care, she may be carried in.[8]

Traditionally, the most promising of the midshipmen was given the honor of commanding just such a rich prize, and David Geisinger was unquestionably the most deserving of the lot. It is probably no coincidence that Geisinger, like the *Atalanta*, hailed from Maryland. Geisinger might even have had some practical experience on board one of his native clipper-brigs; his earliest assignment, the USS *Syren*, was not dissimilar. Blakeley would be sorry to lose him, but if he succeeded in bringing the *Atalanta* in he would certainly be made lieutenant. Blakeley then wrote

the letter to Secretary of the Navy William Jones that would secure
Geisinger's promotion:

> Midshipman David Geisinger having served some time under my com-
> mand, I beg leave to recommend him to the notice of the Department.
> I have given him the charge of the Atalanta. When the boarders were
> ordered to board the Rein Deer, Mr. Geisinger was the first person on
> board of her.[9]

Nearly a year after Geisinger's first request, Captain Blakeley could at long
last deliver his promised recommendation to the honorable secretary. But
there was another little hogshead of spirits that he wished sent off to America as soon as possible:

> Having exhausted every means within my power to reclaim Midship-
> man Thomas N. Bonneville, I am at length compelled to send him home
> in the Atalanta. Reprimand, suspension, advice, and encouragement
> have been tried in vain. Nothing could have the effect to render him
> attentive to his duty. Scarcely a day has passed without a report of him
> from some officer.[10]

Captain Blakeley, perhaps sharing a glass of captured claret with the most
valued of his junior officers in his great cabin, announces his not wholly
unexpected decision to Geisinger. The two men probably talk briefly
together of the service, of the war, and of their future prospects. Blakeley
tells his eager young protégé of his own numerous experiences as prize master and commander. He gives fatherly advice about governing a ship's company, along with various methods of dealing with malcontents, before dropping the bomb about Bonneville. After Blakeley announces his decision,
Geisinger's messmates probably slap him heartily on the back and caution
him against picking fights with the blockading British and, above all, they
beg him, please do not drink up all the wine.

Midshipman Geisinger was ordered to carry back to the United States not
only all of his captain's official dispatches but those belonging to Minister
Crawford as well. There would be some rough sailing ahead, so Blakeley could
spare only eight able seamen aside from Mr. Bonneville, to make up the prize
crew. But Robert R. Stewart, a prominent Philadelphian "of one of the best
families," who had reportedly embarked at L'Orient as a passenger, volun-
teered to go aboard the brig. "I found him of much service in various
instances," recalled Midshipman Geisinger in the very last entry of his *Wasp*
journal, "and a jovial companion." A multitude of pens hastily scribbled out

last-minute letters to far-off friends and family upon the wardroom's great table, atop the numerous folding desks, and astride any dry and reasonably horizontal surface. One such anonymous letter was published in the *Savannah Republican*. It captures the pride and confidence felt by every man aboard:

> There are but few disappointments in life without their attendant bene-
> fits, and but few pains unaccompanied by pleasure. Yesterday, I fully
> believed and expected to have been deprived the pleasure of writing a sin-
> gle line by this opportunity, other than public service: But a disappoint-
> ment has detained the Atalanta longer than was expected, and I am
> indebted to that circumstance for the time I now indulge in writing to
> friends. . . . The Wasp has been one of the most successful cruisers out of
> the United States. She has been the favorite of Fortune, and we offer
> thanksgiving to divine Providence for [its] support and protection. . . . She
> has now been three months and five days at sea, with a complement of 173
> men, whose ages average only 23 years—the greatest part so GREEN, that
> is, so unaccustomed to the sea, that they were seasick for a week. In that
> time, however she has destroyed 12 English merchant vessels and their
> cargoes, the whole value of which, I presume, was not worth less than
> TWO HUNDRED THOUSAND POUNDS STERLING—the thirteenth
> merchantman we are now dispatching for the United States—she is the
> first we have attempted to send in, but being an uncommon fast sailer we
> have great hopes of her safe arrival; and for my part, with judicious man-
> agement I have no doubt of it. . . . Besides these merchant vessels, we have
> whipped two of his Britannic Majesty's sloops of war, and comparatively
> speaking, have lost NOTHING. . . . The Wasp is a beautiful ship and the
> finest sea boat, I believe in the world. Our officers and crew, young and
> ambitious—they fight with more cheerfulness than they do any other
> duty. Captain Blakeley is a brave and discrete [*sic*] officer—as cool and
> collected in action as at a table. The Atalanta is at this moment ordered to
> proceed; and Mr. Stewart waits at my elbow for this. Adieu.[11]

The enthusiasm expressed in this letter was shared by all. Alone for the first time in his own comparatively spacious great cabin, prize master David Geisinger opened his private, sealed orders. They are today considered to be the finest surviving example of the type ever written. He was to carry his prize into Savannah, Charleston, or Wilmington, in that order of preference:

> It is my positive orders that you keep a sharp look out on the top gal-
> lant yard from day light until dark and that during the night a strict

and careful look out be kept, and that on immediately *any sail* being discovered, no matter what her appearance may be, that you avoid her by all the means in your power. The time of your arrival is of little interest compared with your getting in *safely*. The vessel is undoubtedly British and but very few suspicions are entertained of her cargo being of the same character. . . . Speak nothing, avoid everything and bear in mind that a safe arrival is the only consideration. Time and place are secondary matters. Wishing you as I firmly believe you will have a speedy and safe passage and relying confidently on your care and attention.[12]

The *Wasp* and the *Atalanta* began their solitary journeys on 23 September 1814. David Geisinger could hardly have imagined that he would never see his gallant captain nor his courageous corvetteers again. The *Wasp* simply vanished over the hazy southeastern horizon and was never again seen by those who knew her. The tragic disappearance of the *Wasp* remains one of the greatest mysteries in the annals of American naval history.

Geisinger's voyage home lasted some forty-five tempestuous days. At first, he enthusiastically recorded every event, however minute, regarding the course, speed, and the exact set of the sail. But as the glamour of command wore off, he would instead dash off but a few brief comments about the weather. There were only two events that broke the monotony and the nausea. At 7:00 A.M. on Wednesday, 26 October, a strange brig was spied three points on the lee beam. A quarter of an hour later, a second sail appeared through the low, gray clouds, just "a head" and slightly to windward. The moderate wind was then blowing from the north, and with "a heavy sea running," the *Atalanta* hauled "close on a wind and turned." The fatigued crew took two reefs out of the topsails and then set both topgallants against the freshening gusts.

The second sail, a single-masted cutter flaunting English colors that had initially been in chase of the brig, altered its course in pursuit of them. Geisinger now faced his severest test yet. If the armed cutter, which he "supposed . . . to be a Providence or Bermudian privateer," came up with him, he must surely be taken. Eleven men were not enough to work the ship in these dangerous seas and also man the guns. But the cutter did not know his situation. If he acted boldly, appearing to be a heavily armed and reasonably well manned Yankee privateer, he might bluff his smaller antagonist into bearing away, there being, of course, no profit in fighting your enemy's privateers. "*At 9 fired a gun to windward and hoisted an American Ensign,*" he wrote defiantly with a bold underline in his journal. It worked. The cutter quickly bore around in pursuit of the first sail, obviously an easier prey.

On Friday evening, 4 November, the *Atalanta* swifted safely into Savannah Harbor. Although he forgot to mention any particulars of his homecoming, either in his journal or in his official letter to the secretary, Geisinger did experience a little trouble carrying his floating fortune into port. "In coming over the bar last night without a pilot," tattled the *Savannah Republican,* "she went ashore on the North Breaker, but was soon gotten off, after the loss of her rudder and her keel was a little damaged."[13] As per Blakeley's instructions, Geisinger dutifully reported himself to the station's senior naval officer, Commo. Hugh Campbell. Robert R. Stewart immediately departed for Washington, bearing his precious bundle of dispatches, and then fades completely from the naval record, while Midshipmen Geisinger and Bonneville both transferred overland to New York several days later. Of the eight members of the prize crew, all transferred over to the nearby prize-brig *Epervier,* but only three remained aboard at the time when it too disappeared without a trace in the summer of 1815.[14] The patriotic citizens of Savannah, as well as Geisinger, expected to see the *Wasp* glide proudly in on the heels of its lovely prize. Savannah was, after all, Blakeley's destination of choice. Two *Wasp* sightings were reported in the papers on 15 November:

> By a gentleman from St. Mary's, we learn that a neutral vessel arrived at Amelia [Island] on the 11th instant, the captain of which informed [him] that he was boarded by the United States ship Wasp on the 7th, and she was in the act of burning an English vessel. There was a report in our town yesterday that the Wasp was off our bar, and was chased off by the Lacedemonian, there being no pilot to bring her in. Why do not the commissioners of the pilotage do their duty?[15]

The *Lacedemonian,* a 38-gun frigate, was indeed Savannah's primary blockader, but its logbook does not show that it chased anyone away from the bar on that date, nor on any other. It was, however, sailing in company with the brig *St. Lawrence.* On the crisp, clear Monday morning of 21 November, with "Tybee Lighthouse 38 miles" distant and just within sight of Charleston, the captains of the *Lacedemonian* and the *St. Lawrence* decided to improve their crews' gunnery skills. Perhaps they had just received some intelligence (quite possibly the alluded to newspaper article) that an American cruiser was daily expected in. "[At] 10, hove to and exercised with the great guns and fired with shot at a cask and Marines with blank cartridges," reported the frigate's master. "[At] 12, reloaded and secured the great guns."[16] The reports of the heavy guns rolled inshore a considerable distance. Brothers Ben and James Freemen were each on opposite ends of Hunting Island when the unseen reports of naval gunnery, coming in from "a little south of Stono's Inlet," rattled the windows of their respective lodgings. All three Charleston papers reported both seeing and hearing a naval engagement just south of the bar, beginning at 10:00 A.M. and lasting until just past noon. The local tern-schooner *Beaufort Packet*, then three miles out to sea, raced in and reported seeing a running fight in the same direction. One of the witnesses to this "battle" was young Whitemarsh Seabrook. In 1844, as the governor of South Carolina, he recalled his experiences that day:

> The day was calm and the firing heavy and obviously very near. It was evident that two vessels of unequal size were engaged, and the gradually diminishing sounds of their broadsides showed that it was a running fight, and that they were opposite each other. Shortly afterwards, in a conversation with a gentleman of St. Helena . . . he stated that two Negroes who were on Coffin's Island, the eastern most of the Hunting Islands . . . informed him that one of the vessels was much larger than the other, and that while they continued in sight, they were very near each other. It further appears . . . that the engagement commenced off the eastern end of Coffin's Island, and that the vessels . . . steered about southeast. Two or three days before the event alluded to, it was reported that the Wasp was seen off Savannah Bar, and about three months after it, I well remember reading in a newspaper that a British frigate stationed off this coast had not been heard from for a long time. I then came to the conclusion . . . that the fight was between the Wasp and the missing frigate, and that both were sunk by an accidental explosion of the magazine of the former. Blakeley was a daring and chivalrous commander . . . and was not likely to surrender to an enemy unless greatly his superior.[17]

This electrifying story spread up and down the coast, and it was picked up by all the major southern papers. The event even made the national *Niles' Weekly Register* of Philadelphia. "If Blakeley did attempt to fight her," lamented the editor, "it must have been under the most desperate resolutions, and the havoc terrible."[18] After the peace, officers visiting Savannah from the frigate *Severn*, a former blockader, let it be known that whatever might have happened off the coast that day, neither the referenced frigate nor any of the others on the station had been involved. And so, by the steady passage of time, the affair "ceased to be spoken of, and was by many forgotten, or only remembered as a riddle or a dream." The *Lacedemonian's* captain could hardly have guessed that his two-hour target practice would have caused such turmoil ashore. These were by no means the last of the *Wasp* sightings. One of the *Severn's* officers, a lieutenant, did report that the *Wasp* had been captured in the English Channel by a frigate. "There have been several other vague reports of the capture of the Wasp," wrote one northern editor, "from English officers on the coast, from Jamaica, etc."[19] One rumor, described as "very doubtful," appeared out of Kingston the following April:

> By his Majesty's ship Medina, which arrived on Tuesday last, we learn that Rear Admiral Durham had received an official letter from Capt. Patterson, of the Myrmidon, 20 gun ship, stating the capture by that vessel, of the American ship Wasp, of 22 guns, after an obstinate engagement of two hours, during which both vessels suffered severely.[20]

The *Myrmidon* was never engaged, at least according to its logbook. Although no British frigate had gone missing from the North American station during the war, as suggested by Governor Seabrook, one of their heavy sloops of war did. It had set out on a cruise from Bermuda in midsummer 1814 and was never heard from again.[21] The captain's orders might have taken it across the path of an incoming Blakeley at the tail end of his cruise. The missing British sloop of war was the HMS *Peacock*, formerly the HMS *Loup Cervier*, and prior to its capture from the Americans in 1812, it had been none other than the original *Wasp*! It is ironic in the extreme to imagine a possible meeting. In addition, there was also an unsubstantiated postwar story describing how two British frigates had chased an unknown corvette into a squall somewhere off the southern coast, "about the time the Wasp ought to have arrived." When the weather cleared, the stranger was no longer to be seen, and it was thus thought to have foundered.[22] No particulars were ever offered and no marked wreckage or uniformed bodies were ever reported to have washed up along the shore. However, one brief account, dated 21 January 1815, puts the *Wasp* in waters close enough to make it feasible sometime around the previous Christmas:

> LATEST FROM THE WASP. We learn from a friend who arrived here yesterday from Beaufort, N.C. that a Portuguese brig had arrived at that port,

in 14 days from Turks Island, laden with salt. The Portuguese Captain informed, that he was boarded off [Grand] Turks Island by the U.S. sloop of war Wasp, on a cruise. It is 32 days since the Wasp boarded the above brig.[23]

There were a great many other sightings of the *Wasp* long after the *Atalanta* had left it. The last substantiated sighting of Blakeley's corvette occurred on 9 October 1814 about three hundred miles northwest of the Cape Verde Islands. The Swedish brig *Adonis*, sailing from Rio de Janeiro and bound toward Falmouth, England, had been out just over six weeks when the menacing corvette appeared in the offing. At 8:00 A.M., "[we] discovered a strange sail giving chase to us and firing several guns, she gaining very fast." The brig's captain, Mr. J. G. Molen, has been described as warm, convivial, and a mariner who bore "every appearance of being a highly respectable man." But he was not one to be easily fooled. The young officer who boarded his vessel later on that day might have faked a reasonably good British accent, but there was no getting around "the English doctor's uniform" that adorned him. When this boarding surgeon learned that the brig contained two American naval officers bound home via England on parole, he immediately left the ship. "He shortly after returned," reported Captain Molen, "took the American gentlemen with him, and went a second time aboard the sloop." The two officers in question were Midshipmen Stephen Decatur McKnight and James Lyman, both formerly of the frigate *Essex*, the former a nephew of his most famous namesake. Blakeley was delighted to hear of their presence on board the *Adonis*, especially as he now had only three of his original eight midshipmen. The *Adonis*'s log reported the rest:

In about half an hour he returned again with Messrs. McKnight and Lyman and they informed me that the vessel was the United States Sloop of War the Wasp, commanded by Captain Bleaky, or Blake . . . that [they] had now determined to leave me and go on board the Wasp—paid me their passage in dollars at 5s. and 9d. and having taken their luggage on board the Wasp, they made sail to the southward. Shortly after they had left, I found that Lieut. McKnight had left his writing desk behind, and I immediately made signal for the Wasp to return, and stood towards her. They, observing my signals, stood back, came along side, and sent their boat for the writing desk, after which they sent me a log line and some other presents, and made all sail in the direction for the line; and, I have reason to suppose, for the convoy that passed on Thursday previous.[24]

When the *Adonis* eventually reached England after the peace, Captain Molen gave proper notification at the Falmouth Post Office, explaining first, that the *Wasp* had boarded him and second, that McKnight and Lyman had elected to join it. But nobody took even the slightest interest. At the insistence of his relatives several years later, Commo. Stephen Decatur launched an inquiry into the fate of his long-absent nephew and his companion-in-arms. The puzzle was not solved until 1820, when Molen, who had remained unacquainted with the *Wasp*'s famous disappearance, finally came forward with his logbook. Had not a person of as high a standing as Decatur made such an effort, this important sighting of the *Wasp* might never have been reported. Even with the considerable publicity surrounding this tragic disappearance, it still took nearly six years for that latest chapter to come to light. Thus it is clear that there could have been many more such unreported, casual contacts with Blakeley's corvette. Readers of *The New Hampshire Gazette* were treated to "another report relative to the Wasp" in 1815:

> The Norfolk, Va. Beacon of November 22 contains the following paragraph: "A young gentleman in this borough, who had a brother, a lieutenant on board the Guerriere, and another, a midshipman aboard the Wasp, received a letter yesterday from his mother at King's Creek, near Williamsborough, in which she announces a reprint of a letter from her son a lieutenant on the Guerriere, informing her that he had heard from the Wasp; that she was on the coast of the Brazils." (The source where this comes from is most respectable, yet it ought perhaps to be received with some caution by anxious friends.)[25]

The two brothers were, of course, Robert and William Randolph of the *Guerriere* and *Wasp*, respectively. During the latter half of 1815, the frigate *Guerriere* was actively involved in Decatur's successful naval campaign against Algiers. So, for a letter to reach Robert in the Mediterranean, it would first have had to leave the *Wasp* off Brazil, presumably about late November 1814, via some passing neutral merchantman. It would probably have arrived in the United States some time after the peace. From there, it would have been posted on to Robert's last known location, the frigate *United States,* blockaded in the Thames. Robert, however, had since transferred over to the frigate *President* in New York. Following their capture in January 1815, Robert was paroled ashore in Bermuda. After the peace, he returned to New York, rejoining Commodore Decatur on board the *Guerriere* in that city, and together, they sailed off to do battle against the pirates of the Barbary. It is not unreasonable to suppose that any forwarded letter might take an unusually long time in catching up with its fleet-footed addressee.[26]

Curiously, the surviving British correspondence of the Brazil station refers to His Majesty's brig *Kangaroo* having been chased by a strange ship "off the coast" either in late October or early November.[27] Strangely, the incident went unrecorded in its log. *Wasp* sightings were not restricted to the western Atlantic, either. On 3 November, several hundred miles to the southwest of Cape Finisterre, the British brig *Reynard* had a brief encounter with a hostile corvette. At 1:00 P.M., Captain St. Clair spied "a sloop of war" to leeward, flying English colors. The private signals were given, but "she made a mistake in answering." As the *Reynard* was lightly armed, it prudently made all sail away, "supposing her to be an American ship of war."[28] Exactly twenty-four hours later, the menacing ship was once again seen, this time alongside some unfortunate schooner "which was in distress."[29] The *Reynard* arrived in the Tagus on 14 December and reported the sighting to the port's commander, Vice Admiral Fleming. He, in turn, made his own report to the Lords Commissioners of the Admiralty: "On the 2nd of Novr. . . . [St. Clair] had fallen in with a Corvette which he thinks was an American that . . . he perceived that she carried 20 guns, that from the inferior force of the Reynard, he did not feel himself justified in bringing her to action which she did not seek."[30]

The *Reynard* arrived back in Gibraltar Bay on the thirty-first and was once again chased off Finisterre "by a small frigate of the enemy." The challenger was enticed away by "other objects." News of this strange predator spread rapidly throughout the shipping community. HMS *Garland,* for example, had "joined a convoy" of his country's merchantmen on 8 January 1815, and quickly "gained information that a small American frigate was a few leagues to the eastward" off Tenerife.[31] The *Jasper,* a sister brig to the *Reynard,* had been "chased by an Enemy's ship [and] that . . . he succeeded in getting clear of her [but] did not conceive it to be prudent to bring her to action . . . but her captain was fully resolved to go to the bottom rather than have struck his colors."[32] Cdr. Henry Jenkinsen must have considered the stranger (referred to elsewhere as a "corvette") to be a viable enough threat to make such a bold statement to his superiors. However, he did not see fit to mention any of these proceedings in his brig's logbook.

The commander of the 32-gun frigate *Aquilion,* Capt. Thomas Burton, next spotted this "strange ship of war" bearing defiantly down upon him in the early morning hours of 23 January 1815. Burton recorded in his log: "Observed the stranger to be an enemy corvette."[33] The frigate bore off in chase, but the log gives no further particulars, until ten days later, when Burton's lookout spied a smoldering vessel "burnt to the waterline," wallowing in the swells. This third disturbing sighting caused Admiral Fleming to comment in an official letter to Whitehall: "The American of Twenty guns, ship rigged, which was chased by the Aquilion, and I have reason to believe was the same which lately pursued the Jasper," he reported, "[and] this vessel, with another ship of the same description, has generally been taken for the Wasp."[34] Another story appeared in March 1815:

> Letters from Washington state authentically, that an officer of the Argus had arrived there in the cartel San Phillipe, and reported that having touched at Santa Cruz (Tenerife) they there learnt correctly, from the crew of an English brig, prize to the Wasp, on the 9th Jan. that the Wasp had, on days previous, put into Mogador (Morocco) for supplies. This accounts for this interesting vessel to be about the end of December.[35]

These by no means exclusive sightings, if nothing else, give testimony to the *Wasp* fever that was then sweeping the roughly triangular area from coastal Spain, down to the northwest coast of Africa, and out again to the Canary Islands. The following article first appeared in the 13 December 1815 edition of the *Norfolk Weekly Beacon:*

> The Wasp Sunk. Not withstanding the reports which we have heretofore published, a conversation with an officer of the first standing and respectability in the navy, permits us to entertain no doubts of the loss of the U.S. sloop of war Wasp, and that her end was as glorious as her cruise had been brilliant. All readers of newspapers must recollect that, about a year ago, there was an account of a British frigate putting into Cadiz, much cut to pieces, and 100 men killed and wounded, reporting her having an engagement with a large American frigate, off that port. It was known at the time we had no frigate in that quarter, and that the Wasp was believed to be cruising in that neighborhood; but little was said or thought about it at the time, as the report was not generally credited. We now learn from a source which cannot be doubted, that there was an action between an English frigate of the largest class, and an American ship, and that it was undoubtedly the Wasp. Lieut. Conkling, who commanded the schooner Ohio, one of Commodore Sinclair's

squadron on Lake Erie, and who was captured in August, 1814, off Fort Erie, and sent to England, has lately reported himself to his commanding officer, to whom it appears he related having met one of the lieutenants who was aboard the above mentioned frigate, and was informed by him, that the ship they engaged was not a frigate, as was stated, and that his commander as well as every person on board, could see by her battle lanterns being lighted, and from the flashes of her guns, that she was a corvette ship mounting 22 guns, and that they themselves believed that it was no other than the Wasp. But having been so gallantly beaten off, and having suffered so severely, they were reluctant to acknowledge how inferior the force had been which inflicted such severe chastisement on them. It appears by the lieutenant's own accounts, that the action lasted several hours, and that the frigate sheered off to refit, intending to renew the action at day light, which was not far off, if circumstances would admit it. But at earliest dawn there was no vestige of their gallant enemy. From the crippled state of the ship, the short time intervening between the separation and daylight, the lieutenant believed it impossible that they could have been out of sight, had their opponents been above water. The above account essentially coincides with the opinions of the best informed naval men about the seat of government, who generally agree in the belief that the Wasp was the vessel engaged with the frigate above alluded to.

This article is the nucleus of what has become the most common and popular explanation for the disappearance of the *Wasp*—namely, that it had been sunk in a night action with an English frigate off the island of Tenerife. A detailed examination is therefore long overdue. This is especially appropriate, considering that the names *Wasp* and Blakeley are more closely identified with their fate than with their considerable achievements in the English Channel. They have become almost synonymous with disappearance at sea. The *Norfolk Beacon* account was almost universally accepted in the United States until the officer in question printed a "denial" in the *Pittsburgh Mercury*.[36] Oddly, he did so through intermediaries, and in addition, he so carefully worded his statement, according to Dr. Johnson, Blakeley's biographer, as to negate only the specific part about having spoken to a lieutenant, as opposed to another category of officer, such as a master or midshipman. This might have been done, Johnson explained, in order not to betray a confidence. David Geisinger held the same opinion. In later years, he relayed to Johnson the semiofficial version told to him by his then commander at the

Washington Navy Yard, Capt. John H. Aulick, one of Blakeley's former midshipmen in the *Enterprize:*

> That an officer of our navy that was a prisoner in England at the close of the last war, (he thinks an officer to the brig Syren) told him that he there saw and conversed with a British officer, who said that the frigate in which he had been recently cruising, had had a night action with a vessel which he took to be a sloop of war, though her captain maintained she was a frigate. That the vessel suddenly disappeared in the darkness of the night, and that they on board the frigate believed he had sunk.[37]

Fellow *Wasp* veteran Robert R. Stewart, "a very respectable inhabitant of Philadelphia," wrote to Johnson in March 1847 with his views on the subject:

> The action between a British frigate and an American ship of war off Cadiz, I think very probable, as it came from various sources. One in particular reported to me by Mr. Jas. Robinet of this city, (since dead) who, during the latter part of the war, and after the peace, was a clerk in Mr. Hackney's counting-house in Cadiz. He told me that when the frigate entered Cadiz, he went on board her and inquired the news, and was informed nearly as related by Mr. Johnson, with a slight difference as to the killed and wounded on board the frigate.[38]

But Dr. Johnson was of the stubborn opinion that the battle had taken place off Charleston, his hometown,[39] and he then labored on to prove that such a severely damaged frigate could have somehow managed to put into Cadiz, on the other side of the Atlantic Ocean. He further stated, without citing his source, that the frigate in question was HMS *Horatio* but its logbook denies the affair. The *Horatio* had patrolled the North American station in November and had then sailed off Cadiz by the first of the year. A tempestuous following sea smashed in the stern windows during January 1815 and thus might have given the *Horatio* the appearance of having fought an action. On 24 February Admiral Fleming reported that another frigate, "His Majesty's ship Hyperion arrived here . . . with the loss of her topmasts and sails." The *Hyperion* was a superb 18-pounder, 32-gun frigate, the largest of its class. On the thirteenth and fourteenth of February, however, it had been severely ravaged in a storm off Cape Finisterre.[40]

Someone obviously had been cruising these rich waters, and the senior British naval officer on the Cadiz station was of the opinion that this someone was the *Wasp*. The idea that the *Wasp* could have seriously damaged a heavy frigate of the Royal Navy is a romantic notion, but without concrete evidence it is not an overly realistic one. Certainly, no such "cover-up" or suppression of the facts on the Royal Navy's part, as has been suggested, especially one with such a large casualty list, could long stand unnoticed. However, as only mere scraps of the Cadiz station's correspondence survive to the present day, it is possible that there were some other, more sensational sightings. But in their absence, the discussion must be limited to those few recorded incidents that do survive. The important point is this. Even though the *Wasp* may never have left the Brazilian coast, the Royal Navy was of the opinion that it had returned to the scene of its late mischief.

Chronologically and geographically, the aggressive, ship-rigged intruder spotted off Tenerife could indeed have been the *Wasp*. This assertion does not necessarily negate the Randolph letter written "off the Brazils," but it would the aforementioned Amelia Island and Turk's Island sightings. Assuming, for the sake of discussion, that Blakeley was the Tenerife intruder, then the following scenario, one of countless possible scenarios with infinite variations, might explain his actions: Finding the pickings slim in Brazilian waters, Blakeley may have elected to return to the rich seas off the Canaries, the path of homeward-bound Indiamen. Such a deliberate backtrack across the Atlantic, however, would have gone against his orders. If this was Blakeley's plan, it was a clever one because during his necessary absence of several months, the British would have stopped looking for him in the east. The *Wasp* might have cruised past Tristan d'Acunha on its eastern passage, and then followed the African coast northward. Cruising back up into the waters around Tenerife, Blakeley could have destroyed several more merchantmen and sent a cartel into Santa Cruz, as reported in the newspapers, while replenishing his stores in Mogador. The corvette may have had several distant run-ins with the Royal Navy and not engaged any. It is quite possible that Blakeley participated in a prolonged chase and possibly even a distant running fight with an English frigate off Tenerife and that no record of it has yet come to light. There must necessarily have been few or no English casualties for the incident to have been so long overlooked, however. Possibly the *Aquilion* was the culprit, if indeed there was a culprit. Not all chases were necessarily recorded in the logbooks, let alone the details of them. Caught up in a seasonal storm, quite possibly the very one that had nearly enveloped the *Hyperion*, the *Wasp*'s weakened rigging, still patched and spliced after two fierce actions, could finally have given way. In hurricane alley, succumbing unnoticed to the volatile sea is not uncommon. Then again, there is always the possibility that Blakeley continued on with his orders and was truly spotted off Turk's Island and then again off Amelia Island not long afterward, as reported in the papers.

Why did Blakeley separate from the *Atalanta* in the first place? The route taken home by the prize brig was essentially the same one laid out by the secretary for his own return. The *Wasp* could easily have kept up with the *Atalanta*. By sailing within signaling distance of the *Atalanta*, Blakeley could have in effect doubled his horizon, increasing his chances of finding even more prey or avoiding British cruisers. In the latter scenario, they could have better protected one another by sailing together than if each was acting alone. Ideally, Crawford's dispatches were far safer on board the *Wasp* than on board a sparsely manned prize. The same applies to Blakeley's official correspondence to the secretary of the navy. There was every reason for both vessels to stick together and little justification for their separation. The admittedly scant evidence suggests that it was indeed Blakeley's intention to depart from the strict letter of his instructions. That is, that he was not going to follow his prescribed route home but planned on doing some independent roving instead.

There was another possibility regarding the *Wasp*'s fate. It was thought in some circles that the *Wasp* had wrecked somewhere on the western coast of Africa, and that the survivors were either killed by the "Arabs" or had been captured and sold into slavery. This story first appeared in print some ten years after the peace. An English whale ship, the *Spring Grove*, experienced just such a tragedy on 23 November 1824. Only through the determined efforts of the British consul at Mogador, Morocco, the "distinguished philanthropist, Mr. Wiltshire," were some of the crew rescued from bondage. One of the grateful whalers related to Mr. Wiltshire the following tale:

> He says that an Arab chief in whose hands they fell, could speak a little English; and contrived to inform them, that, some years ago, an English ship was lost on the African Coast, that the crew reached the shore, to the number of three hundred men, well armed; that his own tribe, consisting of five hundred men; attacked them and were repulsed; that he solicited the assistance of a neighboring tribe to renew the attack, with an additional force of four or five hundred men; that the British drove them back a second time; and were making good their retreat for some settlement of security, when they were a third time surrounded by a body of thirteen hundred; and that the British fought till three fourths of their number fell, and the remainder were cut to pieces, after laying

down their arms and after killing 250 Arabs. The name of the ship and the time of the shipwreck are both unknown.[41]

The editors of both the prominent *Niles' Weekly Register* and the *Federal Gazette* felt that not only was it possible for the unidentified ship to have been the *Wasp*, but it was certainly probable. The Arabs might easily have mistaken the shipwrecked Americans for English mariners, so concluded the story, although the number of castaways seemed a bit too high, even allowing for great quantities of British prisoners. But the *National Intelligencer* could not, in all conscience, blindly accept this heroic tale of closure. The Arab story too closely resembled another, earlier tale. The *Wasp* may well have wrecked on the Barbary coast, but the above story is mere hearsay, with no concrete evidence whatsoever being offered. It is an ending as valiant, and in many ways as comforting, as the nighttime frigate battle. The true fate of the *Wasp* will probably never be known. It most likely was lost in a storm, somewhere off Africa or the Carolinas, or anywhere in between. Indeed, not only did the *Wasp* and *Epervier* share this same enigmatic fate, but so too did the old *Wasp* while in its enforced English service. Add to this grim tally Blakeley's old *Hornet*, last seen laboring at its moorings in a violent tempest off Tampico in 1829, and the larger corvettes *Albany* and *Levant*, lost in 1854 and 1860, respectively. One day, the wreckage of the *Wasp* will be found. Explorers, perhaps searching for submerged mineral deposits, will come across curious little mounds of ancient, deeply rusted iron. If examined, they will reveal themselves to be the remains of carronades. They might find copper bolts and brass fixtures lying about, perhaps the ship's engraved brass bell or even a dress sword hilt belonging to one of the officers. With luck, one day the answer to the "where" of the *Wasp* may be learned, and the investigation into the "why" can begin.

18. No More Shall Blakeley's Thunder Roar

*T*he late warrant officers' wives—Ann Martin, Mary Bartlett, and Mary Ford—met on 24 August 1815 with Jane Moulton, Mary Stone, and Sally Herrick, the spouses of their husbands' subordinates, in the Newburyport home of Judith Mullen. The one quality that these women now shared was that their half-pay had ceased during the previous month, and they were all now equally destitute, regardless of their late husbands' rank. Their collective hopes were by now also bankrupt. Experienced sea wives knew very well the cause of a ship being six months or more overdue, in spite of the frequent hopeful rumors. Mary Bartlett had earlier written to the secretary of the navy, Benjamin Crowninshield, on her own for suggestions of what to do next. Her initial letter was dated 8 August 1815:

> Sir, I have taken the liberty in consequence of the anxiety, I am under respecting my husband, Gideon M Bartlett, who was boatswain's mate of the U S Ship Wasp, Captain Blakeley, to ask of you, being the head Officer of the Navy Department, what information you have respecting the said vessel [when] last heard from, which was when I believe when her prize, which arrived at Savannah, left her. It has been reported [that] the government is in possession of some information as makes it amount

almost to a certainty that the Wasp was lost near Cape Hatteras. It is also said that she was ordered to cruise round Cape Horn. I wish also to be informed if there is any money that is to be paid by the government for the sinking of the British vessels of war [and] also for the prize sent into Savannah, and when it is to be paid, also if in case she is lost at sea, any provisions is to be made for the widows & children of the officers and crew and how much. My situation is very distressing. I have no means of support but what I derived from my husbands half monthly allowance, which was stopped about the middle of July in consequence of the bill running out. I am in poor health with an infant that is sickly. We are under the necessity of applying to the county home of the poor for some assistance. I have no friends that can help and my health is such that I cannot do but very little besides taking care of my family. I beg of you that you will be explicit and give me all the information I ask, as it will afford some consolation that I have all the news respecting the ship that the government are in possession of.[1]

Mary and Judith had long been friends, and besides, there had always been a close kinship between the merchant sailors' wives of the town, even more so since the declaration of this unpopular war three years before. This vocal duo had recently turned to their husbands' immediate naval superiors for help. Because Newburyport possessed no permanent naval presence, they were forced to do some traveling. Isaac Hull, still the commander of the Portsmouth Navy Yard, was both sincere and sympathetic, but he had no funds at his disposal. With the covert support of the yard's financial agent, the still grieving Henry S. Langdon, Sr., the women were allowed to help themselves to all the government stores that they could carry. But the rent could not be paid with dried peas and sailcloth. They next made the same request of William Bainbridge. Not only did the commodore come up empty of funds, he refused to "give" anything to the travel-worn widows. Out of the goodness of his heart, however, he was willing to deal on the purchase of some of the more necessary items. Judith declined and returned home. She now thought Mary's direct plea a sound idea, but suggested that perhaps if the various spouses spoke with one unified voice, then their chorus must certainly bring on swifter and better results than if each acted alone. And thus was born this day's meeting. Even though the number of Merrimack men serving on board that damned corvette was unusually large, they were on average very young and only a small percentage were married. Besides themselves, Judith and Mary could convince only five others to come that afternoon. Judith composed a letter to the honorable secretary and then presented it for everyone's approval.

> Dear Sir, We, your humble petitioners are aware that you, in your Honorable station, must need have numerous & repeated [requests?], and nothing but the most extreme necessity would induce any of us to trouble you. We are several here, who have husbands (if alive) on board the United States Sloop of War Wasp. Some of us have two, some three, and some four children, & were left in very poor circumstances, all of our dependence being on our half pay, which has ceased, & here let me beg leave to acquaint you sir, that since Nov[embe]r last, we have been obliged to take goods, such as Mr. H. had in the shop, or otherwise to have taken treasury notes, which would have been a great loss, to us. You, Sir, no doubt are well persuaded that we are in distressed circumstances, having no other means left us to still the cries of our children, than by applying to the noble, generous, public-spirited Federalists (or rather Tories of Newburyport) for assistance, who would only reproach and tell us that our husbands ought not to have been [con]cerned in the late inglorious war as they call it, and tell us the poor house is good enuf for such. When you, kind sir, consider our circumstances, we believe, from what we have heard of you, that you will devise means, as soon as possible, to render us assistance, and so to keep us the ensuing winter from calling upon our *poor town*. For the great Mr. B. would not let us one pound of wool to spin, unless we did it at half price . . .[2]

Everyone approved, and so one by one, they signed their names. At the last minute, Judith recalled reading in Captain Blakeley's published dispatches that Boatswain Joseph Martin had been killed in the action with the *Avon* and, as she was under the impression that her husband was next in line to succeed him. She added, "Sir, please to send a line to Judith Mullen who's husband Enter'd as Quarter Master & since the first Boatswain was killed, we heard, was made Boatswain." This might mean an extra dollar or two per month in any possible pension.[3]

On the day before their meeting, Acting Secretary Benjamin Homans had written his response to Mary Bartlett's first letter. He assured her that in spite of all the rumors circulating to the contrary, no information had been received from the *Wasp* since the date of the *Atalanta*'s capture. He confirmed that there was indeed reason to be anxious. "That ship was not ordered to go round Cape Horn," he assured her, "[and] not farther south than the equator, in which course very little might be apprehended for her safety." If the ship was never heard from again, which was looking extremely likely, the payment of an official pension must be a subject for Congress to decide. Sadly, it was out of his hands.[4] His response to Judith's letter was also noncommittal, and longer in coming.[5]

If the Federalist merchants of Newburyport were unjustified in their chastisement and abandonment of the navy widows, they did at least have reason to be alarmed and even a bit angry. The war had nearly ruined their town. In the three years since its declaration, the city's total assessed valuation had dropped from over $6 million to just under $4 million. Average wealth had fallen from the town's all-time high in 1807 at $5,089 per person to just $2,716 at the war's end. The only real exception to this financial decline was the town's wealthiest merchant, and incidentally, its most enterprising smuggler, Gideon Bartlett's uncle, William. Although he had somehow maintained his $500,000 fortune, he declined to assist his nephew's widow. Affairs became so bad during the final days of the conflict that the town fathers were beginning to draw up petitions to the state government, demanding an immediate cessation of all hostilities and a separate peace with England. Only the arrival of news of the peace in February 1815 stopped the secession drive. That same year, 237 Newburyport families were at least partially dependent upon the cash-strapped town for their support, a charitable service that was then costing the taxpayers more than ten thousand dollars per annum. Thus the *Wasp* widows were not alone in their poverty. While it is true that the town's merchants had prospered, the conditions that had made their labors exceptionally lucrative were no longer present. With all Europe now at peace, the demand for New England's products fell off dramatically. No longer did France need Newburyport's vessels to run in overpriced goods from distant colonies past vigilant English blockaders. No longer would English merchants pay outrageous prices for commodities smuggled into Canadian ports in the dead of night. New patterns of commerce were slowly beginning to shape the town's future. Newburyport-to-Europe runs became rare. Local ships sailed south to load Georgia cotton and Virginia tobacco for voyages to the east. Few vessels that departed the city after the war ever returned. Before long, local shipowners moved their operations south to Boston or New York. Local maritime artisans lost the bulk of their business and closed up shop. Newburyport gradually lost its importance as an international center of trade.[6]

Help did finally arrive, but it was a great while in coming. On 20 April 1816, Congress approved and sent on to the president for his signature "An Act Respecting the Late Officers and Crew of the Sloop of War Wasp," providing twelve months' pay for the families, in addition to the fifty thousand dollars in prize money awarded for the destruction of the *Reindeer* and *Avon*. The monies were to be distributed through local navy agents selected by the secretary. In addition, all widows were entitled to a pension amounting to one-half their husbands' former pay for a period of five years, subject to renewal and payable twice yearly. However, should the widow "intermarry" (remarry), her pension benefits would immediately cease. In order to receive such a pension, she would first have to procure legal affidavits attesting to her true identity. She would have to prove that she had indeed married her late husband (a sworn statement from the local minister would suffice). In addition, she would be required to produce witnesses, usually friends of long standing, who would attest under oath that, to their knowledge, she had not remarried. If there were minor children involved, copies of additional documents such as baptismal records, their authenticity once again sworn to in front of the local magistrate, would also have to be forwarded to Washington.

Judith Mullen received her pension until 1818, when she married Thomas Drawn, a Newburyport chair-maker. She remained in her hometown until her death in 1852. The outspoken Mary Bartlett had given birth to her only child, William Gideon Bartlett, on 10 July 1814, while her husband was still repairing his ship's rigging in L'Orient. Tired of the widow's life of solitude, Mary remarried in 1820 to another local mariner, John Brown; they too lived out their remaining days on the quiet and steady Merrimack. Ann Martin never remarried, choosing instead to care for her invalid mother in their Portland home. She was still on the pension rolls as late as 1845 but then disappears from the records. Mary Ford also did not remarry. She lived out her conservative life alone on the shores of her native Merrimack until her death in 1856. Neither Sally Herrick nor Jane Moulten received a pension and there are no records of their fates.

With the exception of the captain, none of the *Wasp*'s commissioned officers ever married or had children, so their survivors' story cannot be told with information gleaned from the navy's pension files. Mrs. Mary Baury, for example, cared little about Frederick's long-overdue promotion to lieutenant, dated December 1814, nor his acceptance into the Society of the Cincinnati. She just wanted her son back. When, by mid-1815, it began to look as though her wish might never be granted, she firmly resolved that her third and sole remaining son, Alfred, would not follow his older brothers, Frederick and Francis, into the military. Alfred L. Baury became one of Boston's most esteemed and respected clergymen. Alfred's son, mariner

Frederick Francis Baury, however, was intrigued with the glorious life that his surnamesake had led. When the Civil War broke out, Frederick joined the Union Navy as a master's mate on board the frigate *Congress*. In that capacity he fought in one of the navy's bloodiest actions when his frigate was destroyed by the Confederate ironclad *Virginia* (previously the *Merrimack*). He survived intact, however, and just like his famous uncle, he eventually reached the rank of acting lieutenant before returning to the merchant marine in 1869.

Great sadness reigned over Portsmouth during the years immediately following the peace. The death of his son was a blow from which Henry Langdon never fully recovered. The loss of his wife in 1818, followed soon after by the deaths of several more of his fourteen children, at length drove the elder Langdon into seclusion from both business and society. He died in Cambridge, Massachusetts, in 1857, after many years of loneliness and "great infirmity." With the best wishes of his nervous parents, Messidor Toscan had joined the navy in April 1814 as a midshipman, but he saw none of the glory that had so inspired his entry. Like his older brother, he too died in his country's service, but his lingering death in August 1818 was a result of the ignoble yellow fever. The elderly Elijah Hall kept faithful to the belief that his son and his only heir, Ashton, would one day return to him. He kept up this desperate hope for one full year longer than most of the other Portsmouth families. Finally, in the summer of 1816, Hall wrote the honorable secretary asking for all that was left to him, the ceremonial sword presented to his son by Congress. He died before this lone treasure could be delivered. The loss of the *Wasp* was not the sole maritime disaster to strike the city during the war. The privateer brig *Portsmouth* also vanished mysteriously at the same time. Many a Granite State clergyman used the common fate of these two tragic ships as examples of the just rewards awaiting all those who would dare set out in search of glory and wealth. "To death alas, how mortals bow," decried a local broadside balladeer, "where are the Wasp and Portsmouth now?"

Midshipman Robert Byrd Randolph, the younger brother of William, transferred to New York in the fall of 1814, where he rejoined Commodore Decatur, then preparing the frigate *President* for sea. Their planned commerce-destroying cruise to the East Indies was thwarted by an alert blockading squadron off Long Island, however, and, after a day-long chase that culminated in a bloody action lasting several hours, Blakeley's old *President* hauled down its colors. In his official report to the secretary describing the events leading up to his loss, Decatur specifically mentioned Randolph's superb performance as the commander of the frigate's forecastle batteries. Randolph and his brother mids were paroled ashore in Bermuda several days later, with complete freedom to roam about the island. Soon after their arrival, the *Bermuda Gazette* published a somewhat mean-spirited and certainly controversial report, received from "Lieutenant the Honorable Sir George James Percival" of the *Tenedos,* an officer belonging to one of the four heavy frigates that had mauled the haughty *President* into submission. Percival reported that the famed American commodore had secretly hidden sixty-eight heavily armed boarders within the recesses of the *President*'s cavernous sail room. Their stated purpose was to rise up against the unsuspecting British prize crew, recapture their ship, and thus effect their escape. Percival belonged to the intersquadron prize crew and claimed to have personally witnessed the concealment.

Although the story might well have been true, it was the worst possible affront to Decatur's character. Officers who had hauled down their flag were honor bound not to take up arms again. Those captains that went back on their sacred word to accept the conditions of quarter were forced to endure the hiss of the civilized world. The other Royal Navy officers involved nevertheless requested that the *Gazette*'s editor, Edmund Ward, put a lid on the story because the war was over and there was no real purpose in pursuing the matter any further. Ward ignored them and reprinted the story, stating this time that he was absolutely convinced that the tale was true, and he reiterated his belief that Decatur had himself directed the concealment. Randolph, who loved the then painfully wounded Decatur as a father, became enraged at this blatant insult. When he "happened" upon the hapless Ward while walking the streets of Hamilton one evening, he instantly attacked him "in a most violent and unprovoked manner with a stick." The timely arrival of several British officers saved Ward from any further beating, while Randolph's close friend Midshipman Christopher T. Emmett (the son of the esteemed counselor Thomas Addis Emmett of New York) hurried the vindicated attacker away. Randolph reportedly escaped prosecution by concealing himself in a sea-chest aboard the cartel. Midshipman Randolph was an immediate hero to everyone in his profession, and the grateful Decatur soon after arranged for his promotion. Lieutenant Randolph sailed away later that year in Decatur's new flagship *Guerriere,* and fought his third major action, this time against the 46-gun Algerian flagship *Meshouda.* It was at this time that he received his brother William's final "off Brazil" letter.

With the dueling death of his mentor Decatur in 1820, Randolph lost his most important naval connection and so languished for many a year as a backwater lieutenant. He set out on a two-year cruise in the *Constitution* in 1826, and when its purser, John B. Timberlake, took his own life midvoyage near the Balearic Islands, Randolph agreed to assume his position. This seemingly innocent opportunity for profit soon turned disastrous, however, when it was discovered that Timberlake's accounts were short by more than nine thousand dollars. This was thought by some to have been the reason for his suicide. Amos Kendall, the navy's fourth auditor, determined that Randolph was solely responsible for the money and then prematurely and rather harshly labeled him a "public defaulter," while completely exonerating the late Timberlake. Randolph protested his innocence and demanded a court-martial to clear his name. About this time, all of the dead purser's accounts and papers conveniently vanished, leaving poor Randolph very little in the way of evidence with which to vindicate himself. The indecisive court-martial eventually found Randolph guilty, and then took the rather unusual step of bypassing Blakeley's old UNC classmate, Secretary of the Navy John Branch, and referring the matter directly to President Andrew Jackson for punishment. There were complicated and sinister forces at work, however. The late purser's widow, Peggy, had remarried Senator John Eaton, the very same man who would soon become Jackson's secretary of war. If Timberlake were held liable, then the debt would fall upon Peggy and thus by law upon the senator. Jackson therefore confirmed Randolph's guilt and instructed the secretary of the navy to dismiss Lieutenant Randolph from the service outright. The railroaded Randolph was shocked. When Randolph learned that the president was planning to receive visitors in the private cabin of his steamboat, peacefully anchored off nearby Alexandria, Virginia, he hatched a plan to avenge his good name, in just the same manner as he had done with Edmund Ward.

Randolph was not recognized amid the steady stream of callers on 6 May 1833. President Jackson mechanically rose from his chair, just as he had done a hundred times before that afternoon. However, the meek and passive visitor, seemingly just an average man in his thirties and appearing, like all the others, to be seeking political favor, did not accept the president's outstretched hand. Robert Randolph suddenly grasped Andrew Jackson by the nose and "proceeded to turn it until blood flowed in a steady stream." Randolph, who was subsequently recognized by several others in attendance, dashed out of the cabin and into the crowd of startled well-wishers, effecting yet another dramatic escape. Thus was born the infamous "Jackson-Randolph Affair," the first recorded incident involving a direct attack upon a sitting president. In 1833 there were no laws on the books specifically directed against assaulting the president, so Randolph remained safe, just as long as he kept out of the District of Columbia. Of course Jackson's political opponents embraced Randolph as a hero, and their repeated, successful attempts at blocking both Randolph's prosecution and extradition created a constitutional crisis. Randolph, who had just inherited a fortune from his late uncle, the former senator John Randolph of Roanoke, never paid his unjust debt, nor was he ever punished for his assault. Sadly, Robert Byrd Randolph is known today not for serving so valiantly beside Stephen Decatur during two wars, but simply as the man who "tweaked Jackson's nose."[7]

What the lucky Thomas Bonneville did from the time of his departure from Savannah up until his resignation in New York on 13 March 1816, is unclear. It is likely, however, that Captain Blakeley's letter delivered its intended effects and the wayward midshipman sat languishing on shore, counting the days with nothing at all interesting to do. "After the war," Thomas's father, Nicholas de Bonneville, finally emigrated from Paris and for a brief while the reunited clan lived peacefully in New York. "Not long after," however, Marguerite and Nicholas decided to return to Paris, and quite possibly they took Thomas with them, a move necessarily requiring a naval resignation from the latter. After Nicholas died in 1828, Marguerite sold the family bookshop and returned to the New World, rejoining her eldest son, Benjamin, in St. Louis, Missouri. Marguerite died in that city in 1846 at the age of seventy-nine. Perhaps Thomas resettled there as well.[8]

On the other hand, Midshipman David Geisinger felt the positive impact of Blakeley's other letter almost immediately. On 9 December 1814, Geisinger received his well-deserved promotion and thus became the first lieutenant of the swift new brig *Fire Fly,* then fitting out as part of Stephen Decatur's Algiers-bound squadron. When the victorious squadron returned home, Lieutenant Geisinger found ample employment in many of the navy's finest ships.[9] Between 1824 and 1832, Geisinger served at the Philadelphia Navy Yard, and during this latter period he met and married Catherine Russell Pierce of Maryland. They had at least four children, their first-born being Johnston Blakeley Geisinger. Tragically, young Johnston died during his thirteenth year while attending an academy in Lawrenceville, New Jersey. In 1829, the State of Maryland honored David Geisinger with a fine sword for "gallantry" in commemoration of his "two brilliant and well fought actions" against the British.[10] On 11 March 1829, he was promoted to master commandant.

Commander Geisinger sailed from Boston in March 1832 in command of the sloop of war *Peacock.* He sailed in company with the brig *Boxer,* under the command of Lt. William F. Shields, one of the fortunate fellows that Blakeley had tried unsuccessfully to rate as acting midshipman on board the *Wasp* in 1813. Their diplomatic cruise around the world lasted nearly two years. The two sloops arrived at Vunglam, China, in January 1833, after first cruising off Quallah Battoo, Sumatra, prepared to chastise the natives for their recent piracy, just in case Commodore Downs had not sufficiently accomplished this same goal two years before (which he had). At Bangkok, Minister Edmund Roberts and Commanders Geisinger and Shields were met with the utmost cordiality and were entertained in the "greatest splendor." On 20 March 1833, they signed the first treaty between the United States and an oriental power. In September, this same diplomatic team signed a similar treaty in Mocha, Arabia, with the receptive sultan. After his triumphant return two years later, Commander Geisinger commanded Boston's naval rendezvous until his promotion to captain on 24 May 1838. From 1841 to 1845, Geisinger commanded the powerful sister-frigates *Brandywine* and *Columbia* during successive Mediterranean cruises, and in 1847 he was given command of the East India Squadron, hoisting his commodore's broad pennant on board the new frigate *Congress*. He returned home in 1850 and was given the command of the United States Naval Asylum in Philadelphia until 1855, when he was placed on the reserve list. Commodore Geisinger died on 5 March 1860, at the age of sixty-nine.

Johnston Blakeley's daughter, Udney Maria,[11] was born in Boston on 10 November 1814, amid a flurry of barely contained excitement. As the true extent of her husband's escapades became fully known on the western side of the Atlantic, Jane Anne Blakeley looked anxiously forward to his triumphant return. She had long marveled at the lavish receptions given thus far to the victorious commanders earlier in the war: Hull, Bainbridge, Jones, Lawrence, Warrington, and especially Decatur. This last officer and his wife, Susan Wheeler Decatur, were the toast of Washington society. In nearly every major seaport in the nation, they were wined, dined, and honored with swords, sets of plate, and memberships in every prestigious society. The accomplishments belonging to these men could in no way rival those unparalleled achievements of her husband. Her captain had taken two equivalent enemies on his cruise, while all the others had done only half as well. Just wait until the *Wasp*'s captain returned home, she must have thought gleefully. But as the bleak winter slowly turned into spring, Jane Anne's deep-seated fears began to mold themselves into a cruel reality. By the fall of 1815, she had given up all hope whatsoever. At this time, Capt.

Isaac Hull took over the command of the Boston Navy Yard. Jane Anne, who had returned briefly to Portsmouth following the peace, went south again to Massachusetts with him, alongside her particular friends Ann Hart Hull, Isaac's war bride, and Hortensia Chew, the wife of Purser Thomas Chew.[12] Occasionally, another report of the *Wasp* would appear in the newspapers—"A London paper mentions a report that the U.S. Sloop of War Wasp had sunk two British sloops near Maranham"—but no longer were they taken seriously.[13] The *Wasp* was nearly a year and a half overdue before editorialists nationwide finally conceded the loss. The North Carolinians took it the hardest:

> THE WASP—We believe that little or no doubt now exists in regard to the fate of this vessel. She has probably long ere this, "mingled with the sands of the ocean"; and her gallant crew, by an inscrutable degree of providence, been consigned to a watery grave. Where all are unfortunate, all deserve a tear of compassion.—But there was one, alike preeminent in fame and rank whose loss his country will long deplore—and whose memory should be particularly embalmed in the heart of every North Carolinian—for Blakeley was a native of this state. That Blakeley perished in *a contest which we believe unwise and unnecessary,* does not lessen our estimation of his character. We should despise ourselves if, on this account, we could withhold our tribute of respect for one so useful and so "famed for deeds of arms"—who has twice conquered the foe; and who still triumphantly displayed those colours, which he had determined shall never waver while he lives. There is one circumstance, which independent of other considerations, gives a "touching pathos" to the subject of this article. Captain Blakeley was a husband and a father! His distressed consort was doomed, for many a mournful month, to all the horrors of suspense, and to have that suspense only terminated by the agonizing conviction that "Wife nor child, more would he behold, Nor friends nor sacred home."[14]

Johnston Blakeley was promoted to a full-fledged captain on 24 November 1814, just two weeks after his daughter's birth, and thus became one of only twenty-one officers to traverse the entire rank structure from midshipman to captain between the navy's birth during the Quasi-War and the end of the War of 1812.[15] Congress had also authorized a handsome sword for Captain Blakeley and each of his officers, along with a gold medal struck in honor of the capture of the *Reindeer.*[16] Not to be outdone, the legislature of the State of North Carolina authorized a sword of their own tastes. Governor William Miller, however, thought it best to put things on hold until the state's favorite son returned. In December 1816, when no doubt at all remained of Blakeley's fate, the Raleigh legislature, once described as "economical to the verge of parsimony," amended the bill to allow the state to financially "adopt" the fatherless Udney Maria. "Probably no child in America was the center of so much interest and sympathy as she," wrote Dr. Kemp S. Battle.[17] North Carolina made Udney Maria their ward and promised to pay all the future costs of her education. Today, this is still considered to be one of the most remarkable resolutions ever passed by that legislative body. Jane Anne Blakeley, still in Boston at this time, was petitioned by Governor Miller to estimate what her daughter's actual monetary needs might prove to be. Jane Anne sought advice from Blakeley's godfather, Edward Jones:

My Dear Sir, Yesterday's mail brought me a letter from Messrs. Macon & Stokes, in which one was enclosed from his excellency Gov'r Miller, and also the resolutions passed in the Senate of North Carolina making provision for the education of my daughter. Your opinion, my kind friend must guide me in the manner of my drawing on the state, and you must also let me know what sum you think I ought to mention as adequate to the present expenses of my child. She is too young at the present time to receive any advantages from what is called education, but her comfort depends upon having it in my power to keep a woman to take care of her, to do her washing &c, to pay the Doctor's bill when her health makes one necessary; all these things I can explain to you, my best friend, but cannot make such a statement to strangers. My friends here say that if my little girl was placed at a good boarding school, her expenses would nearly amount to six hundred dollars annually, do you think that this sum would be thought too large? I suppose by education is meant her maintenance also, you know how little I have it in my power to do for her and this reflection has caused me more anguish than I can describe, and from which I have been most kindly relieved by the liberality of the State of N. Carolina. You know that the sword intended for Capt. Blakeley was voted to be presented to me, but understanding my child is not a son, it has been politely requested that I should name any thing more suitable for a female, which I have done in my reply to the letter from Messrs Macon and Stokes. I hope you will have the goodness to inform me by return of post whether I must draw quarterly or annually, at what time I should commence and for how many years they will think proper to continue the expense of a young lady's education, in short my dear sir I am so totally ignorant of everything concerning this business that I must depend entirely on you for every necessary information. I fear from the silence of Mrs. Jones that she has been ill but [I] sincerely hope by this time she is quite well. My best love to her, in which my family most cordially unite. Kiss my dear Johnston for me and believe me my dear sir, your obliged sincere friend, Jane A. Blakeley.[18]

Six hundred dollars a year it would be. This sum also just happened to exactly match her pension, which was payable biannually for five years commencing on 20 April 1816. In addition to these considerable sums, Jane Anne received seventy-five hundred dollars as the captain's share of prize money awarded for the destruction of the two British sloops of war and the nine hundred dollars remaining of Johnston's uncollected back pay, in addition to his share of the *Atalanta* spoils.[19] Nor was her request for a sword substitute considered out of line, either, especially since the U.S. Congress had already presented her with one. The six-piece, handcrafted silver service eventually presented to Udney Maria was magnificent in its own right. Both the tea and coffee pots offered refreshment through crisply defined eagle-headed spouts, while wreaths of laurel, swords, crossed cannon, and still more eagles embellished their sides and lids. These patriotic themes continued on across the milk jug, both basins, and even the dainty sugar tongs. Each of these items, except the last, of course, bore the following inscription: "In grateful remembrance of the gallantry of Captain Johnston Blakeley, late of the U.S. Navy, who during a short cruise in the Sloop of war 'Wasp' in the year 1814 captured the two British Sloops of war 'Reindeer' and 'Avon,' and was afterwards lost at sea. This Plate is presented to his daughter Udney Maria Blakeley by the State of North Carolina."[20]

As noted in the closing of Jane Anne's letter to Mr. Jones, Mrs. Jones did indeed suffer from a running bout with some sort of ocular malady, and this could well have been the reason she had not written to Jane Anne recently. Mrs. Jones traveled to both Boston and Philadelphia after the war to seek relief from the best medical minds of her day. The "Johnston" whom Jane Anne desired Edward to kiss was in fact the latest addition to the Jones family, Johnston Blakeley Jones. In 1827, Edward Jones retired from his post as solicitor general and began to live the quiet life of an Irish country squire at Rock Rest. He became active in local church affairs and continued supporting the University at Chapel Hill both with funds and donations of books to the school's library. Edward devoted much time to raising his six surviving children,[21] often reading to them by the fireside on long winter nights from both the family bible and his rare first editions of Shakespeare. He taught his children about the law, and to those too young to remember, he told and then retold the story of the young Irish orphan whom he had taken in, later to become the famed fighting captain from North Carolina. Edward's mind "underwent some decay" in later years, and this kept him from continuing with an occasional private legal practice. "Colonel" Edward Jones, as he was sometimes later called, died "peacefully and without suffering" on 8 August 1841, while living out his seventy-ninth year. He was buried in the graveyard of the Episcopal Church in Pittsboro, where most of his final Sundays were spent. In late 1816, *Analectic Magazine* gave the thirsty public the first of only a few minibiographies of Johnston Blakeley, which fortunately included as its frontispiece a very handsomely engraved portrait.[22] The *National Intelligencer* reviewed the article, and a great many of the smaller papers across the country reprinted it for their interested readers, complete with a surprising number of errors.[23]

Jane Anne also remarried. She described in her own words what transpired: "I was married in Boston Mass. on the twenty-second of June 1819, by the Rev. Dr. J. S. J. Gardiner, Rector of the Trinity Church, to Robert Abbott, of the Island of St. Croix."[24] The mysterious groom might well have been a friend of Jane Anne's father, "the late John Hoope, Esq., of the Island of St. Croix."[25] Her mother, Mrs. Mary Hoope, additionally described her latest son-in-law as "Doctor Abbott."[26] By "intermarrying," Jane Anne forfeited the final two years of her pension, but new legislation allowed the minor children of deceased military officers from the War of 1812 to receive a pension in the same amount. Since Udney Maria could draw upon these funds until her sixteenth year, Jane Anne was actually now better off financially. Udney Maria attended a Philadelphia boarding school, courtesy of the State of North Carolina, up until her sixteenth birthday. By November 1830, the good doctor clearly wanted to get out and abroad, for no self-respecting man of that day, no matter how kind or understanding, could long stomach being known simply as the second husband of a nationally famous and heroic man's widow. The Abbotts thus departed the United States for St. Croix in mid to late November.[27]

Before they could embark upon their new life together, however, there was some unfinished financial business to take care of. When Capt. Johnston Blakeley had sailed off into oblivion, he had taken certain sums of the government's money with him. Cash was required on board a man-of-war for various needs, such as recruitment, the purchasing of stores, the paying of hospital bills in foreign ports of call, and the like. And as far as the fourth auditor of the treasury was concerned, Blakeley was a debtor to the United States to the tune of $3,528.64, and these sums had to be accounted for. In January 1823 Robert Abbott petitioned both the House of Representatives and the Senate for a bill to annul the debt. If Blakeley could not produce the money, his papers, or his vouchers, then legally Jane Anne, and thus her new husband, would become responsible. To date, Jane Anne had received a total of about $8,300 (much of the prize money was held in trust for Udney Maria) for her late husband's actions in the war, but he had possessed neither a home nor any properties other than what he sailed away with in his cabin. No will of Johnston Blakeley's was ever found. Jane Anne could not (and Robert Abbott would not) pay back these funds. This was all mere formality, of course, but a necessary formality. The power of the pursestrings lay with the legislative branch, and only they could remove Blakeley's name from the defaulter's list. And this they did most handsomely. "The Committee are of the opinion from the general reputation of Captain Blakeley that the money received by him was applied to the public service," reported the Committee of Claims, "and that if he had lived to return the whole would have been satisfactorily accounted for." On 3 March 1823, the president signed into law a bill crediting Blakeley's account in full for the lost funds. Purser Lewis Fairchild's good name was not so fortunate. He possessed neither the clout nor perhaps even the liable heirs to petition for the erasure of his equally innocent debt, a sum amounting to more than $25,000.

And so Blakeley's remaining family lived out their days on the little Danish island. While the fate of Jane Anne and her new husband after they left the United States is not known, Udney Maria left a brief although tragic record for posterity. On 19 May 1841, she wed Baron Joseph Von Bretton, MD, at St. John's Episcopal Church, in Christiansted, St. Croix. The next 2 March both she and her baby died during childbirth and were buried together in the parish churchyard. Sadly, she thus left no direct descendants to carry on her father's name. But the Blakeley name lives proudly on in his country's navy. No fewer than three ships have been named in Johnston Blakeley's honor: The torpedo boat USS *Blakeley* (TB 27) served with distinction from 1900 to 1920; a destroyer of the same name (DD 150) graced the navy's honor roll from 1918 to 1945; and finally the destroyer escort *Blakeley* (DE 1072) was christened in one of the captain's old haunts, the Charleston, South Carolina, Navy Yard, on 18 July 1970.

Ironically, its current mission is to attack enemy submarines, the commerce raiders of the modern world.

The following account of Johnston Blakeley's epic cruise was printed in newspapers throughout the country following his disappearance. The poem, anonymously written, is entitled simply "On the Wasp, Sloop of War":

No more shall Blakeley's thunder roar
    Upon the stormy deep;
Far distant from Columbia's shore
    His tombless ruins sleep;
But long Columbia's sons shall tell
    How Blakeley fought, how Blakeley fell.

Too long on foaming billows cast,
    The battles fury bray'd;
And still unsullied on thy mast
    The starry banner wav'd;
Unconquer'd will Columbia be
    While she can boast of sons like thee.

O sleep—the battles rage no more
    shall animate thy breast;
No sound on Lethe's silent shore
    disturbs the warriors rest;
No wave molests its peaceful tide
    No navy on its waters ride.

Nor will the muse refuse a tear
    O'er Reilly's course to flow;
Or one less gen'rous and sincere
    On Tillinghast bestow;
Farewell! no warlike sound again
    Can rouse you from the wat'ry main.[28]

$\mathcal{N}otes$

CHAPTER 1. CHOOSE NOW FOR MR. B

1. This date is still suspect. Episcopal Church records in Seaford, County Down, Ireland, record a son "John Blakely" born to John and Marie Blakely on 11 October 1781. (There is or was a Seaford in nearly each of Ireland's counties.) "Johnston" is sometimes interchanged with "Johnson" which sometimes describes the "Son of John." Prior to this finding, the closest any writer had ever come to Johnston Blakeley's date of birth was "October of 1781." Letter, researcher Sean Callahan to author, 16 September 1992. A more definitive genealogical search is currently in process by the author.

2. Kemp S. Battle, *Captain Johnston Blakeley: A North Carolina Naval Hero and His Daughter* (Raleigh, N.C.: Capital, 1902).

3. Moses Thomas, "Biographical Sketch of the Late Captain Johnston Blakeley," *The Analectic Magazine and Naval Chronicle* 7 (January–June 1816), 208–13. Other equally credible but comparably brief contemporary sources tell how Mrs. Blakeley and a child (or children) died—in Charleston, in Philadelphia, or even during the Atlantic crossing. Despite their differences, however, they all agree about the death of Johnston's younger brother. Although the scarcity of surviving pre–Civil War genealogical data from the south inhibits a more precise study, it is probable that the culprit was yellow fever.

4. *The Wilmington Chronicle and North Carolina Weekly Advertiser,* 22 October 1795.

5. *Newburyport Herald and Country Gazette,* 1 June 1816.

6. "Captain Johnston Blakeley," unpublished U.S. Navy officer data files compiled by Christopher McKee.

7. W. Hooper, "Biographical Sketch of Edward Jones, Esquire," *North Carolina University Magazine* 5 (October 1856): 337–60.

8. H. W. Howard Knott, ed. *Dictionary of American Biography* (New York: Scribners, 1936): 2:535–36.
9. Hooper, "Biographical Sketch," 349. Most sources erroneously state that Jones welcomed Blakeley to Wilmington; see, for example, Battle, *Captain Johnston Blakeley*, 3.
10. Edward Jones's obituary notice ascribed his failure as a merchant to an "unguarded zeal in endeavoring to serve a friend." Could this allusion have referred to Edward's "adoption" of the widowed and quite possibly indigent John Blakeley and his son?
11. *Hall's Wilmington Gazette*, 2 March 1797.
12. Ibid., 9 April 1797.
13. Henry Mauger London, "Captain Johnston Blakeley," *North Carolina University Magazine* 16 (May 1899): 254.
14. Thomas, "Biographical Sketch," 209.
15. James Johnson, "Biographical Sketch of Johnston Blakeley, Late of the U.S. Sloop of War Wasp." *North Carolina University Magazine* 3 (1854): 1–16.
16. Battle, *Captain Johnston Blakeley*, 4.
17. Kemp S. Battle, *History of the University of North Carolina* (Spartanburg, S.C.: Reprint Company, 1974), 1:109.
18. Johnson, "Biographical Sketch," 3.
19. University of North Carolina Archives, Philanthropic Society Records, Series 1, Vol. 2, Special Collections, University of North Carolina Library, Chapel Hill, N.C.
20. Johnson, "Biographical Sketch," 2.
21. Ibid. A 1789 copy of Adam Smith's *Wealth of Nations*, vol. 3, survives in the North Carolina Collections at Chapel Hill with Johnston Blakeley's name stamped on the title page.
22. Battle, *History of the University of North Carolina*, 1:153–65.
23. Ibid.
24. Ibid.
25. Thomas, "Biographical Sketch," 209.
26. Hooper, "Biographical Sketch," 358.
27. Battle, *History of the University of North Carolina*, 1:154.
28. Hooper, "Biographical Sketch," 357.
29. Ibid., 357–58.
30. Hooper, "Biographical Sketch," 341–48.

CHAPTER 2. PRESIDENTIAL STUDIES

1. For the best account of the life of Commo. Thomas Truxtun, see Eugene S. Ferguson, *Truxtun of the Constellation* (Annapolis, Md.: Naval Institute Press, 1982).
2. Thomas Truxtun to Lt. John Lewis, 11 and 13 August 1800, Truxtun Letter Book [hereafter TLB], Historical Society of Pennsylvania [hereafter HSP], Philadelphia, Pa.

3. Log of *President,* 8 October 1800, William M. P. Dunne, "Operational Histories of the Ships of the United States Navy" (private collection of resource data files and unpublished manuscript).

4. Ibid., 13 October 1800.

5. Truxtun to Chaplain John Thompson, 14 November 1800, Truxtun Collection, HSP.

6. Log of *President,* 9 January 1801, Dunne, "Operational Histories."

7. Thomas Truxtun to John Gay, 31 December 1800, Truxtun Collection, HSP.

8. Log of *President,* 17 February 1801, Dunne, "Operational Histories."

9. Pay Roll of the *President,* Record Group [hereafter RG] 45, Records of the Office of the Secretary of the Navy, National Archives, Washington, D.C. Published minibiographies (see, for example, Thomas, "Biographical Sketch"; Johnson, "Biographical Sketch") of Johnston Blakeley have not given a correct view of his true naval origins. They state that Blakeley first acquired his sea legs aboard the *President* following its return from the Quasi-War. Wilmington was not a naval port, they argue, and therefore it took the Navy Department a whole year to figure out what to do with the North Carolinian. It was also claimed that only the considerable influence brought to bear by Counselor Jones saved Blakeley from the ravages of the PEA. It is unreasonable, however, to assume that the influence of a mere state solicitor general, unknown inside the navy department, could outweigh the considerable clout wielded by the vast majority of those dismissed outright, many of whom boasted battle experience.

10. "1801, March 3, Retained in the Naval Service, under Peace Establishment of this date," in "Captain Johnston Blakeley, U.S.N.," chronological service record compiled 20 April 1932. Contained within the ZB File, Naval Historical Center, Washington, D.C.

11. Samuel Smith to Truxtun, 28 April 1801, Letters Sent by the Secretary of the Navy to Officers, Microcopy 149 [hereafter M-149], RG 45, National Archives. The midshipmen ordered to be retained on board the *President* following its West Indian cruise were James P. Leonard, Joseph Bainbridge, Benjamin F. Reed, Johnston Blakely [*sic*], William F. Nichols, Archibald K. Kearney, Philemon C. Blake, John Orde Creighton, Edward Giles, Henry Casey, Sidney Smith, James Biddle, and Sloss H. Grenel. In addition, ten other midshipmen came over from six different vessels, including such notables as Lewis Warrington from the *Chesapeake* and Charles L. Ridgely from the *Patapsco.*

12. Dale to the Commandant of Marines at Toulon, 7 December 1801, Dale Letter Book [hereafter DLB], United States Naval Academy Library [hereafter USNA], Annapolis, Md.

13. Dale to the President of the Board of Health, Toulon, 9 December 1801, DLB, USNA.

14. Dale resigned from the naval service on 17 December 1802, ZB File.

15. Robert Smith to Johnston Blakeley, 17 June 1802, M-149.
16. Smith to Blakeley, 25 August 1802, M-149.

CHAPTER 3. RODGERS'S BOY

1. Dunne, "Operational Histories." The *Constellation* (Captain Alexander Murray) departed Philadelphia on 14 March 1802; the *Chesapeake* (Morris's first flag) left Hampton Roads on the following 2 April; and the *Adams* (Capt. Hugh G. Campbell) sailed from New York on 10 June.
2. See Howard P. Nash Jr., *The Forgotten Wars* (London: A. S. Barnes and Company, 1968), 190–208.
3. Evans, Wederstrandt, et al., to Rodgers, 10 March 1803, Area 4 File, RG45, National Archives, Washington, D.C.
4. Dunne, "Operational Histories." The *Constellation* had returned home the previous December and the *Adams* was at this time away convoying merchant shipping in the eastern Mediterranean.
5. The Master's Log of the *John Adams* is one of the main sources of detail for this important chapter in Blakeley's career. G. W. Blunt White Library MS collections, Log #227, Mystic Seaport, Mystic, Conn.
6. *South Carolina State Gazette and Timothy's Daily Advertiser,* 8 May 1800.
7. Quarter Bill of Frigate *John Adams,* John Rodgers Papers, HSP.
8. Glen Tucker, *Dawn Like Thunder* (New York: Bobbs-Merrill and Company, 1963), 138.
9. *Wadsworth Journal,* 22 May 1803; Dudley Knox, *Naval Documents of the Barbary Wars* [hereafter NavDoc BW] (Washington, D.C.: U.S. Government Printing Office, 1938), 2:417.
10. P. C. Coker, *Charleston's Maritime Heritage, 1670–1865: An Illustrated History* (Charleston, S.C.: Cokercraft Press, 1987), 140; Dunne, "Operational Histories." The *John Adams* carried only six 24-pounder carronades on the quarterdeck.
11. The light winds were variable, shifting from the southwest to the west-northwest, with a period of near calm from 8:00 P.M. to about midnight. Master's Log of *John Adams,* G. W. Blunt White Library MS collections, Log #227.
12. Nicholas Nissen to James Leander Cathcart, 4 June 1803, NavDoc BW, 2:439–40.
13. Circular of Thomas Appleton, U.S. Consul, Leghorn, Italy, 1 November 1801, Nav-Doc BW, 1:613. See also William M. P. Dunne, "The South Carolina Frigate," *The American Neptune 47* (winter 1987): 22–32.
14. Fletcher Pratt, *Preble's Boys* (New York: William Sloane Associates, 1950), 264–65. Pratt observed that a large proportion of the victorious commanders of single-ship actions during the War of 1812 had been involved in Preble's 1804 campaign against the pasha. In fact, there were but two exceptions to this rule, Oliver Hazard Perry and Johnston Blakeley. While he could find not even the slightest influence by Preble upon Perry, he enhanced the career of the much less

known Blakeley to suit his purposes. Pratt's work is a lively, well-written account of the lives of many of the U.S. Navy's most celebrated commanders, and it is a splendid introduction to the age of American fighting sail. Unfortunately, it is rife with imaginative, unreferenced, tall tales. The most glaring involved Blakeley: "Blakely [*sic*] was duly gazetted to the [*Congress*] and did some recruiting duty for her, but was pulled out of it because the news of the loss of the Philadelphia made it necessary to support Preble without delay. The John Adams was to return to the Mediterranean at once with a load of stores. . . . She arrived off Tripoli at the peak of the fighting, and Blakely had an opportunity to see how a great commander led his men in action as well as to learn from the old man's lips something of his method." The problem with this story is that surviving records clearly indicate that Blakeley did not return to the *John Adams* until 1809. But Pratt needed Blakeley back on board his old frigate lest the North Carolinian's two great 1814 victories stand out as stark exceptions to his work's overriding theme. The truth is that Blakeley never served under Preble, never observed the great man in action, and quite possibly may never even have met him. If any label of influence could rightfully be applied to Johnston Blakeley, it must surely be "Rodgers's Boy."

CHAPTER 4. THE SPIRIT OF YANKEE ENTERPRISE

1. Robert Smith to Isaac Chauncey, 23 September 1805, NavDoc BW, 6.
2. Ibid.; Smith to Alexander Murray, 25 October 1805.
3. Chauncey to Smith, 10 March 1806, Letters Received by the Secretary of the Navy from Officers below the Rank of Commander, Microcopy 149 [hereafter M-149], RG45, National Archives.
4. Johnston Blakeley to Smith, 8 April 1806, M-148.
5. Blakeley to Smith, 15 March 1806, M-148.
6. Smith to Blakeley, 19 March 1806, M-149.
7. Smith to Blakeley, 5 May 1806, M-149.
8. See Smith to Cathcart, 6 May 1806, NavDoc BW, 6.
9. See Smith to Alfred Hazard, 20 March 1805, M-149.
10. See Christopher McKee, *A Gentlemanly and Honorable Profession* (Annapolis, Md.: Naval Institute Press, 1991), xi–xiii, 47–48, 98–100, 139–40, 160–64.
11. Blakeley to Smith, 8 July 1806, M-148.
12. Blakeley to Smith, 25 September 1807, M-148.
13. McKee, *A Gentlemanly and Honorable Profession,* 161, 164.
14. Circular to Lieutenants, 20 April 1807, RG45 Circulars, National Archives Microfilm Publication M-977, "General Orders and Circulars," 11 September 1798–22 April 1842, Roll 1, Washington, D.C.
15. See Ralph Ketcham, *James Madison* (Charlottesville: University of Virginia Press, 1992), 441–73.

16. See "Master Commandant Philemon Charles Wederstrandt," unpublished U.S. Navy officer data files compiled by Christopher McKee.

17. Wederstrandt to Smith, 12 December 1808, Letters Received by the Secretary of the Navy from Commanders, Microcopy 147 [hereafter M-147], RG45, National Archives.

18. Smith to Wederstrandt, orders dated 5 May 1808, M-149.

19. Wederstrandt to Smith, 2 August 1808, M-147; Decatur to Smith, 24 May 1808, Letters Received by the Secretary of the Navy from Captains, Microcopy 125 [hereafter M-125], National Archives.

20. Wederstrandt to Smith, 16 June 1808, M-147.

21. Wederstrandt to Smith, 29 June 1808, M-147.

22. Wederstrandt to Smith, 24 July 1808, M-147.

23. Johnson, "Biographical Sketch." It is quite possible that the referenced "Julia" was none other than the orphaned "Miss B.," the young woman that had broken young Johnston's heart back at Rock Rest so many years before; she had settled in Savannah.

24. Smith to Wederstrandt, 1 June 1808, M-149.

25. See Wederstrandt to Smith, 8 July 1808 and 27 July 1808, M-147.

26. Smith to Decatur, 6 June 1808, M-149.

27. Wederstrandt to Smith, 8 July 1808, M-147.

28. Wederstrandt to Smith, 1 August 1808, M-147.

29. Smith to Wederstrandt, 8 August 1808, M-149.

30. Wederstrandt to Smith, 2 August 1808, M-147.

31. Smith to Wederstrandt, 2 August 1808, M-149.

32. Wederstrandt to Smith, 15 September 1808, M-147.

33. Johnson, "Biographical Sketch."

34. Wederstrandt to Smith, 15 September 1808, M-147.

35. Capt. John Smith to Robert Smith, 6 and 17 January 1809, M-147.

36. Ketcham, *James Madison*, 458.

37. Wederstrandt to Smith, 29 September 1808, M-147.

38. Capt. John Smith to Robert Smith, 6 January 1808, M-149.

39. Johnson, "Biographical Sketch." The "celebrated Counselor Emmet" was Thomas Addis Emmet, the prominent and popular New York lawyer, destined to become the state's wartime attorney general. He was the brother of Robert Emmet, the founding father of the Society of United Irishmen, executed five years before for his involvement in the bloody Dublin uprisings in 1798. It is a pity that nothing further survives of the meeting that so impressed Blakeley.

40. Ketcham, *James Madison*, 461–66.

41. Enclosure contained with letter: Wederstrandt to Robert Smith, 23 November 1808, M-147.

42. Wederstrandt to Smith, 29 December 1808, M-147.

43. McKee, Wederstrandt data file. Wederstrandt would eventually make a complete recovery, however; he is known to have made several postwar merchant voyages, including one to India in 1816. He would live on to the very ripe old age of 78.
44. Smith to Blakeley, 9 February 1809, M-149.

CHAPTER 5. SOME REFRACTORY CHARACTERS ON BOARD

1. See Charles Goldsborough to Johnston Blakeley, 31 March 1809, M-149.
2. Josiah Fox to Charles Gottlieb, 18 November 1807, Josiah Fox Papers, Peabody and Essex Museum, Salem, Mass.
3. Fox to Evans, 17 April 1809, Josiah Fox Papers.
4. Evans to Hamilton, 12 June 1809, M-147.
5. See "Captain Samuel Evans," unpublished U.S. Navy officer data files compiled by Christopher McKee.
6. Evans to Hamilton, 13 June 1809, M-147.
7. Evans to Hamilton, 5 April 1809, M-147.
8. Evans to Hamilton, 10 June 1809, M-147.
9. Evans to Woods, enclosure with Evans to Hamilton, 29 June 1809, M-147.
10. Evans to Hamilton, 5 July 1809, M-147.
11. Hamilton to Evans, 8 July 1809, M-149.
12. Evans to Hamilton, 23 June 1809, M-147.
13. Evans to Hamilton, 20 July 1809, M-147.
14. Evans to Hamilton, 18 September 1809, M-147.
15. Evans to Hamilton, 2 October 1809, M-147.
16. Evans to Hamilton, 26 October 1809 and 17 November 1809, M-147.
17. Evans to Hamilton, 23 November 1809, M-147.
18. Ibid.
19. Evans to Hamilton, 2 December 1809, M-147.
20. Evans to Hamilton, 3 December 1809, M-147.
21. Evans to Hamilton, 5 December 1809, M-147.
22. Evans to Hamilton, 7 December 1809, M-147.
23. Unless otherwise noted, the details of this cruise were taken primarily from Evans's lengthy report to Secretary Hamilton, dated 19 June 1810, M-147.
24. Note: John Pettigrew is not to be confused with Blakeley's classmate of nearly identical name (Pettegrew) at UNC, Chapel Hill.
25. Evans to Hamilton, 3 March 1810, M-147.
26. Hamilton to Blakeley, 21 June 1810, M-149.
27. "Captain Johnston Blakeley," ZB File.
28. Evans to Hamilton, 13 July 1810, M-147.
29. Hamilton to Blakeley, 18 July 1810, M-149.
30. Hamilton to Blakeley, 21 August 1810, M-149.

31. Hamilton to Blakeley, 23 August 1810, M-149.
32. Hamilton to John Dent, 23 August 1810, M-149.
33. Dent to Hamilton, 15 September 1810, M-147.
34. Dent to Hamilton, 16 September 1810, M-147.
35. Hamilton to Blakeley, 17 September, 1810, M-149.
36. Hamilton to Blakeley, 20 September, 1810, M-149.
37. Hamilton to Blakeley, 26 September, 1810, M-149.
38. Dent to Hamilton, 27 September 1810, M-147.
39. See "John Herbert Dent," unpublished U.S. Navy officer data files compiled by Christopher McKee.
40. John Rodgers to Benjamin Crowninshield, 11 February 1815, Benjamin Crowninshield MSS, Peabody and Essex Museum, Salem, Mass.
41. Charles W. Thompson to Smith Thompson, 7 January 1823, Miscellaneous Letters Received by the Secretary of the Navy, Microcopy 124 [hereafter M-124], RG45, National Archives.
42. Campbell to Hamilton, 26 November 1811, M-125.
43. Campbell to Hamilton, 25 February 1811, M-125.
44. Dent to Hamilton, 5 November 1810, M-125.
45. Blakeley et al. to Dent, 1 November 1810, enclosed with Dent to Hamilton, 5 November 1810, M-125.
46. Dent to Hamilton, 11 October 1810, and 11(?) November 1810, M-125.
47. "Proceedings of a Court Martial convened . . . for the trial of Garret Barry . . . ," 12 December 1810, Judge Advocate General's Records, Microcopy 273 [hereafter M-273], case no. 80, National Archives.
48. "Proceedings of a Court Martial convened . . . for the trial of John Clear, Seaman . . . ," 21 December 1810, M-273, case no. 88.
49. "Afflicted with a disease of a syphilitic nature," according to the corvette's surgeon, Burrows would be carried ashore at Newport the following March. Daniel McCormick to Hamilton, 8 March 1811, M-125. He would relieve Blakeley once again in 1813, this time of the command of the brig *Enterprize*. A painful malady of the groin would, in both cases, prevent this unfortunate officer from long filling Blakeley's shoes, and a British canister shot received well below the beltline would deprive young Burrows of his life at the very moment of his greatest glory.
50. Hamilton to Blakeley, 21 November 1810, M-125.

CHAPTER 6. DELAY, DISAPPOINTMENT, AND DISASTER

1. Johnson, "Biographical Sketch," 3.
2. *The Analectic Magazine and Naval Chronicle*, front piece of vol. 7, January–June 1816.
3. *Newburyport Herald and Country Gazette*, 21 June 1816.
4. Johnson, "Biographical Sketch," 3.

5. Blakeley to Hamilton, 8 January 1811, M-148.
6. Hamilton to Blakeley, 4 March 1811, M-149.
7. Thomas, "Biographical Sketch," 210.
8. Ibid.
9. Blakeley to Hamilton, 22 May 1811, M-148.
10. Williams to Blakeley, 21 May 1811, M-148.
11. See Blakeley to Hamilton, 19 May 1811, M-148, and Log of *Enterprize,* 15 May 1811, RG24. *Guerriere's* death at the hands of "Old Ironsides" one year later has long been considered the birth of the modern American navy.
12. "Proceedings of a Court Martial of Midshipman Robert Ward . . . ," 5 September 1811, M-273, no. 103.
13. Log of *Enterprize,* 5 August 1811, RG24 (emphasis added).
14. David Lyon, *The Sailing Navy List: All the Ships of the Royal Navy—Built, Purchased, and Captured* (London: Conway, 1993), 130.
15. Coker, *Charleston's Maritime Heritage,* 154.
16. Log of *Enterprize,* 13 August 1811, RG24. Three years later Captain Blakeley would once again come across a cluster of four strange sails, three of them British sloops of war. But on that later day, far away in cooler Irish waters, the North Carolina captain would not be quite so cordial.
17. Blakeley to Hamilton, 31 August 1811, M-148.
18. *Enterprize* 1798–1823, Dunne, "Operational Histories."
19. Robinson to Robert Smith, 27 January 1805, NavDoc BW, 5:309–11, 358–59.
20. "Fox #773," Josiah Fox Papers.
21. Robinson to Samuel Barron, 18 February 1805, NavDoc BW, 5:479–80.
22. Robinson to Smith, 13 April 1805, NavDoc BW, 5:358–59.
23. Blakeley to Hamilton, 7 October 1811, M-148. Naval historians have continually pointed to the conversion of the *Enterprize* from a schooner into a brig as a clear example of the conservatism of Capt. Thomas Tingey. Having earned considerable experience as a sea officer in the Royal Navy, the intransigent Tingey was thought to have favored the safer, long-established brig-rig. But the squaring and thickening of the *Enterprize's* top-hamper was the brainchild of Blakeley, not Tingey.
24. Robinson to Smith, 13 April 1805, NavDoc BW, 5:358–59.
25. James Johnson, "The Fate of the Wasp," *Southern Quarterly Review* 15 (1849): 449–60.
26. "Thomas G. Tillinghast," unpublished U.S. Navy officer data files compiled by Christopher McKee.
27. Thomas G. Tillinghast was appointed midshipman on 1 January 1808, and lieutenant on 24 July 1813. Unpublished U.S. Navy officer data files compiled by Christopher McKee.
28. Johnson, "Biographical Sketch," 11.
29. Blakeley to Hamilton, 16 April 1812, M-148.
30. Hamilton to Blakeley, 19 May 1812, M-149.

31. Hamilton to Tingey, 16 May 1812, M-149. Considering the long-standing debate over the "French influence" on American naval design, it is curious that the navy had an interest in the model of an obscure French frigate.
32. Log of *Enterprize*, 21 May 1812, RG24.
33. Ibid., 29 May 1812.
34. Archibald McClaine to Edward Jones, dated Wilmington, 18 November 1790, Captain Johnston Blakeley, MSS, North Carolina Department of Cultural Resources, Raleigh, N.C. This is one of the few surviving letters received by Edward Jones that specifically deals with the subject of slavery. Archibald McClaine, Jones's legal mentor and then a congressman from North Carolina, had written to Edward as far back as 1790 concerning a piece of legislation that would prohibit the importation of slaves into North Carolina. In this letter, the like-minded legislator had applauded the "religious enthusiasm" that Jones had displayed in his support both of the bill and the cause of abolition.
35. Blakeley to Hamilton, 2 June 1812, M-148.
36. See Samuel Carter, *Blaze of Glory* (New York: St. Martin's Press, 1971).
37. Lewis Heermann to Paul Hamilton, 20 March 1812, M-148. See also Heermann to Hamilton, 25 May 1812, M-148, for a detailed view of the yellow fever epidemic.
38. See William S. Dudley, ed., *The Naval War of 1812* (Washington, D.C.: Naval Historical Center Publications, 1985), 1:421.
39. Blakeley to Hamilton, 3 August 1812, M-148 (emphasis in original).
40. Shaw to Hamilton, 17 August 1812, M-125.
41. Log of *Enterprize*, 13–18 August 1812, RG24.
42. Dudley, *The Naval War of 1812*, 1:237–46.
43. Log of *Enterprize*, 18–22 August 1812.
44. Shaw to Hamilton, 23 August 1812, M-125.
45. Hamilton to Blakeley, 30 August 1812, M-148.
46. Log of *Enterprize*, 6–17 October 1812, RG24.
47. Shaw to Hamilton, 27 October 1812, M-125.
48. Blakeley to Hamilton, November 29, 1812, M-148.
49. Log of *Enterprize*, 8–10 December 1812, RG24, and Blakeley to Hamilton, 23 January 1813, M-148.

CHAPTER 7. CHAINED TO THE MOORINGS

1. Blakeley to Hamilton, 23 January 1813, M-148.
2. See McKee, *A Gentlemanly and Honorable Profession*, 183–85.
3. *The Analectic Magazine and Naval Chronicle* 7 (1816): 210.
4. Kearney to Hamilton, 17 March 1813, M-148.
5. Washington to Blakeley, 2 April 1813, M-125.
6. Blakeley to Jones, 22 March 1813, M-125.
7. Blakeley to Hamilton, 8 April 1813, M-148.

8. Log of *Enterprize,* 10 April 1813, RG24. This was to be the last of the *Nonsuch*'s deep-sea cruises.

9. Dent to Jones, 20 February 1813, John H. Dent Letterbook, MSS, South Caroliniana Library, University of South Carolina, Columbia, S.C.

10. Hugh G. Campbell to Johnston Blakeley, copy dated "St. Mary's," 15 May 1813, M-125.

11. Campbell to Blakeley, 7 April 1813, enclosure with Judge Advocate General's Records for case no. 133.

12. Campbell to Blakeley, copy dated "St. Mary's," 15 May 1813, M-125.

13. Jones to Campbell, 24 April 1813, M-149.

14. Log of *Enterprize,* 13 June 1813.

15. Hull to Jones, 3 July 1813, M-125.

16. Blakeley to Hull, dated 29 July 1813, enclosure with Hull to Jones, dated 31 July 1813, M-125.

17. Hull to Jones, 2 August 1813, M-125.

18. Johnson, "Biographical Sketch," 6.

19. Hull to Jones, 2 September 1813, M-125.

20. Battle, *Captain Johnston Blakeley,* 9. Historian Dr. Kemp S. Battle has suggested that Blakeley was promoted solely for capturing the powerful *Fly.*

CHAPTER 8. THE *Argus* ACCURATELY EXTENDED

1. William Jones to Burwell Bassett, 2 February 1813, Letters Sent to Congress, from Dudley, *Naval War of 1812,* 2:26–27.

2. William James, *The Naval History of Great Britain* (London: Bentley, 1837), 4:225.

3. Ibid., 5:93–95.

4. See Howard I. Chapelle, *The History of the American Sailing Navy* (New York: Bonanza, 1989), 256–63.

5. Naval architect and maritime historian Howard I. Chapelle thought Doughty had independently come up with the two radically different designs on his own initiative, presumably for the sake of variety. See Howard I. Chapelle, *The History of the American Sailing Navy: The Ships and Their Development* (New York: Bonanza, 1989), 255–63. Increasingly busy, Doughty also designed the 44-gun frigate *Columbia* (later renamed the *Essex*) and the 74-gun *Columbus* and oversaw their construction in the Washington Naval Yard. The *Argus, Essex,* and *Columbus* were burned, along with much of Washington, D.C., during September 1814.

6. William Jones to Amos Binney, 22 April 1813, M-149 (emphasis added).

7. A third copy of the plan, showing somewhat greater detail but still rather roughly drawn, signed by Doughty and noted as being "examined June 1st 1813," survives in the National Archives. "Construction Draught for the Sloops of War Wasp, Peacock and Frolic copied from the original which was drawn by William Doughty Naval Constr. and approved by the Honorable William Jones, Secretary of the

Navy," CR 41-5-6-C, Cartographic Branch, U.S. Navy Records of the Bureau of Ships, RG19, National Archives.

8. "Vessels Built by Josiah Barker," Josiah Barker Papers, Massachusetts Historical Society, Boston, Mass. Barker also designed and built at least one heavy corvette for the postwar navy (the *Boston* of 1825), along with an earlier, privately financed corvette for the renowned merchant William Gray: an enormous eight-hundred-ton, flush-decked privateer called the *Union*.

9. William Jones to William Bainbridge, 14 August 1813, M-149 (emphasis in original).

10. Amos Binney to Josiah Barker, 16 June 1813, Josiah Barker Papers.

11. "Samuel Hart's bill for copying draught of sloop of war, June 21st," dated 2 July 1813, Accounts of Amos Binney (Boston navy agent), Fourth Auditor Settled Accounts, Records of Accounting Officers of the Treasury Department, RG217, National Archives.

12. Chapelle, *History of the American Sailing Navy*, 258.

13. In 1814 the *Frolic*'s sailing master, James B. Wright, an officer with intimate knowledge of the construction of both sloops, would declare to his British captors "that it would puzzle anyone to discover the slightest difference between her [the *Frolic*] and the Wasp." William James, *Naval Occurrences* (London: Egerton, 1817), 358.

14. Chapelle, *History of the American Sailing Navy*, 258.

15. *Contract for the Building of the Sloop of War Wasp*, dated 6 May 1813, microfilm copy in the Newburyport Public Library, Newburyport, Mass.

16. John J. Currier, *History of Newbury, Mass.* (Boston: Damrell and Upham, 1902), 488. See also the *Newburyport Herald*, 21 September 1813.

17. William Jones to William Bainbridge, 14 August 1813, M-149.

18. Bainbridge to Jones, 20 August 1813, M-125.

19. Jones to Bainbridge, 26 August 1813, M-149.

CHAPTER 9. THE AUTUMN OF DISCONTENT

1. A beautiful portrait of the corvette *John Adams*, painted at the occasion of its second launch following rebuilding in 1830 in Norfolk, Virginia, depicts the grandeur of a launching. See Coker, *Charleston's Maritime Heritage*, 142.

2. Currier, *History of Newbury, Mass.*, 488.

3. *Newburyport Herald*, 21 September 1813.

4. *Newburyport Herald*, 17 September 1813.

5. The exact order of events was preserved in a contemporary commemorative pamphlet. *An Account of the Funeral Honors Bestowed Upon the Remains of Capt. Lawrence and Lieut. Ludlow* (Boston, 1813), broadsheet reprinted in Roscoe Freeman, *The Picture History of the U.S. Navy* (New York: Bonanza, 1956), photo 341 [hereafter *Funeral Honors*].

6. *Newburyport Herald*, 3 September 1813.

7. A map engraved for the *American Coast Pilot* clearly details the harbor circa 1809. In Currier, *History of Newbury, Mass.*

8. Benjamin Labaree, *Patriots and Partisans* (New York: Norton, 1975).

9. Raymond P. Holden, *The Merrimack* (New York, Rinehold, 1958), 133–46.

10. Labaree, *Patriots and Partisans*, 181.

11. Ibid., 185.

12. Ibid., 187.

13. Abigail Jones was a great cause for concern to her husband, because of her mental state. She would slowly deteriorate to the point that she would be described as both "a distracted person and a lunatic" after the war, entirely incapable of self-care. Pension Application File, War of 1812, for Abigail Jones, no. 667, RG15, National Archives.

14. Marshall Sales invoice for a "large patent camboose with furniture," dated 16 July 1813. Accounts of Amos Binney (Boston navy agent), Fourth Auditor Settled Accounts, RG217.

15. "General indent for a sloop of war of 22 guns of stores," unaccompanied document, undated but labeled "Baltimore," found in M-125 among the November 1813 correspondence. This document must be considered the official such indent, as the builder in Baltimore, Erie Kemp, was drawing up all specifications for the six sloops of war. (Hereafter "Baltimore Indent.")

16. *Newburyport Herald*, 2 September 1813.

17. Johnston Blakeley to William Jones, 2 September 1813, M-125.

18. "Alterations and extra work on Ship Wasp . . . Boston October 1814," Navy Area 7 Files, Microfilm Series M-625, Roll 77, June 1814 to December 1815, RG45, National Archives [hereafter "Alterations"].

19. William Bainbridge to William Jones, 25 September 1813, M-125.

20. Jones to Bainbridge, 30 September 1813, M-149 (emphasis in original).

21. *Newburyport Herald*, 24 September 1813.

22. Pay and Muster Roll, U.S.S. Wasp, 1813–14, RG24.

23. "Master James E. Carr," unpublished U.S. Navy officer data files compiled by Christopher McKee.

24. James Carr received his appointment as sailing master on 4 August 1807. Unpublished U.S. naval officer data files compiled by Christopher McKee.

25. John Rodgers to Paul Hamilton, 10 October 1809, M-125.

26. "Baltimore Indent."

27. Bainbridge to Jones, 7[?] October 1813, M-125.

28. James M. Perry, "The U.S. Sloop of War Wasp," U.S. Naval Institute *Proceedings* 87 (1961): 86. Exchange of four partially quoted letters between Johnston Blakeley and William Bainbridge beginning on 11 October 1813. Source not given, nor yet found.

29. "Alterations."

30. Ibid.

31. Jones to Bainbridge, 29 September 1813, M-149.
32. Euphemia Smith, *History of Newburyport* (Newburyport, Mass.: 1854), 201.
33. Log of Gunboat *No. 81*, RG24. If this was the Charlestown to Boston bridge, this entry proves that the *Frolic* was indeed built in Barker's private yard, and not, as some have suggested, in the navy yard. Chapelle, *History of the American Sailing Navy*, 256.
34. *Newburyport Herald*, 14 October 1813.
35. Jones to Bainbridge, 13 October 1813, M-149.

CHAPTER 10. TWO CONNECTICUT YANKEES IN NEWBURYPORT

1. McKee, *A Gentlemanly and Honorable Profession*, 162.
2. Thomas English to Paul Hamilton, 20 July 1810, Acceptances, Midshipmen, taken from "Lieutenant James Reilly," unpublished U.S. naval officer data files compiled by Christopher McKee.
3. Tyrone G. Martin, "The Captain's Clerk," unpublished biographical data file for *Constitution*'s Midshipman James Reilly.
4. Ibid.
5. James Reilly was appointed midshipman on 1 January 1808, and lieutenant on 24 July 1813. Unpublished U.S. Navy officer data files compiled by Christopher McKee.
6. Lewis Fairchild was appointed midshipman on 20 June 1806, and purser on 29 September 1813.
7. "Purser Lewis Fairchild," unpublished U.S. Navy officer data files compiled by Christopher McKee.
8. Possibly "Andrew Cock." Document is illegible.
9. "Chaplain Lewis Fairchild," from Martin, "The Captain's Clerk."
10. Lewis Fairchild to Robert Smith, 18 January 1808, M-148.
11. McKee, *A Gentlemanly and Honorable Profession*, 353.
12. Ibid., 350–63.
13. Isaac Hull to William Jones, 9 September 1813, M-125.
14. Hull to Jones, 23 September 1813, M-125.
15. Frederick Baury Papers, Massachusetts Historical Society (hereafter MHS), Boston, MA.
16. Anonymous typescript, Baury Family Papers, MHS.
17. "Midshipman Frederick Baury," unpublished U.S. Navy officer data files compiled by Christopher McKee.
18. Frederick Baury was appointed midshipman on 18 May 1809, and lieutenant on 9 December 1814. McKee, unpublished U.S. Navy officer data files.
19. Frederick Baury to Polly Baury, 11 September 1809, Baury Family Papers. Frederick's surviving collection of letters to his mother, a delightful series beginning just after his naval appointment, are a rare and revealing look at the life of a midshipman in the prewar navy.

20. Ibid., Frederick Baury to Polly Baury, 2 October 1809.

21. Frederick Baury to William Eustis, 15 July 1810, William Eustis Papers, MHS.

22. Frederick Baury to Paul Hamilton, 15 July 1810, M-148.

23. Frederick Baury to Polly Baury, 6 October 1811, Baury Family Papers. Baury's candid assessments of Hull, written two years apart, are both extraordinary and important. The brave commander of America's most celebrated single-ship victory, the August 1812 battle between the *Constitution* and the *Guerriere,* has long been described as a crack sailor, universally beloved. While acknowledging the captain's merits, the statements by young Frederick seem to call into question the praise heaped upon the captain today. One should not by any means interpret Baury's remarks as an indictment against Hull's character. They simply show that the great men of history, even the beneficiaries of generations of uncritical accolades, were not flawless, and even the best of them had their detractors.

24. "Midshipman Frederick Baury," from Martin, "The Captain's Clerk."

25. Linda Maloney, *The Captain from Connecticut* (Boston: Northeastern University Press, 1977), 175.

26. William Eustis to William Jones, 16 September 1813. William Jones Papers, Historical Society of Pennsylvania, Philadelphia, Pa.

27. Frederick Baury to Polly Baury, 7 October 1813, Baury Family Papers. This is Baury's last surviving letter.

28. Additional data can be found in the David Geisinger Papers, Maryland Historical Society, Baltimore, Md. A twenty-three-year-old mariner from Frederick County, Maryland, he was, with the sole exception of David Glasgow Farragut, the navy's single most valuable midshipman to come through the War of 1812 intact.

29. David Geisinger was appointed midshipman on 15 November 1809, and lieutenant on 9 December 1814. Unpublished U.S. Navy officer data files compiled by Christopher McKee.

30. Stephen Cassin to William Jones, [?] September 1813, M-125.

31. Jones to Cassin, 14 September 1813, M-149 (emphasis in original).

32. Ibid.

33. William J. Morgan, *The Autobiography of Charles Wilkes* (Washington, D.C.: Naval History Division 1978), 46–47. The famous admiral and explorer Charles F. Wilkes Jr. joined the navy as a midshipman just after the close of hostilities against Great Britain. His observations on the regional divisions that existed in the officer corps are especially relevant when discussing the *Wasp*'s mixed wardroom. Wilkes's autobiography also provides interesting insight about Blakeley's immediate supervisor, Commodore Bainbridge.

34. Log of Gunboat *No. 81,* 23 October 1813, RG24.

35. Muster Roll of U.S.S. *Wasp,* RG24.

36. Log of Gunboat *No. 81,* 24 November 1813, RG24.

37. *Newburyport Herald,* 25 November 1813.

38. William Jones to Johnston Blakeley, 16 November 1813, M-149.

39. Rodgers to Hamilton, 24 September 1812, M-125, and "Surgeon William M. Clarke," unpublished U.S. Navy officer data files compiled by Christopher McKee.

40. William M. Clarke was appointed surgeon's mate on 25 November 1809, and surgeon on 24 July 1813. Unpublished U.S. Navy officer data files compiled by Christopher McKee.

41. "William M. Clarke, U.S.N.," ZB File.

42. William Bainbridge to William Jones, 15 December 1813, M-125.

43. Muster Roll of U.S.S. *Wasp*, RG24.

44. Blakeley to Jones, [?] December 1813, M-124. Note: this has faded to near illegibility.

45. John Larkin was appointed midshipman on 12 October 1812. He resigned in Boston on 31 December 1813. Unpublished U.S. Navy officer data files compiled by Christopher McKee.

46. "Midshipman John Larkin," unpublished U.S. Navy officer data files compiled by Christopher McKee.

47. Muster Roll of U.S.S. *Wasp*, RG24. By the time that Blakeley was finally able to put to sea in May 1814, no fewer than forty-one able and ordinary seamen would desert, almost one-quarter of his total enlisted complement. This figure counts only those he was unable to recapture.

48. "Proceedings of a Court Martial . . . of Boatswain Thomas Jackson," 15 December 1813, M-273, Vol. 6 (no case number).

49. Blakeley to Jones, 20 December 1813, M-124.

50. 27 August 1814, "Remarks and Occurrences and historical events on Board the U.S. Sloop of War Wasp of 18 guns, Johnston Blakeley, Esquire, Commanding, by Midshipman David Geisinger," 2 May–23 September 1814 [hereafter "Geisinger Journal"], Manuscript Division, Library of Congress [hereafter LOC], Washington, D.C.

51. *Newburyport Herald*, 4 January 1814. Little is known of Miss Hoope other than what was written in Blakeley's brief nineteenth-century biographies (see, for example, Thomas, "Biographical Sketch"). Her father, according to these accounts, was "formerly a merchant in New York" and a close friend and confidant to Blakeley's father when both were engaged in the mercantile trade. The Hoope family may well have been the New York "friends" with whom Lieutenant Blakeley camped out in 1806 after leaving the *Hornet*. Perhaps it was they who had earlier looked after young Johnston during his boarding-school years in Flatbush. But pension file records suggest otherwise. See Pension Application File, War of 1812, for Jane Anne Blakeley, no. 118, RG15. Note: this and all the following pension files are listed alphabetically by last name of petitioner in Virgil D. White, *Index to War of 1812 Pension Files*, 2 vols. (Waynesboro, Tenn.: National Historical Publishing, 1992). The Hoope family appears from these documents to have had a rather strong postwar Philadelphia connection. Mrs. Mary Hoope, Jane's mother, was deposed before John Swift, Esquire, the mayor of Philadelphia and with whom she claimed to have had a "long standing" acquaintance, for the purpose of obtaining a

pension for her daughter. So too was Jane Anne's sister, longtime Philadelphian Frances N. Hoope. After the war, Johnston's only child, Udney Maria, attended an unnamed boarding school in Philadelphia up until her sixteenth birthday. Perhaps the Hoopes had moved to the nation's capital from New York after young Johnston headed south for home in the mid-1790s. Furthermore, Jane could not have been Johnston's childhood sweetheart, as some writers have supposed, since when Mary Hoope went before Mayor Swift on 19 August 1837, she was described as being "upwards of sixty-four years old." In December of 1813, therefore, Mary Hoope would have been only about forty years of age, or only about seven years older than the bridegroom. Thus Jane Anne was probably then around twenty-one, and thus a dozen years younger than her husband. She may not even have been born when Johnston studied his English and Latin in Flatbush, if that was indeed where the Hoopes actually resided.

52. "Old Act Navy Minor File No. 118" for Jane Anne Blakeley, Pension files, National Archives, Washington, D.C.

CHAPTER 11. A DULL, HARMLESS DRONE

1. *Newburyport Herald,* 29 January 1863.
2. Ibid., 14 January 1814.
3. Frederick Baury to William Jones, 4 January 1814, M-148.
4. Blakeley to Jones, 2 January 1814, M-124.
5. William Jones to William Bainbridge, 14 January 1814, M-149.
6. Blakeley to Jones, 16 January 1814, M-124.
7. Log of Gunboat *No. 81,* RG24.
8. Hull to Blakeley, 12 January 1814. Isaac Hull Letter Book, New York Historical Society [hereafter NYHS].
9. Proceedings of the "Trial of Sailing Master William Harper," 28 December 1813 and 15 January 1814, M-273, Roll 6, case 156.
10. Thomas, "Biographical Sketch," *The Analectic Magazine and Naval Chronicle I* (November 1813), 396–403.
11. Ibid.
12. Dudley, *The Naval War of 1812,* 2:289–92.
13. Edward McCall to Isaac Hull, 7 September 1813, in Dudley, *The Naval War of 1812,* 2:235.
14. Lt. David McCreary, R.N., to Commander Alexander Gordon, R.N., 6 September 1813. "The next morning we observed a man of war brig in the offing. At 9:00 A.M. discovered her to be the Enterprize, gave chase, which she observed, and made all possible sail from us, distant about six miles, beating to the westward with a light breeze. Showed our colors and fired a gun at 2:40 P.M. coming up with the enemy fast, who fired her stern gun at us, and showed American colors at each mast head." Dudley, *The Naval War of 1812,* 2:234.

15. The *Boxer* had been forced to abandon many people ashore on a hunting expedition when the *Enterprize* unexpectedly hauled into view. See William James, *The Naval History of Great Britain* (London: Bentley, 1837), 6:75.

16. Hull to Jones, 18 September in Dudley, *The Naval War of 1812*, 2:242.

17. Ibid., 2:289–92.

18. *Newburyport Herald,* 21 January 1814.

19. *The Analectic Magazine and Naval Chronicle* 7 (January–June 1816).

20. Muster Roll of U.S.S *Wasp,* RG24.

21. *Newburyport Herald,* 4 February 1814.

22. Ibid., 8 February 1814.

23. Smith, *History of Newburyport,* 199.

24. David F. Long, *Ready to Hazard* (Hanover, N.H.: University Press of New England, 1981), 167–87.

25. See McKee, *A Gentlemanly and Honorable Profession,* 129–30; and J. N. Reynolds, *Voyage of the Frigate Potomac* (New York: Harper, 1835), 520–21.

26. *Newburyport Herald,* 11 February 1814.

27. "Statement of the Cost of the United States Sloop of War Wasp," enclosed with letter, Amos Binney to William Jones, dated Boston, 10 August 1814, Navy Area 7 File, National Archives.

28. Blakeley to Jones, 21 February 1814, M-124.

29. Logbook of Gunboat *No. 81,* RG24.

30. Blakeley to Jones, 28 February 1814, M-124.

CHAPTER 12. PROVISIONING ON THE PISCATAQUA

1. The official Jones-Bainbridge spar dimensions were recorded in Bermuda immediately following the *Frolic*'s capture. The *Wasp*'s would have been sparred nearly identical. "Dimensions of the United States Sloop of War Frolic. Hull: Length between perpendiculars: 118.00 Feet, Breadth moulded: 31.06 Feet, Depth from top of Gun deck beam to Limber Streak: 14.06 Feet . . . Masts, Yards, etc.: Main mast, length feet, inches: 75.0; masthead: 12.0; main topmast: 45.0; masthead: 6.9; main top gallant mast: 22.6; royal pole: 12.0; skysail: 6.0; main yard: 67.6, 4 [arms]; main topsail yard: 50.6, 4; main topgallant yard: 34, 2; main royal yard: 22.9, 1.4; main skysail yard: 15.3; foremast: 67.6, 4; fore topmast: 42, 6; fore top gallantmast: 21.0; royal 12(?), 5 ½; sky, 17(?); fore yard: 60.9, 3.8; fore topsail yard: 45.6, 3.8; fore topgall't yard: 30.6, 1.10; fore royal yard: 20.6, 1.03; fore skysail yard: 13.9; mizen mast: 63.9, 10 [head]; mizen topmast: 32.0, 5; mizen topgallant mast: 16.0; mizen royal pole: 8.0; skysail: 5.0; cross jack yard: 51.4; topsail yard: 38.3; mizen topgallant yard: 25.6, 1; mizen royal yard: 17.0, 1; mizen skysail yard: 11.6; spanker boom: 50.6; spanker gaff: 38.0; bowsprit: 32.0; jib boom: 35.3; flying jib boom: 38.9; ringtail boom: 22.6; ringtail yard: 11.3; lower studding and swinging boom: 40.9; lower studding and swinging yard: 20.4; main topmast studding

swinging boom: 35.6; main topmast studding swinging yard: 19.6; fore topmast studding swinging boom: 31.8; do. yard: 17.4; main top gall. S.S. boom: 23.8; do. yard: 13; mizen top gal S.S. Boom: 19.9; do. yard: 10.10; mizen royal S.S. boom: 15.10; do yard: 8.9; mizen royal S.S. boom: 13.3; do. yard: 7.06. Tops $^{36}/_{100}$ of their respective topmasts. The Diameter of fore and main masts of the number of feet in length $^{32}/_{100}$ in inches if of southern pine, and $^{35}/_{100}$ if of white pine. The Diameter of the Mizen Masts of the number of feet in length $^{25}/_{100}$ in inches if of southern pine, and $^{28}/_{100}$ if of white pine. The diameter of the topmasts of the number of feet in length $^{30}/_{100}$ in inches of southern pine, and $^{35}/_{100}$ if of Spruce. The diameter of the Yards of the number of feet in length $^{20}/_{100}$ in inches if of southern, and $^{22}/_{100}$ if of northern. A true copy, signed H[ugh] Pigot Captain [HBMS Frigate *Orpheus*]." Enclosure with Alexander Cochrane to William Croker, dated Bermuda, 17 May 1814, Admirals' Letters to Admiralty, North America Station section for 1814, ADM 1/506, 710, Public Record Office [hereafter PRO], Kew, England.

2. Log of the United States Frigate *Congress,* for 1–2 May 1814, RG24.
3. Jones to Blakeley, 14 March 1814, Confidential Letters Sent to Captains of Ships of War, RG45, National Archives.
4. Log of H.B.M. Frigate *Tenedos,* 25 April 1814, Dunne, "Operational Histories."
5. Log of *Congress,* 18 April 1814, RG24.
6. Ibid., 19 April 1814.
7. Ibid., 30 April 1814.
8. Ibid., 4 May 1814.
9. *Newburyport Herald,* 4 April 1814.
10. Log of *Congress,* 30 March 1814, RG24.
11. Ibid., 20 April 1814.
12. Ibid., 22 April 1814.
13. Ibid., 24 April 1814.
14. *Newburyport Herald,* 24 April 1814.
15. Pay and Muster Roll of U.S.S. *Wasp,* RG24.
16. Richardson's sons would not learn of his fate for another twenty-three years. Pension Application File, War of 1812, for "Widow of Henry Richardson USMC," no. 1385, RG15.
17. Hull to Jones, 25 March 1814, Isaac Hull Papers, NYHS.
18. Ibid., 23 April 1814.
19. Blakeley to Jones, 15 March 1814, M-124.
20. Blakeley to Jones, 7 and 22 March 1814, M-124.
21. "Baltimore Indent," M-125.
22. William Jones to Charles Ridgely, 16 March 1814, M-149.
23. Ebenezer Clough to William Jones, 1 January 1814, Acceptances, Midshipmen, 1810–14, RG45, from "Midshipman Ebenezer Clough," unpublished U.S. Navy officer data files compiled by Christopher McKee.

24. Isaac Hull to William Jones, 23 April 1814, M-125.
25. Ebenezer Clough was appointed midshipman on 9 November 1813. Unpublished U.S. Navy officer data files compiled by Christopher McKee.
26. McKee, *A Gentlemanly and Honorable Profession,* 459–61.
27. James Carr to Johnston Blakeley, 19 April 1814, enclosure with Hull to Jones, 21 April 1814, M-125.
28. Nathaniel Stoodly to Isaac Hull, 28 April 1814, M-125.
29. McKee, Clough data file, unpublished U.S. Navy Officer data files.
30. McKee, *A Gentlemanly and Honorable Profession,* 61.
31. "Midshipman Thomas N. Bonneville," unpublished U.S. Navy officer data files compiled by Christopher McKee.
32. Marguerite Brazier Bonneville to Paul Hamilton, 9 May 1811, Appointments, #3256, from McKee, Bonneville data file.
33. Katherine Few to Lt. E. H. Cummings, USMC, 28 March 1812, M-124.
34. See Jack Fruchtman Jr., *Thomas Paine* (New York: Four Walls Eight Windows Press, 1994), 36, 395, 406, 417–18, 425–26, 433–34.
35. He was also the brother of Benjamin Louis Eulalie de Bonneville, the somewhat controversial army officer who would later work toward, with middling success, the exploitation of the nation's fur trade in the western territories. Benjamin was also a member of the first graduating class at West Point in 1815 (at the age of seventeen) and would later serve with great distinction during the Mexican War. See *Dictionary of American Biography,* ed. W. J. Ghent, 1:438.
36. Thomas N. Bonneville to William Jones, 26 September 1812, M-148.
37. Bonneville to Jones, 7 July 1813 and 8 November 1813, M-148.
38. Thomas N. Bonneville was appointed midshipman on 10 April 1812. Unpublished U.S. Navy officer data files compiled by Christopher McKee.
39. Henry Shurburne Langdon Jr. was appointed midshipman on 5 October 1812. Unpublished U.S. Navy officer files compiled by Christopher McKee.
40. Charles Morris to William Jones, 28 December 1813, M-125.
41. James A. Spalding, *What I Know about the Parrots and Toscans of Portsmouth, Greenland, Brookfield, Middletown, and Lancaster all in New Hampshire* (typescript in the New Hampshire Historical Society, Concord, N.H.), 70–85. Built in 1800, the cupolaed "Toscan Bungalow" may still be seen today in present-day Greenland, New Hampshire.
42. John Howells, *The Architectural Heritage of the Piscataqua* (Portsmouth, N.H.: Abby White Howells, 1965), 144.
43. Ibid.; Spalding, *What I Know,* 80.
44. Frank Toscan was appointed midshipman on 9 November 1812. See Sen. Charles Cutts to Paul Hamilton, 2 November 1812, M-124.
45. Isaac Hull to William Jones, 20 May 1813, M-125.
46. Frank Toscan to William Jones, 30 September 1813, M-148.
47. See ZB File for Ashton Stoodly Hall, Naval Historical Center, Washington, D.C., and *Boston Transcript,* 2 May 1908.

48. Ashton Stoodly Hall was appointed midshipman on 9 November 1813. Unpublished U.S. Navy officer files compiled by Christopher McKee.

49. Ashton Hall to William Jones, 1 January 1814, Acceptances, Midshipmen, 1810–14, from "Midshipman Ashton S. Hall," unpublished U.S. Navy officer data files compiled by Christopher McKee.

50. Theodore Armistead to Paul Hamilton, 6 April 1812, M-124, and Acceptances, Midshipmen, 1810–14, dossier 3599, from "Midshipman William Randolph," unpublished U.S. Navy officer data files compiled by Christopher McKee.

51. William Randolph was appointed midshipman on 14 April 1812. Unpublished U.S. naval officer data files compiled by Christopher McKee.

52. "Court of Enquiry Relating to the Capture of the U.S. Frigate Chesapeake by H.B.M.S. Shannon, off Boston, June 1, 1813," typed MSS, Special Collections, Naval Historical Center.

53. William Randolph to William Jones, 25 September 1813, M-148.

54. Robert Byrd Randolph, William's older brother, was appointed midshipman on 7 June 1811. He had begun his career as Decatur's captain's clerk. Unpublished U.S. Naval officer data files compiled by Christopher McKee.

55. William House was appointed midshipman on 26 December 1812. Unpublished U.S. Naval officer data files compiled by Christopher McKee.

56. William House to William Jones, 14 April 1813, M-148.

57. House to Jones, 13 November 1813, M-148.

58. The enigmatic eighth gentleman might have been either the unidentified "connection of Capt. Charles Stewart of the Navy," or, most likely, that Irish captain's unspecified "nephew." Blakeley had unsuccessfully tried to bring aboard both these men as acting midshipmen the previous December after John Larkin's illness forced his resignation. See Johnston Blakeley to William Jones, 19 December 1813, M-124. Or the mystery midshipman may well have been the ambiguous "Robert R. Stewart of Philadelphia," who came home with prize-masters Geisinger and Bonneville (having allegedly entered in L'Orient, France), and who bore the State Department dispatches. Charles Stewart, after all, hailed from the city of brotherly love as well. Strangely, the Stewart name appears neither in the muster book nor on the Geisinger journal's careful list of L'Orient newcomers.

59. Isaac Hull to William Jones, 2 May 1814, M-125.

60. Johnston Blakeley to William Jones, 2 May 1814, M-124.

CHAPTER 13. THE TESTING BEGINS

1. "Proceedings of the court of inquiry into the capture of the U.S.S. Frolic by H.B.M.S. Orpheus and H.B.M. Schooner Shelbourne," held 5 December 1814, on board the United States Frigate *Guerriere*, M-273, Roll 8, no. 204 [hereafter "*Frolic* Proceedings"].

2. James, *Naval Occurrences*, 334–40.

3. William M. P. Dunne, "Pistols and Honor, " *The American Neptune* 50 (fall 1990): 245–59.

4. Letter, William M. P. Dunne (Stephen Decatur's biographer) to author, dated 1 September 1992.

5. John Shaw to Paul Hamilton, 2 March 1812, M-125.

6. See Joseph Bainbridge to Paul Hamilton, 5 December 1812, M-148; Samuel Hambleton to David Porter, 12 May 1812, Misc. MSS, NYHS; and Joseph Bainbridge's petition for debt relief to the House of Representatives, Committee on Naval Affairs, ca. January 1822, Bill no. 132, National Archives. Unpublished U.S. Navy officer data files compiled by Christopher McKee.

7. Statements for the cost of building the sloops, dated 10 August 1814, and 12 March 1814, for the *Wasp* and *Frolic,* respectively, may be found in the Navy Area 7 File, RG45.

8. Joseph Bainbridge Jr. to William Jones, 22 December 1813, M-147.

9. Jones to Bainbridge, 16 January 1814, enclosure with *Frolic* court-martial proceedings, M-273.

10. "An Abstract of the Log of the Late United States Sloop of War Frolic, Captured by His Majesty's Ship Orpheus, on the 20th Day of April, 1814," for 20 February 1814. Copy dated New Providence, 25 April 1814, signed by Alexander Cochrane. Enclosure with Adm. Alexander Cochrane to Adm. William Croker, dated Bermuda, 15 May 1814, Admirals' Letters to Admiralty, North America Station section for 1814, ADM 1/506, 12986, PRO [hereafter referred to as the "*Frolic* Extract"].

11. "Journal kept on board the U.S. Vessel of War Frolic, Joseph Bainbridge Commander, of 18 guns," 20 February–20 April 1814, author unidentified, unbound, New York Public Library [hereafter NYPL] Mss. Collections. Note: eight of the missing pages are in the Chicago Historical Society [hereafter CHS] Collections, Chicago, Ill. Unless otherwise noted, all references are from the NYPL portion. Hereafter referred to as the "*Frolic* Journal."

12. "*Frolic* Journal," 24 February, this date at CHS.

13. "*Frolic* Journal," 12 March 1814.

14. Ibid., 17 March 1814.

15. Ibid., 29 March 1814.

16. Joseph Bainbridge to William Jones, 3 June 1814, M-147.

17. Later historians, if they refer to this fight at all, declare that the pirate was sunk by a single broadside, and that it took with it over one hundred souls to the bottom well. See Theodore Roosevelt, *The Naval War of 1812* (New York: Putnam, 1910), 2:46.

18. "*Frolic* Extract," 17 April 1814. Whether this brig was Spanish property or, most likely, American is unclear, but in either case it had been unlawfully detained and rudely mistreated. Bainbridge, at any rate, did not see fit to detain, molest, or destroy her.

19. Ibid., 18 April 1814.

20. Ibid.; James, *Naval Occurrences*, 337.

21. John Rodgers to Benjamin W. Crowninshield, 11 February 1815, *Proceedings of the Massachusetts Historical Society, 1887–89*, 2d ser., 4.207 (emphasis in original).

22. Joseph Bainbridge to William Jones, 3 June 1814, M-147.

23. Log of H.B.M. Frigate *Orpheus*, Admiralty: Captains' Logs, ADM 51/2615, for 20 April 1814, PRO. See also unidentified officer's journal excerpted in James, *Naval Occurrences*, 335–6.

24. James, *Naval History of Great Britain*, 6:290–91.

25. "A Report of the Sailing Qualities of His Majesty's Ship 'Florida' as Found on Strict Observation Thereof, Between the Fifth of September, 1815, and this Date [January 1819]," Navy Board and Admiralty Letters, ADM 95/49, 2169, PRO.

26. Lewis Warrington to William Jones, 24 January 1814, M-147.

27. Testimony of Capt. Richard Walter Wales, R.N., H.B.M. Brig *Epervier* court-martial minutes, Admirals' Letters to Admiralty, courts-martial for November, 1814 through January, 1815, ADM 1/5447, 20479, PRO.

28. Thomas Fleming to Lords Commissioners of the Admiralty, dated H.M.S. Ship *Elizabeth* at Gibraltar, 22 September 1814, Admirals' Letters to Admiralty, ADM 1/157, Channel Fleet section for 1814, PRO.

29. Lewis Warrington to William Jones, February 1814, M-147.

30. *Savannah Republican and Evening Ledger*, 5 November 1814.

31. Only a half-dozen married able seamen are specifically identified in the navy's pension file as having belonged to the *Wasp*. However, there probably were other married men whose widows never filed for a postwar pension. Pension Application File, War of 1812, for Sarah Atkins, no. 44, RG15.

32. Brindlecomb's marriage to Sarah Stacey in July 1797 preceded the baptism of their first-born David by only three weeks. Because such situations were scandalous in puritanical New England, one wonders if David Jr. was not the result of some overly enthusiastic courting by David Sr., perhaps before heading off on some lengthy sea voyage, only to find a startling surprise awaiting him at the pier nine months later. Ibid., for Sarah Brindlecomb, no. 164.

33. Hannah Lowther was rather sickly, yet she strained herself to the utmost to maintain her modest home. She looked forward to receiving not only the bulk of her husband's steady pay but a respectable bounty in prize money as well. Ibid., for Hannah Lowther, no. 724.

34. Ibid., for Nabby Phippen, no. 951.

35. Stone had joined the service earlier in the war, either in 1812 or 1813. Ibid., for Mary Stone, no. 1142.

36. After the war, Charlotte Brown confessed that the cause of her late husband's duplicity involved his place of birth, England. Because he was a subject of the Crown, he rightfully feared the consequences of his being made a prisoner during time of war; the penalty for taking up arms against one's king was death. Francis Brown, on one hand, was far too common a name to warrant instant recognition

by any potential captors, unless Francis had either deserted from the Royal Navy or had performed some other, more serious misdeeds back in the old country. Andrew Passenger, on the other hand, was so obviously a pseudonym that it alone might have invited a prisoner of war agent to do some extra digging. As far as the U.S. Navy was concerned, he was Andrew Passenger, able seaman. He would later send his wife several letters from Portsmouth, New Hampshire, playfully addressing them to Charlotte Passenger. Little did he know how this would complicate her postwar affairs, placing her in the awkward position of having to prove that both names represented the same man. Ibid., for Charlotte Passenger, no. 933.

37. McKee, *A Gentlemanly and Honorable Profession,* 219.

38. Pension Application File, War of 1812, for Mary Bartlett, no. 83, RG15.

39. Sarah Anna Emery, *Reminiscences of a Nonagenarian* (Newburyport, Mass.: William H. Huse Company, 1879), 277.

40. Enoch would soon introduce a tender yellow pear to Boston society that would, from then on, proudly bear his family name. Donald A. Doliber, "Unforbidden Fruit: The Bartlett Pair," *The Essex Genealogist* 8 (1988), 4:16.

41. Martin had the good fortune not to remain in the *Chesapeake* under James Lawrence's short tenure, and so he had not been killed, maimed, imprisoned, or otherwise inconvenienced in Halifax the previous summer. If Martin had been a devoted follower of Captain Evans he had probably served under Blakeley in the corvette *John Adams* during its 1809–10 commission. As Captain Evans's increasing blindness (his reason for giving up command of the *Chesapeake*) threatened to keep him forever away from another floating command, Martin might well have sought out Captain Blakeley, Evans's longtime protégé and a known, safe commodity for employment. Pension Application File, War of 1812, for Elizabeth Martin, no. 744, RG15.

42. John R. Spears, *A History of Our Navy* (New York: Scribners, 1899), 3:81–83.

43. "Geisinger Journal," 4 May 1814, LOC.

44. William Gilkerson, *Boarders Away* (Lincoln, R.I.: Andrew Mowbray, 1993), 2:156–216.

45. Lewis Warrington to William Jones, 12 May 1814, M-147.

46. Gordham Lincoln invoice for small arms, dated 24 September 1813, Accounts of Amos Binney (Boston navy agent), Fourth Auditor Settled Accounts, RG217, National Archives, Washington, D.C.

47. Gunners Stores listed in the "Baltimore Indent," M-125.

48. "Statement of the Cost of the United States Sloop of War Wasp," Boston, 10 August 1814. See section for Cordage, p. 2, Navy Area 7 Files, RG45.

49. John Bullus to William Jones, 11 December 1813, M-124.

50. Research courtesy of Capt. Kenneth A. Johnson, U.S.N.

51. Blakeley to Jones, 21 February 1814, M-124.

52. "She [the *Frolic*] had mounted twenty 32 pound carronades and two long eighteens," Hugh Pigot to Alexander Cochrane, 25 April 1814, enclosure with Alexan-

der Cochrane to William Crocker, dated Bermuda, 15 May 1814, Admirals' Letters to Admiralty, North America Station section for 1814, ADM 1/506, 12986, PRO.

53. Charles Ridgely to William Jones, 8 September 1813, M-147. Perhaps Blakeley had proofed his cannon (despite the secretary's "advice") with similar results on his missing twentieth.

54. Thomas Tingey to William Jones, 28 August 1813, M-125.

55. Benjamin Syman to William Jones, 8 November 1813, M-124.

56. Johnston Blakeley to William Jones, 11 September 1814, M-124.

57. Testimony of Lt. George Budd, *Court of Enquiry Relating to the Capture of the Frigate Chesapeake*, Naval Historical Center.

58. See Pension Application Files, War of 1812, for Lucy Flagg, no. 32; Ann Martin, no. 745; and Elizabeth Manley, no. 765, RG15. Mrs. Martin was both respectable and responsible, a woman active in the affairs of her community; Mrs. Manley presumably was not. Mrs. Manley's pension was first sent to a court-appointed guardian, instead of directly to her (this intermediate step was reserved mostly for minors), because, as the local magistrate noted with mild disgust, she was "a person given to excessive drinking and idleness."

59. "Geisinger Journal," 20 May 1814, LOC.

60. Johnston Blakeley to William Jones, 20 May 1814, M-124.

61. M. Florence Bourne, "Thomas Kemp, Shipbuilder and his Home, Wades Point," *Maryland Historical Magazine* 49 (1954), 271–89.

62. Taylor Peck, *A History of the Washington Navy Yard and the U.S. Naval Gun Factory* (Annapolis, Md.: Naval Institute Press, 1949), 47, 61, 64–68, 259. Chapelle erroneously states that it was burned "on the stocks." Chapelle, *The History of the American Sailing Navy*, 256–58, 280.

63. Research courtesy of Capt. Kenneth A. Johnson, U.S.N.

64. John Orde Creighton to William Jones, 18 July 1814, M-147.

65. Ibid.

CHAPTER 14. THE CARNAGE WAS DREADFUL

1. "Geisinger Journal," 3 June 1814, LOC.

2. Johnston Blakeley, "A List of British Vessels Captured by the United States Sloop of War Wasp, etc.," enclosure with letter, Johnston Blakeley to William Jones, dated 10 July 1814, M-124.

3. "Geisinger Journal," 9 June 1814, LOC.

4. Gordon Lincoln, also receipt dated 23 September 1813, from William Fitz for transportation of small arms from Boston to Newburyport, Accounts of Amos Binney (Boston navy agent), Fourth Auditor Settled Accounts, RG217.

5. Gilkerson, *Boarders Away*, 1:25–47.

6. Ibid., 1:104–6.

7. Samuel Leech, *Thirty Years from Home* (Boston: Gleasons, 1843), 180.

8. "Geisinger Journal," 14 June 1814, LOC.

9. Ibid., 17 June 1814.

10. Blakeley, "A List of British Vessels," M-124.

11. "Geisinger Journal," 22 June 1814, LOC.

12. David Steel, *Steel's Elements of Mastmaking, Sailmaking, and Rigging* (Largo, Fla.: Edward Sweetman, 1982), 204–6.

13. "Geisinger Journal," 27 June 1814, LOC.

14. *Savannah Republican and Evening Ledger,* 8 November 1814, unidentified London paper quoted.

15. James, *Naval History of Great Britain,* 3:126–29.

16. Lt. William Chambers to Adm. William Croker, dated "28 St. Aubyrn St., Plymouth," 25 August 1814, Lieutenants' Letters to Admiralty, ADM 1/2824, 428, PRO.

17. Manners probably did not possess a strong dislike for the Americans; a close relation had earlier married the daughter of Benjamin Rush of Philadelphia, one of the signers of the Declaration of Independence. Johnson, "Biographical Sketch," 8–9. William Manners was made lieutenant on 14 August 1806, and master and commander on 7 February 1812, letter researcher Graham Salt to author, 21 March 1994.

18. William W. Bowers, *Naval Adventures during Thirty-five Years of Service* (London: R. Bentley, 1833), 276–79.

19. James, *Naval History of Great Britain,* 6:294–97.

20. *Savannah Republican and Evening Ledger,* 8 November 1814, a reprint of a letter from an unidentified London Paper, dated 26 July 1814.

21. Lt. William Chambers to William Donnet, Vice Admiral of the Red, 7 July 1814. Enclosure with the minutes of proceedings, "at a Court Martial held on board His Majesty's Ship Salvadore del Mundo," dated 12 August 1814, for the loss of the *Reindeer* [hereafter "*Reindeer* Court-Martial"], Admirals' Letters to Admiralty, courts-martial for July through August, 1814, ADM 1/5444, 07976, PRO.

22. Bowers, *Naval Adventures,* 277.

23. "Geisinger Journal," 29 June 1814, LOC.

24. Johnston Blakeley, "Minutes of the Action between the Wasp and the Reindeer," enclosure with Johnston Blakeley to William Jones, 22 September 1814, M-124.

25. *The New Hampshire Gazette,* 7 February 1815.

26. Bowers, *Naval Adventures,* 277–78.

27. Pension Application File, War of 1812, Navy Invalid, for "William Thompson Boatswain of U.S.S. Wasp," no. 1526, RG15.

28. *Newburyport Herald,* 16 September 1814, reprinted from an unidentified English paper.

29. *Savannah Republican and Evening Ledger,* 8 November 1814, reprinted from an unidentified English paper.

30. Bowers, *Naval Adventures,* 278.

31. Blakeley, "Minutes of the action," M-124.

32. Chambers to Donnet, 7 July 1814, "*Reindeer* Court-Martial."

33. *Newburyport Herald,* 16 September 1814.

34. "Geisinger Journal," 14 July 1814, LOC.

35. *Newburyport Herald,* 16 September 1814.

36. *New Hampshire Gazette,* 7 February 1815.

37. Chambers to Donnet, 7 July 1814, "*Reindeer* Court-Martial."

38. Bowers, *Naval Adventures,* 278.

39. James, *Naval History of Great Britain,* 6:295.

40. *Newburyport Herald,* 16 September 1814. "No Norse Viking, slain over his shield, ever died better," wrote Theodore Roosevelt in *Naval War of 1812,* 2:52.

41. Chambers to Donnet, 7 July 1814, "*Reindeer* Court-Martial."

42. Spaulding, *What I Know.*

43. James, *Naval History of Great Britain,* 6:294–95.

44. Pension Application File, War of 1812, Navy Invalid, for "William Thompson Boatswain of U.S.S. Wasp," no. 1526, RG15.

45. "Geisinger Journal," 29 June 1814, LOC.

46. Johnston Blakeley to William Jones, 22 September 1814, M-124.

47. Any naval mind, picturing the action as Blakeley described it, would have been, to say the least, perplexed. One such confused tactical enthusiast was John Thomas Serres (1759–1825), Admiralty draftsman and marine painter to King George III, who later created a series of four stunningly beautiful watercolors of the *Wasp-Reindeer* engagement. Although these were painted with great technical accuracy, especially regarding the relative size of both vessels, it is clear that Serres was unable to make heads or tails of Blakeley's official report, the only official contemporary account ever published. Did the American captain mistake starboard for larboard? If so, he thought, at which particular mention? His solution (no doubt after throwing up his hands!) was to draw the two sloops attacking each other bow on, exchanging larboard broadsides on opposite tacks in his first painting. His second view, entitled "The Wasp with her Gib Boom in the Reindeer's Lee Rigging," shows the bow-rake perfectly, suggesting the influence of one of the unofficial published accounts. But he mistakenly brings the two sloops together in his third view, "Vessels Are Alongside Each Other," in full contact for the boarding scene on the *Wasp's* starboard side, with both bows pointing in the same direction. There is an awkward, glaring discontinuity between the four views, as if in deliberate acknowledgment of his many unanswered questions. Edgar P. Richardson, *American Paintings and Related Pictures in the Henry Francis du Pont Winterthur Museum* (Charlottesville: University Press of Virginia, 1986), 138–43.

48. *Newburyport Herald,* 16 September 1814, reprinted from an unidentified English paper.

49. Roosevelt, *The Naval War of 1812,* 2:53.

50. James, *Naval Occurrences*, 360.
51. Only the cover letter, Chambers's report, and the court's decision survive. See "*Reindeer* Court-Martial." Two clues to the proceedings are available in the form of brief notes scribbled in the margins of Chambers's report. "Their Lords do not understand," began the nearly illegible scribing, "the shortness of complement, how 8 men could be absent if there were 118 present and loaded aboard . . . when she went to sea." The *Reindeer*'s full roster included 121 names, so how could Chambers claim as an excuse that he was eight short? Trivial perhaps, but here is expressed the paternalistic view that 118 Englishmen ought to be able to cope successfully with any heavily manned foreign sloop of war. But the heart of their embarrassment lay within the second jotting: "How came this vessel to have only 24-lbers?" Below is written the name "Sir Robert Calder," quite possibly Manners's immediate Plymouth superior, who was responsible for the caliber's reduction. See Letter from Vice Adm. William Donnet to Adm. William Croker, dated "[HMS] Salvadore Del Mundo, Hamoaze," 8 July 1814, Admirals' Letters to Admiralty, Plymouth Station section for 1814, ADM 1/834, 0428, PRO.
52. Roosevelt, *Naval War of 1812*, 2:54.

CHAPTER 15. L'ORIENT

1. William Chambers to Johnston Blakeley, 29 June 1814, dated "H. M. Late Sloop Reindeer," M-124.
2. *Newburyport Herald*, 16 September 1814, reprinted from an unidentified English paper. This article was doubtless the source of the most common misconception concerning the *Wasp*'s origin. Blakeley's response to the cartel plan has not survived.
3. "Geisinger Journal," 30 June 1814, LOC.
4. Bowers, *Naval Adventures*, 277–79.
5. *Newburyport Herald*, 16 September 1814.
6. Also referred to as the *Packet of Lisbon* in some English correspondence.
7. Actually, according to Steel's Naval List of 1813–14, the *Hibernia* was the flagship of Vice Adm. Sir Edward Pellew, while Sidney Smith was aboard as his flag captain.
8. Andrew Allen to Thomas Chambers, dated "Paquet of Lisbon," 5 July 1814, enclosure with William Donnet to Adm. William Croker, dated "[HMS] Salvadore Del Mundo, Hamoaze," 8 July 1814, Admirals' Letters to Admiralty, Plymouth Station section for 1814, ADM 1/834, 0428, PRO.
9. Thomas Chambers to Johnston Blakeley, 1 July 1814, M-124.
10. Blakeley to Chambers, 1 July 1814, M-124.
11. Thomas Chambers and Richard Johns (sailing master) to Johnston Blakeley, "United States Ship of War Wasp at sea," dated 1 July 1814, enclosure with William Donnet to Adm. William Croker, dated "[HMS] Salvadore Del Mundo, Hamoaze,"

8 July 1814, Admirals' Letters to Admiralty, Plymouth Station section for 1814, ADM 1/834, 0428, PRO.

12. Thomas Chambers to "The Right Honorable Lords of the Admiralty," dated 25 August 1814, Lieutenants' Letters to Admiralty, ADM 1/2824, 428, PRO.

13. Vice Adm. William Donnet to Adm. William Croker, 8 July 1814, Admirals' Letters to Admiralty, Plymouth Station section for 1814, ADM 1/834, 0428, PRO.

14. Blakeley to Jones, 10 July 1814, M-124.

15. Blakeley to Jones, 8 July 1814, M-124.

16. "At 5 sent the following Men to L'Orient Hospital vis . . . Mr Toscan & Mr Langdon, Midshipmen, Mr Swett, Master's Mate, Wm Thompson, Boatwn Mate, John Dick 2d Master, Andrew Passenger, Nathl Seammon, John Bennet, Robt Jarvis, Simon Cassallies, Caleb Wheadon, Henry Herbert, John Thurston." Two other seamen went ashore at a later, unspecified date: On 27 July, "came on board from the Hospital, Mr. Levett M. Mate & Wm Preston Seaman." Total number recorded by Midshipman Geisinger as being hospitalized: fifteen. From "Geisinger Journal," LOC.

17. Blakeley to Jones, 10 July 1814, M-124.

18. Blakeley to Jones, 27 August 1814, M-124.

19. *Savannah Republican and Evening Ledger,* 8 November 1814, reprint of 23–26 July, unidentified "English papers." The unidentified English master was probably Thomas Spearpoint, captain and former part-owner of the schooner *Jenny.* One wonders at the nature of the "simple question" that Spearpoint directed toward the deputy consul!

20. C. S. Forester, *The Age of Fighting Sail: The Story of the Naval War of 1812* (Garden City, N. J.: Doubleday, 1956), 214–16.

21. Ibid.

22. Chase C. Mooney, *William H. Crawford, 1772–1834* (Lexington: University Press of Kentucky, 1975), 41. Blakeley may have traveled overland to Paris to meet with Crawford, or the American minister may have come to Brittany to see his countrymen. Neither Geisinger's journal nor Blakeley's three surviving L'Orient-penned letters are clear on whether Blakeley and Crawford ever met. It would be fitting, however, to think that a personal meeting with Blakeley and even a possible brief friendship were in part responsible for Crawford's change of heart.

23. William H. Crawford to James Monroe, 17 August 1814, Letters Received by the Secretary of State from France, State Department records, National Archives.

24. "Geisinger Journal," LOC. Geisinger's Journal is the source for nearly all surviving details of the *Wasp's* stay in France.

25. Spalding, *What I Know,* 81.

26. Blakeley to Jones, 27 August 1814, M-124.

27. There were fifteen new arrivals: On 19 July, "Joined the Ship Antonio Martin"; 20 July, "Jnn Mede, Ward Room Stewd"; July 23, "Saml Langford & Wm H. Wilkins"; 25 July, "the following men joined the Ship this day - vis - Richd Collins [Note: Manners's clerk of the same name returned home on the *Lisbon Packet*],

Anthy Cappeau, Sam C. Dudley, Shubael Young"; 26 July, "Samuel Smith"; 27 July, "John Taylor & Richd Fisher"; 2 August, "Jno Brown & Casper Urich"; and on 7 August, "Nathan Matherson." However, two of these were discharged on the eve of sailing: 6 August, "Discharged Wm Simmons & John Bennet, Seamen, they being Frenchmen." From "Geisinger Journal," LOC.

28. "At 3 died at the French Hospital at L'Orient, Henry Herbert Seaman," from "Geisinger Journal," 20 July 1814.

29. Five wounded seamen only are noted as returning to the ship: On 27 July, "came on board from the Hospital, Mr. Levett M. Mate & Wm Preston Seaman"; and on 2 August, "John Dick, John Bennet & Simon Cassallics, Return'd on board from the Hospital." From "Geisinger Journal," LOC.

30. Pension Application File, War of 1812, for William Thompson, RG15.

31. Pension Application File, War of 1812, for Charlotte Passenger, no. 933, RG15.

32. "Run, Berent Johnson, Sea, & Peter Pedro," from "Geisinger Journal," 1 August 1814, LOC.

33. *Newburyport Herald*, 17 September 1813.

34. Johnson Blakeley to William Jones, 7 July 1814, M-124.

35. Blakeley to Jones, 27 August 1814, M-124.

36. "Geisinger Journal," 1 September 1814, LOC.

37. Log of HMS *Armada*, 1 September 1814, Masters Logs, ADM 52/4417, 198628, PRO.

38. Roosevelt, *Naval War of 1812*, 2:56.

CHAPTER 16. THE *Wasp*, TO BE SURE

1. Nelson had originally ordered "England confides every man to do his duty," but Lieutenant Pasco nervously recommended a change of verbs since, as he explained to his commander, "confides" was an alpha-numeric code, and would thus have to be spelled out, consuming far too much space aloft, whereas there was a special code for "expects" already in the fleet's vocabulary. Nelson happily approved the change, remarking as he descended to the quarterdeck, "that will do Pasco, make it directly." James, *Naval History*, 3:425, 6:102.

2. The *Tartarus* was one of six vessels built to Constructor Henslow's *Thais* class of fire ships. Launched at the Davy Yard in Topsham in August 1806, it was reclassed and rearmed as a sixth-rate sloop of war in 1806. Its dimensions were: 108', 9" on the gundeck; 29', 7" moulded breadth; 9' depth of hold; and it displaced a mere 422 tons. It mounted twenty-two 24-pounder carronades on the main deck and eight 18-pounder carronades on the spar deck alongside two long-nine pounder chase guns. See Lyon, *The Sailing Navy List*, 149.

3. Ibid., 131, 140–42. H.B.M. Brig *Kangaroo* was another member of the common *Cruiser*-class.

4. Log of H.M.S. *Tartarus*, 1–3 September 1814, Masters Logs, ADM 52/1380, 198628, PRO.

5. Vice Adm. Herbert Sawyer to Adm. William Crocker, 15 August 1814, Admirals' Letters to Admiralty, Cork Station section for 1814, ADM 1/626, 0428, PRO.

6. No *Tiger* appears on surviving Baltimore privateer registration lists. See Jerome R. Garitee, *The Republic's Private Navy: The American Privateering Business as Practiced by Baltimore During the War of 1812*, American Maritime Library, vol. 7 (Middletown, Conn.: Mystic Seaport Press/Wesleyan University Press, 1977), 274–82. See also Fred W. Hopkins Jr., *Tom Boyle* (Cambridge, Md.: Tidewater Publishers, 1976), 38–55.

7. Boyle later bragged of escaping from several squadrons of enemy sloops of war sent specifically out to nab him. Had Blakeley inadvertently saved Boyle? Garitee, *The Republic's Private Navy*, 160.

8. Lt. George Lloyd to Vice Adm. Herbert Sawyer, 2 September 1814, enclosure with letter, Vice Adm. Herbert Sawyer to Adm. William Crocker, 15 August 1814, Admirals' Letters to Admiralty, Cork Station section for 1814, ADM 1/626, 0428, PRO. A separate, nearly identical copy appears with the court-martial records, Admirals' Letters to Admiralty, courts-martial for October, 1814, ADM 1/5446, 4710, PRO.

9. Progress book of H.M. Sloop *Avon*, Navy Board and Admiralty records: Progress and Dimension Books, ADM 180/12, 17051, PRO.

10. *London's Naval Chronicle* 32 (July–December 1814), 243.

11. James, *Naval Occurrences*, 364–65.

12. *Niles' Weekly Register* 7 (1814), 207–8.

13. Arbuthnot was made lieutenant on 28 April 1810 and commander on 27 October 1813. "Master and commander" was the equivalent rank of master commandant in the American navy and Arbuthnot too would have been called captain by courtesy.

14. The action occurred on 10 July 1813. See James, *Naval History of Great Britain*, 6:15–16. Assigned to this same frigate, Arbuthnot had led an earlier boat expedition on the coast of France in September 1810. See ibid., 5:100–101.

15. Minutes of proceedings, "at a Court Martial held on board His Majesty's Ship Salvadore del Mundo," dated 1 October 1814, for the loss of the *Avon* [hereafter "*Avon* Court-Martial"], enclosure with Vice Adm. Herbert Sawyer to Adm. William Crocker, dated "His Majesty's Ship Trent, Cork Harbour, 6 September 1814," Admirals' Letters to Admiralty, ADM 1/5446, 4710, PRO.

16. Blakeley, "Minutes of the action," 10 September 1814, M-124.

17. Testimony of Lt. John Harvey, "*Avon* Court Martial." Never having seen any official Admiralty documents (they too were suppressed from the public for nearly a century), British historian William James misrepresented the particulars of this battle. "The Wasp fought more warily in this action than in Reindeer's," James concluded. "She would not come fairly alongside, so as to give the Avon an opportunity of boarding." Arbuthnot clearly had no intention of boarding just yet. At this point, he wished only to rejoin the *Castillian*, for the *Avon* was a fast, fleeing sloop of war possessing the critical weather-gauge. During the court-martial Lieutenant

Harvey had no right to bemoan the *Wasp*'s "advantageous" position: "By being on our starboard quarter and from her superiority in sailing," he testified, "she was able to keep the position she pleased." At this critical opening moment, James tells us, the *Wasp* deliberately discharged a broadside of star and bar shot into the *Avon*'s rigging. These devices instantly cut away the slings of its gaff, he tells us, and "on the immediate fall of the latter, the boom mainsail covered the quarterdeck guns on the side engaged, the only ones that would at this time bear." Actually, carronades were incapable of firing such projectiles, and if the few long 12s had managed to perform such a feat under these unfavorable conditions, it would have been worthy of praise, not scorn. The gaff did in fact come down early in the fight, but nowhere do any of the participants record any disabling of the guns underneath. It certainly did not slow the *Avon*'s flight. Only much later, when the brig's main topsail was shot from the yard, was its progress finally checked. James, *Naval History of Great Britain,* 6:297–99.

18. Pendergrast's chest wound proved mortal, and he would leave behind, according to the Cork newspapers, "an amiable wife and two children." *Savannah Republican and Evening Ledger,* 17 November 1814. From a letter dated Cork, Ireland, 12 September 1814, reprinted from "an English paper."

19. First printed in the *Savannah Republican and Evening Ledger,* 5 November 1814.

20. *The Star* (Raleigh, N.C.), 10 November 1814, 6:178.

21. Cdr. Edward Flynn to "Adm. of the White Sir Richard Bickerton, Bart.," no date, His Majesty's Sloop Caphalus, at sea, enclosure with Adm. Richard Bickerson to Vice Adm. Herbert Sawyer, 9 September 1814, Admirals' Letters to Admiralty, Portsmouth Station section for 1814, ADM 1/1243, 2019, PRO.

22. Lt. George Lloyd to Vice Adm. Herbert Sawyer, 2 September 1814, enclosure with Avon court-martial, Admirals' Letters to Admiralty, courts-martial for October 1814, ADM 1/5446, 4710, PRO.

23. Ibid.

24. Even James, a harsh critic of the increasingly substandard late-war British gunnery, doubted that the *Castillian* could have finished the job. James, *Naval History of Great Britain,* 6:299.

25. Arbuthnot last appears in the April 1817 edition of Steele's Navy List.

26. James, *Naval Occurrences,* 362–66.

27. See the Logs of H.M.S. *Castillian*: Captains' Logs, ADM 51/2197, 1084, and Ships' Logs (also referred to as "Deck Logs"), ADM 53/352, 1084, PRO.

28. *Savannah Republican and Evening Ledger,* 5 November 1814.

29. James Arbuthnot to Herbert Sawyer, 2 September 1814, enclosure with *Avon* court-martial, Admirals' Letters to Admiralty, ADM 1/5446, 4710, PRO.

30. Quoted in James, *Naval Occurrences,* 365–66.

31. Ibid., 362–66.

32. *Niles' Weekly Register* 7, 1814, 203, quoted from a "London paper of October 6th."

33. Pratt, *Preble's Boys,* 272.

34. *Niles' Weekly Register 7,* 1814, 165.
35. *Newburyport Herald,* 2 September 1814; *New Hampshire Gazette,* 20 December 1814.
36. *The Star,* 2 December 1814.
37. James, *Naval History of Great Britain,* 6:299.
38. *Savannah Republican and Evening Ledger,* 17 November 1814.
39. Sadly, however, Blakeley's name is virtually unknown today outside the field of early American naval history. Most people remember the *Wasp* merely as an aged aircraft carrier, or, at best, as the smaller sloop of war that Jacob Jones took into action in 1812 against the English brig *Frolic.* Many who ought to know better are surprised to learn of this "second" *Wasp.*

CHAPTER 17. ADIEU

1. Johnston Blakeley to William Jones, 11 September 1814, M-124.
2. *New Hampshire Gazette,* 22 November 1814.
3. Johnson, "The Fate of the Wasp," 449-60.
4. Garitee, *The Republic's Private Navy,* 280.
5. *Savannah Republican and Evening Ledger,* 5 November 1814.
6. Perry, "The U.S. Sloop of War Wasp," 92.
7. A detailed listing of the *Atalanta's* stores may be found at the end of David Geisinger's *Atalanta* Journal, currently held in the Maryland Historical Society, Baltimore, Md.
8. Blakeley to Jones, 23 September 1814, M-124.
9. Blakeley to Jones, 23 September 1814, M-124.
10. Ibid.
11. *Savannah Republican and Evening Ledger,* 5 November 1814. The style of writing closely resembles that of the solitary Philadelphian, Midshipman William House. The letter implies that its author was either a friend or possibly a familial acquaintance of Mr. Stewart, but this is impossible to confirm without identifying the addressee. It also suggests that the addressee would soon have an opportunity of speaking with the courier. The style is undeniably different from that of the succinct James Reilly or the disjointed, run-on Frederick Baury. Thomas Tillinghast, however, wrote in a somewhat similar fashion.
12. Blakeley to Geisinger, 23 September 1814, manuscript collections of the U.S. Naval Academy Museum, Annapolis, Md. (emphasis in original).
13. *Savannah Republican and Evening Ledger,* 5 November 1814.
14. The three who perished on board the *Epervier* were Able Seamen John Davis, Samuel C. Battista, and John Dudley. Quarter Master Christopher Jefferies and Seamen David Stephens, Caesar Pearce, John Whitney, and Morris Roberts either left the service in Savannah or transferred to other navy ships at New York or off Algiers. Two pay rolls of the *Epervier* survive, one dated 3 May 1815 and the other dated 14 July 1815. The author is indebted to the *Epervier's* biographer, Capt.

Joseph R. McCleary, U.S.N., for generously sharing his biographical files for this project. One muster roll survives as well, dated 24 April 1815. All three reside in RG24, National Archives.

15. *Savannah Republican and Evening Ledger,* 15 November 1814.

16. Log of H.M. frigate *Lacedemonian,* 9–23 November 1814, Captains Logs, ADM 51/2517, PRO. See also Masters Logs, ADM 52/4164, for the same dates.

17. Johnson, "The Fate of the Wasp."

18. *Niles' Weekly Register 7,* 1814, 207.

19. *Newburyport Herald,* 31 March 1815.

20. Ibid., 28 April 1815.

21. Dunne, "Operational Histories."

22. Spears, *History of Our Navy,* 4:103.

23. *New York Mercantile Advertiser,* 21 January 1815.

24. David Porter, *Journal of a Cruise,* Classics of Naval Literature Series (Annapolis, Md.: Naval Institute Press, 1986), 551–67.

25. *New Hampshire Gazette,* 15 December 1815.

26. For Robert to receive this letter in the Mediterranean, send a response to his younger brother, probably Peter Byrd Randolph, and then, in turn, get off yet another letter to his mother at least one year would need to transpire. Giving Mrs. Corbin sufficient time to contact her third son, Peter, who in turn wrote to his local newspaper, one might expect that a November 1815 publication is not too far out of line. All things considered, it made pretty good time.

27. No exact date or position given. One uncited source gives the date as 11 November 1814, but the log is silent on this date. Notes enclosed with letter, researcher Graham Salt to author, 21 March 1994.

28. Position at noon: Lat. 41.58N / Long. 14.48W, "Virgo NE 194 miles," Log of *H.M.S. Reynard,* Masters' Logs, ADM 52/4280, PRO.

29. Ibid., Position at noon: Lat. 43.32N / Long. 15.28.

30. Vice Adm. Flemimg to "Their Lordships," 4 January 1815, Admirals Journals, ADM 50/108, 5518, PRO. Noon position given in *Reynard's* log on 14 November 1814: Lat. 41.58, Long 14.28, Masters' Logs, ADM 52/4280, PRO.

31. Position at noon: Lat. 34.44N / Long. 15.28W, 8 January 1815. Log of *H.M.S. Garland,* Ships' Logs, ADM 53/573, PRO.

32. Letter quoted in *Elizabeth's* Log dated 2 January 1815, Admirals Journals, ADM 50/108, 5518, PRO. See also the logs of HMS *Jasper:* Captains Logs, ADM 51/2485; Masters Logs, ADM 52/4518; and Ships Logs, ADM 53/738, PRO.

33. Position at noon: Lat. 38.47N / Long. 12.17W. See Logs of HMS *Aquilion,* 32-guns: Captains Logs, ADM 51/2134, and Masters Logs, ADM 52/4019, PRO. Note: the *Aquilion* sailed in company with the *Reynard* on 20 and 21 November 1814, also in company with the brig *Papillon.*

34. Vice Adm. Flemimg to "Their Lordships," 1 March 1815, Admirals' Letters to Admiralty, Lisbon Station section for 1815, ADM 1/351, 38, PRO.

35. *Newburyport Herald,* 3 March 1815. Mogador, incidentally, was a favorite watering hole for privateers, particularly for those sailing out of Boston. Admirals' Letters to Admiralty, Mediterranean Station section for 1815, ADM 1/430, 14, PRO.
36. *Pittsburgh Mercury,* 2 January 1816.
37. Johnson, "The Fate of the Wasp," 457.
38. Ibid.
39. Dr. James Johnson lived three miles upstream from the city on the Cooper River in a private villa called "Belvedera." See Coker, *Charleston's Maritime Heritage,* 178.
40. Log of *Hyperion,* 14 February 1815, Captains' Logs, ADM 51/2452, PRO.
41. *Niles' Weekly Register* 25 (4 June 1825), 214.

CHAPTER 18. NO MORE SHALL BLAKELEY'S THUNDER ROAR

1. Mary Bartlett to Benjamin W. Crowninshield, dated Newburyport, 8 August 1815, M-124.
2. Judith Mullen et al., to Benjamin Crowninshield, 22 August 1815, M-124 (emphasis in original). The type of assistance offered to the widows, more than any other incident, best portrays the differences between Hull and Bainbridge, the "Old Ironsides" legendary fighting captains.
3. How Judith heard of her husband's promotion is not known. Strangely enough, Judith Mullen is not listed among those eight married women who signed a power of attorney with Boston agent Amos Binney, so how she received her half-pay up till this point is unclear, as well. Mary Stone, Jane Moulton, Mary Bartlett, and Mary Ford all appeared on Lewis Fairchild's final payroll list, for the accounting period ending 30 June 1814 at Boston and signed by Amos Binney on 2 July. They were joined by Abigail Jones, wife of the ship's cook Richard Jones, and Martha Johnson, Ann Martin, and Nabby Phippen, wives of John, "Johnathon," and Joseph, respectively. Ledger dated Boston, 2 July 1814, "for the sloop Wasp," Accounts of Amos Binney (Boston navy agent), Fourth Auditor Settled Accounts, RG 217.
4. Benjamin Homans to Mary Bartlett, 21 August 1815, M-124.
5. Benjamin Homans to Mary Bartlett, 20 October 1815, M-124.
6. Labaree, *Partisans and Patriots,* 180–205.
7. See *Official Letters, With Comments, and Observations Relative to the Capture of the President, American Frigate: and Concealment of Men aboard that Ship; Together with the Correspondence between the Secretary and the Commander in Chief, and the editor and the Royal Gazette; and a Letter substantiating the Charge of Concealment. Selected from the Royal and weekly Gazettes, of Different Dates* (St. George, Bermuda: Edmund Ward, 1815). See also Sister Claude de Chantel Kennedy, *Biography of a Colonial Town: Hamilton, Bermuda, 1790–1897* (Hamilton, Bermuda: The Bermuda Book Stores, 1961), 106–7. Randolph wrote the editor of the *Commercial Advertiser* in March 1815 and gave his version of the affair: "As soon as I read the scurrilous

remarks in the Royal Gazette . . . I walked to the King's square with the determination to chastise the editor. I soon fell in with him and executed my purpose in the most ample and satisfactory manner. There was no American officer in the company except Midshipman Emmett, and Mr. Ward, the editor, was accompanied by Lieutenant Sammon of the Royal Navy, but by neither of these officers was I interrupted or assisted in the operation. Having previously obtained my passports, and being advised that the editor of the *Royal Gazette* was taking measures to employ the civil authorities against me, I left the island the next day for the United States. . . . R. B. Randolph, Midshipman, Late of the U.S. Frigate *President.*" See also John M. Belohlavek, "Assault on the President," *Presidential Studies Quarterly* 12 (summer 1982), 361–69.

8. Fruchtman, *Thomas Paine,* 433.
9. As a lieutenant, David Geisinger served aboard the following vessels: *Fire Fly* (Mediterranean), *Macedonian* (1815 North Atlantic and Boston), *Independence* (1816, receiving ship at Boston), *John Adams* (1818–20 in the West Indies and the Gulf of Mexico) and *Constitution* (1820–24 in the Mediterranean). From David Geisinger Papers, Maryland Historical Society, Baltimore, Md.
10. David Geisinger's second son, George Francis, grew to be a wealthy and generous philanthropist. The Geisinger Medical Center in Danville, Pennsylvania, was dedicated to his memory. See C. A. Abney Metzer, *In Search of Kate* (St. Louis, Mo.: Genealogical Research and Productions, 1978), 103–22.
11. North Carolina historian Dr. Kemp S. Battle searched hard but in vain to find the source of this "singular" name. Perhaps it was of Dutch East-Indies origin. The child is also referenced as "Maria Udney." See Battle, *Captain Johnston Blakeley,* 13.
12. Maloney, *The Captain From Connecticut,* 273–74.
13. *Newburyport Herald,* 15 July 1815.
14. *Newburyport Herald,* 13 February 1816, noted as being "from a Raleigh, N.C. paper" (emphasis added).
15. McKee, *A Gentlemanly and Honorable Profession,* 272–73.
16. This act was later amended to include mention of the *Avon* on the same coin as well.
17. Battle, *Captain Johnston Blakeley,* 13.
18. Jane Anne Blakeley to Edward Jones, 5 March 1817, Mary B. Hardin Collection, P.C. 557, North Carolina State Archives, Raleigh, N.C.
19. The *Atalanta* received only $7,281.33 at the postwar auction, there being little need for a narrow privateer hull incapable of carrying the usual amounts of cargo. Jane Anne had to wait until March 1822 to receive her late husband's 15 percent share, or $1,092.20. Pension Application File for Jane Anne Blakeley, RG15.
20. The service was last known to have been in the possession of a "Laura E. Smith of Jeb Street," Greensboro, N.C. The North Carolina historical archives in Raleigh retain an old, sadly undated black and white photograph of the six items. Their heights are given on the back of the photograph in inches: Tea Pot, 11 3/4; Coffee

Pot, 10 ¼; Milk Jug, 9¼; Basin, 6½; Covered Basin, 8½; and the Sugar Tongs, 1½ inches long. All information written on the back of the service photograph, Captain Johnston Blakeley, MSS.

21. Johnston, Du Ponseau, Charlotte, Frances, Louise, and Elizabeth Jones. William S. Powell, ed. *Dictionary of North Carolina Biography*, vol. 3 (Chapel Hill: University of North Carolina Press, 1985), 317.

22. Thomas, "Biographical Sketch."

23. *Newburyport Herald*, 21 June 1816.

24. Jane Anne Abbott to Samuel Southand, dated Philadelphia, 20 November 1819, Pension Application File, War of 1812, for Jane Anne Blakelely, no. 118, RG15.

25. *Newburyport Herald*, 4 January 1814.

26. Ibid.

27. R. S. Smith to Samuel Southand, 3 December 1830, Pension Application File, War of 1812, for Jane Anne Blakeley, no. 118, RG15.

28. *Newburyport Herald*, 23 July 1816.

Bibliography

Primary Sources

Chicago Historical Society, Chicago, Ill.
> "Journal of a Cruise on Board the U.S. Sloop of War Frolic of 18 Guns, Joseph Bainbridge Commanding," unsigned partial MSS. Contains some of the missing pages torn from the *Frolic* Journal. The majority of the 1814 USS *Frolic* Journal is at the New York Public Library.

Historical Society of Pennsylvania, Philadelphia, Pa.
> William Jones Papers
> John Rodgers Papers
> Commo. Thomas Truxtun Collection, includes Letter Book

Library of Congress, Manuscript Division, Washington, D.C.
> "Remarks and Occurrences etc. on Board U.S. Sloop of War Wasp of 18 Guns, Johnston Blakeley, Esquire Commanding," 2 May–23 September 1814, MSS, by Midshipman David Geisinger, USN

Maryland Historical Society, Baltimore, Md.
> Midshipman David Geisinger Papers. Contains Midshipman Geisinger's *Atalanta* Journal.

Massachusetts Historical Society, Boston, Mass.
> Josiah Barker Papers
> Baury Family Papers
> Midshipman Frederick Baury, MSS
> William Eustis Papers

National Archives, Washington, D.C.
> General Records of the Department of State, Record Group 59, Microcopies M34, T164, T373, T379, T212, and T223.

M-124. Miscellaneous Letters Received by the Secretary of the Navy, Micro-copy 124, Naval Records Collections of the Office of Naval Records and Library, Record Group 45. Oddly, all of Master Commandant Blakeley's cruise and most of his corvette's commissioning letters are contained here.

M-125. Letters Received by the Secretary of the Navy from Captains, Micro-copy 125, Naval Records Collections of the Office of Naval Records and Library, Record Group 45.

M-147. Letters Received by the Secretary of the Navy from Commanders, Microcopy 147, Naval Records Collections of the Office of Naval Records and Library, Record Group 45.

M-148. Letters Received by the Secretary of the Navy from Officers below the Rank of Commanders, Microcopy 148, Naval Records Collections of the Office of Naval Records and Library, Record Group 45.

M-149. Letters Sent by the Secretary of the Navy to Officers, Microcopy 149, Naval Records Collections of the Office of Naval Records and Library, Record Group 45.

M-273. Judge Advocate General's Records. Records of U.S. Navy courts of inquiry and courts-martial. Microcopy 273.

Navy Area 7 Files and Navy Area 8 Files for New England, Naval Records Collection of the Office of Naval Records and Library, Record Group 45. Con-tains several valuable documents relating to the costs, designs, and alterations of the two Massachusetts sloops of war.

Old Subject File, Naval Records Collection of the Office of Naval Records and Library, Record Group 45.

Pension File Records, Veterans Records, War of 1812 Pensions and Pension Applications, Record Group 15.

Records of Accounting Officers of the Treasury Department, Letters Received and Sent by the Accountant of the Navy, Record Group 217. The many surviving financial receipts give important details.

U.S. Navy Records of the Bureau of Ships, Record Group 19.

Naval Historical Center, Washington Navy Yard, Washington, D.C.
"Court of Enquiry Relating to the Capture of the U.S. Frigate Chesapeake by H.B.M.S. Shannon, off Boston, 1 June 1813," typed MSS, Special Collections ZB File, Personnel Files

Newburyport Public Library, Newburyport, Mass.
Contract for the Building of the Sloop of War Wasp

New York Historical Society, New York, N.Y.
Isaac Hull Letter Book
Isaac Hull Papers
"Journal of a Cruise on Board the U.S. Sloop of War Frolic of 18 Guns, Joseph Bain-bridge Commanding," unsigned partial MSS, Miscellaneous Manuscripts—U.S.

Navy, 1799–1851. Contains the majority of the 1814 USS *Frolic* Journal.
Commodore John Rodgers, Letter-books and manuscripts
North Carolina Department of Cultural Resources, Raleigh, N.C.
Captain Johnston Blakeley, MSS. Mostly typescripts of secondary newspaper accounts from the national *Niles' Weekly Register,* but does contain several Jane Anne Blakeley letters as well as photographs of the state's silver service award.
North Carolina State Archives, Raleigh, N.C.
Mary B. Hardin Collection, P.C. 557
Peabody and Essex Museum, Salem, Mass.
Benjamin Crowninshield, MSS
Josiah Fox Papers
Public Record Office, Kew, England
Royal Navy, MSS. This collection contains most of the surviving British naval records, correspondence, and courts-martial transcripts for this period.
South Caroliniana Library, University of South Carolina, Columbia, S.C.
Captain John Herbert Dent, Letterbook 1811–14, MSS
United States Naval Academy Library, Annapolis, Md.
Dale Letter Book
University of North Carolina Library, Chapel Hill, N.C.
University of North Carolina Archives, Philanthropic Society Records, Series 1, Vol. 2, Special Collections

Secondary Sources

"Action of the U.S. Sloop Wasp with H.M.S. Sloop Avon, August 1, 1814." *Naval Chronicle* 32 (1814): 243–45.

Adams, Henry. *History of the United States of America during the Administrations of Thomas Jefferson and James Madison.* New York: Literary Classics of the United States, 1986.

The Analectic Magazine and Naval Chronicle. Philadelphia, Pa. Various issues, 1813–16.

Ashe, Samuel A. "Johnston Blakeley." In *Biographical History of North Carolina from Colonial Time to the Present.* Vol. 1, 157–62. Greensboro, N.C.: C. L. Van Noppen, 1906.

Barnes, James. "The Cruise of the Wasp." *Harper's Weekly* 40 (1896): 1027.

Battle, Kemp S. *Captain Johnston Blakeley: A North Carolina Naval Hero and His Daughter.* Raleigh, N.C.: Capitol, 1902. Little more than a very brief hardcover pamphlet, this book, the only other stand-alone biography of Johnston Blakeley, is of little concrete value.

———. *History of the University of North Carolina.* Vol. 1, *From 1789 to 1868.* Spartanburg, S.C.: Reprint Company, 1974.

Belohlavek, John M. "Assault on the President: The Jackson-Randolph Affair of 1833." *Presidential Studies Quarterly* 12 (summer 1982): 361–69.

Boudroit, Jean. *Corvette La Creole, 1827: Historique de la Corvette 1650–1850.* Collection Archeologie Navale Francaise. Paris: Boudroit, 1990. The history of the development of the corvette in the French navy, which particularly details *La Creole,* a ship-rigged sloop of war remarkably similar to the *Wasp.*

Bourne, M. Florence. "Thomas Kemp, Shipbuilder and his Home, Wades Point." *Maryland Historical Magazine* 49 (1954): 271–89.

Bowers, William W. *Naval Adventures during Thirty-five Years of Service.* London: R. Bentley, 1833.

Bradford, James C. *Command under Sail: Makers of the American Naval Tradition.* Annapolis, Md.: Naval Institute Press, 1985.

Carter, Samuel, III. *Blaze of Glory: The Fight for New Orleans, 1814–1815.* New York: St. Martin's Press, 1971.

Chapelle, Howard I. *The History of the American Sailing Navy: The Ships and Their Development.* New York: Bonanza, 1989.

Chenney, Robert K. *Maritime History of the Merrimack-Shipbuilding.* Newburyport, Mass.: Newburyport Press, 1964.

Coker, P. C., III. *Charleston's Maritime Heritage, 1670–1865: An Illustrated History.* Charleston, S.C.: Cokercraft Press, 1987.

Conner, Robert D. "Captain Blakeley in the War of 1812." *North Carolina Review,* 6 April 1913.

Cooper, James Fenimore. *The History of the Navy of the United States of America.* London: Bentley, 1839.

———. *Lives of Distinguished American Naval Officers.* Philadelphia, 1846.

Crisman, Kevin J. *The Eagle: An American Brig on Lake Champlain during the War of 1812.* Shelburne, Vt.: New England Press, 1987.

———. "The Jefferson: The History and Archaeology of an American Brig from the War of 1812." Ph.D. diss., University of Pennsylvania, 1989.

Currier, John J. *History of Newbury, Mass.* Boston: Damrell and Upham, 1902.

De Kay, James Tertius. *Chronicles of the Frigate Macedonian, 1809–1922.* New York: Norton, 1995.

Doliber, Donald A. "Unforbidden Fruit: The Bartlett Pair." *The Essex Genealogist* (1988), 4:16.

Dudley, William S., ed. *The Naval War of 1812: A Documentary History,* 2 vols. to date. Washington, D.C.: Naval Historical Center Publications, 1985–.

Dunne, William M. P. ("The Naval Scribe"). "Pistols and Honor: The James Barron–Stephen Decatur Conflict." *American Neptune* 50 (fall 1990): 245–59.

———. Resource data files for "Operational Histories of the Ships of the United States Navy, for American Naval Vessels *President, Congress, John Adams, New York, Hornet, Argus, Enterprize, Wasp,* and *Frolic.*" Unpublished manuscript, Hampton Bays, N.Y.

———. "The South Carolina Frigate: A History of the United States Frigate *John Adams.*" *American Neptune* 47 (1987): 22–32.

Dye, Ira. *The Fatal Cruise of the Argus: Two Captains in the War of 1812.* Annapolis, Md.: Naval Institute Press, 1994.

Elting, John R. *Amateurs to Arms: A Military History of the War of 1812.* Chapel Hill, N.C.: Algonquin Books, 1991.

Emery, Sarah Anna. *Reminiscences of a Nonagenarian.* Newburyport, Mass.: William H. Huse Company, 1879.

Ferguson, Eugene S. *Truxtun of the Constellation: The Life of Commodore Thomas Truxtun, 1755–1822.* 1956. Reprint, Annapolis, Md.: Naval Institute Press, 1982.

Freeman, Roscoe. *The Picture History of the U.S. Navy.* New York: Bonanza, 1956.

Fruchtman, Jack, Jr. *Thomas Paine: Apostle of Freedom.* New York: Four Walls Eight Windows Press, 1994.

Garitee, Jerome R. *The Republic's Private Navy: The American Privateering Business as Practiced by Baltimore during the War of 1812.* American Maritime Library, vol. 7. Middletown, Conn.: Mystic Seaport/Wesleyan University Press, 1977.

Gilkerson, William. *Boarders Away: With Steel-Edged Weapons and Pole Arms.* 2 vols. Lincoln, R.I.: Andrew Mowbray, 1991–93.

Guttridge, Leonard F., and Jay D. Smith. *The Commodores.* Annapolis, Md.: Naval Institute Press, 1986.

Hall's Wilmington Gazette. Wilmington, N.C. Various issues, 1795–99.

Hanks, Carlos C. "How Ended the Gallant Wasp." U.S. Naval Institute *Proceedings* 68 (1932): 1137–38.

Holden, Raymond P. *The Merrimack.* New York: Rinehold, 1958.

Hooper, Rev. W., LL.D. "Biographical Sketch of Edward Jones Esquire, Late Solicitor General of the State of North Carolina." *North Carolina University Magazine* 5 (1856): 337–60.

Hopkins, Fred W., Jr. *Tom Boyle: Master Privateer.* Cambridge, Md.: Tidewater Publishers, 1976.

Howells, John. *The Architectural Heritage of the Piscataqua.* Portsmouth, N.H.: Abby White Howells, 1965.

Hubinger, Bert. "Little Wasp, Big Sting." *Naval History* 8 (July/August 1994): 30–34.

Hunt, Livingston. "Our Last Yardarm Fight: The Wasp and the Reindeer." *Harvard Graduate Magazine* 37 (1929): 418–28.

James, William. *The Naval History of Great Britain.* Vols. 1–6. London: Bentley, 1837.

———. *Naval Occurrences . . . etc.* London: Egerton, 1817.

Jarrett, Calvin D. "In Command of the Wasp." *Sea Classics* 5 (1979): 24–29, 66.

Johnson, James. "Biographical Sketch of Captain Johnston Blakeley, Late of the U.S. Sloop Wasp." *North Carolina University Magazine* 3 (1854): 1–16. Although brief, this article is very useful.

———. "The Fate of the Wasp, Sloop of War." *Southern Quarterly Review* 15 (1849): 449–60.

Kennedy, Sister Claude de Chantel. *Biography of a Colonial Town: Hamilton, Bermuda, 1790–1897.* Hamilton, Bermuda: The Bermuda Book Stores, 1961.

Ketcham, Ralph. *James Madison: A Biography*. Charlottesville: University Press of Virginia, 1992.

Knox, Dudley. *Naval Documents of the Barbary Wars*. Vols. 1–7. Washington, D.C.: U.S. Government Printing Office, 1938.

Labaree, Benjamin W. *Patriots and Partisans: The Merchants of Newburyport, 1764–1815*. New York: Norton, 1975.

Leech, Samuel. *Thirty Years from Home*. Boston: Gleasons, 1843.

London, Henry Mauger. "Captain Johnston Blakeley." *University of North Carolina Magazine* 16 (May 1899): 253–58.

London's Naval Chronicle. July–December 1814.

Long, David F. *Ready to Hazard: A Biography of Commodore William Bainbridge, 1774–1833*. Hanover, N.H.: University Press of New England, 1981.

Lyon, David. *The Sailing Navy List: All the Ships of the Royal Navy—Built, Purchased, and Captured*. London: Conway, 1993.

Maloney, Linda M. *The Captain from Connecticut: The Life and Naval Times of Isaac Hull*. Boston: Northeastern University Press, 1977.

Martin, Tyrone G. *The Captain's Clerk*. Unpublished MS. Tryon, N.C. Biographical data files pertaining to naval officers who served on board the United States frigate *Constitution*.

———. *A Most Fortunate Ship: A Narrative History of Old Ironsides*. Annapolis, Md.: Naval Institute Press, 1997.

McKee, Christopher. *A Gentlemanly and Honorable Profession: The Creation of the U.S. Naval Officer Corps, 1794–1815*. Annapolis, Md.: Naval Institute Press, 1991.

———. U.S. Navy Officers Biographical Data Card files, 1794–1815, compiled from primary records, unpublished.

Metzer, C.A. Abney. *In Search of Kate*. St. Louis, Mo.: Genealogical Research and Productions, 1978.

Mooney, Chase C. *William H. Crawford, 1772–1834*. Lexington: University Press of Kentucky, 1975.

Morgan, William James. *Autobiography of Rear Admiral Charles Wilkes, U.S. Navy, 1798–1877*. Washington, D.C.: Naval History Division, 1978.

Nash, Howard P., Jr. *The Forgotten Wars: The Role of the U.S. Navy in the Quasi War with France and the Barbary Wars, 1798–1805*. London: A. S. Barnes and Company, 1968.

Nautical Research Journal. Silver Spring, Md.: Nautical Research Guild.

Newburyport Herald and Country Gazette. Newburyport, Mass., 1811–16.

The New Hampshire Gazette. Portsmouth, N.H., 1813–16.

New York Mercantile Advertiser, 21 January 1815.

Niles' Weekly Register. Philadelphia, Pa. Various issues, 1808–14.

Official Letters, With Comments, and Observations Relative to the Capture of the President, American Frigate: and Concealment of Men aboard that Ship; Together with the Correspondence between the Secretary and the Commander in Chief, and the editor and the Royal Gazette; and a Letter substantiating the Charge of Concealment. Selected from the Royal and weekly Gazettes, of Different Dates. St. George, Bermuda: Edmund Ward, 1815.

"Official Report of the Battle between the Wasp and the Avon." *Niles Weekly Register* 7 (1814): 192.

"Official Report of the Battle between the Wasp and the Reindeer." *Niles Weekly Register* 6 (1814): 115.

Paullin, Charles Oscar. *Commodore John Rodgers: Captain, Commodore, and Senior Officer of the American Navy, 1773–1838.* Annapolis, Md.: Naval Institute Press, 1966.

Peck, Taylor. *A History of the Washington Navy Yard and the U.S. Naval Gun Factory.* Annapolis, Md.: Naval Institute Press, 1949.

Perry, James M. "The U.S. Sloop of War Wasp." U.S. Naval Institute *Proceedings* 87 (1961): 84–92.

Petrejus, E. W. *Modeling the Brig of War "Irene."* Hengelo, Holland: N. V. Uitgeversmaatschappij "De Esch." English ed., 1970. The most complete account of the design of the *Cruiser*-class sloop of war of which *Reindeer* and *Avon* were but two examples.

Pittsburgh Mercury. 2 January 1816.

Porter, Captain David. *Journal of a Cruise.* Reprint, Classics of Naval Literature Series, Annapolis, Md.: Naval Institute Press, 1986.

Pratt, Fletcher. "Johnston Blakeley: The Carolina Sea Raider." U.S. Naval Institute *Proceedings* 76 (1950): 996–1007.

———. *Preble's Boys: Commodore Preble and the Birth of American Sea Power.* New York: William Sloane Associates, 1950.

Reynolds, J. N. *Voyage of the Frigate Potomac.* New York: Harper, 1835.

Richardson, Edgar P. *American Paintings and Related Pictures in the Henry Francis du Pont Winterthur Museum.* Charlottesville: University Press of Virginia, 1986.

Riley, James. *Riley's Narrative: An Authentic Narrative of the Loss of the American Brig Commerce, Wrecked on the Western Coast of Africa, in the Month of August, 1815, etc.* 1859. Reprint, Elm Grove, Wis.: Sycamore Press, 1963.

Rogers, Robert Cameron. *Will o' the Wasp: A Sea Yarn of the War of 1812.* New York: Putnam, 1896. A whimsical Victorian fantasy, reportedly a "true" account of the *Wasp*'s last days—"brought before the public for the first time!" Farcical but fun.

Roosevelt, Theodore. *The Naval War of 1812.* New York: Putnam, 1910.

Savannah Republican and Evening Ledger. Savannah, Ga., 1814–15.

Smith, Euphemia Vail. *The History of Newburyport.* Newburyport, Mass.: Smith, 1854.

South Carolina State Gazette and Timothy's Daily Advertiser. Columbia, S.C. 8 May 1800.

Spalding, James A. *What I Know about the Parrots and Toscans of Portsmouth, Greenland, Brookfield, Middletown, and Lancaster all in New Hampshire.* Typescript in the New Hampshire Historical Society, Concord, N.H.

Spears, John R. *The History of Our Navy.* 6 vols. New York: Scribners, 1899.

The Star. Raleigh, N.C., 1814–16.

Steel, David. *Steel's Elements of Mastmaking, Sailmaking, and Rigging.* Reprint, Largo, Fla.: Edward Sweetman, 1982.

Thomas, Moses. "Biographical Sketch of the Late Captain Johnston Blakeley." *The Analectic Magazine and Naval Chronicle* 7 (January–June 1816): 208–13.

Tucker, Glen. *Dawn Like Thunder.* New York: Bobbs-Merrill and Company, 1963.

Wadsworth Journal. 22 May 1803.

White, Virgil D. *Index to War of 1812 Pension Files.* 2 vols. Waynesboro, Tenn.: National Historical Publishing Company, 1992.

The Wilmington Chronicle and North Carolina Weekly Advertiser. Wilmington, N.C. 22 October 1795.

Winslow, Richard E. *Wealth and Honor: Portsmouth during the Golden Age of Privateering, 1775–1815.* Publication no. 12. Portsmouth, N.H.: Portsmouth Marine Society, 1988.

Index

McClaine, Thomas, 118, 130, 208
McKee, Christopher (historian), 123
McKnight, Stephen Decatur, 265, 266
Mede, John, 228
Medina (ship), 264
Medway, 195
merchants, economic effects of war on, 277
merchant service, 30, 47–48, 123–24
Merrill, Orlando, 107, 113, 119, 120
Merrimack River, 113
Merrimack (sloop of war), 107, 279
Meshouda (cruiser), 37, 280
Milan Decree, 49
Miller, William, 228, 285
Milne, Sir David, 22
Minorca, 28–29
Mogador, Morocco, 268, 271, 272
Molen, J. G., 265, 266
Monroe, James, 227
Mooney, Charles, 226
Mordiew, John, 198
Morocco, 26, 43
Morris, Charles, 165
Morris, Richard Valentine, 16, 31–34, 37–40, 42–43, 174
Moulton, Jane, 274, 278
Mullen, John, 208
Mullen, Judith, 274–78
mumps, 9
Murdock, Bartlett, 191–92
Murray, Alexander, 16, 45–46
Mustapha, Bobba, 26
Myrmidon (frigate), 264

Napoleonic Wars, 80
National Intelligencer, 273, 287
Nautilus (schooner), 42
Navigator (publication), 114
navy, U.S.: Blakeley's entry into, 14–18; change in policy following embargo, 58–59; completion of, 20; condition of

in 1812, 81–82; cutbacks, 25; expansion of, 101–2, 226
Negroes, 83, 93
Nelson, Horatio, 235
Neptune (barque), 198–99
Nereide (frigate), 238, 247
Newbury, Mass., 113
Newbury Bar, 113
Newburyport, Mass., 113–16, 120, 123–36; Blakeley's departure from, 147–50; economic effects of war on, 277
The Newburyport Herald and Country Gazette, 115, 147, 249
Newell, John, 95–96, 141
New England coast, patrol of, 53–54, 56–57, 95
New Hampshire Gazette, 249, 266
New Orleans, La., 82–83, 85–88
newspapers: honor of Blakeley, 289; on *Wasp-Avon* battle, 249–50. *See also* specific titles
New York, and embargo, 56
New York Columbian, 250
New York (frigate), 16, 24, 32, 34, 38, 40, 43
Nicholson, John B., 35, 112
Niles' Weekly Register, 239, 249, 263, 273
Nissen, Nicholas, 27, 39
No. 81 (gunboat), 121, 131, 132, 134, 140
No. 83 (gunboat), 121, 132, 139
Non-Intercourse Act, 58
Nonsuch (schooner), 92–93
Norfolk, Va., 48
Norfolk Weekly Beacon, 268–69
Norris, Otho, 112
North Carolina, honor of Blakeley, 284–85

O'Brien, Richard, 28
Ohio (schooner), 268
Olivia (brig), 193
Ontario (corvette), 105, 194
"On the Wasp, Sloop of War," 289

About the Author

Stephen Duffy is an independent scholar who holds a degree in electrical engineering. A lifelong maritime enthusiast, Mr. Duffy is a founding member of the Southwest Florida Model Shipwrights. Following a presentation at the 1993 International Maritime History Symposium in Annapolis, he was encouraged to develop his paper on the cruise of the *Wasp* into a full-length biography of Johnston Blakeley. Mr. Duffy resides in Sarasota, Florida, where, in his spare time, he is slowly constructing a model of the *Wasp*.